Metaphysical Africa

AFRICANA RELIGIONS

Edited by
Sylvester A. Johnson, *Virginia Tech*

ADVISORY BOARD:
Afe Adogame, *Princeton Theological Seminary*
Sylviane Diouf, *Historian of the African Diaspora*
Paul C. Johnson, *University of Michigan*
Elizabeth Pérez, *University of California, Santa Barbara*
Elisha P. Renne, *University of Michigan*
Judith Weisenfeld, *Princeton University*

Adopting a global vision for the study of Black religions, the Africana Religions book series explores the rich diversity of religious history and life among African and African-descended people. It publishes research on African-derived religions of Orisha devotion, Christianity, Islam, and other religious traditions that are part of the Africana world. The series emphasizes the translocal nature of Africana religions across national, regional, and hemispheric boundaries.

Metaphysical Africa

Truth and Blackness in the Ansaru Allah Community

MICHAEL MUHAMMAD KNIGHT

The Pennsylvania State University Press
University Park, Pennsylvania

Library of Congress Cataloging-in-Publication Data

Names: Knight, Michael Muhammad, author.
Title: Metaphysical Africa : truth and blackness in the Ansaru Allah Community / Michael Muhammad Knight.
Other titles: Africana religions.
Description: University Park, Pennsylvania : The Pennsylvania State University Press, [2020] | Series: Africana religions | Includes bibliographical references and index.
Summary: "Describes the Ansaru Allah Community/Nubian Islamic Hebrews (AAC/NIH), a 1970s religious movement in Brooklyn that spread, in part, through the production and dissemination of literature and lecture tapes. Tracks the development of AAC/NIH discourse to reveal surprising consistency and coherence behind the appearance of serial reinvention"— Provided by publisher.
Identifiers: LCCN 2020033926 | ISBN 9780271087092 (cloth)
Subjects: LCSH: York, Dwight, 1935- | Nubian Islamic Hebrews—History. | Nuwaubian movement—United States—History. | African Americans—Religion.
Classification: LCC BP605.N89 K58 2020 | DDC 297.8/6—dc23
LC record available at https://lccn.loc.gov/2020033926
Copyright © 2020 Michael Muhammad Knight
All rights reserved
Printed in the United States of America
Published by The Pennsylvania State University Press,
University Park, PA 16802–1003

The Pennsylvania State University Press is a member of the Association of University Presses.

It is the policy of The Pennsylvania State University Press to use acid-free paper. Publications on uncoated stock satisfy the minimum requirements of American National Standard for Information Sciences—Permanence of Paper for Printed Library Material, ANSI Z39.48–1992.

TO JIBREEL, FROM AZREAL

Contents

Acknowledgments *ix*

List of Illustrations *xi*

Introduction: "The Most Dynamic Pamphlets in History" *1*

1 | "I Am the Raisin-Headed Slave": The Nubian *Ahl al-Bayt*, Sudanese Mahdiyya, and Global Blackness as Islamic Revival *28*

2 | Heralds of the Reformer: Visions of Blackamerican Muslim History *75*

3 | "The Covenant Is Complete in Me": Nubian Islamic Hebraism and the Religion of Abraham *113*

4 | Between Zion and Mecca: Bilal as Islamic and Hebrew *135*

5 | The Sudan Is the Heart Chakra: The AAC/NIH as Sufi Tariqa *147*

6 | Islam Is Hotep: Ansar Egyptosophy *167*

7 | The Pyramidal Ka'ba: Malachi Z. York and the Nuwaubian Turn *187*

8 | Nuwaubian Ether: Ansar Legacies in Hip-Hop *221*

Coda: The View from Illyuwn *237*

Notes *245*
Bibliography *260*
Index *276*

Acknowledgments

First, this project would never have manifested without Sadaf. Beyond the ways that Sadaf makes every project possible, perhaps especially this one, she also endured this book's added burden of numerous cardboard boxes marked "NUWAUBIAN," which claimed an increasing amount of space in our home.

Juliane Hammer's formative presence in my work and the significance of her mentorship and friendship cannot be overstated. My thinking about American Islam and Islamic studies has also been informed by the guidance of Carl Ernst and Omid Safi. My sense of the AAC/NIH's globalizing imaginary and the place of the Sudan in its narratives was particularly enhanced by numerous conversations with Cemil Aydin regarding transnational Muslim networks. Ali Asani was instrumental in helping me think about Islam in terms of its diverse local expressions. Laury Silvers introduced me to the field and to a world of possibilities for my work that I could never have accessed otherwise. I am grateful for my mentors and hope that this work reflects the best of what they gave me.

A version of my presentation on AAC/NIH Sufism received editorial attention from Ilyse Morgenstein Fuerst, and her careful reading and insightful notes sharpened my discussion not only in the piece she read but in this book at large.

This book is much stronger than it would have been if it had entered the world without first passing through the gates of three insightful and rigorous anonymous reviewers. Their careful reading and valuable suggestions made a substantial impact on the work.

Pat Bowen is a remarkably generous scholar with a truly collaborative spirit, and this project was enhanced by his eagerness to share resources. Likewise, Paul Greenhouse graciously shared material and insights from his years of documentary fieldwork with the community to inform my analysis. I am so appreciative of how they model mutually supportive scholarship. My sincere thanks to those invaluable conversation partners who have left their marks on this work, including Zaheer Ali, Kate Merriman, Megan Goodwin, Atiya Husain, Matthew Hotham, and Samah Choudhury.

This project began with energetic encouragement and support from Edward E. Curtis IV and Sylvester Johnson, for which I cannot adequately thank them. Penn State University Press has been a supportive and encouraging publisher, and I owe gratitude to everyone there who worked to bring this book into the world, particularly Patrick Alexander, Alex Vose, and Laura Reed-Morrisson. Suzanne Wolk's editorial precision was a savior for the manuscript's execution as a book.

This was the last project that Allison Cohen negotiated for me before parting with Gersh Agency for life on the editorial side. Allison is a superstar agent and brilliant editor, and I hope that we work together again.

Peace to my colleagues, students, and friends at the University of Central Florida.

As always, everything that I do exhibits my debt to my mother.

Illustrations

1. AAC/NIH poster, ca. 1980 2
2. AAC/NIH pamphlet, ca. 1980 3
3. Advertisement for public classes, 1987 5
4. Advertisement for the Upper Room, ca. 1972 46
5. Al Haadi Al Mahdi, *Hadrat Faatimah (AS): The Daughter of the Prophet Muhammad (PBUH), Part 2* (1988), front cover 54
6. The *Ahl al-Bayt*: 'Ali, Fatima, and their sons, Hasan and Husayn. From Al Haadi Al Mahdi, *Hadrat Faatimah (AS): The Daughter of the Prophet Muhammad (PBUH), Part 2* (1988), 53 55
7. The Prophet Muhammad Leaving Medina for Mecca, AAC/NIH poster, ca. 1988 55
8. *Hadrat Faatimah (AS) Pleads for Her Land*. From Al Haadi Al Mahdi, *Hadrat Faatimah (AS): The Daughter of the Prophet Muhammad (PBUH), Part 2* (1988), 112 56
9. Ansaru Allah Community, *The Final Link* (1978) 65
10. Ansaru Allah Community, *Sayyid Saadik Al Mahdi Visits the Ansaars in America 1981* (1981) 67
11. Al Mahdi with Sadiq al-Mahdi during Al Mahdi's travels in the Sudan in the 1970s. From Ansaru Allah Community, *Are the Ansars (in the West) a Self-Made Sect?* (n.d.), 7 67
12. Al Haadi Al Mahdi, *About the Raatib* (1987), front cover 68
13. *Silsilati: My Lineage*. From Al Haadi Al Mahdi, *The Book of the Five Percenters* (1991), 379 68
14. Al Haadi Al Mahdi, *Why the Nosering?* (1986), front cover 71
15. "An understanding that very few understand." From Ansaru Allah Community, *Id with the Ansars* (1977), front cover 81
16. Advertisement for Al Mahdi, *The Book of Lamb* (1979) 88
17. Advertisement for Al Haadi Al Mahdi, *Who Was Noble Drew Ali?* (1988) and *Who Was Marcus Garvey?* (1988) 98
18. AAC/NIH portrait of Allah ("Messenger Clarence 13X"). From Al Haadi Al Mahdi, *The Book of the Five Percenters* (1991), 37 108
19. "We Are Family: The Nubian Nation," AAC/NIH poster, ca. 1990 112
20. "Peace in the Lamb," AAC/NIH poster, ca. 1992 115

21. The AAC/NIH six-pointed star and crescent. From Al Haadi Al Mahdi, *Gospel of Barnabas, Book Two* (1984) 118

22. Al Haadi Al Mahdi, *Should Muslims Observe the Sabbath?* (1985), front cover 124

23. "As Sayyid Al Imaam Isa Al Haadi Al Mahdi," AAC/NIH poster, ca. 1988 128

24. Tents of Nubia, *The Truth, Edition 16: Muhammad Was a Hebrew* (1993) 133

25. Al Mahdi holding his Mihjan staff, as displayed on the inside cover of many AAC/NIH publications is. From Al Haadi Al Mahdi, *The Book of the Five Percenters* (1991), inside front cover 145

26. Advertisement for the Sons of the Green Light, 1985 164

27. Al Mahdi, *Eternal Life After Death* (1977), front cover 175

28. Ansaru Allah Community, *Al Imaam Isa Visits Egypt 1981* (1981), front cover 179

29. Al Haadi Al Mahdi, *Gospel of John, Chapter One* (1984), front cover 184

30. "The Savior," Dr. Malachi Z. York, 1993 194

31. York as Chief Black Eagle, head of the Yamassee Nation. From York-El, *The Constitution of U.N.N.M.: "The United Nuwaubian Nation of Moors"* (1992) 201

32. Pharaoh Akhenaten. From York, *El Katub Shil el Mawut (The Book of the Dead): Coming Forth by Day* (1990s) 209

33. Dr. York publicity photo, 1986 223

34. Dr. York, "You Can't Hide," twelve-inch vinyl (1986) 223

35. Afrika Bambaataa and the Soul-sonic Force, *Return to Planet Rock* (1989) 234

36. *El Maguraj*, Nuwaubian pilgrimage manual, 1990s 239

37. Extraterrestrial wearing Ancient and Mystic Order of Melchizedek fez. From Holy Tabernacle Ministries, *Savior's Day 1996: Man of Many Faces Brings Us One Message* (1996) 241

Introduction
"The Most Dynamic Pamphlets in History"

Many experienced their first glimpse of the imam via a poster that appeared on subway station walls around the turn of the 1980s. He stands in a white robe and turban, his hands open in invitation. His forehead bears the bruise associated with frequent *sujdah* (prostration); his upper left cheek bears three parallel scars, his tribal marks. His body is framed by two territories—a red outline of the United States, captioned "WEST," and a green outline of Africa, marked "EAST"—and a variant of the Prophet Muhammad's seal, reading *la ilaha illa Allah* (there is no god but Allah). Above his head, in elegant Arabic calligraphy, we find *bismillahir rahmanir rahim* (in the Name of Allah, Most Gracious, Most Merciful); at his feet, the caption *al-Mukhlas*, rendered in Arabic with the English translation "The Purifier."

"NOW!!!" the poster commands, "RECEIVE THE ANSWERS TO LIFE-LONG QUESTIONS!!!" Promising "the most dynamic pamphlets in history," the poster offers a list of 116 publications. Scanning the titles, a reader might recognize some as anchored in Islam: *Ninety-Nine Plus One Names of Allah*; *Why Allah Should Not Be Called God*; *Why the Veil?*; *Why the Beard?*; *Fast of Ramadaan*; *Series of Hadith*; *Bilal*; *Qur'an Arabic Lesson One*. Other titles seem to express a Christian orientation (*Christ Is the Answer*; *Understanding the Book of Revelation*; *Opening of the Seventh Seal*; *Leviathan: 666*) or a commitment to the recovery of African heritage (*Yoruba*; *Great African Kings*; *Ancient Egypt and the Pharaohs*; *Science of the Pyramids*; *Tribal Encyclopedia*). Still others suggest an interest in various "metaphysical" traditions commonly grouped together

FIGURE 1 AAC/NIH poster, ca. 1980.

as "New Age" (*What's Your Astrology Sign Brother?*; *Science of Healing*; *The Lost Children of Mu and Atlantis*). At the bottom right corner, the poster invites its reader to visit the Ansaru Allah Community at its flagship location on Brooklyn's Bushwick Avenue: "DO IT NOW! TIME IS RUNNING OUT!" (fig. 1).

Throughout cities in the northeastern United States, the Ansar became a well-known presence through male members' soliciting donations and peddling literature while dressed in their white turbans and robes (fig. 2). Community members even became visible on MTV, appearing in the videos of affiliated artists such as KMD and The Jaz (featuring a very young Jay-Z, whose lyrics reference Ansar concepts). Throughout the 1980s, the Ansar remained a compelling presence in the heartlands of Black Islam, particularly cities of the northeastern United States.[1]

FIGURE 2 *Al Imam Isa Visits the City of Brotherly Love (Philadelphia)*, ca. 1980.

In the early 1990s, the community relocated from Brooklyn to a commune in the Catskills, and in 1993 it migrated to a 476-acre property in rural Georgia. The latter move accompanied an apparent self-reinvention using a bricolage of materials that included contemporary UFO-centered religions, Freemasonry, New Age modes of mysticism and healing, and traditions of ancient Egypt and Mesopotamia. Popularly known as Nuwaubians, the community members now regarded their leader as a visitor from the planet Rizq, in the nineteenth galaxy, Illyuwn. For outside observers, the community's definitive features would become its eclectic references and seemingly incoherent self-identification, as it followed its leader in and out of various affiliations, faith convictions, codes of dress, and ritual practices in accordance with his whims.

In 2002, the man from the poster having been taken into police custody, a force of three hundred FBI, ATF, and local law enforcement personnel stormed the community's land with armored trucks and helicopters, seizing weapons and cash and taking control of the property. Media coverage of the event marveled at the commune's unique architecture (including a black pyramid with gold trim seemingly styled after the Kaʻba in Mecca), and at the community's interest in pharaonic Egypt and belief that its leader was an extraterrestrial. As of this writing, the man from the poster, a convicted sexual predator in his seventies, is serving a sentence of more than one hundred years at the ADMAX facility in Florence, Colorado.

This book examines the public discourse of a community that has defied easy categorization, in part because both the community and its leader appear to have undergone numerous intellectual and aesthetic makeovers since its origins at the end of the 1960s. Self-identified through the 1970s and '80s as the Ansaru Allah Community (AAC) and/or the Nubian Islamic Hebrews (NIH), the community provoked questions of religious categorization and the modes through which its boundaries are constructed, in both popular and academic contexts (fig. 3). What exactly did it mean to be an "Islamic Hebrew"? Were members of the community Muslim or Jewish? Did they blend different religious traditions in a new mash-up all their own? When they changed their community's name and dress codes, did they also switch religions? How did the community make sense of these changes? And how were categories of "Islam" and "Judaism" affected by the community's interest in the themes of ancient Egypt and UFO religion?

FIGURE 3 Advertisement for public classes, 1987.

Scholarship on the AAC/NIH begins with a sectarian polemic. The main secondary source on the community in the 1980s, Abu Ameenah Bilal Philips's *The Ansar Cult in America* (1988), was published by Riyadh-based Tawheed Publications with the stated intention of exposing Al Hajj Imam Isa Al Haadi Al Mahdi—the man from the poster—as a heretical charlatan who had transgressed the boundaries of Islam. The tract includes remarks on an earlier draft from Saudi Arabia's Presidency of Islamic Research, Ifta and Propagation, which offers suggestions on how to better clarify the AAC/NIH's "falsehood, shamefulness, and remoteness from the correct path"; Philips comments that the finished volume represents his fulfillment of that mandate.[2] The book's introduction, by Ahmad Muhammad Ahmad Jalli, associate professor of Islamic theology at King Saud University, places the AAC/NIH within what Jalli terms the "Baatinite (esoteric) movement," a phenomenon that he defines as including all of Shi'ism, along with the Druze, Baha'ism, the Ahmadiyya, and other traditions. This apparently monolithic "Baatinite movement," Jalli says, has "attempted to destroy the Islamic faith and lead a revolt against the teachings of Islamic law by employing free interpretations of the religious texts, claiming that all texts have an outer obvious meaning known only to the masses and an inner hidden meaning known only to a select few initiates." Such groups, he warns, "wear the cloak of Islaam while striving to destroy it from within."[3] Relying on post-1975 media and interviews with estranged former members, Philips divides AAC/NIH history into four stages of development: "Foundation," "Mahdism," "The Christ" (in which Al Mahdi identifies himself as the returning Jesus), and finally "God Incarnate" (in which Al Mahdi exploits Sufism's "mystical short-cuts" and the "aberrant philosophy" of medieval Andalusian master Ibn al-'Arabi for his own gain).[4]

Philips's division of AAC/NIH history into clear "stages," each marked by clear doctrinal shifts, name changes, and redesigned symbols and uniforms, became the standard narrative by which the community would be understood, perhaps informing even its own narratives. Scholarly treatments have defined the community as marked by constant change, serial mass conversions, and abrupt pivots between identities. These accounts, however, disagree with one another as to the community's precise trajectory. Among claims found in academic literature, we read that the AAC/NIH started as a Jewish group and later became Muslim;[5] started as a Muslim group and later became Jewish;[6] "began to sound more specifically Islamic" after 1973, its leader claiming descent from the Prophet in 1988;[7] started as a spinoff from the Nation of Islam but later abandoned racialist doctrines to become Qurʾan-centered "fundamentalists";[8] developed unique doctrines to compete with "orthodox" Muslims and then became more Bible-centered;[9] sought greater conformity with "orthodox" Muslims by the start of the 1990s;[10] grew open to reform in the 1980s with input from the Sudanese Mahdiyya but ignored Mahdiyya objections to its Bible usage;[11] broke ties with the Sudanese Mahdiyya in 1980;[12] and ultimately reoriented itself around Christ's imminent return.[13] Rather than attempt to sort this out with a comprehensive engagement of the community's immense literary output over time, scholarship has taken it for granted that the community has no interest in making sense to itself or outsiders. As NRM (New Religious Movement) studies supplanted Islamic studies as the primary academic field giving attention to the AAC/NIH, the community began to be treated as a movement of esotericist deconstruction, led by a gnostic trickster for whom instability, self-contradiction, and doctrinal incoherence serve as teaching exercises.[14]

This book takes a different approach. Examining decades' worth of AAC/NIH books, pamphlets, newsletters, and lecture tapes, it tells a story not only of transformations but also of continuities. I resist assumptions that the movement pinballed at random between categories of "Islam," "Judaism," "New Age," "UFO religion," and "Egyptian religion." Instead of emphasizing serial reinvention, the following discussion examines rhetorical threads through which the community maintains its sense of coherence.

Specifically, this book engages the Ansaru Allah Community/Nubian Islamic Hebrews with an interest in the movement's vision of "metaphysical Africa." I owe the term to Catherine Albanese's "metaphysical Asia," which she employs in *A Republic of Mind and Spirit* to describe the ways in which Americans reinvented Asia "according to their Americanized metaphysical categories."[15] Metaphysical Asia signifies the reconstruction of essentialized "Eastern spirituality" under an American metaphysical rubric that features themes of mental powers, energy, healing, and the mind-body relationship, and includes not only practices of meditation and physical wellness but also traditions popularly termed "magical" or "occult." Finally, the concept of metaphysical Asia speaks to the ways in which an interest in "Eastern spirituality" engages "world religions" such as Hinduism and Buddhism while potentially rewriting them in American conceptual vocabularies.

American metaphysical religion, while marked by claims of "universal" wisdom and spirituality, often expresses the governing prejudices of its mostly white advocates. Among the traditions that typically undergo appropriation under the "New Age" rubric—Hinduism and yoga, Tibetan Buddhism, Zen, indigenous American religions, Amazonian shamanism, Taoism, Christian gnosticisms, Jewish Kabbalah—we do not typically encounter traditions of Africa (apart from pharaonic Egypt). Nor does the New Age pool of resources typically include Islam, beyond a particular construction of Sufism that imagines Sufi traditions and figures such as Rumi as separate from Islam.[16]

Parallel to the white intellectual traditions covered in Albanese's account, there were also African American esoteric traditions that often resonated with white esotericisms and white imaginaries of a vast, undifferentiated "Orient" but sometimes differed in their resources. Susan Palmer, author of a monograph on the Nuwaubians, observes that what she calls the "black cultic milieu" is essentially unknown to "white New Agers."[17] In contrast to white practitioners, Black metaphysical religionists have often claimed timeless and universal spiritual truths in ways that prioritized Africa (not only Egypt) and Islam (not only Sufism) as their centers. In the early twentieth century, the Great Migration of African Americans from the rural south into northern cities provoked transformations of African-derived hoodoo tradition, characterized by increasing commercialization in a metaphysical marketplace of mail-order companies and individual practitioners advertising goods and services in Black newspapers. Practitioners claiming titles such as "African scientist," "Mohammedan scientist," "Mohammedan Master of Stricter African Science," and "Arabian Mystic Seer and Master of the Ancient Mysteries," and claiming origins in Nigeria, Zulu South Africa, and the Sudan advertised their expertise to serve clients' medical, spiritual, and magical needs.[18] These Africa-centering practitioners did not exist in a separate universe from Black religious thought and liberation struggles. The patron of occult "African science" could also have an interest in the glories of ancient Black civilizations, the true place of Black people in the Bible, the Egyptian and Ethiopian origins of Freemasonry, Black liberation in the United States, and anticolonial movements across the globe. The question of Jesus Christ's true race, esoteric reinterpretations of Christ's divinity and recovery of his "lost years" spent undergoing initiation in Egypt and India, the lost "Oriental" powers of occult African, "Mohammedan," and "Hindoo" sciences, and resistance against both domestic and worldwide white supremacy do not need to be compartmentalized into distinct "religious," "magical," and "political" dimensions. These concerns often occupied the same spaces and compelled the same thinkers.

Across the twentieth century, metaphysical Africa developed as a tradition of sacred geographies and enchanted genealogies, affirming Blackness as a unique spiritual gift and destiny. Melanin theorists argued that thanks to greater melanin concentrations in the pineal gland, Black people were naturally inclined toward greater mental, emotional, and physical wellness, extraordinary philosophical insight, sensitivity to other humans' magnetic fields, and the ability to access information from unexpected places—as in Frances Cress Welsing's claim that George Washington Carver obtained his botanical knowledge from the plants themselves, as they "talked to his melanin." In Afrocentric thought, melanin theory sometimes serves as a counter to "ancient aliens" narratives that reduce human agency and attribute marvels of the ancient world to extraterrestrial intervention. While white occult writer Robert K. G. Temple argued that the Dogon tribe in Mali possessed advanced knowledge of the star Sirius B that could only be attributed to the tribe's tutelage under extraterrestrial teachers, Welsing suggested that the Dogon achieved this knowledge independently through their extrasensory intuition, a power credited to superior pineal glands.[19]

This "metaphysical Africa" can also include Egyptocentrism, the identification of pharaonic Egypt with Black Africanity, particularly the construction of biological, historical, and spiritual or philosophical linkages between pharaonic Egypt and African diasporas in the Americas.[20] Egyptocentrism (and Egyptosophy, a romanticization of ancient Egypt as the original source of all esoteric and/or occult knowledge)[21] has become a prominent dimension of Afrocentrist thought, though Afrocentrism and Egyptocentrism should not be conflated and sometimes even appear in tension with each other. Some Afrocentrists prefer the wisdom traditions of Yoruba over those of the pharaohs, or identify with enslaved Hebrews rather than with their Egyptian oppressors.[22] The African Hebrew Israelite community founded by Ben Ammi in the 1960s, to take just one sample from a diverse pool of Black Hebrew traditions, identifies Israel as "northeast Africa."[23] Other seekers of metaphysical Africa, envisioning the entire continent as a singular cultural entity, conceive of a comprehensive "African spirituality" that includes Yoruba and Kemetism, as well as the African roots of "Abrahamic" religions. Advocates of African spiritualities might assert that the West has unfairly misrepresented indigenous traditions of Egyptian *neteru* and Yoruba *orishas* as polytheistic, or instead defend polytheism against Western monotheist hegemony; these claims can also appear in the same argument.[24]

Islam entered into this matrix through various portals: occult practitioners who envisioned Africa as a land of magical, mysterious "Mohammedan science"; Masonic orders' appropriations of Islam to evoke a "mystic Orient";[25] non-Muslim writers such as J. A. Rogers and Edward Blyden, who praised the "Muslim world" as a realm of greater egalitarianism and historical Black glory; transnational Ahmadiyya networks and other Muslim diasporas; and what Cemil Aydin terms a "Third World internationalism" characterized by interactions between anticolonial, pan-Islamist, and pan-Asianist movements throughout the world. Aydin points to the encounter in London between Caribbean pan-Africanist Marcus Garvey and Sudanese-Egyptian pan-Islamist Duse Mohamed Ali, and their continued collaboration when Ali visited Garvey in the United States.[26] American visions of Islam as innately connected to Blackness did not develop from one singular root, but rather from a multiplicity of entangled genealogies. In Duse Mohamed Ali's *African Times and Orient Review*, we find writings by Muslim religious reformers, pan-Africanists, and pan-Asianists, but also by theosophists such as Annie Besant, whom the journal praised as "among the first rank of sane thinkers."[27]

Muslim movements such as the Moorish Science Temple and the Nation of Islam emerged from this context of polyculturalism, transnational connections, and creative activity. Noble Drew Ali engaged New Thought narratives of Jesus as an initiate of mystery schools, composed his *Holy Koran* by appropriating metaphysical texts such as Levi H. Dowling's *Aquarian Gospel of Jesus the Christ*, and claimed mystical initiation at the Pyramid of Cheops. As an Islamic prophet, he taught African Americans that they were not "Negroes" but rather Moors and "Moslems," and that he was divinely chosen to restore their lost nationality and religion. A close read of the Supreme Wisdom Lessons, the teachings of Nation of Islam founder Master Fard Muhammad and his student successor, Elijah Muhammad, reveals metaphysical webs in which the Nation developed, engaging popular imaginaries of Moses as a master occultist and Jesus as a mystery school initiate, as well as New Age discourses on the power of the mind, magnetic attraction, and godhood as realization of one's inner nature.[28] The Lessons did not present their knowledge as new or historically specific, but rather as the timeless truth of a primordial, self-created Black Man who was a "righteous Muslim" by his very nature.

Elijah Muhammad's vision of Islam informed his vision of Blackness. As Edward E. Curtis IV has observed, the Nation "constructed black identity in terms of a shared history that was defined by its Islamic character."[29] This construction both opened and limited the Nation's encounter with African cultures and spiritualities. While Elijah Muhammad conceptualized Blackness as eternal and divine, he was by no means an Afrocentrist. Elijah recognized pharaonic Egypt as a Black achievement, but his ideas about non-Muslim African cultures also upheld white supremacist tropes. Elijah's "Asiatic" Blackness was definitively *not* African; while Ben Ammi reconceptualized Israel as "northeast Africa," Elijah redefined the African continent as "East Asia." The Messenger spoke disparagingly of non-Muslim African cultures and condemned the "savage dress and hair-styles" of African cultural revivalism in the 1960s, lamenting that many Black people in America, seeking the "love of Black Africa," had embraced "the jungle life."[30]

The Nation's aspirations toward globalized Muslim "orthodoxy" after Elijah Muhammad's death in 1975, coupled with immigration reform that radically changed American Muslim demographics, altered the relation between Islam and Blackness. In the later twentieth century, numerous Afrocentrist intellectuals viewed Islam as an alien culture of Arab supremacy that had only entered Africa via invasion and slavery. Afrocentrists subjected Islam to the same critiques with which the Nation had denounced Christianity, presenting Islam as non-Black and even as a force of anti-Blackness. In what Sherman Jackson has termed "Black Orientalism," conversion to Islam lost much of its capital as a performance of Black "racial/cultural 'orthodoxy,'" becoming repositioned as an embrace of Arab and South Asian cultures and even as a rejection of Blackness. When "Blackamerican Muslims began to show signs of being culturally and intellectually overrun by immigrants," Jackson writes, "they began to draw the charge of cultural apostasy."[31] For many who sought to recover an indigenous African spirituality, Islam became untenable.

While some Afrocentrists treated Islam as inauthentically African, many Muslim communities also treated Black African cultures as illegitimate experiences of Islam. Writing on troubled histories between Black and Muslim identities, Su'ad Abdul Khabeer argues that amid "chronic disavowal" of Blackness in Muslim communities, "American Muslims, Blacks and non-Blacks, rarely think of Africa as an archive for Islamic authenticity and authority," and "Africa (save Egypt, Morocco, and Mauritania) has been effectively erased from the Islamic tradition."[32] As scholarly networks associated with the Salafiyya movement came to represent a dominant school of thought in Black Sunni communities, particularly in cities of the northeastern United States, numerous Black converts traveled to Saudi Arabia for religious training and returned home as authoritative community leaders. In the 1980s, the Saudi government established a "satellite school" in Virginia to prepare Americans for study at the Islamic University of Madinah. As Saudi Arabia became increasingly privileged as the archive of "true Islam," local traditions of Black Islam were further marginalized as heretical and illegitimate.³³ In turn, this trend bolstered Afrocentrist repudiations of Islam as Arab cultural hegemony.

A controversy of critical importance to the Ansaru Allah Community was Islam's place in metaphysical Africa. The AAC/NIH can be found at a nexus of competing priorities, as Al Mahdi invoked a metaphysical Africa that upheld Islam as timelessly Black. The AAC/NIH constructed a metaphysical Africa that affirmed and absorbed Afrocentric objections to "orthodox" Islam as a legacy of Arab violence against Black people, but also relocated Islam's true heartland in the Sudan—*bilad as-sudan*, translated in AAC/NIH literature as "Land of the Blacks." Between anti-Islamic Afrocentrism and Muslim anti-Blackness, or between Black Orientalism and Black Salafism, AAC/NIH media navigated these conflicts in complex and compelling ways. This book explores various ways in which the AAC/NIH, formulating truth through its own metaphysical Africa, envisioned the connection between Blackness and Islam.

REINTRODUCING ANSAR HISTORY

The AAC/NIH began not as a "spinoff" or "offshoot" of movements such as the Nation of Islam or Moorish Science, but rather as a small circle of young Sunni Muslims in Brooklyn with links to the State Street Mosque led by Granada-born Daoud Ahmed Faisal (d. 1980). Faisal established the Islamic Mission of America (IMA) in 1928. The IMA identified as Sunni, though Pat Bowen observes that "Sunni" signified "the Muslim world in general" rather than a concrete sectarian identity, noting that the IMA relied on translations of the Qur'an that came through networks of the Ahmadiyya—a South Asian Muslim movement scorned and persecuted as "heretical" throughout the twentieth century.³⁴ By the early 1960s, friction between immigrant and Black segments at State Street inspired a handful of Black members to leave under the leadership of Hafis Mahbub, a Pakistani member of the Sunni revivalist Tablighi Jama'at who had taught at the masjid. These attritioned State Street members formed the Ya-Sin Mosque, which claimed a more strict adherence to Muslim legal traditions (characterized in part by women's use of full-face veils) while also addressing the specific needs of African American Muslims, and later gave rise to the Dar ul-Islam movement.³⁵

The future Al Imam Isa Al Haadi Al Mahdi, then Dwight York (b. 1945), spent part of his teens and early twenties connected to State Street Mosque. The circumstances of Al Mahdi's conversion remain disputed. It has been claimed that Al Mahdi's introduction to Islam came through members of the Nation, whom he reportedly encountered during a 1965–67 incarceration for felony assault and other charges. This narrative seems to start with Abu Ameenah Bilal Philips, who provides no details of Al Mahdi's criminal history but simply remarks, "In prison it may be presumed that Al Mahdi came in contact with Elijah Muhammad's teachings as well as those of Noble Drew Ali's," after which he converted at State Street and began to "concoct" a "black nationalist version of Islaam."[36] If Al Mahdi had converted in Brooklyn "around 1965," as Philips suggests, this would have been before his incarceration, not after his release. Resisting the prison conversion narrative, Al Mahdi would claim that he first attended State Street's Friday prayers in 1957, at the age of twelve, when Faisal essentially took him in as a son and renamed him Isa ʿAbd'Allah ibn Abu Bakr Muhammad.[37] Paul Greenhouse, a documentary filmmaker who has done extensive fieldwork with the community, encountered reliable claims that his mother was already a member of State Street Mosque, and that in the late 1960s Al Mahdi would walk up and down the street to perform public dhikr, the recitation of divine names, with a talking drum.[38]

At State Street Mosque, Al Mahdi would have encountered Sufis, Salafi revivalists, former Nation and Moorish Science Temple members, white converts (probably including author Maryam Jameelah, who converted at State Street in May 1961, received her new name from Faisal himself, and became a close friend of Faisal's wife, Khadijah),[39] followers of Sayyid Abu A'la al-Mawdudi and Sayyid Qutb, Tablighi Jama'at networks, UN diplomats from Muslim-majority countries, and various diasporic communities that had started with Muslim seamen. Of particular relevance for Al Mahdi, State Street's Muslim diasporas included a Sudanese-American community that had been planting roots in Brooklyn since the arrival of merchant marines in the 1940s. Anthropologist Rogaia Mustafa Abusharaf reports that these seamen came from Dongola, the same part of the Sudan that Al Mahdi later claimed as his own place of origin, and regarded State Street Mosque as their "home away from home." Some had learned of Satti Majid, the Dongolawi scholar who traveled to the United States with a vision of spreading Islam, connected with Yemeni Muslims in Brooklyn, and mentored Faisal before leaving the country in 1929.[40] Faisal's establishment of his Islamic Mission, writes Abusharaf, "marked the birth of an African Muslim religious body in North America." At State Street, the Dongolawis "managed to reproduce in revealing ways the community they left behind," providing Brooklyn seekers with access to an indigenous African

Islam.⁴¹ Rather than an isolated bubble of local "heterodoxies" without exposure to a larger "Muslim world," Brooklyn offered an Islamic education that was both locally embedded and transnationally connected. Among the groups accessible at State Street alone, one could choose between Islamic revivals that privileged the Sudan and Pakistan as their natural centers.

It was in this context that young Dwight York learned of Muhammad Ahmad (1845–1885), a Sufi revolutionary from Dongola who declared himself the awaited Mahdi, called for Islam's restoration to its pure and original form, raised an army of followers, drove British and Turko-Egyptian oppressors from the Sudan, and led a short-lived Islamic state until his death in 1885. In the years during which a newly paroled York navigated State Street's complex terrain and embarked on a path of Afrocentric Sufism, the Mahdiyya made international headlines amid political turmoil in the Sudan. When the Sudan regained its independence in 1956, the Mahdiyya, also known as Ansar (Helpers), established the National Umma Party, their own political party, and took power. In May 1969, the young government fell to a military coup led by Ja'far Muhammad al-Numayri. The following year, after a failed attempt to assassinate al-Numayri, the Ansar revolted, prompting a government assault on their stronghold at Abba Island that resulted in the massacre of a thousand Ansar. Among those killed was the Mahdi's grandson, Imam Hadi al-Mahdi, whose nephew and successor, Sadiq al-Mahdi, fled the country. During his exile in Egypt, Sadiq articulated the Ansar platform against the Muslim Brothers; while the Brothers relied on a "traditional pattern" and conformed "to the Sunni school of thought and are bound by the four Sunni schools of law," the Ansar, Sadiq explained, "draw from all schools of thought and we are not bound by any school of law. We recognize the original texts and seek new formulation, conscious of changes in time and place."⁴²

In addition to Brooklyn's Sudanese community, the future Al Mahdi would have encountered visions of African spirituality from non-Muslim diasporic networks. New York was home to a Yoruba spiritual and cultural revivalist movement driven by increased Caribbean migration and African American conversions to Afro-Cuban traditions. Black converts to Santeria, recognizing that West African traditions had been transformed by their diffusion across the Atlantic, shifted attention from Cuba to West Africa and sought to "purify" African traditions. As Yoruba revivalists pursued linkages to an "older primordial moment in Africa," Tracey E. Hucks explains, they produced a distinctly American construction of African spirituality.⁴³

When the Harlem-based Yoruba Temple disseminated literature that offered "reconnection to the continent of Africa, and a rationalization for the collective return to African religion and culture," this vision of Africa did not include Islam.[44] Against Nation and Sunni leaders alike who disparaged non-Muslim African societies as "primitive" and presented Islam as a "civilizing" influence, Yoruba Temple media implicated Islam in the erasure of indigenous African cultures.[45] Speaking to the various legacies of Malcolm X, however, the Yoruba Temple honored Malcolm's birthday a year after his assassination with a parade through Harlem.[46] According to one of Greenhouse's informants within Al Mahdi's circle, another point of intersection between New York's Muslims and Yoruba Temple was Al Mahdi's own mother, who reportedly participated in a Yoruba revivalist community while also attending State Street Mosque.

Yoruba Temple literature made claims of its own about the Sudan. In *Tribal Origins of African-Americans* (1962), Yoruba leader Oseijeman Adefunmi argued that West African cultures bore ancestral connections to ancient Egyptian and Nubian kingdoms, as European invasions of North Africa provoked mass migrations across the Sahara (which Adefunmi labeled a greater "Sudan"). Specifically, Adefunmi reported that Yoruba ancestry could be traced to the ancient Nile city of Meroë, capital of the Kushite kingdom and a little more than one hundred miles from modern Khartoum, which meant that many of the West Africans taken to the Americas as slaves were Nubians.[47]

Back in Brooklyn, Al Mahdi's public drum/dhikr marches and private study circles produced a new faction in the State Street universe. Given a critical lack of extant sources prior to the 1970s, we must rely partially on the community's retroactive accounts in later materials and Philips's interviews with former members in the 1980s. With this caution in mind, it appears that circa 1967–69, Al Mahdi headed a small group called Ansar Pure Sufi and operated a "Pure Sufi" bookstore. One of Philips's informants recalled joining in 1968 after getting "fed up" with the Dar ul-Islam and seeing Al Mahdi's group show up at a Dar celebration of the Prophet's birthday. They "looked different," he recalled, with their tarbushes, nose rings, and bone earrings, and a Dar brother told him, "Stay away from them 'cause they are crazy." He also reported that in its early days, the group consisted of fifteen members at most, "dropping off to about five when times got rough."[48] By 1969 they had become the Nubian Islamic Hebrew Mission in America (NIHMA), and in 1971 they established a headquarters at 452 Rockaway Avenue in Brooklyn's Brownsville neighborhood, approximately a mile from the Dar's Atlantic Avenue masjid.[49]

As among the Dar, NIHMA women fully veiled their faces. The male members of NIHMA became known for peddling literature and other products throughout New York, dressing in distinct uniforms, and visiting other masjids to engage Muslims on issues of doctrine.[50] "When you see Nubian brothers on the street," explained a 1972 issue of the periodical the *Muslim Man*, "you'll notice that they wear tall black tarbushes [with green tassels], clean neat suits that button down the front, or the familiar *selawa*. With the silver nose rings and signet rings, their dress alone tells you a lot about the Muslim man."[51]

The earliest surviving NIHMA pamphlets attribute authorship to Al Mahdi under the name Isa Abd Allah ibn Abu Bakr Muhammad, and they typically begin with the page-one declaration, "Muslims must realize they are alone in Their Sorrow." Contrary to narratives of constant reinvention, early NIHMA newsletters express remarkable consistency with later material. *Back to the Beginning: The Book of Names* (1972), for example, informs readers that Adam was Black; that African Americans were descended from Kedar, son of Ishmael, who was Black and "the real Arab"; that Black people are Nubians and not only the true Arabs but also the true Hebrews; that white people are Amorites; that Muhammad Ahmad was the anticipated Mahdi; that true Muslims must abide by the Sabbath; and that hadith traditions are generally unreliable and must not be privileged over the Qur'an and other revealed scriptures, such as the Torah and Psalms. The pamphlet makes positive connections to Arabic, Hebrew, and Yoruba, and also features images of the Star of David, the Kundalini "sleeping serpent," and the Egyptian ankh, along with a serpent eating its tail captioned "Never ending life from Africa." A star's six points are captioned (clockwise from the top): Allah, Shango, Obatala, Man, Elohim, YHWH.[52] In other pamphlets from the early 1970s, Al Mahdi articulates themes that remained crucial to his teachings for decades to come, such as the notion of Black suffering as the spell of Leviathan, Al Mahdi breaking the spell in 1970, and a promise that Black oppression would end in the year 2000. In early publications, Al Mahdi also asserts that white people (Amorites) are cursed with leprosy and pale skin.[53] In harmony with his later writings on Jesus, he interprets the Qur'an and Bible to argue that the angel Gabriel had intercourse with Mary and was Jesus's biological father.[54]

Speaking to divisions affecting Muslim Brooklyn, NIHMA newsletters proclaimed a need for the Black man to "speak his own language," meaning "Arabic or Kufic in its purest form" rather than the corrupted "Pakistanian Arabic" and other diluted forms learned from immigrant Muslims.[55] These newsletters established connections between Islam and Africa that remained major concerns in AAC/NIH media for decades, expressed in Al Mahdi's vision of the Sudan as the center of divine creative activity, his treatment of "Sudan" as a name for the whole of Africa, his incorporation of the ankh, and his claims that Yoruba traditions derive from Islam.[56] The connections found shared expression in advertisements from his NIH "tribe" for a June 4, 1972, festival at 452 Rockaway that promised "dress of Islamic countries," Islamic poetry, the "Al Ansaru Allah Dance Troupe," African drumming, and Merchants of Oyo—a group led by Al Mahdi's brother, Obaba Oyo (born David Piper York Jr.), that sold African imports (including bone jewelry that AAC/NIH members wore for a time) and Islamic literature, and traveled the country showcasing Oyo's jewelry designs.[57] Oyo, who also worked as a fashion designer for the Harlem-based New Breed Clothing brand, which popularized dashikis in the 1960s, formed his own African Islamic Mission (AIM) in Brooklyn's Bedford-Stuyvesant neighborhood. An AIM pamphlet from 1975 identifies Oyo's family as "Islamic Hebrew" and quotes Genesis to prophesy that Black suffering under the "iniquity of the Amorites" would end in the year 2000.[58] The AIM became known for reprinting books on Black history and Islam, both popular books and rare and out-of-print titles, ranging from general history and cultural materials, to Nation of Islam and Moorish Science texts, to the writings of Muslim apologist Ahmed Deedat, to classical proto-Afrocentrist works.[59]

NIHMA pamphlets defended the right of American Muslims to identify with Sufism, lamenting that "many Muslims are under the impression, and are indoctrinating others with the fallacy that you must be from the East in order to elevate yourself to the degree of a Sufi."[60] Al Mahdi's Sufism identified Khidr as Melchizedek, the immortal priest mentioned in the Hebrew Bible; located the "Temple of Khidr" at the seventh heaven;[61] and described the progressive opening of chakras as the soul's ascension toward the plane of divine reality ("Allah and Al Khidr") and then the seventh and final plane of Blackness.[62] Al Mahdi affirmed the Nation and Five Percenter declaration "the Black Man is God" but nuanced its theological impact by distinguishing between "God" and "Allah," which Al Mahdi did not regard as simply a matter of straightforward translation. For Al Mahdi, these terms signified different things: "God" did not refer to the transcendent creator of the worlds but was an acronym for Gomar Oz Dubar, three "Kufic" words meaning wisdom, strength, and beauty. The Black man is God because he has been granted these attributes; Allah, however, is giver of the attributes and cannot be contained within them.[63]

In the early 1970s, Al Mahdi identified himself as the grandson of the Sudanese Mahdi,[64] presented his organization as an authorized branch of Faisal's

Islamic Mission of America,[65] and constructed an Islamic Egyptosophy with the narrative that Hajar, mother of Ishmael, was the daughter of Imhotep.[66] Whether for his teachings, fashion choices, or aggressive proselytizing and peddling, Al Mahdi attracted negative attention from other Muslim groups in the city. In the summer of 1973, followers of Al Mahdi were attacked by a group from the Mosque of Islamic Brotherhood (MIB), a Black Sunni movement based in Harlem, for peddling newspapers in Manhattan; four MIB members were arrested.[67] The MIB complained in a September 1973 editorial of "numerous little cults" linking Islam with "eccentric nonsense," "mythology and esoteric foolishness" that resembled "the more barbaric aspects of primitive pagan societies." The editorial specifically targeted the AAC/NIH in its mention of "cult" followers wearing "rings in their noses, bones in their ears," which were elements of AAC/NIH dress code at the time.[68] Nonetheless, Al Mahdi presented himself during the early 1970s as exhibiting greater compatibility with Black Sunni movements than with the Nation of Islam: "To all those Muslims who for the past three years have found and are still finding fault with us, at least we proclaim the Kalimah of ALLAH and adhere to the Five Pillars of Faith."[69]

AAC/NIH pamphlets from 1973, identifying the community as the Nubian Islamic Hebrews, also display the designation "Al Ansaru Allah, the Helper of Allah." On the back cover, these pamphlets offer a manifesto titled "Goals and Purposes of the Nubian Islamic Hebrews" to parallel the mission statements found in the Nation of Islam's *Muhammad Speaks* and in the newspapers of Sunni groups such as the Islamic Party of North America. "Goals and Purposes" declares the intention to teach children "Arabic, Aramaic, Hebrew, and all the African dialect as they can learn" and to incorporate practices of "African drumming, Islamic drumming, Chanting, and dancing," and expresses an ultimate ambition to "go home, to build our own country which is in Africa." The statement also defines the group as "non-sectarian" and as committed to "Islam in its pristine purity as taught by the Qur'an and the Sunnah."[70]

Community literature from the later 1970s describes the period of 1970–74 as the first half of a "tribulation," during which the devil infiltrated the community and caused desertions.[71] In February 1974, months before Al Mahdi instituted the practice of begging for donations, the movement struggled: during the New York Police Department (NYPD)'s investigation of a shooting at the Ya-Sin Mosque that left four dead, a grocery store owner identified with the "Islamic Hebrews" told detectives that his group no longer used its St. John's Place location and did not have a masjid at the moment but owned a green bus and gathered at the homes of its members.[72] During the "tribulation" period, Al Mahdi traveled to the Middle East and Africa, where he made a pilgrimage to Mecca and experienced a mystical vision of Khidr/Melchizedek at the junction of the two Niles in the Sudan. These travels seem to correspond to the community's phasing out its Nubian Islamic Hebrews name in favor of Ansaru Allah Community.[73] Mailing addresses that appear in the pamphlets of this period also suggest at least a coincidental relationship between the name change and the move from the Rockaway apartment to 496 Flatbush.[74] Surprisingly, given the spirit of Al Mahdi's usual treatment of Saudi Arabia, pamphlets published shortly before and after the move also feature the Saudi coat of arms on their back covers, in addition to Al Mahdi's own six-pointed star and upward-pointing crescent.[75]

The Ansaru Allah name affirmed links to the Sudanese Ansar, which also accompanied the adoption of new dress codes for the "Ansar of the West" that more closely mirrored the "Ansar of the East." Overall, the community's rhetorical strategies remained consistent. NIHMA literature had already recognized Muhammad Ahmad as the Mahdi, prioritized Khidr as a mediator between worlds, identified Al Mahdi as a direct "student under Sheik Al-Khidr of Nubia," and even depicted Al Mahdi as a miracle worker with supernatural insights and powers.[76] Community media continued to advocate biblical scriptures as essential to Muslim life (arguing that Muhammad only adhered to the way of Abraham and *fitrah*, "the natural practices of all the Prophets") and maintained the six-pointed star and upward-pointing crescent as its symbol.[77]

From the later 1970s through 1983, the group identified itself as Ansaru Allah (often transliterated in double-vowel style as Ansaaru Allah). This name did not erase the community's prior history, deny previous NIHMA teachings, or mark a new emphasis on "Islam" over "Judaism." Reflecting on the community's earlier identification, a 1978 editorial remarked, "In between the years 1970 and mid-1973, we were known as Nubian Islamic Hebrews. And we do not deny that we still are."[78] Considering past "tribulations" in the newsletter titled *Id with the Ansars* (1977), Al Mahdi explains, "We did not propagate the Scriptures as profoundly" as the community did later in the decade. "We started out with Genesis... as we became more knowledgeable of the Scriptures... [we] worked our way through the Old Testament and the New Testament up to the Qur'an, into which we are now delving heavily."[79] Al Mahdi's claim of progressing through Hebrew and Christian scriptures to a Qur'an-centered methodology, however, does not correspond with the community's observable rhetorical strategies; in *Id with the Ansars*, the newsletter that makes this claim,

Al Mahdi's New Testament citations (primarily from the book of Revelation, which he identifies as Christ's *Injil*, mentioned in the Qur'an) are nearly double the combined references to passages from the Hebrew Bible and Qur'an.[80]

Siddiq Muhammad, Philips's informant who had joined the movement in 1968, reports that around June 1974, as Al Mahdi's command that followers beg on the streets led to a massive flood of revenue, "things started to really change."[81] A short passage in *Id with the Ansars* hints that an intellectual shift had also occurred in the community—not an abrupt turn from one religious identity to another, but rather an intensified focus on Al Mahdi himself. The community's investigations of scripture had produced new understandings of its leader's significance, as "the Lamb (Al Masih) has become known to the people as the person he was prophesied to be, rather than by what he calls himself."[82]

Literature from the late 1970s reports that Al Mahdi (born in 1945, an even century after the birth of the Sudanese Mahdi)[83] launched his movement in 1970 (a century after the Mahdi established his mission), upon the opening of the seventh seal mentioned in the book of Revelation. While sources from earlier in the decade present Al Mahdi as the Mahdi's grandson, 1977's *Muhammad Ahmad: The Only True Mahdi!* and later materials name him as the Mahdi's great-grandson.[84] The seventh seal signified the Qur'an, which was "opened" with Al Mahdi's arrival as its master translator and interpreter. His mission was to teach the 144,000 helpers of Allah (Ansar Allah) in preparation for Christ's return in the year 2000. While AAC publications such as *Al Imaam Isa Visits Egypt 1981* featured a photo of Al Mahdi with the caption "Our Savior Has Returned," Al Mahdi's precise connection to Christ remained so ambiguous that some apparently believed that Al Mahdi identified himself as the returning Jesus. Al Mahdi insists in *I Don't Claim to Be . . .* (1981) that he "never claimed to be Christ" and that his pamphlets were misunderstood. He explained that Jesus would not return as an embodied reincarnation, but that the *spirit* of Jesus would "descend into a person" and then "disperse amongst his followers," the 144,000 foretold in Revelation as followers of Muhammad's household, his *ahl al-bayt*.[85] Al Mahdi also deployed Jesus during this period to articulate his relationship to Elijah Muhammad; the first appearance of Jesus was heralded by John the Baptist, who was endowed with the spirit of the biblical Elijah. Al Mahdi (whose first name, Isa, is the Arabic equivalent of Jesus) thereby projected the relationship between Elijah/John and Jesus onto Elijah Muhammad and himself.[86]

In AAC literature dating from the late 1970s through the 1980s, we can observe themes relating to esoteric knowledge and advanced technology in ancient Egypt, emphasis on a globalizing Black Islam that featured both the Sudanese Mahdiyya and Elijah Muhammad as key ingredients, antagonism toward Arab Sunnis and their African American "puppets," discussions of chakras and other New Age reference points, and claims of Al Mahdi's interaction with several transcendent figures, including Khidr, Jesus, ancient pharaohs, and extraterrestrial sages. These themes do not follow one another in distinct "phases" but can be found in the same publications, along with continued commitments to "traditional" Islamic knowledge marked in part by details such as commitment to Maliki jurisprudence[87] and the study of classical Arabic.

Again, changes in names and symbols have limited illustrative power. A number of publications from 1982 refer to the movement as United Muslims in Exile, though this name change did not reflect a reorientation of discourse or practice or supplant Ansaru Allah as the movement's identity. Nor did the AAC/NIH's changes of symbols and flags consistently signify new doctrinal orientations, though these changes sometimes corresponded to shifting claims and the visual cultures of its opponents. Around the turn of the 1980s, the community used a white, green, red, and black flag bearing the *shahadah* (testimony to Allah's oneness and the prophethood of Muhammad), along with the double-bladed sword of 'Ali. This design echoed the MIB flag, which displayed the *shahadah* in the same style of Arabic with a single-bladed sword. Ironically, it was the MIB, not the Ansar, that employed a black, red, and green color scheme (as opposed to the Garveyite pan-Africanist flag, which consisted of the same colors but positioned the red stripe above the black) and gave as its flag's inspiration the Sudanese Mahdiyya (while being careful to explain that Muhammad Ahmad, a "great champion of justice," was "known to many as the Mahdi" without acknowledging that he personally claimed that title for himself).[88]

From 1983 to 1987, community literature simultaneously used the names Ansaru Allah Community and Nubian Islamic Hebrews. It was also during this time that Al Mahdi added "Al Haadi" to his name, becoming As Sayyid Al Imaam Isa Al Haadi Al Mahdi and emphasizing his claim to be the son of Muhammad Ahmad's son Sayyid Hadi Abdulrahman al-Mahdi (1918–1971). In 1984, Al Mahdi established a Sufi order, Sons of the Green Light, which he promoted throughout AAC/NIH literature as adjacent to the larger community. From 1987 to 1991, without erasing its Ansar identity, the community rebranded itself the Original Tents of Kedar. It was as the Original Tents of Kedar that the community adopted the Mahdiyya flag.[89]

During the late 1980s, the character of Yanaan/Yaanuwn, who was first mentioned at least as early as 1983 as an intergalactic sheikh who sometimes occupied Al Mahdi's body, entered into new prominence and became increasingly identified with Al Mahdi. Original Tents of Kedar books frequently display an image of Al Mahdi with the Ansar masjid and a flying saucer in the background and a caption identifying him as "As Sayyid Isa Al Haadi Al Mahdi (Yanaan)."[90] When asked, "Who is Yanuwn?" during a session open to the public circa 1988, Al Mahdi confirmed, "I am an extraterrestrial incarnated."[91] Al Mahdi's 1991 commentary on the book of Revelation claims that Yanaan is the nineteenth elder in Khidr's order, and also an appearance of Khidr himself in human form.[92] In his interpretation of Rev. 1:7 ("Here he is coming upon the clouds"), Al Mahdi reveals that the Buraq, Muhammad's steed during his ascension, was not a winged animal but a fleet of spaceships within the Mothership, which will descend to earth to gather the saved 144,000.[93]

A survey of AAC/NIH media from the 1970s to the early 1990s reveals considerable stability. Despite changes in name, flag, symbols, and clothing, the AAC/NIH did not abandon the resources that had previously authorized its truth claims in favor of a whole new set of materials. In a single pamphlet from 1983, Al Mahdi hits notes that observers would treat as marking separate phases of his career, presenting his body as a medium through which Khidr, Jesus, an ancient Egyptian pharaoh, and Yanaan speak. Rather than presume that Al Mahdi's choices perform a postmodernist mysticism designed to break down all categories and produce enlightenment through incoherence, we can examine the ways in which items related to one another within the particularities of his own toolbox and the world of preexisting connections that made this toolbox possible—and even intelligible—to a community.

At the start of the 1990s, Al Mahdi and numerous followers relocated to the community's Jazzir Abba campground in the Catskills (named after Abba Island in the Sudan). Rebranding Jazzir Abba as Mount Zion, Al Mahdi also changed his own name to Rabboni Y'shua Bar El Haady and embarked on reforms that led observers to call this period his "Jewish" phase. Shortly thereafter, the community relocated en masse to Georgia. Material from 1992–93 identifies the community as the Tents of Abraham or Tents of Nubia, renames Al Mahdi Dr. Malachi Z. York or affectionately calls him the Lamb (again, a designation used for him since the 1970s),[94] and tells a story of the movement's changes. At Mount Zion in 1992, York reportedly informed community members that they would "stop living the life of a Muslim" because Islam was about to become increasingly associated with terrorism, and Sunni Arabs would never accept African American Muslims as equals.[95]

In 1993, the community, having adopted the name Holy Tabernacle Ministries, migrated to its Tama Re commune in Eatonton, Georgia. Post-1993 media intensified York's attention to pharaonic Egypt, new resources such as ancient Sumerian religion, indigenous American sovereignty movements, and narratives of extraterrestrial civilizations, while simultaneously denigrating and reconstructing Jewish, Christian, and Muslim traditions. In the second half of the 1990s, the community came to be known as the United Nuwaubian Nation of Moors (UNNM). York also led numerous Masonic lodges, such as the Ancient and Mystic Order of Melchizedek, which adhered to the lessons of his earlier Sufi order and simply switched out references to Khidr with Melchizedek (a move consistent with York's historical conceptualization of the figure).

York regularly acknowledged his Brooklyn past, often explaining, "I came giving you what you wanted, so you would want what I have to give."[96] Though the community had always acknowledged changes in name, symbol, and prescribed dress, and made claims of an intellectual progression, it was only after the move to Georgia that York retroactively spoke of his mission as having passed through a sequence of distinct phases or "schools." Amid these narratives of change, however, there are continuities. Even in his ostensibly "post-Islamic" work, while distributing lecture tapes with titles such as "Islam Is Poison," York still praised figures such as Elijah Muhammad and Daoud Faisal, claimed a connection to the Sudanese Mahdiyya, treated the Qur'an as a meaningful source for his teachings, and wrote of restoring Islam to its "pristine purity."[97]

In 2004, roughly two years after his arrest and the government raid on Tama Re, York was convicted of multiple charges relating to RICO (Racketeer Influenced and Corrupt Organizations) conspiracy, including racketeering and the interstate transportation of minors for sexual abuse. In 2005, upon government confiscation of the land, bulldozers purged Tama Re of its pyramids and statues. In the years since York's conviction, Nuwaubians have sought to free him through a number of strategies, including assertions of his innocence and claims that his trial was illegitimate, by challenging federal jurisdiction, whether on the grounds of legal sovereignty (as a Native American tribal leader) or diplomatic immunity (as a Liberian consul). While increasingly decentralized and intellectually diverse, the community continues to develop without his physical presence.

OUTLINE OF THE BOOK

The chapters of this book focus on various resources and strategies through which AAC/NIH formulated and communicated its truth. Chapter 1 explores key themes in Al Mahdi's metaphysical Africa. It discusses Al Mahdi's construction of the Sudan as a land of mystical knowledge, deeply connected to human origins and the coming fulfillment of divine plan; as a refuge for Muhammad's "unmistakenly black" daughter Fatima and son-in-law 'Ali, as they fled persecution by "pale Arabs" Abu Bakr and his daughter A'isha; as an archive of timeless Islamic knowledge, because Fatima and 'Ali left secret scriptures in the protection of Nubian custody; as the center of the modern Nubian Islamic revolution against both European and Turko-Egyptian exploitation and oppression; and as the site from which Al Mahdi found his footing in the American context, from which to navigate between anti-Muslim Afrocentrism and the anti-Blackness of encroaching Arab and South Asian Sunni hegemonies.

Chapter 2 examines the ways in which Al Mahdi constructed an ostensibly contradictory genealogy of forerunners—most significantly Elijah Muhammad and Al Mahdi's Sunni mentor, Sheikh Daoud Faisal—that includes Noble Drew Ali, Malcolm X, Allah (the former Clarence 13X), and Marcus Garvey (whom Al Mahdi claims had become Muslim), all of whom appear as figures of authorization in his claim to inherit a singular tradition of Nubian Islam in the West.

Chapter 3 complicates the popular narrative, put forth in academic literature and retroactively embraced in community media, that the AAC/NIH passed through distinct "Muslim" and "Jewish" phases. Apart from a period in 1992–93 in which the community did appear to shed coded markers of its Muslim identity (such as turbans for men and face veils for women) in favor of practices that could code as Jewish (such as Al Mahdi changing his title from imam to rabbi and wearing a yarmulke), these various sources do not agree as to how exactly we can date the "Muslim" and "Jewish" phases. Even at different points in community literature, we find multiple ideas of when the movement was most invested in the "Hebrew" dimension of its Nubian Islamic Hebrew identity. Highlighting significant continuities in the community's literature across these allegedly distinct phases, and the ways in which the community conceptualized itself in materials contemporary to the supposed mass conversions, this chapter problematizes the notion that we can easily carve AAC/NIH history into a series of successive affiliations.

Chapter 4 focuses on a figure who became an important site of both linkage and rupture: Bilal ibn Rabah, an Ethiopian who rose to prominence as one of the early companions of the Prophet Muhammad. In modern Muslim discourses, Bilal's legacy became particularly meaningful as evidence of Islam's racial egalitarianism. Al Mahdi, however, charged that "pale Arabs" had reduced Bilal to a condescending anti-Black stereotype—a slave who can sing—while denying the Blackness of other early Muslims, including the Prophet himself. Promising to reveal Bilal's true significance, Al Mahdi presented Bilal as protective custodian of the Mihjan, the scepter that had belonged to all of the Israelite prophets, which he carried on an epic quest from Ethiopia to Mecca in order to bequeath it to the awaited Ishmaelite prophet, Muhammad. This chapter discusses Bilal's significance in AAC/NIH discourse for the connections that he enabled between Israelite and Ishmaelite prophethood, the relevance of his Ethiopian Israelite backstory in Al Mahdi's imaginary of metaphysical Africa, and his polemical utility as Al Mahdi weaponized his legacy against "pale Arab" Sunnis and their Black allies—including W. D. Muhammad, who had briefly referred to his followers (and to African Americans at large) as "Bilalians."

Chapter 5 explores the AAC/NIH's underexamined relationship to Sufism, marked not only by its origins as Ansar Pure Sufi but also by its founding of an in-house Sufi order, Sons of the Green Light, in 1984. I argue that Al Mahdi was perhaps the most successful Sufi master in the United States through the 1970s and '80s, while academic studies of American Sufism have completely ignored his community in part because of the flawed categories and prejudices that continue to inform the study of American Islam more broadly.

Chapter 6 pushes back against the notion that the AAC/NIH embraced Egyptosophic spirituality only late in its history as part of a post-Muslim makeover. I demonstrate that an investment in pharaonic Egypt appeared early in the AAC/NIH archive and remained present throughout its overtly "Islamic" and "Jewish" material. When the community migrated to a compound that it declared its "Egypt in the West" and decorated the property with sphinxes, ankhs, and pyramids, this reflected not a sudden embrace of Egyptosophy out of nowhere but rather the turning of a rhetorical dial that the community already possessed.

Chapter 7 examines the community's exodus from New York to rural Georgia in 1993 and its development as the United Nuwaubian Nation of Moors (UNNM). This chapter surveys key themes of Nuwaubian discourse that are typically taken to highlight the "random" and "incoherent" nature of the community's narratives—Egyptosophy, UFO religion, claims of Native American heritage, and Freemasonry—and calls attention to the various ways in which these themes are historically linked both within the community's own archive and in broader African American intellectual traditions. Things certainly do change, but I resist the assumption that the Nuwaubian-era community has surrendered its attempt to achieve a rationally satisfying argument or a meaningful narrative of its own history.

Chapter 8 examines Al Mahdi's theories of music and sound and briefly expands the scope of community media to include artists whose work may or may not have been published by official AAC/NIH institutions. While Al Mahdi did own a recording studio and music label, and made use of music in numerous ways (and was even an aspiring R&B star himself), not all artists who disseminated AAC/NIH messages in pop culture did so through his personal resources in the music industry. Though the Five Percenter presence in hip-hop has been extensively documented, the AAC/NIH made a substantial contribution to hip-hop culture that has gone largely unnoticed. This chapter seeks to make a critical intervention in a growing body of scholarship that examines hip-hop's varied relationships to Islam but has thus far ignored Al Mahdi's community.

In the coda, I offer a short reflection on the arguments advanced in preceding chapters and the key themes of the work, particularly the problems of overemphasizing the community's apparent instability and engaging the eclecticism of its archive through frameworks of "syncretism."

Before we proceed, a few notes, the first regarding names. As the community identified itself as the Ansaru Allah Community (AAC) and/or Nubian Islamic Hebrews (NIH) for most of its history prior to the government's raid on Tama Re, sometimes privileging one name over the other, I usually refer to it as the AAC/NIH. The community's leader has become notorious for employing a plethora of aliases, but he was known for much of the period covered here (with slight variations in spelling) as As Sayyid Al Imaam Isa Al Haadi Al Mahdi. Throughout this book I generally refer to him as Al Mahdi, while occasionally using the other names he adopted when discussing those periods of his life and AAC/NIH history (he remained Al Mahdi even when literature referred to him as Isa Muhammad, for example; these names were not mutually exclusive). When discussing the community and its leader after significant transformations in the early 1990s, I use the names by which they identified themselves at that time.

Al Mahdi's names aside, the question of authorship remains complicated. AAC/NIH media usually reflect the official voice of Al Mahdi himself, though works often describe him in the third person without attribution to another author, and Al Mahdi has been accused of writing by committee. Each of Al

Mahdi's wives reportedly headed an aspect of the community's operations, meaning that one wife would have supervised the production of media content. In her memoir, Al Mahdi's former wife Ruby S. Garnett recalls the research department: "Book shelves lined the wall in that section; full of all kinds of books that . . . the sisters used to do research out of. The sisters work area was stationed right there in front of the bookshelves, and there were rows of computers where some of them sat quietly typing and looking through books and some were making photo copies of things."[98] One survivor of Al Mahdi's abuse informed me that it was her job to read books that he wanted to appropriate (she particularly enjoyed reading Zecharia Sitchin), and could identify content in Al Mahdi's works that she had personally written. When he spoke through these publications, Al Mahdi operated not only as an individual author but as a collective of thinkers. I am not interested in determining which materials "really" come from his own pen; nor, for that matter, am I overly concerned with the issue of Al Mahdi's plagiarizing material from outside sources. I thus refer to the community and Al Mahdi himself interchangeably as the producer of AAC/NIH discourse. When I write, "Al Mahdi argues x," I present Al Mahdi as an assemblage of actors who participate in his ongoing construction.

This approach also helps to move consideration of the AAC/NIH beyond Al Mahdi's abuse and exploitation of community members and to decenter him as our primary interest, even while exploring thousands of pages attributed to him. The Ansaru Allah Community's significance is not reducible to Al Mahdi's discourse or crimes; its media represent not a singular "cult leader" but a *community* that has included thousands of members through five decades and counting. Beyond "official" membership, the community's narratives also inform countless readers who have encountered its pamphlets, books, and tapes. Taking these media seriously, I take the community and its extended sphere of conversation partners seriously as well.

CHAPTER 1

"I Am the Raisin-Headed Slave"

The Nubian Ahl al-Bayt, Sudanese Mahdiyya, and Global Blackness as Islamic Revival

> The history of Arabia needs rewriting.
>
> —DRUSILLA DUNJEE HOUSTON
>
> Mohamet, the founder of Islam, was an Arab. What is an Arab? . . . Arabia is but an extension of Africa where black people from the southwest, and white, or nearly white people from the northwest met to mingle their cultures and their blood. . . . Mohamet, himself, was by all accounts a Negro.
>
> —J. A. ROGERS

As African American thinkers and communities engaged moral geographies that relocated Blackness and redefined its meanings, various maps both overlapped and competed with one another.[1] Which territory should provide the ideal moral geography—the presentation of Africa as a singular, united cultural entity, or the similarly imagined "Muslim world"? Some Muslims reject pan-Africanism as a racialist or secular nationalist ideology antithetical to Islam; some Afrocentrists reject notions of a global Muslim *umma* because of the inequalities and anti-Black racism that this construction elided, even rejecting Islam itself as anti-Black. This chapter discusses AAC/NIH engagements with that tension, which Al Mahdi answers with his own moral geography and a religio-racial mythic history that anchors Islam in a timeless *bilad as-Sudan*, "land of the Blacks." After introducing the question of Islam's relationship to Blackness as conceived by numerous Muslim and non-Muslim thinkers, I examine AAC/NIH narratives of racial history as they inform key themes of AAC/NIH media: the Blackness of Arabic, presentations of conflicts in the original Muslim community as racialized power struggles between Black Arabs and "pale Arab" imposters, the centrality of the Sudan as a Black Islamic archive, embodied practices such as the veil and nose ring, and AAC/NIH ideas of the "wrong Africa," Yoruba revivalism.

Community media report that it was in the Sudan, at the junction of the two Niles, that Allah created Adam out of black clay. It was also in the Sudan that the members of Muhammad's family found sanctuary as Black refugees in flight from Islam's takeover by "red" and "pale" Arabs. The Sudan became a site at which interwoven Muslim eschatological expectations and hopes of Black liberation found their fulfillment, as the anticipated Mahdi rose from the Sudan in the nineteenth century to defeat Anglo-Egyptian colonial oppression. Finally, the Sudan provides the AAC/NIH with an embodied link to Nubian Islam, as Al Mahdi presents himself as the great-grandson of the Sudanese Mahdi, himself a direct descendant of the Prophet. Al Mahdi speaks to what Zareena Grewal terms "the moral geography of the Dark world" espoused by Malcolm X, and to the "transnational moral geographies of newly arrived revivalist immigrants" that supplanted it.[2] AAC/NIH media deflect anti-Muslim Afrocentrism not by rehabilitating Arab slavery and anti-Blackness, but by decentering "pale Arabs" as Islam's natural authorities and constructing the Sudan as Islam's true heartland. For Black people to study Arabic and live in accordance with the Qur'an does not require a disavowal of Afrocentrism or capitulation to the Arabian Peninsula's current occupants, because the Arabic language, the Qur'an, the authentic Sunna, and Islam itself are Nubian. Monotheism is Black. In his metaphysical Africa, Al Mahdi challenges both sides of the Afrocentrism-Islam debate on their own terms, always claiming the origins, center, authenticity, and authority.

MALIK VS. OMOWALE

Drusilla Dunjee Houston's *Wonderful Ethiopians of the Ancient Cushite Empire* would find a warm reception among Afrocentrist readerships in the later twentieth century. Writing in 1926, Houston also speaks to controversies that persisted for later Afrocentrists and African American Muslims: racial identities in ancient Egypt and Arabia, and the sources of their great pharaonic and

Islamic civilizations. Houston presents both Egypt and Arabia as originally colonies of Ethiopia, insists that modern Nubians in Egypt maintain a timeless race pride that keeps them from miscegenation with Egyptians, Arabs, and Turks, and distinguishes between Arabia's earliest Black inhabitants and "the Semitic race, which is in possession of Arabia today." Houston emphasizes Muhammad's descent from Abraham's "Hamitic" concubine, Hajar, but she also follows an "Islam-by-the-sword" narrative to treat Muhammad's religion as emblematic of "the primitive nature of the Semitic Arabian." She deduces that Semitic Arabs could not have produced Islamic civilization from their own "bare life" but relied on Black influence.[3]

Like their contemporaries among pan-Africanists and Black Israelite movements, African American Muslims in the 1920s and '30s recalibrated the meanings of Africanity. Noble Drew Ali taught that Black people in the United States must reclaim their nationality as Moors, descendants of Moabites from Canaan who migrated, with the pharaohs' permission, to northwest Africa and founded the Moroccan empire.[4] Recovering genealogical links to Islamic heritage was not strictly the concern of "heterodox" movements: Muhammad Ezaldeen, a former Moorish Science member who studied in Egypt and later formed possibly the first African American Sunni movement, the Addeynu Allahe Universal Arabic Association, emphasized the identification of Noah's son Ham—and by extension, in the era's biblically informed narratives of race, all Black people—as an Arab.[5] Conversion to Sunni Islam did not signify a "color-blind" erasure of race but instead reclaimed "Hamitic-Arab" racial heritage.[6]

The Nation of Islam witnessed (and contributed to) profound changes in the ways in which Black intellectuals envisioned Africa. Affirming the Black Man as father of civilization while still enforcing Victorian ideals of respectability, civilization, and progress, Elijah Muhammad exhibited complex views on Africa. For Elijah, reclaiming Black prestige did not immediately mean correcting popular misconceptions about African cultures, but rather insisting that global Blackness could not be reduced to what he perceived as Africa's limitations. In the Supreme Wisdom Lessons, Master Fard Muhammad asks Elijah, "Why does the devil call our people Africans?" Elijah answers, "To make our people of North America believe that the people on that continent are the only people they have and are all savage. . . . The original people live on this continent and they are the ones who strayed away from civilization and are living a jungle life. The original people call this continent Asia but the devils call it Africa to try to divide them. He wants us to think that we are all different."

The macrocosmic Black Man's greatness, according to the Lessons, was not located in the continent that devils had named "Africa"; instead, his universe lay beyond Africa and what Elijah called its "jungle life." In a 1934 editorial, Elijah argues for a global Muslim Blackness that transcends what he regards as the embarrassment of non-Muslim African cultures. The forces of white supremacy promote images of Africa's "savage" cultures to keep Black people in North America from recovering their full dignity in Islamic—that is, *Asiatic*—civilization. "We were never told by our enemies who made slaves of us that the Moslems (Asiatics) who were brought over here were from the Nile in Egypt," he writes. "No, they taught us we were from the jungles of Africa, and that all of our people lived there.... Why does not the white man teach you to go to Egypt, Arabia, Persia, Yemen, or Afghanistan? No, he knew that if you went East you would learn who you were."[7]

After visiting Africa in 1959, Elijah called the continent "ugly looking," populated with "near nude" women nursing babies in public, and proclaimed that the Nation must go to Africa not to learn from Africans but "to civilize people.... We don't consider the people of Africa's jungle as anything for us to follow.... I am already civilized and I am ready to civilize Africa." The ancient Shabazz tribe had established civilization at the "best part of our planet," the Nile Valley and the holy city of Mecca; however, the tribe's journeys further into Africa were linked to its having "strayed from civilization," which Elijah connected to the Shabazz tribe's developing kinky hair and thick lips in the new climate.[8] In the 1960s, Elijah guarded his mosques against Afrocentrism with decrees against "adopting the African dress and hair styles." Drawing a firm distinction between African and Muslim identities, Elijah warned that his Nation accepted only "the style of real Muslim people," and threatened exile to Muslims who wore "the headpiece of traditional and tribal African people who are other than believers in Islam." The newspaper *Muhammad Speaks* reprinted this 1968 statement in 1974, perhaps speaking to renewed disputes concerning the relationship between Africa and Islam.[9] However, Edward E. Curtis IV's investigation of *Muhammad Speaks* content through the later 1960s and '70s highlights Nation authors who also celebrated African achievements in settings such as the Songhai Empire, while defending the Nation against a new tide of "Africanists" who disparaged Muslims for "allegedly exploiting 'Mother Africa.'"[10]

In encounters with Black and non-Black Sunni communities that had been escalating since the 1950s, Elijah Muhammad would reconstruct his link to the "Muslim world." In the 1950s, he asserted that the Prophet Muhammad, "an Arab, was a member of the black nation."[11] Losing interest in approval from transnational Muslim communities, Elijah later identified the Prophet as "a white man" who represented an "Old Islam" for white people. In contrast to Old Islam, Elijah foretold a "New Islam" that would be "established and led by Black Muslims only."[12] In the early 1960s, as the Saudi government established transnational organizations such as the Muslim World League (MWL) and World Assembly of Muslim Youth to export its brand of Sunni revivalism, Elijah proclaimed that his right to speak came only from the divine: "I will say that neither Jeddah nor Mecca have sent me! . . . I am sent from Allah and not from the Secretary General of the Muslim League! There is no Muslim in Arabia that has the authority to stop me from delivering this message."[13] An early example of Saudi efforts to redirect African American Muslim practices appears in Malcolm's short post-Nation career, when he became a guest of state during his pilgrimage to Mecca and obtained scholarships for members of his new organizations, Muslim Mosque, Inc. and the Organization of Afro-American Unity, to study in Saudi Arabia.[14]

When Malcolm X returned from his post-Nation travels in early 1964, he brought not one but two recovered identities back with him. In Mecca, Malcolm had earned the honorific name of hajji for his pilgrimage; he famously used this to supplement Malik El-Shabazz, the name that Elijah Muhammad had given him, becoming El-Hajj Malik El-Shabazz. In Nigeria, he received another name: Omowale, meaning "the child has come home" in Yoruba.[15] These names seem to represent two heartlands for Malcolm's global vision: one Islamic, the other African. Even as Malcolm treated these heritages as interconnected, some voices in the Black freedom struggle and American Muslim communities would perceive rupture or even irreconcilable contradiction between them.

Twentieth-century efforts to recover African spiritual traditions that had been suppressed in the violence of transatlantic slavery, as with efforts to restore African Muslim traditions, were transnational and polycultural, the product of new connections. As early as the 1940s, increased Cuban migration to the United States facilitated new opportunities for African Americans to encounter Afro-Cuban traditions. Tracey E. Hucks explains that in the 1950s and '60s, amid anticolonial movements and intensifying imaginaries of Africa as "a single continental entity," African American religious thinkers reconceptualized Afro-Cuban traditions as pathways to an indigenous African spirituality. This progression becomes readable in the trajectory of Oseijeman Adefunmi. Born Serge King and raised Baptist, as a child he wondered, "Who is the African

God?" In 1959, Adefunmi underwent initiation into the Shango priesthood in Cuba and later felt a shift in his center of gravity from the Caribbean to Africa. In his pursuit of authentic African religion and his establishment of successive communities, such as the Sango Temple and Yoruba Temple, Adefunmi embarked upon a project of re-Africanizing the Afro-Cuban spiritual tradition[16] and searched for the "purest African form," which he viewed as having been diluted in the Americas.[17]

In Harlem (which he renamed "New Oyo"), Adefunmi's Yoruba Temple promoted an African neotraditionalist revival by marketing African clothes, saint candles, and herbal remedies, not to mention distributing Adefunmi's books and pamphlets throughout the city.[18] Yoruba Temple literature portrayed Islam as a force of alien invasion and exploitation: "The first people to penetrate Africa for slaves in modern times were the Arabs, who ever since they brought their religion to Egypt in 636 A.D. have been plundering the coasts of East Africa for people to be used as slaves"—a trade that continues, Adefunmi wrote in 1962, "to this day." Recognizing that Muslims were among the enslaved Africans taken to the New World, Adefunmi asked why Islam perished in the Americas while Yoruba traditions survived. Unable to impose their hegemony, enslaved Muslims could not compete against genuinely African spiritualities, he explained, and "the Mohammedan influence which was not indigenously African to begin with quickly perished under the impact and dynamism of African culture."[19]

Advocating non-Islamic conceptions of Black spirituality in 1962 Harlem, Adefunmi confronted an African American Islamic renaissance. Rethinking Islam's brand prestige as resistance to white supremacy, Adefunmi argued that Islam remained more palatable to white Western tastes than Yoruba did, given Islam's monotheism and the West's negative portrayals of indigenous African spiritualities: "Because of the western deprecation of African religion with its Gods, dancing and drums, many blacks are making a superficially intellectual association with Islam, which is a religion acceptable to the white majority and known to be accepted by many Africans." Adefunmi suggests that Islam's rigid legalism will never constrain the imagination and passion of African intellects: "The African, being supremely creative and cosmopolitan, will eventually revolt against a culture which debars plastic sculpture and other traditionally African expressions such as dancing, syncopated singing, smoking and drinking."[20]

During this same period, Brooklyn's State Street Mosque suffered from antagonism between African American and immigrant Muslims. Many Black members were alienated by the mosque's requirement that they carry identification cards to prove themselves "orthodox" Muslims. Others criticized Faisal himself as insufficiently "orthodox" and lacking in scholarly credentials. These critiques were not mutually exclusive. In 1962, a handful of Black converts left State Street to follow the mosque's Qur'an teacher, a member of the Pakistan-based Tablighi Jama'at, and start a Sunni revivalist community. Their masjid, Mosque Ya-Sin, sparked the rise of the Dar-ul-Islam Movement, the most successful Black Sunni community prior to the death of Elijah Muhammad.[21]

Al Mahdi, only twenty-two years old in 1967, formulated a construction of Islam that spoke from and to the divisions in Brooklyn's Muslim communities, while also engaging non-Muslim visions of metaphysical Africa. For Al Mahdi, this meant an Afrocentric Sufism that emphasized loud dhikr with the *duff* and talking drums, identification with historical Nubia and Sudanese folk Islam, mystically guided apocalyptic anticolonialism, rigorous study of Arabic, claims of a "back to the scriptures" textualist revival, and aesthetics that incorporated Egyptian ankhs, nose rings, tarbushes, bones worn in the ears, and, in the case of Al Mahdi himself, tribal scarification. The Mosque of Islamic Brotherhood's newspaper compared these practices to "the more barbaric aspects of primitive pagan societies."[22]

In 1965, the year of Malcolm X's assassination, changes in U.S. immigration policy radically transformed American Islam. As a result of the Hart-Celler Act, which abolished national-origin quotas that had been in force since 1924, the United States received immigrants from Muslim-majority nations on an unprecedented scale.[23] Once perceived as a Black religion, Islam became reimagined as a setting in which Black people depended on Arab and South Asian immigrants for tutelage.[24]

By the time of Elijah Muhammad's death in 1975, Black Islam was being challenged by Saudi encroachment and changing relations between African American and immigrant Muslim communities. W. D. Muhammad's statements upon succeeding his father confront these tensions: "I am not asking any of you to come with me, that I am going to direct you or lead you to Arab world leadership.... I tell you that the Arab world has to look this way for understanding."[25] On February 25, 1975, the day before the Nation's annual Saviors' Day celebration and W. D. Muhammad's first day as head of the Nation of Islam, he told his ministers, "Don't think any Arab is coming here to tell you anything.... I don't care if he's been reading the Holy Qur'an since the day Arabia became sandy. He's not coming here to lead these sheep."[26]

Mustafa el-Amin quotes a 1978 address in which W. D. Muhammad declares, "I am not going to the Arabs.... I am not going to Sunnism, I am not going to

Wahhabism.... I am going to the Kaʿba." To regard Islam as "Arab religion" is "sheer stupidity," W. D. Muhammad argues, and serves "the plan of the devil to keep our people away from their last hope, by making them think that to identify with al-Islam is to identify with the Arabs."[27] W. D. Muhammad even suggested that the first Muslims were not of the same race as modern "light-skinned, Caucasian rich Arabs." In an argument that would register with AAC/NIH narratives, W. D. Muhammad asserted, "The original Arabs were black people and the Caucasians came in and mixed up their blood with them just as they mixed blood with many other black people."[28]

Nonetheless, W. D. Muhammad sought opportunities to engage global Muslim networks. Jeff Diamant's work on Saudi "soft power" in Black Muslim communities sheds light on W. D. Muhammad's interest in accessing Saudi resources, noted in a 1975 disclosure to his officials: "We have not millions but billions that we can get if we show the world that we realize what we already have in our hands." Through organizations such as the MWL, Diamant writes, the Saudi state sought to "alter African-Americans' religious practices." This effort provided W. D. Muhammad with scholarships at the Islamic University of Madinah and other institutions, funding for pilgrimages to Mecca, training for his imams, financial and personnel support for staffing his masjids, and thousands of printed copies of the Qurʾan. This collaboration provoked tension, as evidenced when an MWL official publicly corrected W. D. Muhammad, until W. D. Muhammad began to decline Saudi offers for scholarships and hajj funding in the early 1980s.[29]

Some members of W. D. Muhammad's community resisted movement toward Saudi-centered al-Islam. Others, informed by training and resources obtained through W. D. Muhammad's collaboration with the Saudi project, felt that he had not moved far enough. Siraj Wahhaj, an imam in W. D. Muhammad's community formerly known as Jeffrey 12X, traveled to Saudi Arabia for training under the MWL. He arrived at the position that W. D. Muhammad was not legitimately a Sunni Muslim, broke from his former imam, and upon returning to the United States opened his Masjid at-Taqwa in Brooklyn.[30]

Critiques also came from Black Sunnis outside the post-Nation community, such as the Islamic Party of North America (IPNA), founded by Yusuf Muzaffaruddin Hamid in 1971. Hamid had converted in 1962 and spent much of the '60s traveling Muslim-majority countries, where he engaged movements such as the Muslim Brothers. In Pakistan, he became a student of Jamʿaat Islami ideologue Abul A'la Mawdudi.[31] Upon his return to the United States, he grew disillusioned at the Islamic Center of Washington, D.C., owing to its immigrant leadership's failure to engage the concerns of African American Muslims.³² With other alienated Black Muslims, he left the Islamic Center and started the Masjidul Ummah, later forming the IPNA. In 1972, the "Islam in Africa" issue of IPNA journal *Al-Islam* attacked Islamic Center director Muhammad Abdul-Rauf, who protested with the Nation after a violent confrontation with the NYPD at Mosque No. 7 and proclaimed that the "whole Muslim world" supported the Nation. To the IPNA, this amounted to Muslims "crawling and bowing" before a "polytheistic racial cult."³³ Even as W. D. Muhammad reformed the Nation, the IPNA continued its opposition. In 1976, *Al-Islam* offered editorials titled "Islamic Worker's Response to *Bilalian News*: No Compromise in Islam" and "Elijah and Fard Must Go!" charging that W. D. Muhammad's claim to be a Muslim could not be taken seriously as he continued to express "extremely respectful references" to Fard Muhammad and had not fully denounced his deceased father.³⁴

W. D. Muhammad was not the Saudis' only opening into Black Muslim communities. Numerous converts traveled to Saudi Arabia for scholarly credentials, including Al Mahdi's future adversary, Bilal Philips, later the first Western student at the University of Madinah; Abdullah Hakim Quick, the university's first American graduate; and other figures who would become the backbone of Black Salafism in the later 1980s and '90s.³⁵ Beyond overt Saudi interventions in American Muslim life, the turn of the 1980s also saw the rise of immigrant-centered Muslim institutions, such as the Islamic Society of North America.

In the course of these transformations, Islam lost much of its capital among Afrocentrist intellectuals as a pro-Black alternative to Christianity. In anti-Islamic Afrocentrism, Islam appears as an ideology of Arab racial supremacy, no less guilty than Christianity for its violent suppression of indigenous African traditions and connection to Black enslavement. Blackamerican Muslim movements such as the Nation of Islam, in this view, are correct in their indictment of Christianity but deluded in their search for an authentic connection to Africa through the religion of Arab invaders. One prominent voice of anti-Islamic Afrocentrism, Yosef Ben-Jochannan, explains that he wrote *African Origins of the Major "Western Religions"* (1970) to help African Americans trapped in "mental enslavement" by Christianity, Judaism, and Islam to at least recognize the Black contributions to what he regards as these overtly anti-Black traditions.³⁶

Chancellor Williams's *The Destruction of Black Civilization* (1971) offers a comprehensive history of various African kingdoms and states ("Black Civilization") from 4500 BCE to argue that the "destruction of Black Civilization" occurred repeatedly throughout history whenever Black/African nations opened their gates to outsiders. Arab Islam and European Christianity both opposed "African religion," which had ironically provided the Hebrews with source material. Arabs, whom Williams categorizes as "a white people, the Semitic division of Caucasians," with their own "white superiority complex," appear throughout Williams's history as slave-trading invaders. As white Arab "armies of Islam continued their triumphant march on Africa, destroying its basic institutions wherever they could do so," Williams reminds his reader, "Black Muslims were not spared from destruction by non-Black Muslims." Williams regards Islam as instrumental in slavery's racialization: Egypt's Mamluk "revolt of white slaves" in 1250 CE essentially ended the white slave trade, after which "Black Africa became the exclusive hunting ground for slaves."[37]

Williams's reading of relationships between Arabs, Islam, and Africa offers significant implications for African Americans who look to Islam for their Black historical consciousness. Williams regrets that many "mixed up and confused" Black people in the United States, having rightly rejected the names of their ancestors' "white western slavemasters," have replaced them not with authentic African names but rather with the "Arab and Berber slavemaster's names."[38] Williams provoked critical responses from the IPNA, which published a front-page challenge in *Al-Islam*. In its 1976 editorial "Slaves: 'Set Them Free as a Favor,'" the IPNA charges Williams with attempting to "slander Islam," countering that rather than abolish slavery outright, Islam "adopted a wise and practical plan for the gradual abolition of slavery." The editorial pushes back against conflations of Islam with Arabness, pointing out that Williams and other writers, "ignorant of what Islam teaches," erroneously accept any action by Muslim Arabs as representative of Islam. When Arab slave traders violate Islamic principles, this is not Islam's problem. Acknowledging Arab exploitation of Black slave labor, the unnamed author asserts, "the Arab slave trade in East Africa was just as condemnable in the eyes of Islam as the European slave trade in West Africa."[39] In another *Al-Islam* editorial, the IPNA promoted awareness of African Muslim legal, artistic, and scholarly heritages, refuting "extreme Black Nationalists" and "fuzzy-thinking 'scholars'" who portray Islam as "an 'Arabian thing,' not African." While arguing for Islam's African legitimacy, however, the editorial also resorts to "civilizing mission" arguments: "The human development of those Africans who accepted Islam was far superior to that of the pagans.... Islam thus brought West Africans to the pinnacle of disciplined human development, and what is human cannot be anti-African."[40]

In his foundational Afrocentrist text *They Came Before Columbus* (1976), Ivan van Sertima minimizes Arab Muslim contributions to the African empire of Mali. He writes that while traders became Muslim as "the pragmatic thing to do, since nearly all foreign trade was with the Arabs," Mali's Muslim elites "gave Islam little more than lip service." Securing Mali as a Black African legacy rather than an import from outside, Van Sertima declares, "Arab-Islamic influence on medieval Mali, therefore, was very peripheral."[41]

Echoing arguments from Williams, Molefi Asante writes in *Afrocentricity* (1980) that while Christianity's relationship to anti-Black oppression had been thoroughly documented by Black intellectuals, Islam's historical anti-Blackness had escaped comparable scrutiny. Resisting Islam's image as a pro-Black alternative to Christianity, Asante charges that "the adoption of Islam is as contradictory to Afrocentricity as Christianity had been." Asante remains sympathetic to Elijah Muhammad, but he regards Elijah's essential contribution to the Black freedom struggle as liberation from Christianity, rather than a point of entry into Islam. For Asante, religion is nationalism; the Muhammad of seventh-century Arabia was "a nationalist who strove to bring about a cohesive spirit among his people." This means that Islam inescapably empowers Arabs over non-Arabs: "The African who makes the pilgrimage often flies over numerous sacred cities and sites of his own to march around someone's sacred stone.... Turning one's head to Mecca is symbolic of the same cultural insistence which keeps the convert looking in the direction of another's culture, not his own." Conversion to Islam, in Asante's view, requires the adoption of "non-African" customs and the surrender of African heritage. "If you must change your name," he writes, "choose an African name, not an Arab name. Why go through the trouble of discarding a European name to choose an Arab one?"[42]

Many Afrocentrist seekers, regarding Christianity and Islam as equally anti-Black, sought to recover a singular and self-contained "African religion." The AAC/NIH developed alongside movements that offered this "African religion" through reconstructed Yoruba traditions (such as Oyotunji African Village) and Egyptosophy (such as the Ausar Auset Society), while also engaging a variegated American Islam: W. D. Muhammad's post-Nation community, constructing its legitimacy significantly through creative reinterpretation of the Nation's ideology and connections to non-Black Muslims; Louis Farrakhan's Nation revival, which staked its own claims on the legacy of Elijah Muhammad; Arab and South Asian communities supplanting Black communities as the public faces of Islam in America; and Black Salafi scholars and institutions that increasingly looked to Saudi Arabia as a center of Islamic authenticity and authority. Amid diverse articulations of Islam's relationship to Blackness, the AAC/NIH produced its own metaphysical Africa in which potential conflicts between Islamic and Black authenticities become reconciled.

THE ANSAR RACE EPIC

In texts such as *Tribal Encyclopedia* (1977) and *Polytheism: Worship of the Canaanites* (1977), Al Mahdi offers grand narratives spanning thousands of years in which historical origins reveal unchanging essences, religious and racial taxonomies become intertwined, and Islam becomes the ultimate expression of a timeless, transhistorical Blackness. These narratives resist the location of Islam's center in a non-Black "heartland," privilege Nubians as the true and original Arabs, racialize Islam as Black, and locate "pale Arabs" within whiteness, thereby positioning them as natural enemies of Islam.

According to Al Mahdi, there are three races: Cushites (Nubians/Blacks), Amorites (Europeans, Aryans, "India Asian," etc.), and Edomites ("Oriental" nations). The indigenous peoples of the Americas do not constitute a distinct race of their own; they emerged through intermarriage between Nubians—who had been instrumental in the founding of Inca, Aztec, and Maya civilizations, spreading science and architecture across the Americas and even building pyramids for technologically advanced communication with pyramids in Egypt and the Sudan—and Edomites.[43]

Al Mahdi in turn divides Nubians into three major subcategories—Dongolawi ("Dongaloway," in Al Mahdi's rendering), Jaaliyyan, and Shaqiya—that correspond to identities in the Sudan,[44] describing each by its physical characteristics. The Dongolawi are distinguished by their "long nose, long face, slanted eyes, semi-thin lips, wooly hair, dark complexion," somewhat reminiscent of Al Mahdi himself, as opposed to the Jaaliyyan's "round face, round eyes, wide nose, thick lips, wooly hair, dark skin complexion"; the Shaqiya constitute a mixture of the two.[45] Al Mahdi further identifies the Dongolawi as descendants of Kush/Cush, one of the sons of Noah's son Ham, presents "Cush" as a Hebrew word for "dark-faced," and privileges the Kushites as having been a "pure seed and at one time the largest and most prominent tribe in Sudan."[46]

From his reading of the Qur'anic account (15:28), Al Mahdi writes that Allah formed Adam from black mud/clay. Adam's skin was therefore literally black, though "pale so-called Arabs" conceal Adam's Blackness with allegorical interpretations. Al Mahdi additionally locates the site at which Adam and Eve were created as the junction of the White and Blue Niles in the Sudan and translates *al-Sudan* as "Land of the Blacks." Further connecting the land to Adam and Eve, he highlights the Arabic dual form to render *al-Sudan* specifically as "Land of the *Two* Blacks." Traveling from the Sudan to what is now the Arabian Peninsula before there was a Red Sea dividing them, Adam and Eve arrived at the Garden of Eden in Mecca. After their exile from the garden, they returned to the Land of the Two Blacks, which become the cradle of early humanity.[47] Discussing Adam as Allah's *khalifa* (representative, successor, vicegerent) in the world, Al Mahdi negotiates with Nation of Islam theology: the Black man is not Allah, but because he was created by Allah to signify the divine in this world, he is God (again, "Allah" and "God" are not interchangeable terms for Al Mahdi). Asking, "Who should really be called God?" in *The Forgotten Tribe Kedar* (1974), Al Mahdi answers, "The so-called 'Black Man' whenever he raises himself back to the level he was first on."[48]

"The descendants of Adam," Al Mahdi explains, "lived and ruled in the whole of Africa before the parting of the Earth (Africa) and the Moon (Asia)."[49] The Moon's partition from the earth refers to a Nation narrative, though Al Mahdi's commentary relocates its meaning. According to Elijah Muhammad, the "scientist tribe" of Shabazz was responsible for the separation of the moon from the earth. Al Mahdi interprets Elijah's account as true but allegorical: "If ever you hear talk of the moon parting from the Earth, it is Arabia and Africa. Arabia is the moon and Africa is the Earth." Arabia corresponds to the moon in that both are dry land, while Africa corresponds to the earth as "the mother of life."[50] Arabia and Africa were split during a war between Cain's descendants and Salaam, an advanced civilization that occupied land now covered by the Red Sea. Salaam was founded by the council of twenty-four elders (also referred to as "scientists," again in conversation with the Nation) who descended to earth as the "sons of Allah" mentioned in Genesis 6:2; the leader of the council and ruler of Salaam was Khidr/Melchizedek.[51] Fearful of Salaam's scientific advancement, descendants of Cain attacked the kingdom. They destroyed Mu, Salaam's capital, which led to the sinking of Salaam and the creation of the Red Sea.[52]

Prior to its partition, the land was called Nubala, "the ancient Arabic word for 'Nubia' and Nubia means 'Black.' . . . Those people who live in the whole of Africa, then 'Nubala' before the parting of the Earth and Moon, were Nubians."[53] As the proper name for the continent, Nubia represents wholeness, while Africa maintains fracture—literally, as Al Mahdi traces the name to the Arabic f-r-q root, signifying division.[54]

There was not yet such a thing as white people. Before the flood, all of humanity was Black. To explain white origins, Al Mahdi revisits the "curse of

Ham" narrative that circulated widely in the American context to support white supremacy,[55] but he flips the story to reposition white people as the cursed seed. Al Mahdi writes that after finding dry land, Noah accidentally invented wine and became drunk. Ham encountered his intoxicated father and viewed him with thoughts of "homosexuality and incest," for which Noah cursed the progeny of Ham's son Canaan. Al Mahdi emphasizes that only Canaan's sons fell under the curse; other sons of Ham who fathered Black nations, such as Phut, Cush, and Mizraim (father of Egypt) were unaffected. Canaan's curse, physically marked by albinism, produced the white race.[56] Al Mahdi treats the Nation of Islam's Yakub narrative, in which white people emerged as the result of an ancient Black scientist's eugenics regime, as valid in spirit—correctly observing a connection between whites and the devil—if not in its details.[57] Unlike Elijah Muhammad, who rejected notions of Allah and the devil as immaterial beings, Al Mahdi affirms the existence of both an unseen *shaytan* (Iblis, who, as per the Qur'anic account, became cursed after refusing to prostrate himself before Adam) and a "physical devil," the white race, Canaan's seed.[58] While Al Mahdi often appears to treat Amorites and Canaanites as interchangeable, he also uses "Canaanite" more specifically for peoples born from Amorites who raided Nubian villages to rape Nubian women, namely, "sub-tribes" with dark skin and straight hair such as the Indo-Aryans and Iranians.[59]

Shunned and humiliated for his albinism and leprosy, Canaan and his wife (who was also his sister) fled into the Caucasus Mountains, where they had eleven sons, whose descendants became increasingly animalized, even walking on all fours and eating raw human carcasses. Al Mahdi cites the Qur'an's narrative of the "Companions of the Cave" (18:9–25) and its mention of their dog as evidence of Amorite bestiality.[60] While white men pursued rape in Nubian villages, white women left in the caves copulated with dogs and other animals, evidenced today in white babies born with "dog-straight hair" and tails.[61] Likewise, Al Mahdi traces sexually transmitted diseases to white people who let dogs lick their sores.[62]

Al Mahdi's narrative of Allah sending Abraham to civilize white people echoes the Nation's vision of the devil as able to "clean himself up" but also as requiring Black instruction, as well as its treatment of Moses as a "half-original" prophet who attempted to civilize white devils but ultimately failed.[63] After his own troubles with white people, Abraham journeyed to Egypt and found Imhotep, who brought him to Zoser (Abdul Quddus), a "Master Healer" and priest in Melchizedek/Khidr's order. Al Mahdi reverses the historical relationship between Imhotep—the sagacious author of wisdom literature who was worshipped as a healing god in the Egyptian temple system, as well as in the Greek pantheon as Asclepius—and Zoser, the pharaoh for whom Imhotep served as a scholarly consultant.[64] For Al Mahdi, Imhotep was the pharaoh and Zoser the healing sage.[65] It was thanks to their advanced science that Abraham could deliver the genetically engineered pig to the Caucasus Mountains, giving Canaanites an alternative to eating the cadavers of their own people. Some of the cave-dwelling Canaanites did accept Abraham's teachings and became Yakub's devil "pale Jews," who thought of Abraham as their father and strove to follow him though they were not his biological progeny.[66]

Tribal Encyclopedia and other pamphlets tell us that Allah repeatedly delivered Israel into the hands of the Canaanites as punishment for betraying their covenant. The Israelites were ultimately destroyed, their only surviving remnant today being the Judahite refugees who became the Ethiopian Falasha, who preserved divine law until prophethood passed to the Ishmaelites. Al Mahdi denounced contemporary Black Hebrew/Israelite movements and their leaders, "who believe or make believe that they too are descendants of Israel," for misleading Nubians away from their true Abrahamic lineage: "You are descendants from the loins of his first son Ishmael (PBUH), Ishmaelites."[67] Specifically, Nubians in America descend from Kedar, Ishmael's only son to preserve his seed's purity.[68]

In Al Mahdi's global history, religions correspond to racial essences that inevitably manifest themselves, as articulated in *Polytheism: Worship of the Canaanites*. The text racializes monotheism as Black and polytheism as a symptom of white perversity. Allah sends messengers to specific communities, Al Mahdi explains, and the Canaanites received "many guides" but could not keep to the laws of Islam. Unable to grasp the worship of Allah without partners, the Canaanites repeatedly distorted their guides' teachings and took to worshipping the guides themselves.[69] The first messenger sent to white people was the Buddha; Al Mahdi explains that Siddhartha Gautama himself identified "buddha" as an office parallel to "prophet." The Buddha was sent to the "Hindus," who descended from "Aryans (Albinos) who lived in the Caucasian Mountains" and migrated to the Indian subcontinent with their abducted Nubian concubines. Merging "these two extreme races" of Amorite and Nubian, the Aryan peoples displayed traces of both, having Amorite hair texture and Nubian complexions. Their religious traditions were also hybrid, characterized by "a strict life-style of obedience and study" but "based upon worship of the Devil." In particular, the modern Hare Krishna movement "has become one of the largest devil worshipping societies in the western hemisphere," while also anchored in the worship of a Nubian as a god (Krishna's name translates as "Dark Black," Al Mahdi explains). "Although mankind worships the Nubians," Al Mahdi clarifies, "their goal is to enchant the black converts[,] casting them into a spell." Upon this introduction to Hinduism, Al Mahdi returns to the Buddha, a "Nubian prince," captioning the photo of a Buddha image to note "the kinky hair, a sign of his Cushite (Black) heritage." Against assumptions that the Buddha was "an Indian or what is termed Indo-Aryan," Al Mahdi argues for the Buddha's Blackness with reference to his lineage through Elam, son of Noah's son Shem. Al Mahdi presents Buddha as a secular (but not unbelieving) Nubian philosopher and ascetic: though the Buddha "believed in a Creator, he did not center his attention in converting the Canaanite (Indians) who had previously lost their soul because of selfishness, lust, greed, and etcetera."[70]

Al Mahdi then moves to Zoroastrianism, which he treats as inauthentic yet surprisingly similar to Islam. Prior to the invasion of Persia by Indo-European peoples and the proliferation of Hindu-informed "idol worshipping," Persia had been occupied by Nubians. While Zoroaster attempted to reform Persian religion, "the Indo-Europeans (Caucasian) were not content with the belief in an unseen Creator" and thus reverted to their "concrete gods," myths, and rituals. Finally, Al Mahdi gives a brief and largely innocuous discussion of Confucius, who has "probably affected more Chinese (Edomites) over the centuries" than any other thinker. Confucius was a "humanist" and an "ethical and religious teacher" who did not force religion upon his people. Al Mahdi regards Confucius as a true guide for the Chinese people, but notes, "as close as Confucius was to the truth, he was yet very far" because he excluded the worship of Allah from his teachings.[71]

These racial-religious histories informed Al Mahdi's understanding of differences between Muslim communities. Dismissing criticism that he was not properly orthodox, Al Mahdi shrugs away "orthodoxy" as white heresy: "the word 'orthodox' has no Islamic beginnings. ORTHODOX was made up by the pale man.... Such a word has no place in the Islamic way of life: and there is no such thing as an 'ORTHODOX' Muslim." He adds that true Muslims follow the Sunna but "absolutely DO NOT LABEL themselves with unnecessary titles such as 'Sunni.' The word 'Sunni' is of Persian origin."[72] Because Persians are Amorites in Al Mahdi's thought, tracing "Sunni" to Persian origins racializes it as white. In a 1977 pamphlet, Al Mahdi writes that he only accepts the *Muwatta* of Malik b. Anas (d. 795) as legitimate because it was the lone hadith collection produced first in Arabic; he alleges that other collections were originally Persian and then translated into Arabic.[73]

Al Mahdi constructs a Blackness-affirming Salafism: Islam's "pristine purity" exists at the origins, which rest in *bilad as-sudan*, "Land of the Blacks," while heretical innovation (*bida'*) is linked to Iran, the "land of the Aryans." And just as "pale Jews" make false claims of descent from the Israelites, today's "pale Arabs" are imposters. "The first and true Arab," Al Mahdi writes, was Abraham's son Ishmael, who was Black. "Therefore, the Nubian man (Blackman) is the real Arab. It was the Nubian man who lived and ruled Arabia as well as Africa."[74] Al Mahdi addresses the "real Arabs" question in an episode of his *True Light* cassette tape series[75] and in the pamphlet *Sons of Canaan*. "Many of the present-day inhabitants of Arabia and many parts of North Africa," he explains, are "Pale people (lepers) . . . not the real Arabs."[76] He translates Kedar's name from Hebrew as "mighty and Black skin" and links it to the Arabic q-d-r root, "as in the Night of Power" (*laylat al-qadr*) mentioned in the Qur'an. He also finds Ishmael's protected seed in Solomon 1:5: "I am Black, but comely, O Daughters of Jerusalem, as the tents of Kedar, as the curtains of Solomon."[77] In *The Forgotten Tribe Kedar*, Al Mahdi tells us that the true Arabs, the descendants of Kedar, were tricked and scattered by the pale imposter Arabs, who abducted them and sold them to European slave markets. This is how the progeny of the prophets ended up in American wilderness. As the lone tribe that "remained pure and maintained their original Blackness,"[78] Kedar's line was destined in Genesis 15:13–16 to find itself in a land not its own. "We are this lost but now found tribe," Al Mahdi proclaims, "who were called by the Honorable Elijah Muhammad 'SHABAZZ.'"[79]

THE BLACKNESS OF ARABIC: LANGUAGE OF THE SCRIPTURES

Su'ad Abdul Khabeer has observed the importance of Arabic in U.S. Muslim communities as a signifier of Islamic legitimacy, expertise, and authority, particularly amid tensions between transnational and African American Muslims. In contexts that presume immigrants from Muslim-majority countries to be innately more qualified as authorities than African American Muslims, the study of Arabic theoretically levels the field. "Because of the cultural capital of Arabic among Muslims worldwide," Abdul Khabeer argues, "Arabic will always be a trump in negotiations of symbolic power, even in contexts that do not include Arabs, like those of African American Muslims whose main *immigrant* interlocutors are South Asian." Abdul Khabeer also acknowledges African American Muslim resistance to Arabic for the implication that "'authentic' Muslim identity can only be created through the adoption of foreign cultural forms and practices," a problem exacerbated by Arab slave trading as well as by contemporary dynamics within Muslim communities. Even those who allow Arabic's primacy often challenge assumptions that Islamic authenticity requires wholesale Arab mimesis. "The question posed by some African American Muslims," Abdul Khabeer notes, is "does the value given to the Arabic language extend to Arabs and Arab culture?"[80]

The AAC/NIH answers this question by redefining what it means to be Arab. Confronting Black Salafism on its own terms, Al Mahdi's racial histories present Arabic as inherently Black. While privileging Arabic as crucial for Islamic knowledge and practice, Al Mahdi detaches the language from the "pale Arabs" who had usurped the Nubian birthright. Because the Arabs who enslaved Black Africans were not the real Arabs, one does not have to choose between submission to Arab cultural hegemony and Black Islamic agency. Providing Egyptian and Sudanese Arabic teachers for his community, Al Mahdi promised a more pure Arabic than what one found among "pale" Muslims: "DON'T waste time learning Urdu (Pakistanian Arabic) or any other form of diluted Arabic, until you've learned your own pure form. The Arabic you are being taught by these Horite, Canaanite and Amorite moslems (wolves in sheep's clothing) is below your degree of learning."[81] Arguing for his own credentials with Arabic, Al Mahdi would later attest that he was a native speaker who lost much of his Arabic after coming to the United States as a child. He claimed that to recover his Arabic, he practiced with "a Syrian named Ghalib" at State Street Mosque and later studied Arabic at a university in the Sudan.[82]

Back to the Beginning: The Book of Names (1972) treats the significance of one's name in ways that would be familiar to those versed in Nation of Islam discourse: "Your name is important today in the everyday life of the Nubian (Black) Man and woman, because of the fact that your name is supposed to represent you." The loss of authentic Nubian names, rooted in Nubian languages (Arabic, Hebrew, Yoruba, and others), accompanied the broader physical and ontological violence of slavery. To be stripped of one's true ancestral name was of a piece with being forced to accept Christianity, the replacement of traditional foods with "swine and other poisonous flesh," and imposed nakedness. *Back to the Beginning* walks readers through lists of Arabic, Hebrew, and Yoruba names, grouped by gender and provided in translation and transliteration, along with basic introductions to the respective languages. The artifact reads like an introduction to Muslim life, concluding with a list of "things that a Muslim should have" that includes a prayer rug and beads for reciting divine names. Published early in AAC/NIH history, *Back to the Beginning*'s final

FIGURE 4 Advertisement for the Upper Room, ca. 1972.

pages do not advertise the extensive book catalog found in later publications, but they contain an ad for the Upper Room, an establishment where patrons could enjoy art, music, tea, and food at the community's Rockaway Avenue headquarters. The ad contains six-pointed stars, the Nation's star and crescent, and an ankh, with greetings in Arabic (*salaam alaykum*), Swahili (*jambo*) and Yoruba (*alafiya*) (fig. 4). The pamphlet also advertises Arabic classes alongside Islamic and martial arts classes at the Rockaway location.[83]

Al Mahdi weaponizes his mastery of Hebrew when chastising other Muslims for their lack of attention to the Bible. Arguing against Black Hebrew/Israelite movements, however, he gives primacy to Arabic. He insists that Arabic is the language of the angels and prophets (with special emphasis on Abraham, noting that Abraham was called a "Hebrew" but did not speak a "Hebrew" language) and the original root of all other languages.[84] The original name for the creator of the universe, therefore, is Allah, of which names such as Eloh or El were later derivatives. After going astray, the Israelites lost their right to the divine name and were left with the Hebraic consonants YHWH, which signified what was now ineffable. Al Mahdi argues that these consonants correspond to the Arabic Sufi chant *ya huwa*, literally "Oh He," as the masculine pronoun *huwa* represents a name known only to Allah himself.⁸⁵

Against Afrocentrists, who had their own linguistic recovery projects, AAC/NIH media argue for the Afrocentricity of Arabic. In *Arabic: The First Language* (1977), Al Mahdi positions Arabic, rather than Swahili, as the true Nubian language; in white-run "black history" courses, the devil "teaches you the lie that your language is Swahili or any of the so-called African languages. . . . Swahili is a tongue which is a combination of Arabic and Bantu that was made up exclusively for the purpose of trading slaves during the so-called 'Arab Slave Trade.'" "So, all you back to Africa, Swahili or Yoruba-speaking people," he asks, "whose Africa are you going to? The natives that speak to Tarzan are just as astray as you are. Can't you see now why the Devil must keep you ignorant?" The Afrocentrist marginalization of Arabic keeps Nubians from realizing "not only the Black man's true language, but the first language in existence."⁸⁶

AAC/NIH publications such as *A Family Guide to Easy Arabic Phrases* and *Teach Yourself Qur'aan with Tape* encourage community members to further integrate Arabic into their ritual practice and even their interpersonal communications. Before becoming equipped to speak Arabic as a primary language in the home, AAC/NIH members were expected to learn at least enough Arabic to perform ritual actions such as formal salat and various supplementary prayers (*du'a*). To this end, Al Mahdi's *Muslim Prayer Book* not only provides the ritual prescriptions in their original Arabic with English translations, but also includes Roman transliteration for those who have not yet learned the Arabic script.

AAC/NIH literature presents mastery of both the Arabic language and vocalization as essential to proper engagement with the Qur'an; Al Mahdi's 1982–86 series of commentaries on short Qur'an suras, *As Sayyid Al Imaam Isa Al Haadi Al Mahdi Explains the Secret Meaning of Qur'aan to the A'immah of Ansaaru Allah*, includes attention to recitation (*tajwid*), providing charts of relevant symbols and the rules for specific letters. Discussing the Qur'an's multiple vocalizations, Al Mahdi explains that in AAC/NIH programs, children learn to recite the Qur'an in accordance with the *riwayah* of 'Asim, which he connects to the family of the Prophet as well as to the Sudan. 'Asim's recitation, traceable to 'Ali, became popular in North Africa through the Fatimid caliphate. Al Mahdi writes that after falling from power, the Fatimid dynasty sought refuge in the Sudan, specifically in "the area that encompasses Kordofan, Darfur, Berber, and the town of El Obeid and Khartoum. This area was called Nubia." Here, 'Asim's recitation "continued to be passed down and practiced in purity by the few who knew and respected it," including the Sudanese

Mahdi. Al Mahdi proclaims that his own community has taken responsibility for preserving the 'Asim recitation in the West.[87]

"Now that you have become familiar with the Arabic language," Al Mahdi wrote in 1989, "a step further [will be taken] into a language that will be instituted for the first time here in the West": Nubic. In *Nubic: The Language of the Nubian Americans*, Al Mahdi clarifies that he does not intend to abandon Arabic; rather, Nubic constitutes "an advanced form of Arabic" with a script largely recognizable to readers of Arabic. Al Mahdi advocates Nubic by citing Elijah Muhammad's negative impressions of Africa, in which not all Africanities are to be regarded as equal: "The Nubians of Southern Nubia have lost their way and are living like savage beasts in Africa. . . . These are the same Africans you see in books wearing make-up on their faces and bodies. Isn't it strange how the media only show these jungle bunny, porch monkey-looking Africans as representatives of Africa?" The media erase "Africans such as the Nubians of Nuba (northern Sudan) who are the Muslims that kept their culture. This is the same culture that was passed down by way of the Prophets." Blackamericans come from the northern Sudan, the better of the two Nubias. After generations of erasure by the devil, Al Mahdi has come to reveal Blackamericans' true nationality (Nubian American), homeland (Sudan/Nubia), and language (Arabic/Nubic).[88]

"WE ARE THE ORIGINAL FORM OF ISLAM"

Al Mahdi's Nubian odyssey incorporates historical Islam in his reading of the Prophet, his family, and the power struggles that divided the first Muslim community, asserting both that "original" Islam is Nubian and that "Sunni is a white form of Islam."[89] Al Mahdi writes that the Prophet was descended from the pure, unmixed line of Kedar, designating him as an "unmistakably Black" man, "very dark complexioned" and with "thick lips," contrary to imaginaries of him as a "white Arab with blond hair and blue eyes" promoted by "so-called 'Moslems' from the East."[90] Al Mahdi argues that as proto-Sunni Muslims circulated fictitious hadiths, they destroyed Islam on two levels, producing a corpus of their own opinions to overrule the genuine scriptures and falsely portraying Muhammad as a white man.[91] Editions of *Hadith: Allah's Scripture Comes First* from 1977–79 feature a drawing of a white hand (wearing a crucifix ring) descending from above to present a book titled *Hadith* (with the author attribution "By the Paleman") to several eager Black hands below (wearing rings that display Egyptian ankhs or crescents and five-pointed stars). A cartoon in *The Man of Our Time* (1978) depicts a white man in a suit and tie hovering above a kufi-wearing Black man, holding him by the head and pointing with his other hand to a large book titled "SUNNAH OF MOHAMMAD." Though Al Mahdi did not reject the hadith corpus wholesale, and even published his own hadith collections, he presents excessive reliance on hadiths as an instrument of white control over Black Muslims. Al Mahdi thus absorbs Afrocentrist critiques while preserving the innocence of "true" Islam, centered in the Qurʾan and *authentic* hadiths.[92]

Without identifying himself as Shi'i, Al Mahdi affirms Muhammad's cousin and son-in-law ʿAli as his rightful successor and upholds Shi'i narratives about Muhammad's family experiencing persecution under the early caliphates. He weaves these representations of early Islam as characterized by theft and conquest into his larger history, projecting themes of his Nubian race epic onto conflicts that divided the original Muslim community. This means that while ʿAli and the Prophet's daughter Fatima are Black, Abu Bakr—recognized in Sunni traditions as the first rightly guided caliph—and his daughter Aʾisha, the Prophet's wife, whose fairness caused him to call her "Humayra" (little red one), are white. The power struggles between rival camps among the earliest Muslims become racialized as another episode in Nubians' eternal struggle against Canaan's cursed seed.

AAC/NIH media affirm Muhammad's Blackness from as far back as the record goes, but their allegiance to the *ahl al-bayt* and their racialization of the Sunni-Shi'i conflict developed over time. The earliest work in which I could find affirmation of ʿAli as the rightful successor to the Prophet, *Muhammad Ahmad: The Only True Mahdi!*, was produced in 1977. In the same work, Al Mahdi explains that "the true line of succession is the one according to the Shiʿites for they recognized twelve men as successors . . . and they all came from the tribe of the Quraysh." This pamphlet names the twelve Imams of Ithna Ashʿari ("Twelver") tradition as Muhammad's successors but neglects details of Ithna ʿAshari narratives that provoke tension with his investment in the Sudanese Mahdiyya, such as the twelfth Imam's disappearance as a child, his continued existence in a metaphysical state of *ghaybat* until the end of the world, and his ultimate status as the singular awaited Mahdi. For Al Mahdi, the twelfth Imam is not the Imamate's eschatological conclusion but passes his authority to a successor and continues the chain. Al Mahdi cites hadiths in which the Prophet predicts that the awaited Mahdi would come from him through Fatima, but these hadiths appear in Sunni collections.[93] It appears that Al Mahdi's ʿAlidism intensified after Iran's Islamic Revolution in 1979, but not immediately. A 1982 issue of the *Ansaar Village Bulletin* gives an account of the Prophet's grandsons (and second and third Shi'i Imams) Hasan and Husayn gently teaching an elderly man, and provides a short biography of 'Ali, but in neither case does it touch upon points of sectarian division.[94]

Still treating biblical literature as an Islamic resource, Al Mahdi locates the significance of the *ahl al-bayt* in part through his reading of Revelation. Although *The Holy Gospel: The Revelation of Jesus the Messiah to the World* (1984) could appear to observers as marking a "Christian turn" away from Islam, Al Mahdi's biblical exegesis and focus on Christ lead him to the Prophet's family. For its mention of a woman "gowned in white, wearing a crown of twelve stars upon her head; at her feet was the crescent moon," Al Mahdi reads Revelation 12:1 as a reference to Fatima. His *Holy Gospel* presents an illustration of Fatima in white niqab, wearing the crown of twelve stars, with the crescent at her feet bearing the word *al-islam* in Arabic script. Rather than point immediately to the twelve-Imam line, Al Mahdi deciphers the stars to signify the twelve tribes of Ishmael. Allah had explained their meaning as such to Adam and Eve, who experienced a vision of Fatima as a young girl shortly after their creation. Fatima's crown also contained an onyx stone, which Al Mahdi reads as symbolic of 'Ali's descent from Adam, along with the Black Stone of Mecca, fashioned from black clay that was left over after Adam's creation. When Adam and Eve noticed young Fatima wearing earrings of gold and silver, Allah explained that there was no difference in value between gold and silver but that the two earrings represented Hasan and Husayn.[95]

According to Al Mahdi, the "sharp two-edged sword" of Revelation 1:16 refers to 'Ali's sword, Zulfikar. *The Holy Gospel* refers to the event of Ghadir Khumm, regarded in Shi'i traditions as the moment that Muhammad declared 'Ali his successor, while Abu Bakr and A'isha appear as treacherous conspirators obsessed with personal power. Al Mahdi then turns to the continuation of authority after Muhammad. He presents the Imamate in two cycles: the first consists of the ten Imams that followed 'Ali, starting with his sons Hasan and Husayn and proceeding to the Ithna 'Ashari line's eleventh Imam, Hasan al-Askari. The second cycle starts with the twelfth Imam of Ithna 'Ashari tradition, Muhammad b. Hasan al-Mahdi, through whom Al Mahdi traces an imamate that leads to Muhammad Ahmad, the Sudanese Mahdi. As the nineteenth Imam after 'Ali, Muhammad Ahmad's position conforms to the "mathematical miracle" that ACC/NIH literature finds in the number nineteen.[96]

In his commentary on Revelation, Al Mahdi describes the *ahl al-bayt* suffering persecution and hardship after Muhammad's death, accuses A'isha of breaking the law by rebelling against 'Ali's leadership, charges Sunni scholars with fabricating hadiths to favor A'isha, and notes the Sunni treatment of those who supported Muhammad's grandson Husayn: "His helpers [Ansar] and friends underwent the worst possible killings; women and children were tortured; bodies trampled, heads taken out on the blades of spears." From Karbala, Al Mahdi then turns again to nineteenth-century Sudan, describing the Anglo-Egyptian oppression of Nubian peoples and the rise of the Mahdiyya. Despite the Mahdiyya revolution, the British regained power and persecuted the Mahdi's family, echoing the suppression of the *ahl al-bayt*. Al Mahdi points to his own emergence as the promised leader, citing the hadith that reads, "Hearken and obey although a Black Slave whose head is like a dried grape will be appointed to rule over you."[97] Citing the "dried grape" hadith in *Where Is the Tabernacle of the Most High?* (1986), he then proclaims, "I am the only successor to Ahlil Bayt."[98]

While AAC/NIH literature of the early 1980s connects the oppressors of Muhammad's family to modern forces of European colonialism and white supremacy, its media later in that decade more explicitly racialize divisions among the early Muslims. This shift corresponds to the publication of Runoko Rashidi and Ivan van Sertima's edited volume *African Presence in Early Asia* (1985), which includes a contribution by Wayne B. Chandler on racial conflicts at the origins of Islam. In "Ebony and Bronze: Race and Ethnicity in Early Arabia and the Islamic World," Chandler follows J. A. Rogers, who wrote in volume 1 of *Sex and Race* of an ancient Arabia in which Black rulers saw themselves as racially superior to their "Persian and Turkish subjects,"[99] and envisions pre-Islamic Mecca as a racially stratified society in which Black Arabs lived close to the Ka'ba, while "Red Semites," ancestors of the future Umayyad dynasty, were marginalized on the outskirts. With "strong belief in a Black/Semitic alliance, a central theme of Islam which was never well-received by either group," Muhammad proclaimed, "I was sent to the Reds and the Blacks" and preached a universalist message. He proselytized among the "primitive Semites" because he needed soldiers, and they converted mainly in the hope of war plunder, but he also appealed to "the great Blacks who had laid the cornerstone of culture and civilization in Arabia" and possessed superior military technology. As one of history's great empire builders, Muhammad successfully united the peoples of Arabia into a singular nation under his power, but after his death, racial hostilities resurfaced and destroyed what he had built. The Semitic Muslims, opposing hereditary succession because they could make no credible claim of relation to Muhammad, called for elections as "the only way to guarantee political leverage.... It was this fight for power that created the Sunni Moslem." 'Ali's later refusal to pledge allegiance to Muʿawiyya, the "Semitic governor of Syria," launched a "civil war between Blacks and Semites," and Islam's racial divisions were never resolved, as the Red Semites became the Umayyad caliphate and continued to persecute Muhammad's family, while Black Arabs became the nucleus for Shi'ism. In particular, Chandler identifies the Fatimids (descended from Muhammad's daughter Fatima, whom Chandler claims had ruled from 616 to 633 CE) as a later "Black caliphate" and credits its famed Assassins with a "devastating war of terror against the Christian Crusaders and the Semitic orthodox Sunni Moslems." Chandler also holds Sufism to be a branch sect of the Assassins.[100]

AAC/NIH book catalogs from 1985 onward mention a book titled *The Prophet Muhammad and Ali Were Nubian (Black)*.[101] Though the volume does not appear to have survived, depictions of its cover in advertisements suggest that it was a translated excerpt from a prominent reference for Chandler, *The Book of the Glory of the Black Race*, by ninth-century Afro-Iraqi scholar al-Jahiz (775–868).[102] In 1988, Al Mahdi published a two-volume work, *Hadrat Faatimah (AS): The Daughter of the Prophet Muhammad (PBUH)*, that intensified the presentation of "orthodox" Islam as a white supremacist takeover of Nubian Islam. The covers of both volumes depict Fatima as a Black woman clothed in white niqab, wearing a golden crown with twelve stars, holding gold and silver apples in her hands, with a crescent at her feet. Al Mahdi tells of Fatima's exalted nature, her preexistence of the created universe, her communication with angels from a young age, and her significance for her father's mission, while weaving in references to the nineteenth-century Sudanese Mahdi. *Hadrat Faatimah* also identifies Muhammad as a "Black Arab." When 'Ali leads the Muslim army into battle, their Meccan opponents are described as "Red Arabs."[103]

The second volume emphasizes the suffering of Fatima and her children at the hands of Red Arabs and "so-called Jewish" Canaanites. Al Mahdi writes of young Husayn's abduction by Salah bin Rega, who "planned to make Al Imaam Husayn (AS) his black slave; being that he was so black skinned. In those days Red Arabs had Black slaves." An accompanying illustration depicts white-skinned, hook-nosed Salah kidnapping the Black child.[104]

The account of Muhammad's death furthers these themes. Muhammad dies after consuming lamb meat that has been poisoned by a Jewish woman. During Muhammad's deathbed illness, 'Umar and A'isha deny his request for writing implements, thereby preventing him from making a final statement; after 'Ali argues with 'Umar, they send 'Ali out of the room. According to Al Mahdi, 'Umar knew that the Prophet had wanted to name 'Ali his successor. In an illustration captioned "All gather around to hear the Prophet Muhammad

(PBUH)," Muhammad and an unidentified man and woman (apparently 'Ali and Fatima) standing watch over him all have dark skin; behind them stand a man and veiled woman with light skin ('Umar and A'isha), the woman's eyes giving an impression of scheming or enmity. While Abu Bakr appears in the first volume as a sympathetic figure who follows and supports Muhammad with sincerity, even risking his life to flee Mecca with him,[105] the second volume presents a shift in his character after the Prophet's death. Fatima pleads with Abu Bakr for her rightful inheritance, the land of Fadak; while Fatima and 'Ali appear in the accompanying illustration as Black, Abu Bakr and his entourage, apparently including A'isha, all have lighter skin.[106] Throughout AAC/NIH media, Abu Bakr would appear as a "red" or "pale" Arab in contrast to the Nubian Prophet and his family (figs. 5–8).

"There was much chaos between the Red and Black Arabs after the death of the Prophet Muhammad," Al Mahdi writes, explaining that this chaos "resulted in the division of the Muslim world into many sects."[107] Allah chose Fatima as the one child of Muhammad who would survive him, knowing that of all Muhammad's children, only Fatima could produce a lineage to fight for its due successorship.[108] Driven into exile by A'isha's "malice and jealousy," Fatima and 'Ali fled Arabia, heading to Egypt and then the Sudan. The Muslims' internal strife culminated in the rise of Yazid, "a drunk, a womanizer, and a man of questionable character," who ascended to the caliphate and sent a legion against Husayn's supporters at Karbala, after which Husayn's severed head was brought to Yazid's palace. In the centuries to come, refugees from the Shi'i Fatimid caliphate—recognized by Al Mahdi as descendants of Fatima and 'Ali—fled Egypt for safety in their ancestors' refuge of the Sudan, future birthplace of the true Mahdi with ancestry traced directly to Husayn.[109]

The suffering of Muhammad's family and the tragedies of Karbala, as refashioned by Al Mahdi, speak to several important registers in the context of American Islam throughout the 1980s. A range of post-Nation Sunni discourses emphasized "graduation" from local pro-Black traditions to absorption within a "universal" Muslim *umma*, centered in Saudi Arabia. Meanwhile, Afrocentrist thinkers, despite sympathy for Elijah Muhammad, rejected Islam as an anti-Black ideology of Arab supremacy. AAC/NIH media resist Sunni claims of superior Islamic authenticity by reexamining the original Muslim community, countering Sunni narratives of "golden age" triumphalism with a Shi'i narrative of oppression and tragedy. The discourse of Islam as "color-blind" and of Elijah Muhammad as having no Islamic legitimacy, supported by modern "pale Arab" networks, becomes a repetition of the ways in which pale Arabs

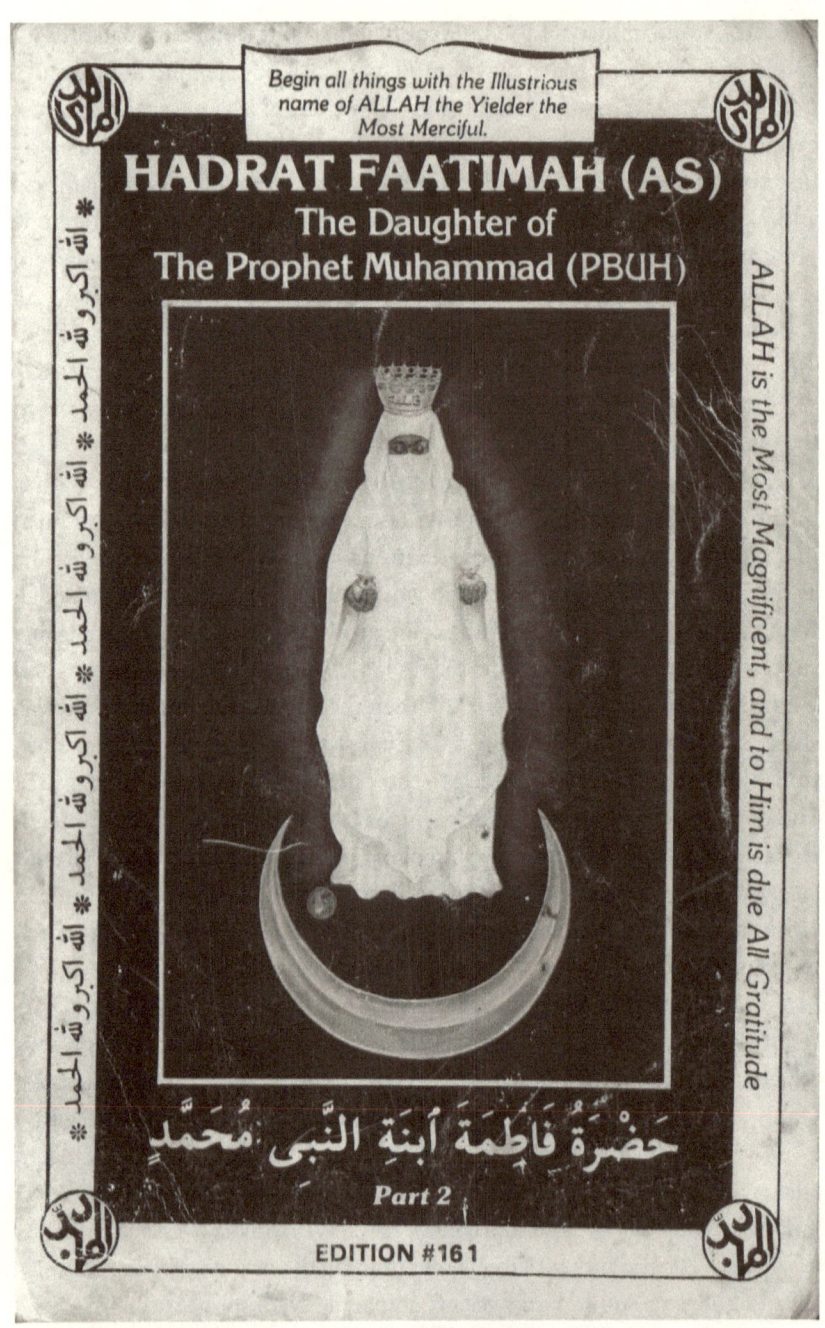

FIGURE 5 Al Haadi Al Mahdi, *Hadrat Faatimah (AS): The Daughter of the Prophet Muhammad (PBUH), Part 2* (1988), front cover.

FIGURE 6 The *Ahl al-Bayt*: 'Ali, Fatima, and their sons, Hasan and Husayn.

FIGURE 7 *The Prophet Muhammad Leaving Medina for Mecca.* Left to right: 'Ali holding his double-bladed sword, Zulfikar; the Prophet, riding his camel and holding the Mihjan; Bilal, holding the Prophet's standard; and Abu Bakr, the "pale Arab," holding a spear.

"I Am the Raisin-Headed Slave" • 55

FIGURE 8 *Hadrat Faatimah (AS) Pleads for Her Land.* With 'Ali, Fatima confronts Abu Bakr, A'isha, and their supporters for her right to inherit the land of Fadak from her father. From Al Haadi Al Mahdi, *Hadrat Faatimah (AS): The Daughter of the Prophet Muhammad (PBUH)*, Part 2, 112.

had stolen Islam from Black people, starting with the Prophet's own family. The theme of Karbala as an eternally repeating injustice finds reflection in the ongoing oppression of Nubians by Amorites (whether European or pale Arab), while Sunni animosity toward the Prophet's household converges with Arab racism against Nubians to become a singular white animosity for the original Black Islam of the *ahl al-bayt*. This timeless hatred is manifested in Arab Sunni antagonism toward the AAC/NIH, a community that has pledged its loyalty to a Black man who is also a direct descendant of 'Ali and Fatima.

Though Islam, in Al Mahdi's view, is properly Nubian, Sudanese, and Black, *Sunni* Islam remains guilty of the anti-Blackness that Afrocentrists have charged. The crucial choice for Nubians in the West is not between Arab-supremacist Islam and Blackness-affirming Afrocentrism, but rather between an oil-funded surge of globalizing white Sunni hegemony and the pure Nubian Islam of the Prophet's family. Islam's true revival begins with a Black man, descended from the *ahl al-bayt*, who sets the stage for his great-grandson to awaken Nubian consciousness in the West.

THE NINETEENTH IMAM: THE SUDANESE MAHDI

The man that Al Mahdi identified as the true Mahdi and his biological and spiritual forerunner, Muhammad Ahmad (1845–1885), emerged from a unique milieu of Sudanese Sufism. In Muhammad Ahmad's lifetime, local Sufi traditions underwent multiple transformations amid the arrivals of "neo-Sufi" orders such as the Tijaniyya and Khatmiyya, the development of a modern Sudanese nationalism among Muslim communities to the north, and colonial interference by Egypt's Turko-Egyptian ruling elite, which abused the Sudan with an unjust tax system and imposed its own ideas of Islamic orthodoxy as a reformist "civilizing mission." The Turko-Egyptian regime, Robert O. Collins observes, regarded the Sudan's popular Sufi leaders as "ignorant peddlers of superstition" and sought to correct the masses; Sudan's indigenous Islamic authorities, in turn, resisted "the orthodox Islam introduced by the Turks which they regarded as heresy."[110] The colonial authorities pursued Islamic reform in the Sudan with control over local education, bringing legions of clerical scholars (*'ulama*) into the Sudan from al-Azhar in Cairo, sending Sudanese clerics for instruction at al-Azhar, and formal shari'a courts with Egyptian judges.[111] The religious conflict between colonizers and the colonized was not only between rural mystics and university-trained jurists but also between competing legal systems, as the Turko-Egyptian institutional networks privileged the Hanafi school, though the Maliki school had enjoyed greater prominence in the Sudan.[112]

Muhammad Ahmad's family claimed to have migrated to Dongola from Egypt in the fifteenth century, boasted *ashraf* (descent from the Prophet) status and a reputation for producing holy men, and was connected to the Sammaniyya, one of the neo-Sufi orders of recent arrival in the Sudan. The order's founder, Muhammad b. 'Abd al-Karim al-Samman (1718–1775), had received initiation into the Khalwatiyya in Cairo and developed the Sammaniyya as his own Khalwati branch. His disciples spread the order as far as Indonesia and Malaysia; Ahmad al-Tayyib al-Bashir (1742–1824), also an initiate of the Qadiriyya, Khalwatiyya, and Naqshbandiyya orders, brought the order to the Sudan circa 1764,[113] with particular success on the White Nile.[114] The Sammaniyya's spread into the Sudan reflected a transition in Sudanese Sufism from local, rural lineages to "more centralized and better-organized supranational orders" that transcended tribal divisions.[115] Muhammad Ahmad became a sheikh in the order and joined his boatbuilder brothers at Abba Island for ascetic hermitage on the White Nile, where he provoked controversy after condemning a circumcision party for its allowance of dancing. Expelled from his brotherhood, he joined a rival Sammaniyya branch and in 1878 participated in the building of its leader's tomb, thereby fulfilling prophesy: the sheikh had foretold that the builder of his tomb would be the awaited Mahdi.[116] In 1881, bolstered by a vision in which the Prophet confirmed his status to an otherworldly assembly that included past Sammaniyya *awliya* (spiritually advanced "friends" of God, popularly rendered as "saints"), he declared himself the awaited Mahdi and called for a return to the pure Islam of the Prophet, which required liberation from the corrupted Islam of the Turko-Egyptian regime. Sudanese nationalism was inseparable from religious liberation; the Mahdi's anti-imperialist struggle was also an Islamic freedom struggle, an uprising of Muslims against the Islam of the state.

The Mahdi raised an army among his followers (Ansar), achieved a series of military triumphs against the imperial powers, and formed a meta-tribal "super-tariqa"[117] and theocratic regime, "the only truly anti-imperialist, Islamic republic of its time in Africa."[118] As the supreme legislative and theological authority, the Mahdi denounced adherence to legal schools (*madhahib*), rejected the ʿ*ulama* as having "distanced themselves from the light of the Prophet," and ordered the burning of books of hadith, Qurʾan commentary, and jurisprudence, reportedly leaving only the Qurʾan and his own devotional text, his *Ratib*.[119] His position as the Mahdi rendered both the colonial ʿ*ulama* and local tariqas obsolete: though Sufi orders had been integral to the Mahdiyya's support, the Mahdi ultimately banned tariqas, prohibited visitation to shrines, and fenced off sheikhs' tombs from public access.[120]

The Mahdi died in 1885, just a few months after capturing Khartoum. Under his appointed successor, the Mahdist state would last thirteen years before falling to British and Egyptian forces. For the nationalist spirit that his short revolution fostered and his seemingly miraculous defeat of Turko-Egyptian and British power, he is regarded as Abu al-Istiqlal, Father of Independence.[121] Despite his claims of transcendent authority and his departure from accepted readings of the law (such as his having five wives at one time),[122] he was also credited with contributing to Sunni revivalism in the Sudan. Maryam Jameelah, who had converted at State Street Mosque and become a member of the Faisals' inner circle, positions the Mahdi's Ansar alongside Muhammad ibn ʿAbd al-Wahhab's (1703–1792) "Wahhabi" movement in what is now Saudi Arabia. "The Mahdist movement," she writes, "was not in vain.... To this day, the Sudanese are the most Islamically-minded in the Arab world."[123]

Upon reconquest in 1898, the Sudan was ruled by an "Anglo-Egyptian Condominium" through the first half of the twentieth century, in which the British colonial overlord and its Egyptian subject theoretically shared control over the territory. The British administration embarked on a program of Islamic reform to suppress destabilizing elements such as Mahdism and local Sufi orders. This meant privileging an al-Azhar model of rational Scholasticism over the less governable authority of the brotherhoods. The British destroyed the Mahdi's shrine, dumped his bones into the Nile and stole his skull, banned the reconstruction of damaged Sufi shrines, set up shari'a courts, built and financed masjids and Qur'an schools, and sought to establish an urban "consultory board of Ulema" to supplant the decentralized authority of rural Sufi orders, while portraying its erasure of Sudanese Islam as a restoration of true Islamic orthodoxy.[124] The British colonial project in the Sudan emphasized reliance on the Qur'an and classical *fiqh* (jurisprudence) to secure itself against dangerous mystical masters and impose a rational secular authority upon the masses.[125]

The Ansar's hopes for apocalyptic redemption did not disappear, but they were projected onto the Mahdi's son, Sayyid 'Abd al-Rahman al-Mahdi, whom many Ansar came to identify as the returning prophet Jesus.[126] Still fearful of the Mahdiyya's revolutionary potential, the British kept surveillance on 'Abd al-Rahman and prohibited him from identifying himself with terms such as Imam or Mahdi. During the First World War, he called for Ansar to support the British against the Turks, whom the Ansar still regarded as "corrupters of Islam."[127]

During the Second World War, an American need for seamen prompted a small migration of Sudanese men to the United States, leading to the start of a community in Brooklyn. "They originated from the same part of the country, Dongola," writes Rogaia Mustafa Abusharaf, and constituted a distinct presence at State Street Mosque, their "home away from home."[128] State Street Mosque was apparently the site at which Dwight York—possibly from the age of twelve in 1957—first experienced African Muslim communities, along with anti-Black racism from non-Black Muslims. Al Mahdi developed his own circle with other young Black Muslims in the late 1960s, which identified as Nubian, adopted an Afrocentric Sufism, and proclaimed Black Islamic power against both white supremacy and non-Black Muslim privilege. These connections did not depend on "influence" from the Nation of Islam; nor did Ansar Pure Sufi originate as the Nation's "offshoot." Inhabiting a transnational Muslim space in which Sufism was organically linked to Black African liberation, young Dwight York took less interest in Harlem's famous Mosque No. 7 ministers (Malcolm X, succeeded by Louis Farrakhan) or the nascent Five Percenter movement than in this anticolonial Black Sufi master rising from the land of classical Nubian and Kushite kingdoms to expel Turko-Egyptian and British oppressors.

The Final Link (1978) (fig. 9) explains that after the seventh seal was broken in 1970 and Al Mahdi established the Ansar in the West, the community endured four years of "persecutions, slander and public humiliation."[129] This period is described elsewhere as the first half of a "tribulation" during which the community lost many of its earliest members.[130] In 1973, in the midst of this turmoil, Al Mahdi traveled with followers to the Sudan and "regained our lost heritage and fused the broken link back together again." It was in the Sudan that they came into the knowledge "that we are indeed the lost tribe of Ismail [Ishmael] (PBUH) and that part of the family [was] destined to rise in the West."[131] An unnamed writer describes the party's travels as yielding a collective self-discovery, a communal echo of Malcolm X's pilgrimage to Mecca and travels in Africa. Al Mahdi's party ventured to Abba Island, where "our brother Ansars accepted us with open arms and hearts, and gave us the confirmation that we sought so diligently for." The Sudanese Ansar confirmed that Al Mahdi was the Reformer and the fulfillment of the prophetic hadith that read, "Hearken and obey although a Black Slave whose head is like a dried grape will be appointed to rule over you." Al Mahdi thus proclaims, "I am the raisin-headed slave" whose arrival had been foretold by Muhammad and the scriptures.[132] In *Are the Ansars (in the West) a Self-Made Sect?*, Al Mahdi treats his travels in the Sudan as proof of his legitimacy against critics outside the community. "For years you have said that the Sudanese will not accept the Ansars in the West," he writes. "You also said that we as a people have lost our spiritual and physical link with Sudan (Africa)."[133]

In the years after Al Mahdi became a member of the State Street community, established Ansar Pure Sufi, and rebranded his movement as the Nubian Islamic Hebrews and Ansaru Allah Community, the newly independent Sudan struggled. In 1958, a military coup led by two generals, one an Ansar and the other belonging to the Khatmiyya, took control of the newly independent Sudan. ʿAbd al-Rahman passed away in 1959 and was succeeded as spiritual head of the Ansar by his son Siddiq, who led the community for only two years before dying in 1961. The Ansar's *shura* council named Siddiq's brother al-Hadi as imam, while Siddiq's son Sadiq became head of the Ansar political party, the Umma Party, and served as prime minister from 1966 to 1967. In 1969, Ja'far Muhammad al-Numayri took power in a coup; a year later the Ansar revolted, resulting in the army's bombardment of their Abba Island base in the White Nile, killing thousands of Ansar (including al-Hadi Al Mahdi) and sending Sadiq into exile.[134]

Apart from brief notes on the end of the Ansar's exile from Abba Island in 1979, Al Mahdi's pamphlets and newsletters throughout the 1970s do not provide extensive commentary on the contemporary Sudan. I have not found any AAC/NIH material that mentions al-Numayri by name, and only sparing mention of the Umma Party. The Sudan in AAC/NIH material appears in somewhat Orientalist fashion as a land of "pure Islam" outside time.

Al Mahdi's followers performed their connection to the Sudanese Ansar via clothing prescriptions of white robes, turbans, and face veils, the Bushwick Avenue masjid's aesthetic echo of the Mahdi's shrine in Khartoum, and the presence of Al Mahdi's alleged genealogy in his pamphlets, displaying portraits of his father, grandfather, and the Mahdi. Also central to this performative linkage was Al Mahdi's connection to his living Mahdiyya family. AAC/NIH media from the late 1970s and early '80s make a prominent photographic display of Al Mahdi's relationship with his claimed cousin and the Sudan's former prime minister, the Mahdi's great-grandson Sayyid Sadiq al-Mahdi (figs. 10–11). The two appear together with a caption locating the moment in the backyard of the Mahdi's house in the Sudan during Al Mahdi's 1973 trip. Sadiq is also shown visiting the Brooklyn masjid in 1978, participating in congregational prayers, and smiling in conversation with cousin Isa. A cartoon drawing of legions of Black men in white turbans and robes from the East and West extending their hands to one another in friendship, with the two arms of a handshake in the foreground labeled "Africa" and "America," appears to have been clipped from a *Muhammad Speaks* cartoon (with Ansar logos added). Imposed upon the drawing are photographs of Sadiq and Isa representing "two halves of the Ansar family," the Ansar of Abba Island and the "lost sheep of Ismail [Ishmael]" in the West. The image is also captioned with Revelation 7:9, which refers to "a great multitude" representing "all nations and tongues" standing "before the throne, and before the Lamb, clothed with white robes."[135]

With the bold headline "THIS IS THE PROOF!" Al Mahdi presents his alleged cousin's address to the community, demonstrating the Sudanese Ansar's full endorsement of the Ansar in the West. Sadiq gives his salaam to the "brother and sister Ansari" and expresses delight upon seeing that the Mahdiyya has spread to the West. Though he spoke on his great-grandfather's legacy of Islamic revival and treating the AAC/NIH as a branch of the Sudanese Mahdiyya, it remains unclear whether Sadiq was aware of the AAC/NIH's doctrinal peculiarities. In his address, Sadiq identifies a core message of Islam as its condemnation of all racial prejudice, insisting "that man, whatever his color, is the same. People have all descended from one stock, Adam (PBUH). They are all one species, and therefore the religion of Islam is the religion of racial unity."[136]

The reproduction of Sadiq's talk includes a moment from the question-and-answer session in which an Ansar asks about the possibility that

Sadiq might send teachers to the Brooklyn community. Sadiq answers, "Yes, insha'Allah. This is what I have promised my brother and I will do." While African American Sunni communities increasingly boasted the credentials of Saudi-supported education, the spiritual leader of the Ansar in the Sudan—a much poorer nation, itself growing dependent on Saudi resources—opened alternative gates to the Islamic archive. But Sadiq does not envision the transmission of knowledge between Ansar communities as a one-sided tutelage of the West by the East. Rather, he expresses a desire for true collaboration in which the Ansar of the West bring their unique American experience and knowledge to the Sudan and participate as true partners in the making of a united Islamic nation. The Ansar of the West can help defeat Christian missionary work in the Sudan "because you have a better experience of what it means to be Christian and Black. . . . And you also have a better understanding of how to address people who might need to be addressed towards Islam from this point of view. This all means that your potential is not only here, but it can also be seen in your homeland of the movement that's in the Sudan."[137]

While Al Mahdi had recognized Muhammad Ahmad as the Mahdi prior to his 1973 trip, it appears to have been after his travels that he identified himself as the Mahdi's grandson (later, great-grandson). Over time, the question of his origins became the center of an elaborate saga, of which some details remained malleable. Al Mahdi's backstory, as articulated in an AAC/NIH poster labeled "The Reformer" from the late 1980s, is as follows: In October 1944, Faatimah Maryam, daughter of a Sudanese merchant seaman from the Nubian Kenazi tribe, traveled from the United States to Egypt for study in Alexandria, where she met a man named Abdul Haadi. "At the time," the poster explains, "the young girl did not know that this young man had such a royal lineage, and in time, their relationship blossomed." At the end of the academic year, they went their separate ways, returning to their homes in the Sudan and later reuniting in Omdurman. "His royal family did not accept her," the poster explains, "and did not want anyone to know about this child [whom she had conceived with Abdul Haadi]." Dejected after giving birth alone, Faatimah "departed for America in shame, accompanied by her father, her brother, [famous musician] Hamza El Din and her young child, Issa." The family settled in New Bedford, where the baby was registered as "male York," receiving his last name from his mother's ex-husband. They raised the boy in the United States until he was seven, when Sheikh Ahmad Hasuwn came from Khartoum to retrieve him. The boy lived at Abba Island on the White Nile until the age of twelve and then returned to America. Living in Teaneck, New Jersey, he spent each weekend in Brooklyn with a family connection, an African American convert to Islam named Umar Abdullah, who brought him to the State Street Mosque for Friday prayers. It was there that Daoud Faisal, knowing the child's secret, took it upon himself to prepare him for his mission. Though it is unclear how Faisal had become aware of the boy's identity, he could have recognized the truth as it appeared on his body: "dark skin, thin lips, long nose and slanted eyes and a mole on his right cheek, with three *shuluk* (tribal scars) on each cheek—the marks of the Dongolowy people fit the description which a pure descendant of the seed of Abraham (PBUH) would possess."

Sadiq's visits to the Brooklyn community around the turn of the 1980s received prominent coverage in AAC/NIH publications, which carefully negotiate Isa's claimed Mahdiyya descent. *The Final Link* and *Are the Ansars (in the West) a Self-Made Sect?* abound with photos of Sadiq and Isa together, quote Sadiq's addresses to the Brooklyn community, and refer to their alliance as "symbolic to the joining together of the two halves of the family; of two hemispheres, the East and the West." However, while Al Mahdi had already claimed descent from Muhammad Ahmad, AAC/NIH publications that emphasize Sadiq's endorsement of the community do not precisely define Al Mahdi's relation to the family. Neither *The Final Link* nor *Are the Ansars (in the West) a Self-Made Sect* specifically identifies the two leaders as cousins or otherwise forges a biological connection between Isa and the Mahdi. A section in *Are the Ansars (in the West) a Self-Made Sect* titled "The Legacy and Heritage of a Great Man and His Heirs" displays portraits of the Mahdi, his son ʿAbd al-Rahman, grandson al-Haadi, and finally Isa, and identifies Isa as the third successor to the Mahdi and "Imam of the Ansars in the West," but does not name him as a grandson or great-grandson. The reader is only told to "study the pictures on this page and see for yourself the resemblance between Al Imam Isa (WU) and Imam Al Hadi Al Mahdi." The newsletter names Isa as Al Hajj Al Imam Isa Abd Allah Muhammad Al Mahdi, minus the "Al Haadi" that would appear in his name throughout sources from 1983 onward and mark his claim to be al-Hadi's son.[138]

The AAC/NIH disseminated the *Ratib*, the Mahdiyya prayer book, in Al Mahdi's personal translation. As a mystical revelation received by Muhammad Ahmad on the mountain of Qadir, the *Ratib* provided the Mahdiyya with a manual of prayers, chants, and exercises that paralleled the competing *Ratibs* of local Sufi orders. Among the Mahdiyya, recitation of the text constituted an important—and for some followers, allegedly the only—Islamic ritual practice. Because the *Ratib* was feared as a public symbol of Mahdism and a call for jihad, the Anglo-Egyptian colonial regime attempted to ban the book in the early decades of the twentieth century but rescinded the ban after prohibition became clearly unenforceable; and the regime ultimately allowed printed editions and public assemblies for recitation.[139] *The Final Link* reports that when Sadiq visited the AAC/NIH, his address to the community included recitations from the *Ratib* and a defense of the text's Islamic legitimacy. The *Ratib*, he insisted, was "not a composition apart from Islam" but simply a compilation of Qur'an excerpts and prayers of the prophets. He also corrected the AAC/NIH recitation of the *Ratib*, pointing out that it was not customary *always* to recite the *entire Ratib* after late afternoon (*asr*) prayer; short sections would do as well.[140] The AAC/NIH's appropriation of the *Ratib* is evident in the book lists found in the back pages of community pamphlets, consistently including a translation, *The Raatib (Unshakable) of Al Imam Muhammad Ahmad Al Mahdi (AS)*, from at least as early as 1977.[141] Advertisements for a forthcoming edition in 1978 describe the *Ratib* as a source of "great spiritual inspiration, strength and patience" for more than nine million Muslims who read the text every day between the late evening prayer (*isha*) and the pre-sunrise prayer (*fajr*).[142]

Al Mahdi's introduction to his 1980 edition asserts that the text "possesses high mystical powers; powers that bind communities," and that it is not a "political work" but merely a collection of excerpts from the Qur'an and hadith literature, along with accounts of Muhammad Ahmad's visionary encounters with the Prophet and Khidr.[143] The 1980 edition includes parallel Arabic text, along with stylized illustrations depicting faceless angels, prophets, and the Mahdi's defeat of British soldiers.[144] The AAC/NIH also disseminated cassette tapes of Al Mahdi reciting the text in English (with salutations upon the Prophet in Arabic), accompanied by drums and background singing, simultaneously evoking imaginaries of indigenous African spirituality and Islamic ritual authenticity.

Though Al Mahdi maintained his ideological investment in the Sudanese Mahdiyya, the formal relationship between the Ansar communities of the West and East—or at least Sadiq al-Mahdi's friendship with the AAC/NIH—seems to have ended in the early 1980s. This could be salient for Al Mahdi's 1983 reintroduction of "Nubian Islamic Hebrews" alongside "Ansaru Allah Community" as a name for the movement. It bears repeating, however, that the name does not reflect a change in the community's official position on the Sudanese Mahdi or its leader's relationship to him. In 1987, after using a sequence of flags to represent the community, Al Mahdi began to promote the black, red, and green Mahdiyya flag as the "Nubian banner." The embrace of the Mahdist flag corresponds to changes in Sudanese politics; in 1986, following the removal of al-Numayri and a decade and a half of rebuilding the Ansar in and out of exile, Sadiq al-Mahdi

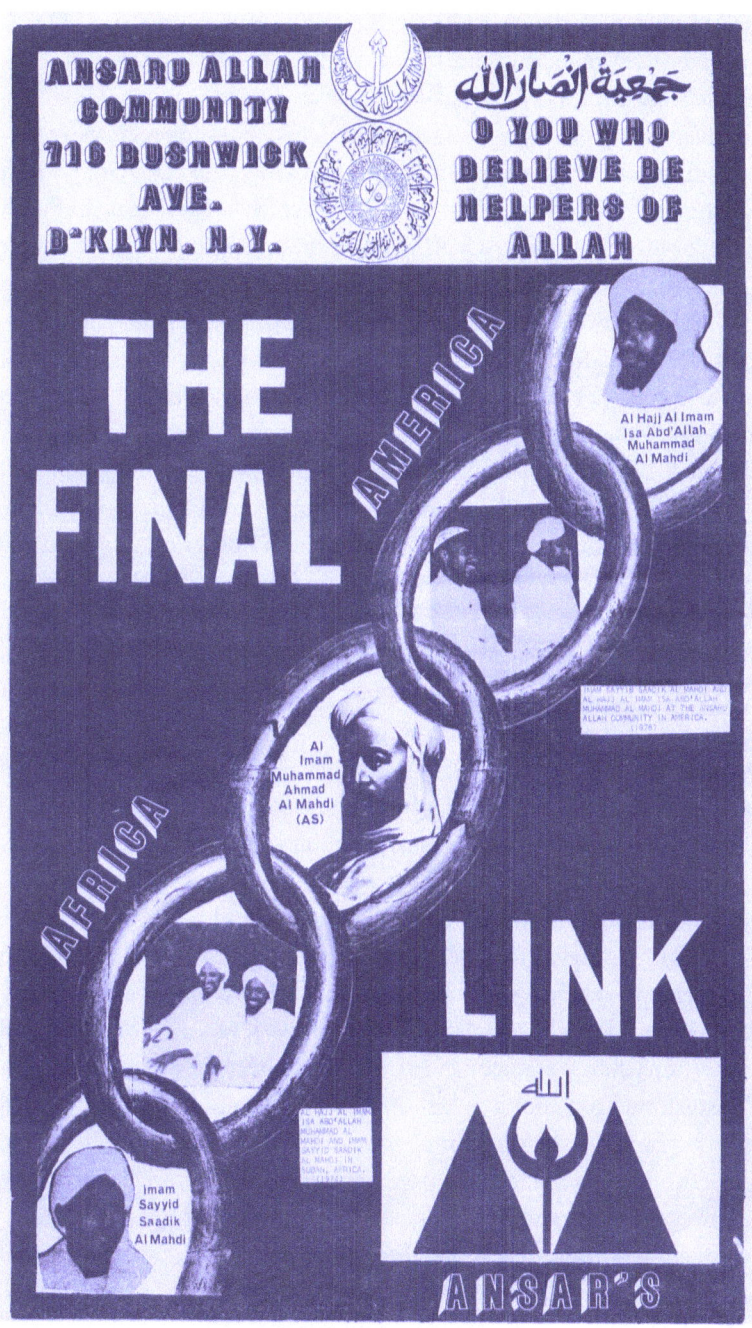

FIGURE 9 *The Final Link*, 1978.

returned to power. During Sadiq's 1987–89 stint as prime minister, Al Mahdi reemphasized the Sudanese Mahdi in such works as *About the Raatib: The Book of the Mahdi* and *The Call of the Mahdi in America*.

Our Flag (1989) provides the Mahdist flag's history (and polemics against other communities' flags) and photos of hip-hop artists such as Doug E. Fresh wearing the flag. As Al Mahdi boasts, Grandmaster Melle Mel wears the flag in the video for his song with AAC/NIH member Van Silk, "What's the Matter with Your World?"[145] *About the Raatib* (fig. 12) and *The Call of the Mahdi in America* include notices for a future "Banner Day for Nubians" and advertisements for medallions, banners, patches, key chains, lapel pins, buttons, stickers, and clothes bearing the flag—"a must for every Nubian who wants to spread the Da'wah."[146] The final pages of *About the Raatib* advertise color portraits of Al Mahdi and members of his genealogy—"beautiful pictures of these Great Leaders, descending from your motherland of Sudan"—available for a one-dollar donation.[147] The back covers of both *About the Raatib* and *The Call of the Mahdi* display the Mahdi's tomb and the AAC/NIH's masjid in Brooklyn, demonstrating architectural resonances between them. Between the two photos, one finds an image of the Mahdiyya flag. Al Mahdi acknowledges that long before his mission, Marcus Garvey's Universal Negro Improvement Association (UNIA) had adopted the red, black, and green flag as symbolic of pan-Africanism in the 1920s, though Al Mahdi would charge that Garvey had placed the colors in the wrong order by not putting black on top.

Displaying illustrations of Sudanese weaponry above the caption "Homemade spears used by the Mahdiyya ... to conquer the British army," Al Mahdi provides in Muhammad Ahmad a template for triumph over white empire. The Sudanese Mahdiyya's nineteenth-century struggle for Nubian liberation from Amorite powers was easily mapped onto the AAC/NIH's late twentieth-century struggle for Nubian Islam in the Americas, as Al Mahdi confronted both American white supremacy and an encroaching Sunni hegemony of "pale Arab" institutions and communities. Al Mahdi's vision of a Nubia-centered Islam in his grand narrative, spanning thousands of years and culminating in the rise of the Sudanese Mahdiyya, would preserve Islam's power as resistance against white supremacy while simultaneously upholding Afrocentrism's resistance against Muslim anti-Blackness. Through this nineteenth-century mystical master, "tall, powerfully built, with the features of a god, cast in black bronze, dressed in flowing white, on a splendid Arabian horse" as he led Nubian armies into battle, Al Mahdi found a transcendent moral geography for Black Islam and his own place in its unfolding destiny (fig. 13).[148]

FIGURE 10 AAC/NIH commemoration of Sayyid Sadiq al-Mahdi, prime minister of the Sudan (1966–67, 1986–89), great-grandson of Muhammad Ahmad, the "Sudanese Mahdi," and alleged cousin of Isa Al Mahdi, visiting the community in 1981.

FIGURE 11 Al Mahdi with his alleged cousin, Sadiq al-Mahdi, during Al Mahdi's travels in the Sudan in the 1970s.

"I Am the Raisin-Headed Slave" • 67

FIGURE 12 Al Haadi Al Mahdi, *About the Raatib* (1987), front cover.

FIGURE 13 *Silsilati: My Lineage.* Al Mahdi (seated in the foreground) with his alleged father, al-Hadi al-Mahdi (1918–1971); grandfather 'Abd al-Rahman al-Mahdi (1885–1959); great-grandfather Muhammad Ahmad, the "Sudanese Mahdi"; and their direct ancestor, the Prophet. From Al Haadi Al Mahdi, *The Book of the Five Percenters* (1991), 379.

RECLAIMING HAJAR: THE VEIL AND NOSE RING

Throughout AAC/NIH history, members of Al Mahdi's community were marked by clothing prescriptions that took different forms over the years, most famously the flowing white robes, abayas, *khimars*, and turbans, to follow the Sudanese Mahdiyya. Echoing Orientalist narratives and apologetic Muslim pamphlets alike, AAC/NIH discourse presents Islam not as a mere "religion" but rather as a comprehensive "way of life." This means that Black liberation depends not only on restoring self-knowledge but also on reclaiming Nubian bodies from the poisonous regimes of Amorite civilization. AAC/NIH media echo what Curtis terms "the Islamized black body" in the Nation's ethics of Black corporeality.[149] In AAC/NIH discourse, the Nation correctly identifies the problem and solution but lacks the full knowledge needed to prescribe a truly Islamic life. Black Sunni communities are also exposed in AAC/NIH literature for their dependence on ill-equipped Arab and South Asian scholars and their failure to adopt authentic practices.[150] Only Al Mahdi can re-Islamize the Nubian body.

AAC/NIH men became publicly visible by peddling, begging, and proselytizing in distinctive Ansar garb. Though both men and women adhered to dress codes that Al Mahdi defined as the "garb of the righteous," pamphlets discussing clothing often focused on dictates for proper women's attire. Examining the Nation of Islam's prescriptions for dress, Curtis notes relationships drawn in *Muhammad Speaks* between immodesty and white people.[151] The embrace of Islamic modesty meant liberation from the norms of whiteness. AAC/NIH media build upon this association: *Al Imaam Isa Visits Egypt 1981* includes a photo of an ostensibly white woman, her blonde hair uncovered and arms exposed in a short-sleeved shirt, captioned with a verse of the Qurʾan: "O Children of Adam, let not the Shaytan cause you to fall into affliction as he expelled your parents from the garden, pulling off from them both your clothing" (7:27).[152] *Disco Music: The Universal Language of Good or Evil?* (1979) contrasts photos of a white woman dancing at a nightclub with pictures of young AAC/NIH girls in white hijabs and robes practicing folk dances, with the caption "Which dance would you rather your child do?"[153]

For Al Mahdi, proper Islamic dress resists U.S. white supremacy and positions his community above illegitimate Muslims. While linking immodesty to whiteness, AAC/NIH literature also connects women's inappropriate exposure with Arab Muslims, revealing the hypocrisy of their claims to true Islam. *Al Imaam Isa Visits Egypt 1981* features a two-page spread, "Women Behind the Veil in Egypt," with photographs of women and commentary on their clothing.

Al Mahdi gives Egyptian women a mixed review, noting that in "an era of decadent modernism" and a "changing cultural scene," the fully veiled face persists as a "symbol of Islaamic stability," while acknowledging that some Muslim women are misled by incorrect translations of the Qur'an (33:53). Though progressive Muslim reformists typically prioritize a Qur'an-centered methodology, arguing that the Qur'an's prescription for dress is more general and less restrictive than the hadith corpus, Al Mahdi makes the opposite argument: hadiths are the refuge of liberals. Commenting on a photograph of a street scene in Egypt in which two women on the left wear full face veils and two women on the right wear hijabs that leave their faces exposed, he captions the former "Al Qur'an" and the latter "Al Hadiyth." The veiled women follow "Allah and the Qur'an," while the exposed women follow "al hadiyth and men."[154]

Al Mahdi defends AAC/NIH veiling against the "distorted" clothing practices of Muslim-majority societies such as Egypt, Pakistan, Morocco, Saudi Arabia, and even the Sudan in his 1984 edition of *Why Do Muslim Women Wear the Face Covering (Veil)?* The expanded 1989 edition gives increased attention to African cultures, privileging Islamic Nubian heritage—"following the laws of our father Abraham"—over "paganistic polytheist" Africans. The AAC/NIH dress code "distinguishes us from the other so-called Muslims" and also those Afrocentrists who "adopted the dress of Africa." Al Mahdi warns his reader, "The wearing of multi-colored dress, dashikies and Galles is not the dress of the righteous but because you did not study your heritage from the beginning ... you went to the East and came back with your new found truth on how Muslims should dress. But in all actuality you've swayed further away from the Siraatu'l Mustaqiym."[155]

In his 1986 booklet *Why the Nosering?* (fig. 14), Al Mahdi claims credit for having introduced the nose ring and other Islamic clothing traditions, such as full veiling for women and white robes and turbans for men, to North America. Al Mahdi recalls that when his followers first began wearing nose rings in 1970, they were mocked as "cannibals"; more than a decade later, however, the nose ring had become a popular fad among Black women who remained unaware of its history and meanings. The AAC/NIH's advocacy of the nose ring challenges Arab Muslims for their anti-Black racism and criticizes Blackamericans who lack an authentic connection to Africa. Against charges that the nose ring is not legitimately Islamic but rather imitates an Israelite custom, Al Mahdi insists that his critics are both unable and unwilling to read *all* of the scriptures in Arabic (significant for the primarily biblical citations through which Al Mahdi argues for nose rings). The nose ring, he claims, is an "Islamic tradition" that distinguishes its wearer as the "seed of Abraham." The first woman to wear

FIGURE 14 Al Haadi Al Mahdi, *Why the Nosering?* (1986), front cover.

the nose ring was Hajar, whom Al Mahdi identifies as Abraham's second wife rather than as his concubine; Hajar was "an educated woman and a psyche" and the daughter of Imhotep, himself a student of Zoser, who in turn was an initiate of Khidr's school. The wearing of nose rings by AAC/NIH women becomes a reference to Hajar, who stands as an embodied point of triangulation between "Abrahamic" or "Semitic" Islam and the wisdom traditions of pharaonic Egypt.

This linkage fails to register with Afrocentrists, whom Al Mahdi accuses of erasing Islam from the African heritage that they hope to recover. Without Islam, however, Afrocentrists remain disconnected from true Nubian Blackness. "By wearing noserings, dashikis, head wrappings, and assorted African attire," Al Mahdi writes, "you may feel you have found your past. But in truth, you have only picked up bits and pieces of a heathen culture and distortions of Al Islaam."[156]

THE WRONG AFRICA: YORUBA REVIVALISM

Advertisements for *The Prophet Muhammad and Ali Were Nubian (Black)* present readers with a loaded question: "Is it true that all Black men were polytheists like the Yoruba of West Africa?"[157] When Al Mahdi argues for Islam as the essential form of African spirituality, Yoruba revivalism appears in his work as a foil. Like his Muslim contemporaries in both the Nation of Islam and Sunni communities, Al Mahdi considers Muslim Africa more civilized and advanced than the "primitive" and "pagan" non-Muslim Africa (an exception is made for pharaonic Egypt) and stresses the Muslim presence among enslaved Africans in the Americas. He also claims superiority for Muslim ancestry: a 1972 NIHMA pamphlet, clearly meant for Al Mahdi's readers in the northeastern United States, claims that while slaves taken from Yoruba regions were sent to the Carolinas and Mississippi to perform hard labor and toil in cotton fields, slaves taken from "Islamic countries" such as the Sudan and Egypt (prized for their "extreme intelligence and the highest learning") were brought to New York and New Jersey.[158]

A cartoon in a 1982 *Ansaar Village Bulletin* depicts worshippers of Shango among Jehovah's Witnesses, astrologers, disco-dancing women, and non-AAC/NIH Muslims doomed to hellfire.[159] As Al Mahdi's metaphysical Africa remains Islamic, he presents Yoruba as a corrupted derivative of Islam and distorted vision of Blackness. In his introduction to *Yoruba* (1978), Al Mahdi writes with regret that many African Americans have wrongly identified Yoruba as "the true religion of all Black people." He attributes this misunderstanding to white supremacist deception: the Amorite "shows you tribes and tribes of people who follow paganistic religions then tells you, 'THESE ARE YOUR PEOPLE.' Yes these are your people who have strayed from the path of ALLAH SUBHANA WA TA῾ ALA."[160]

Privileging polytheism as the essential African spirituality, Yoruba revivalism troubles Al Mahdi's metaphysics of race. As early as 1972, Al Mahdi argued that the Yoruba were originally Muslim,[161] and asserted that Yoruba has "many roots extended from Islam" but nonetheless remains an unacceptable corruption of Islamic monotheism. *Yoruba* walks the reader through a history that starts with Eden in the "Land of the Black," progresses toward Yoruba's rise as a great kingdom ("but a paganistic people who had a diety [sic] for mostly everything"), and leads to the Yoruba's encounter with Islam. Living in Nubia, the Yoruba learned "many of their signs and symbols which . . . proved their relation with Islam prior to them becoming paganistic." In an account without dates, seemingly taking place out of earthly time, a man named Lamurudu brought the Yoruba religion to Mecca. "It was not known as Yoruba at the time," Al Mahdi notes, "but just idolatry or polytheism." Lamurudu's son Oduduwa became "heir to the throne of Makkah" and collaborated with Lamurudu to make idolatry the state religion. They ordered that idols be placed inside the Ka'ba; the son of Oduduwa's priest, however, was a Muslim and destroyed them. Contesting the territory of the Ka'ba led to a civil war that the Muslims ultimately won. Oduduwa and his father were killed, and their supporters fled from Mecca to the Sudan—where Muslims again pushed them out, causing them to seek refuge in distant Nigeria. Oduduwa's seven grandchildren became kings and queens of seven original Yoruba states.[162]

Al Mahdi then analyzes Yoruba deities as parallels to Allah's attributes, demonstrating "the fact that these people were once Muslim." From there, he discusses the slave trade, connecting Muslim and Yoruba tribes as mutual victims of "the paleman" while again affirming African Muslim superiority over non-Muslims. Through European connections to the Arab slave trade, transatlantic slavery brought Muslims from "Nubia, Sudan and other Islamic countries" to North America. "These Blacks," Al Mahdi asserts, "were of extreme intelligence and of the highest learning."[163] In pamphlets from the mid-1980s, Al Mahdi continues this narrative of Nubian Muslims as exceptional Africans, claiming that Amorite slave traders ventured into the Sudan after realizing that they could not control "uncivilized, paganistic" Africans. Amorites thus targeted the Dongolawi, "a special breed who were very intelligent."[164] But integrating learned Sudanese Muslims into American slave society provoked a new crisis for Amorites, as the Muslims taught other slaves their true history. To neutralize Islam's power as a force of liberation, the white devils promoted a slave-making distortion of Islam: "The Amorite then had to bring about a religion that was somewhat Islamic but differed from the Islam that was practiced in Sudan, so he chose the Pakistanis and others to teach you their diluted forms of Islam. . . . This was for you to think that Islam was not your original way of life."[165]

Al Mahdi argues that the devil deceives Black people into believing that cultures of non-Black Muslims such as "Pakistanis" represent Islam's true heartlands, thereby severing Islam from Blackness. Yoruba revivalism and anti-Muslim Afrocentrism thus ironically enforce white supremacist narratives about what it means to be African, leading Nubians in the Americas to forget that "everything originated in the land of the Black (Sudan), and that the original way of life was Islam."[166] As Nubian heritage inescapably means Islamic heritage, and true Islam remains inherently Nubian, both "orthodox" Islam (embodied by "pale Arab" and South Asian Muslims and their African American stooges) and Yoruba revivalism appear in AAC/NIH media as instruments of anti-Blackness, requiring correction by a master teacher.

CONCLUSIONS

From his beginnings at State Street Mosque, watching Black Muslims abandon their Black imam to follow Pakistani Muslims, to the 1970s, in which the Nation of Islam, seeking acceptance and resources from the larger "Muslim world," abandoned Elijah Muhammad's legacy, and through the 1980s, in which immigrant-led Muslim institutions became leading voices of American Islam and Saudi-supported Black Salafi networks rose to prominence, Al Mahdi consistently advocated Black Muslim agency against dominance by non-Black Muslim power.

"The pale and red Arabs now ruling Saudi Arabia will not be able to admit that we (the Mahdiyya) are superior over them," claims the community's 1991 calendar, "because this will mean submitting to Black Arabs (Nubian).... They cannot see themselves following a Black Arab, just like Iblis (CH) would not bow to the Prophet Adam." The calendar charges that Saudis associate Blackness with slave status, but then mentions the familiar hadith "Hearken and obey although a Black Slave whose head is like a dried grape will be appointed to rule over you."[167] For Al Mahdi, the Black slave is mentioned not as a disavowal of racial prejudice but rather as a promise of pure Islam's return. As the prophesied raisin-headed slave, Al Mahdi rescues Islam's Blackness from white supremacist Sunni orthodoxy. "If the Sunni Muslims want to worship the white man and a white god," he told an audience in the late 1980s, "*lakum dinukum wa liya din*—to them be their way of life, and [to] us be ours, we'll find out on *yawm al-akhira* [the Last Day] who's true."[168]

CHAPTER 2

Heralds of the Reformer
Visions of Blackamerican Muslim History

> They all had at least one thing in common, the insight to know that by following all the Scriptures of ALLAH Most Glorified and Exalted the Nubian in the West would be free.... I could fit into Noble Drew Ali's shoes, and don Elijah Muhammad's hat, and put on Shaikh Daa'wud's robe and bear the flag of Marcus Garvey (TWON), which was raised from the Mahdi (AS) of whom I descend.
>
> —AL IMAAM ISA AL HAADI AL MAHDI

During the 1980s, between two competing visions of the Nation of Islam's journey—one in which the forty-year labor of Elijah Muhammad found its fulfillment in his son's reuniting of "lost-found" Muslims with the worldwide Muslim *umma*, another in which Louis Farrakhan faithfully carried on the Messenger's work while the Messenger's son sought to destroy it—the AAC/NIH challenged both sides.[1] Al Mahdi presented himself as Elijah Muhammad's only legitimate successor, the leader best qualified to build bridges between the Nation and "traditional" Islam. To this end he relied on Elijah's promise of a future teacher who would come, the credentials he could boast as a student of Sunni authority Daoud Faisal, and the legitimacy that Faisal's name could bestow upon his claims regarding Master Fard Muhammad. He also challenged Black Sunni communities not only as a defender of Elijah Muhammad's mission against the anti-Black racism of Arab and South Asian Sunni Muslims, but also on Sunni terms: positioning himself against W. D. Muhammad, Al Mahdi boasted a superior command of Arabic, deeper knowledge of Islamic tradition, and a more organic connection to the "Muslim world" via the Sudan. In contrast to scholarship that has positioned Al Mahdi's Islam almost exclusively within "heterodox" African American traditions, or assumed that his discourse progressed toward or away from "Sunni orthodoxy" at various times, this chapter demonstrates that in its constructions of Al Mahdi's Blackamerican Islamic genealogy, AAC/NIH media drew from registers on both sides of a contrived heterodox-orthodox binary. Al Mahdi cited both a Sunni imam and the spiritual head of the Nation of Islam to stake his claim as leader of Blackamerican Muslims.

Ahmad, Jesus' Khalifat (officially dated 1980, more likely published ca. 1984), while focused on popular Muslim arguments that the Bible foretold Muhammad's arrival, opens with an assertion of Al Mahdi's significance as a master teacher whose mission was foretold by his modern predecessors. The booklet offers photographs of Black Muslim leaders, captioned by Al Mahdi's commentary: Noble Drew Ali ("He told his followers to expect me"), Elijah Muhammad ("He knew I was coming and told his followers to follow me"), and Daoud Faisal ("He informed his people that I was here"). Al Mahdi notes that each community has failed to heed its leader's advice.[2] Whether Noble Drew Ali's Moorish Science, Elijah Muhammad's Nation of Islam, and Daoud Faisal's Sunnism were theologically compatible does not affect Al Mahdi's point: to follow these men ultimately requires an embrace of Al Mahdi, whose community best represents their collective legacy and purpose. As he subsumes the patriarchs of Blackamerican Islam into his mandate, Al Mahdi builds complex narrative webs.

Al Mahdi does not simply construct Muslim difference in binary oppositions of heterodox versus orthodox but rather sees it in relation to a larger struggle between global Nubian awakening and opposition to that awakening from the combined forces of white people and "pale Arabs." In this struggle, Malcolm X becomes a tragic figure for having been led astray and then murdered when his usefulness to "pale Arab" devils expired. Al Mahdi asserts both that Elijah lacked knowledge of classical Islam and that Malcolm was wrong to abandon Elijah for pale Arabs. The proper telos of Blackamerican Islam does not become embodied in Malcolm's pilgrimage to Mecca but rather in Al Mahdi's power to bring these legacies together. "It was prophecy," he tells us, "that Marcus 'Musa' Garvey, Shaikh Daa'wud, the Honorable Elijah Muhammad and Noble Drew Ali (TWON) would lay the foundation for your true way of life, Al Islaam, so that I, the Reformer, can continue their missions and bring you the complete teachings of Al Islaam."[3]

Engaging contemporaries like W. D. Muhammad and Louis Farrakhan with varying degrees of critique and polemic, Al Mahdi reworks Blackamerican Muslim histories in ways that increasingly seek to subsume elders of the past—including Elijah Muhammad, Daoud Faisal, Malcolm X, Noble Drew Ali, Marcus Garvey (who Al Mahdi claims had converted to Islam), and Allah (the former Clarence 13X)—within his metanarrative of Blackamerican Islam. In their AAC/NIH reconstruction, these sages lend their authorizing gravitas to Al Mahdi, who appears as their natural heir and successor. Departures and breaks in their respective understandings of Islam, attributed in AAC/NIH media to their incomplete knowledge, find reconciliation and correction in the teachings of Al Mahdi.

SHEIKH DAOUD FAISAL, "FOUNDING FATHER OF ORTHODOX ISLAM IN THE WEST"

Faisal's Islamic Mission of America (IMA) and its headquarters, the State Street Mosque, have received attention as milestones of American Muslim institution building (and also as unfortunate parables of tensions between African American and immigrant Muslims over questions of Islamic authority).[4] Throughout Al Mahdi's career, he consistently drew upon his connection to Faisal and State Street Mosque for evidence of his credentials, often in the most literal sense of displaying signed certificates and claiming an institutional link between Faisal's groups and Al Mahdi's Ansar.

In 1928, Faisal established the Islamic Propagation Center of America in Harlem, and in 1935 he founded the IMA and State Street Mosque. Faisal received formal authorization in 1943 from King Abd al-Aziz ibn Saud and a charter from Sheikh Khalid of Jordan to teach Islam to Americans.[5] Though Faisal opposed the valorizations of Blackness that characterized the Moorish Science Temple of America and the Nation of Islam, he nonetheless presented Islam as the original religion of Black people and the only cure for racism.[6]

Insider and outsider sources alike agree that State Street Mosque was the site of Al Mahdi's early education as a Muslim. As noted in the introduction, according to Abu Ameenah Bilal Philips, Al Mahdi converted to Islam at State Street circa 1965 after a stint in prison;[7] there are also suggestions that Al

Mahdi's mother was already a member of Faisal's community.[8] As Al Mahdi constructed his origin narrative in the 1970s and '80s, he claimed that he was the son of an American woman and the grandson of the Mahdi, and that he came to State Street through Faisal's connections to Sudanese diplomats. Fully aware of his secret identity as heir to the Mahdiyya, Faisal provided the child with religious instruction to prepare him for his mission.[9]

In the earliest extant AAC/NIH publications, Faisal and his organizations maintain a consistent presence. Al Mahdi regularly features pictures and quotations of Faisal and constructs an authorizing lineage from Faisal to himself. One NIHMA pamphlet from 1972–73 displays Faisal's photo on its front cover under the title *Founding Father of Islam in America Today, Here Since 1928 A.D.* Another pamphlet from the period hails him as "King of Muslims in America," reports that King Faisal of Saudi Arabia considers Daoud Faisal his adopted father, and shares the story of "one of many modern-day miracles" in which Faisal caused two pills to mysteriously appear in a bottle for a man who needed them. The pamphlet presents Faisal as a "founding father" not only of Islam in America but specifically of the AAC/NIH: "Who is Shaikh Daoud? He is our father—our patriarch—the Truth the Light—the only voice crying in the wilderness in the last minute of the last day."[10]

In AAC/NIH media, the lineage connecting Faisal and Al Mahdi was not only pedagogical but institutional. The name Nubian Islamic Hebrew Mission in America evokes Faisal's Islamic Mission of America; in 1973, Al Mahdi referred to his organization as "Ansaru Allah Community of the Islamic Mission of America Inc.," presenting the Ansar as a spinoff from Faisal's IMA and his leadership of the Ansar as a Faisal-appointed position.[11]

As the AAC/NIH feuded with other Muslim groups even in these early years, and as the nature of AAC/NIH interest in Faisal became a point of conflict at State Street, AAC/NIH publications deployed Faisal to symbolically or explicitly defend the Ansar. Pamphlets from the early 1970s portray Faisal as vouching for the AAC/NIH against "countless rumors that have spread throughout the various so-called Muslim communities."[12] Problems intensified when Faisal selected an AAC/NIH member to serve as his mosque's caretaker, which caused friction with "people who hadn't been there in years to contribute any of their time or financial support."[13] It appears that in Faisal's later years, the AAC/NIH was opposed by other State Street parties in competition over proximity to him. The claims of a privileged relationship between Al Mahdi and Faisal in AAC/NIH literature speak to a context in which Faisal and the legacy of State Street had become contested territory. *Breaking the Fast* (1973) describes Faisal's visit to the AAC/NIH's Eid al-Fitr celebration (apparently a tradition that persisted through the mid-1970s), where AAC/NIH members greeted Faisal and wife, Khadijah, with "probably one of the warmest welcomes in history," and Faisal led the *maghrib* prayer. The Faisals and Al Mahdi appear together on the pamphlet's front cover. An unnamed author recalls Al Mahdi "in deep thoughts sitting to one side of the room" and reports that Al Mahdi "was thinking back to those memorable days when he was a student under Sheikh Daoud at 143 State Street. He would rush there every Tuesday and Thursday night to be taught, helped, and guided." During one session, Faisal instructed his class to "go forth and spread and teach the truth in the name of ALLAH," which the pamphlet writer connects to Al Mahdi's present mission.[14]

By calling upon "the so-called Negro man in America who calls himself a Muslim to identify with the land as a Muslim from which his ancestors [came]," Al Mahdi positions himself in early AAC/NIH media as a defender of Faisal against those who left him and became the Dar. He lashes out at Black members of State Street Mosque who followed the mosque's Pakistani teacher Hafis Mahbub, a member of the Tablighi Jama'at:

> Today, you see American Negroes grasping the attire and traditional customs of Pakistan and India, two countries where over millions of people are starving because they chose to worship the cow instead of ALLAH. Their homeland isn't totally Islamic, but yet they'll come to America, aristocratically, to teach poor ghetto Negroes Islam. Think, and ask yourselves, do you see them taking on the customs and traditions of the Hausa's of Nigeria, or the garb of the people of Timbuktu, or adhering to the ways of the people inhabiting the area of the junction of the two Niles? All of those people are Muslim, and their way of life is Islam. For realizing this fact, that we are descendants of Muslims who were of great Islamic kingdoms and we are not an inferior people, we, the Nubians of Ansaru Allah are harassed and labeled innovators!derlass[15]

Al Mahdi writes of Faisal's appreciating African Muslim cultures and affirming a larger point that culture does not necessarily violate the bounds of religion, which leads them to collaborate against anti-Black racism in New York's Muslim communities. In this same 1973 column, observing polemical exchanges between the Sunni journal *Al-Islam* and the Nation of Islam's *Muhammad Speaks*, the AAC/NIH writer calls Faisal a "wise man" who cautions against sectarianism.[16] That year, Faisal was called to intervene in a conflict between the AAC/NIH and the Mosque of Islamic Brotherhood (MIB). The MIB, having declared Harlem off limits to AAC/NIH activity, sent an armed force against AAC/NIH peddlers who had violated the ban. With MIB members in police custody, Faisal mediated a truce between the groups, and Al Mahdi's followers did not press charges.[17]

In writings from the late '70s, Faisal continues to function as both an authorizing figure for the AAC/NIH's credentials and a source of partisan friction between the AAC/NIH and other factions. AAC/NIH newspapers from the second half of the 1970s repeat previous boasts of Faisal's endorsement of Al Mahdi, marked by his attendance at the community's celebration of Eid al-Fitr. *Id with the Ansars* (1977) presents Al Mahdi and Faisal together on the front cover with the caption "An understanding that very few understand" (fig. 15). Captioned photographs in this pamphlet tell the story of the Ansar sending a "motorcade of Cadillac limousines" to the home of their "honored guest," Faisal and Khadijah emerging from their limousine with Ansar assistance, and the elders holding court at their seat of honor: "Resplendent in his golden robes, and tajj. The king on his throne accompanied by his dowager consort." Al Mahdi is shown checking on Faisal, "just making sure that our patriarch is having a good time." A photo of Faisal speaking to Al Mahdi presents Faisal's advice in its caption: "'Watch out! There will be many to hate you and trying to stop your growth right in your midst. I know because they did it to me.'" Another photo shows white-garbed boys reciting the Qur'an for Faisal. The caption explains that tears flowed from their eyes, prompting Faisal to ask why they were crying. Al Mahdi answers, "Because not only can they chant Qur'an, they understand it."[18] *Id-ul-Fitr with the Ansars 1979* notes Faisal's absence from the festivities, while providing photographs from previous visits. A piece titled "Our Founding Father" explains, "As you all know, it is a tradition that Shaikh Dau'wd celebrates his 'Idu'l Fitr with the Ansars. . . . But this year we were met with much disappointment due to envy." The article claims that when Al Mahdi's delegation arrived to pick up Faisal, enemies of the AAC/NIH ("Pakistanian Arabs") persuaded Khadijah to keep her husband from attending: "They said that it would look bad for him to celebrate 'Idu'l Fitr with the Ansars." The following pages seek to illustrate the connection between Faisal and the AAC/NIH, including photographs of AAC/NIH men awaiting Faisal's arrival at the Eid celebration, a photo of Faisal embracing an Ansar (the caption has Faisal telling him, "Don't worry, I'm with you [the Ansar] in heart"), and a copy of the "Muslim Missionary Certificate" signed by Faisal and awarded to the Ansaru Allah Nubian Mission. The article proclaims that the AAC/NIH is "not a sect, schism, neither are we an alien community, especially to Shaikh

FIGURE 15 "An understanding that very few understand." Al Mahdi and Faisal together to celebrate the end of Ramadan. From Ansaru Allah Community, *Id with the Ansars* (1977), front cover.

Dau'wd Faisal," and questions whether Faisal is receiving proper care from those "same people who selfishly kept him from joining us on such a warm and joyous occasion."[19]

Al Mahdi's appropriation of Faisal intensified after Faisal's death in 1980. That year, Al Mahdi published *Islam the True Faith: The Religion of Humanity*, a tribute to Faisal. The cover proclaims that Faisal is the "Founding Father of Orthodox Islam in the West." As Al Mahdi consistently treated Faisal as a "founding father of Islam in America," the added qualifier "orthodox" suggests new sensitivity in terms of Al Mahdi's position. In its early years engaging Sunni groups within the State Street orbit, the AAC/NIH does not explicitly situate itself as something other than "orthodox." The pamphlet includes excerpts from Faisal's book (also titled *Islam, the True Faith, the Religion of Humanity*). Al Mahdi's *Islam the True Faith* includes numerous photos of Faisal in candid moments with Al Mahdi and AAC/NIH members, making a visual argument for Faisal's approval of the AAC/NIH, along with the Muslim Missionary Certificate.[20] The back cover of the booklet features advertisements for *Book of the Lamb*.

Faisal's significance in AAC/NIH genealogies remains visible throughout the 1980s. In the second of a 1986 pair of booklets titled *Where Is the Tabernacle of the Most High*, Al Mahdi names Faisal as one of "several Blackmen that have contributed to laying the foundation of Al Islaam in the West," and thus as "instrumental in laying the foundation for the much awaited coming of the Reformer."[21] A 1989 list of AAC/NIH holidays includes November 22, Faisal's birthday, "in commemoration of his being the first man to bring true Al Islaam to you . . . his spirit lives on through the Ansaru ALLAH Community, the new Arabic Kingdom of Illumination."[22] Publications from the late 1980s advertise *Who Was Shaikh Daww'ud?*, a booklet in the vein of pamphlets like *Who Was Marcus Garvey?* and *Who Was Noble Drew Ali?*, and a revised edition of Al Mahdi's earlier *Islam the True Faith: The Religion of Humanity*.[23]

Al Mahdi writes that outside the AAC/NIH, Faisal's contribution has gone unrecognized, as Muslims at State Street refused to listen to him. In a veiled reference to the faction that formed the Ya-Sin Mosque and Dar ul-Islam, he writes that members of State Street Mosque "would rather listen to Pakistanians that fell out of the sky. They wouldn't listen to a man who had already set up a Jamat here in the West." Faisal's successes paved the way for Al Mahdi, but his failures made Al Mahdi necessary. Al Mahdi mentions Faisal's attempt at Muslim communal living, Medinat as-Salaam, which lasted only three years, and then refers to his own Jazzir Abba, the AAC/NIH settlement in Sullivan

County. "It was just not his time," Al Mahdi writes. "There was someone to come that would turn that dream into a reality once again."[24]

According to Al Mahdi, many members of Faisal's State Street Mosque became the AAC/NIH's "backbone." Launching his own mission was not a matter of competing against Faisal; in fact, it came at Faisal's insistence: "I was a faithful attendant of the State Street Masjid in its infancy. . . . It was Shaikh Daa'wud (HWON) who passed on his knowledge and wisdom to me. He also gave me his Seal to be his Successor." While presenting himself as Faisal's student, Al Mahdi also alleges that Faisal's own religious education came at the hands of Al Mahdi's father and grandfather; the Islamic knowledge that Faisal passes to Al Mahdi is actually Faisal's repayment of a debt. The question of why Al Mahdi had previously used the name Isa Muhammad and concealed his connection to the Sudanese Mahdiyya is explained by this relationship: it was Faisal who advised Al Mahdi to change his name in order to prevent his assassination by enemies of the Mahdiyya in the Sudan. A Moroccan sheikh gave Al Mahdi the name Isa Muhammad, which he used until he revealed himself as Isa Al Haadi Al Mahdi, great-grandson and third *khalif* of the Sudanese Mahdi.[25]

Sources from 1972–73 reflect awareness of Nation of Islam teachings—Al Mahdi presents the pig as a genetically engineered amalgamation of cat, rat, and dog, states that white rule has reached its six-thousand-year expiration date, and refers to the twenty-three "scientists" that Elijah Muhammad draws from his reading of Revelation[26]—but does not typically engage the Nation in direct confrontation, whether as collaborator or rival. While Elijah Muhammad becomes an authorizing figure for AAC/NIH discourse only after his death, Daoud Faisal authorizes the AAC/NIH through his participation in the community. Of the figures discussed in this chapter, Faisal virtually monopolizes Al Mahdi's attention in his earliest writings. As the AAC/NIH emerged within a factionalized Brooklyn Muslim milieu, it was seemingly less concerned with groups such as the Nation, Moorish Science Temple, and Five Percenters than with its position relative to other factions at and around State Street Mosque. The Dar was Al Mahdi's first Black Sunni foil, a "proximate other" reflected even in its symbol, an upward-pointing crescent with *five*-pointed star. From Philips's informants, we learn that AAC/NIH members used to make appearances at Dar events, attracting attention for their provocative bone earrings and nose rings.[27] In Al Mahdi's pamphlets from the early 1970s, we find a conversion narrative in which a woman first encounters Islam through attending Ya-Sin Mosque, at which a Dar brother tells her to raise her index finger and repeat some "mumbo-jumbo"; she attends sisters' classes but learns "very little." She decides to "search deeper into Islam" by attending the AAC/NIH masjid, where she learns proper modesty and the "straight path." AAC/NIH publications from the period, including "a non-sectarian journal presenting Islam in its pristine purity as taught by the Quran and the Sunnah," seek to match these Sunni groups largely on their own terms, while contesting "Pakistani" ownership of Islam.[28] To this end, Al Mahdi draws upon Faisal for his own legitimacy as the spiritual and administrative leader of a Blackness-affirming Muslim community. Faisal features in AAC/NIH antagonism toward the Dar, which Al Mahdi critiques as a tragic case of Black men deferring to Pakistani culture as representative of "true Islam" rather than embracing the Muslim cultures of Africa. The power of Faisal's legacy in Muslim histories of New York, along with the State Street Mosque's value as a cautionary parable, remains potent even as Al Mahdi's project increasingly appropriates figures such as Elijah Muhammad.

ELIJAH MUHAMMAD AND THE SECRETS OF *Lam*

With most of Al Mahdi's polemical energy directed toward the Dar, Elijah Muhammad remains essentially invisible in the earliest AAC/NIH sources. One 1973 AAC pamphlet, *Will Send "Elijah" Before the Coming of the Great and Dreadful Day of the Lord*, could encourage the inference that Elijah Muhammad serves as a herald to Isa Al Haadi Al Mahdi in the same way that the biblical Elijah reappeared (in spirit) as John the Baptist to serve as a forerunner to Jesus. While such a reading might have seemed intuitive to some readers, it remains speculative, as the pamphlet makes no explicit mention of Elijah Muhammad or the Nation of Islam.

This virtual silence on Elijah Muhammad did not change instantly after Elijah's passing in 1975. Before 1978, when Louis Farrakhan broke away from W. D. Muhammad's reorientation project to revive the classical Nation of Islam, AAC/NIH literature did not exhibit a meaningful interest in the Nation, or in overtly challenging W. D. Muhammad. A diachronic reading of AAC/NIH media of the late 1970s suggests that Farrakhan's Nation revival provoked intensified AAC/NIH concern with Elijah's legacy. If one were to read AAC/NIH literature exclusively from 1977, she would have a different impression of the community's location of itself in relation to the Nation than she would if she read its publications from 1979.

In Al Mahdi's comparison of his community's symbol to those of other Muslim movements, sources from 1972–73 make subtle references to the

Nation, naming the left-facing crescent as symbolic of "American-born Negroes subject to the influence of the Turks" and discrediting Turkish descent as "half original."[29] In a 1972 pamphlet, Al Mahdi discusses the flag used by "followers of a Mr. Elijah Mohammed" without referencing the Nation by name, and claims that the flag came from "a Mr. W. D. Fard, the son of a Russian woman, Mime, and a Syrian father, Alfonso."[30] He repeats the claim in the 1977 pamphlet *Our Symbol* but otherwise avoids directly engaging the Nation in extant materials from 1977.[31] *Christ Is the Answer* (1977) includes a "False Prophets" section that denounces Father Divine and Sweet Daddy Grace as greedy charlatans and treats Noble Drew Ali more generously as a well-intentioned leader whose legacy amounts to a "start in the right direction," but it does not acknowledge Elijah one way or the other.[32] Another artifact from 1977, a revision of 1973's *Will Send "Elijah" Before the Coming of the Great and Dreadful Day of the Lord* remains officially silent on Elijah but could strike some readers as an esoteric claim on Elijah's legacy in relation to Al Mahdi's mission, particularly when read intertextually with Al Mahdi's developing connection to Jesus. As with the earlier edition, however, this interpretation is by no means self-evident or unavoidable as *the* singular plain-sense meaning. It does not appear that the death of Elijah Muhammad provoked an immediate rhetorical turn.

Al Mahdi seemingly derides Elijah Muhammad in *Khutbat's of Al Hajj Al Imam Isa Abd'Allah Muhammad Al Mahdi, Book Two*, in which he laments that Faisal's decades of work have gone ignored, while "Elijah Muhammad comes on with an Amorite as a leader, and they follow him to the death. To the point to kill another Muslim."[33] Al Mahdi dates the sermon July 5, 1974 (seven months before Elijah's death), but the *Khutbat's* volumes were published in 1977–79, the period in which Al Mahdi's literature started to make claims upon Elijah and the Nation's legacy.[34] The first volume of *Khutbat's* also presents a sermon dated to 1975 (no month provided) in which Al Mahdi attacks unnamed "false prophets" who reject the finality of prophethood. Al Mahdi asks a hypothetical interlocutor, "Who is Khatim An Nabi?" (Seal of the Prophets), adding that if his conversation partner answers, "the Prophet Muhammad," Al Mahdi would then ask, "Which Prophet Muhammad?" These "false prophets," he writes, "received no Revelation. . . . They didn't even receive guidance from the proper teacher."[35] Al Mahdi then criticizes "certain schools of thought out there" that deny the physical resurrection of the dead, as well as those who denounce belief in an unseen "spook" god and instead "believe in ALLAH as a man," and even Muslims who mispronounce *Muslim* as "Muzlam." After these clear jabs, Al Mahdi scoffs, "So foolish men untie the bowtie, it's keeping the blood from going to your head."³⁶ While it's possible that Al Mahdi attacked the Nation and/or Elijah Muhammad from his own minbar prior to Elijah's death, it remains notable that he did not publish these critiques for wider dissemination until the late 1970s.

In the final years of the decade, Al Mahdi began to explicitly articulate his position as the fulfillment and conclusion of Blackamerican Islam's variegated traditions and movements, but he remained cautious concerning Elijah Muhammad. Presenting himself as a master Qur'an translator and interpreter in *The Man of Our Time*, Al Mahdi claims that Marcus Garvey foretold a future arrival of people with a "Book of Light," that Noble Drew Ali had a vision of himself receiving a Qur'an, and that Daoud Faisal "envisioned a clear, precise Qur'an" to clearly articulate Islam. Al Mahdi also mentions that among "the visions most recently revealed," one foresaw the Qur'an coming as a "new book" that bore the Arabic letter *lam* (ل); curiously, Al Mahdi's reference to the vision of *lam* does not name the visionary who experienced it.³⁷

The visionary was Elijah Muhammad. From June through October 1972, Elijah delivered a twenty-week lecture series that was later disseminated as *The Theology of Time*. In his August 20 lecture, he mentions that Master Fard Muhammad had given him a copy of the Qur'an in Arabic, but he was unable to read it. Fard then brought him the English translation by Ahmadiyya scholar Muhammad Ali, promising that when Elijah learned to read Arabic, Fard would give him an Arabic Qur'an. "I made it myself," Fard told him. Elijah narrates that Fard once showed him this Qur'an, "but I couldn't read it. I could only recognize one letter in it."³⁸

What was the letter that Elijah recognized, and what was its value for understanding Black Muslim futures? Did this mysterious narration relate to Elijah's promise one month later that his community would not study the Bible or the "present Qur'an" in the hereafter? "You will have a new book," Elijah said in his September 24, 1972, lecture, "and the new book will replace the present Bible and Qur'an.... A new book is coming and that new book is the thing to which the people must give ear."³⁹ In his August 20 lecture, Elijah stated that he expected Fard to come back in less than a year with the book. Four years later, Fard had not returned, Elijah had passed away, and Imam W. D. Muhammad was dramatically de/reconstructing the Nation. As he articulated his project of redesigning the Nation in broader "mainstream" or "orthodox" al-Islam, W. D. Muhammad presented his reforms as esoteric fulfillments of his father's teachings. In the March 12, 1976, edition of *Bilalian News*, W. D. Muhammad referred to a vision that Elijah had experienced in which he saw a book with letters that were "penetrating the book all the way through" and possessed a "glow or illumination." Elijah knew only one of the letters: the Arabic *lam*, which "seemed to have been all through the book and it stood out through all the writing." W. D. Muhammad first claims that the book of his father's vision could not have signified a future book to replace the Qur'an as Elijah had claimed in *Theology of Time*. To W. D. Muhammad, the suggestion of a "new book" meant that the community did not yet know the Qur'an. The *lam* signifies the *shahadah*, testimony to the oneness of God and the prophethood of Muhammad, which W. D. Muhammad identifies as the Qur'an's dominant principle. When one reads the statement in Arabic (*la ilaha illa Allah, Muhammadu rasul Allah*), *lam* "stands out more than any other letter."[40] W. D. Muhammad employed his father's vision and his own exegesis to produce a new flag for the community, bearing the testimony of faith.[41]

Around the time that Farrakhan broke away from the reformed community to revive the original Nation, Al Mahdi's *Book of ل: To Whom It May Concern: Fear No Longer for I Have Arrived* (ca. 1978–79) and a larger two-volume work, *The Book of Lamb: The Message of the Messenger Is Right and Exact* (1979) stake his own claim as Elijah Muhammad's true successor (fig. 16). *The Book of ل* divulges that the "passing of the covenant of leadership" occurred with Elijah's death and Al Mahdi's anointing as the Reformer. Al Mahdi has come to "explain the teachings of the Honorable Elijah Muhammad and give the Black man in the Western hemisphere his spiritual heritage: his natural and only language—Arabic; his proper way of life following the sunnah of all the prophets of Allah subhana wa ta'ala—Islam; and the complete understanding of all the scriptures of Allah subhana wa ta'ala." In the wake of Elijah Muhammad's passing, his people were "left without guidance, in a state of confusion, void," until the "appointed time" at which Al Mahdi would arrive.[42]

In *The Book of Lamb*, Al Mahdi advocates for Elijah Muhammad as a devout Muslim who "often read the Holy Qur'an in his teachings and was quite aware of what it was saying," and who never claimed prophethood.[43] He introduces his *Book of Lamb* as a defense against Elijah's enemies: "Don't let the devil deceive you into thinking that you were tricked, because the teachings of the Honorable Elijah Muhammad (HWON) were right and exact, only misunderstood and misinterpreted."[44]

Al Mahdi holds that Elijah Muhammad "taught the Black Man many things yet much of what he taught had to be explained at a later date by one who has been chosen as the MUJADDID . . . who would explain the allegorical teachings of his herald."[45] Al Mahdi's claim to be the true *mujaddid*, reformer of Islam for

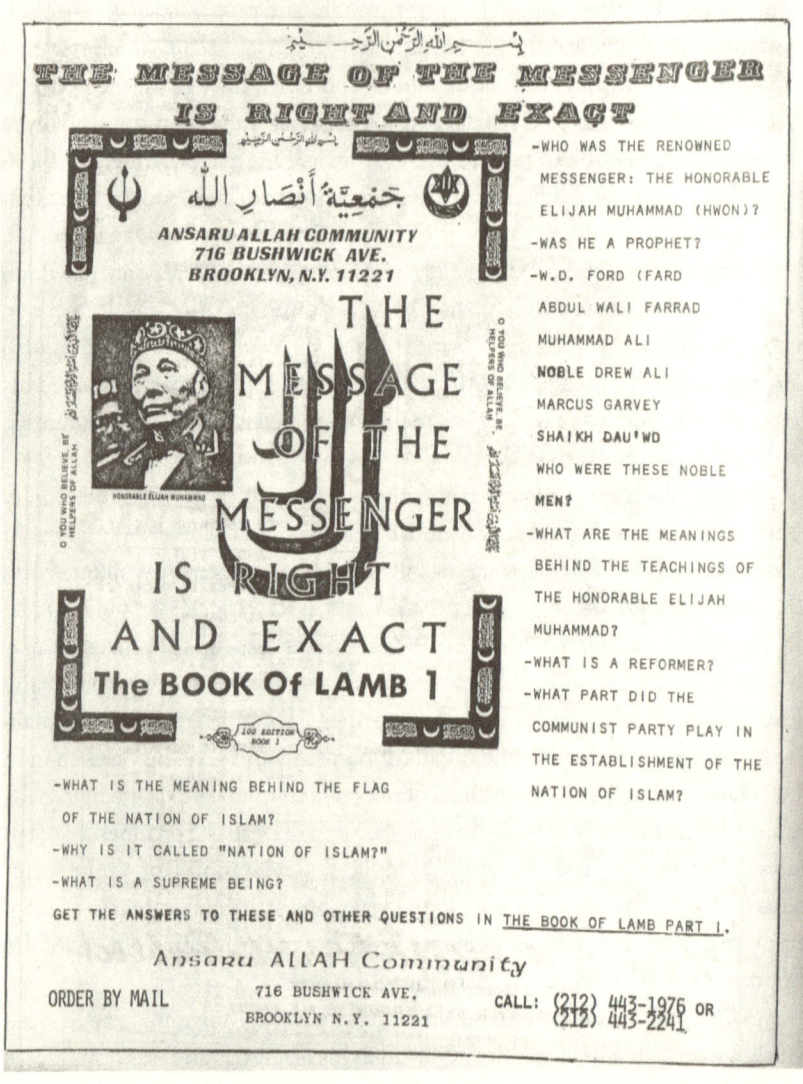

FIGURE 16 Advertisement for Al Mahdi, *The Book of Lamb* (1979).

his century, mirrored an identical claim made by W. D. Muhammad. For both leaders, self-identification as the *mujaddid* territorialized the Nation's past as well as its future.

As competing reformers, both W. D. Muhammad and Al Mahdi creatively reconstruct the Nation of Islam's major doctrinal points, including its racial demonology. In W. D. Muhammad's reading, Fard Muhammad's designation of white people as "devils" was meant to condemn the satanic ideology of white supremacy, rather than the "white race."[46] In Al Mahdi's reading, Elijah Muhammad correctly identifies the race of devils, but Elijah's understanding needs refinement; white people ("Amorites") are indeed devils, but specifically the "Physical Devil" or the "physical manifestation of the devil" in distinction from the supernatural *shaytan*, Iblis, whose existence Elijah had denied.[47] For telling the truth about white devils, Al Mahdi praises Elijah as a divine "warner."[48] In *American Muslims: Muslims in America* (1980), he laments that Elijah's work "has been totally destroyed by his own. Not only do they welcome the Devil into their 'mosque,' but they seek the economic and 'spiritual aid' by the pale Arab (devils)." In contrast, he praises Farrakhan's Nation revival as "the best news we have heard in a long time. You better believe the day will come when the Ansars and Minister Farrakhan will sit down at the same table because we are the only ones who know who the Devil is!"[49]

Like W. D. Muhammad's interpretation of his community's history, in which the Nation's peculiarities only served Master Fard Muhammad's "master plan" to gradually introduce a more "traditional" or "mainstream" Islam, Al Mahdi argues that Elijah Muhammad's role was to prepare Nubians for Islam's arrival in "its pristine purity."[50] Elaborating on the theme of Islam's true six-pointed star versus the Nation's illegitimate five-pointed star, Al Mahdi asserts that even while using the inferior star, Elijah Muhammad recognized the six-pointed star as correct. In a *Muhammad Speaks* column, Elijah had explained that this star was once the Nation's symbol: "The star in our flag today has five points, but our old star had six points. The six-pointed star stood for the word 'Kingdom' in the language of our religion (Islam)." When W. D. Muhammad reprinted the statement, Al Mahdi charges, he edited his father's words: "The star in our flag today has five points, but our old star stood for the word 'Kingdom' in the language of our religion (Islam)."[51]

Al Mahdi restores Elijah Muhammad to his rightful position as a "messenger" (not a "prophet") whose divine mission was to open a portal for the Reformer, a superior teacher who would correct the Nation's mistakes and fulfill its mission, described in the competing claims of both W. D. Muhammad and Al Mahdi as the "second resurrection."[52] It is in *The Book of Lamb* that Al Mahdi explicitly connects Malachi 4:5 ("Behold I will send you Elijah the Prophet before the coming of the great and dreadful day of the Lord") to Elijah Muhammad, because Elijah preceded another "day of the Lord," Al Mahdi's own arrival.[53]

Referring to Elijah's vision that W. D. Muhammad had described in 1976, Al Mahdi explains that Elijah promised the coming of one with knowledge of the Arabic letter *lam*: "He did not understand the meaning of this himself, but he told his followers that this would be a sign for them, and to follow whoever possessed this knowledge. This man who he spoke of was the Reformer (Mujaddidun) ... the one who would properly restore Islam as our way of life."[54]

For Al Mahdi, the *lam* signifies "lamb," as in the Lamb mentioned in the book of Revelation; he recognizes this lamb not as Jesus but rather as Melchizedek, whom he regards as identical to both the angel Michael and Khidr, the mystical teacher of Moses.[55] Al Mahdi also identifies himself with this entity, explaining that while his own body was "born of a mortal," his spirit is that of the Lamb.[56] Elijah Muhammad's vision of the *lam*, the only Arabic letter that Elijah could recognize, was significant in that *lam* is the twenty-third letter of the alphabet, matching the twenty-three years of the Qur'an's revelation.[57] Thirty years stand between 1970, year of the seventh seal's opening, and 2000; thirty happens to be *lam*'s numerical value in the classical Arabic *abjad*. Al Mahdi examines the mathematics of *lam*: to spell out the letter's sound, one first writes *lam* itself, which appears 33,432 times in the Qur'an, followed by an *alif*; Al Mahdi notes that the *lam-alif* combination appears in the Qur'an 45,190 times. The third letter used to write the *lam*'s sound, *mim*, appears 45,919 times. Al Mahdi adds these numbers, arriving at the incorrect sum of 114,541 (it should be 124,541), which he then digit-sums as 1+1+4+5+4+1, getting 16, which he in turn digit-sums as 1+6 to produce 7, the "perfect number."[58] "The ل that Elijah Muhammad saw in 1967," Al Mahdi writes, "is the same ل that sums up the entire universe,"[59] but W. D. Muhammad either misread his father's vision or deliberately misrepresented its meaning "so he could associate himself with the so-called White Arabs in the East."[60] Correcting W. D. Muhammad's attempts at a new name and flag, Al Mahdi argues for his own "banner of the Mukhlasiyna," bearing four *lams* to signify *ladhdha* (the agreeable inner soul), *laffa* (the joining together or mingling of a crowd), *lubb* (the seat in man's heart), and *ludd* (the United States, seat of the Antichrist/Dajjal), along with the word *ladha* (Allah's protection) at the center.[61]

Between *The Book of* ل and *The Book of Lamb*, something changes. In the former work, Al Mahdi makes straightforward claims upon Elijah Muhammad as his divinely appointed forerunner, rendering Al Mahdi the proper heir to Elijah's stewardship over the Nation. In the latter, Al Mahdi still claims Elijah's mantle as his own inheritance, but he also subjects the Nation's teachings to critical dissection. The shift seems to reflect a changing American Muslim milieu, as 1978 also happened to be the year in which Farrakhan parted ways with W. D. Muhammad and sought to revive the original Nation. *The Book of* ل declares,

"You were blinded for 3½ years but you see now that you have been deceived by the Devil; so now come home so we can finish our work!"[62] This blindness could reflect the second half of a "tribulation" described in community literature, corresponding to the period 1974–77.[63] Datable to 1978–79, it would appear that *The Book of* ل identifies the Satanic deception as W. D. Muhammad's reform project that followed his 1975 ascension, and that roughly four years later, Al Mahdi promises a more faithful continuation of Elijah Muhammad's work. In 1978, Al Mahdi would write that there were "no more Yorubas, or Black Jews, or Israelites, or Black Muslims or any of the others," and that the AAC/NIH stood alone;[64] in contrast to the 1978–79 *Book of* ل, the 1979 *Book of Lamb* seems to reflect a post-Farrakhan setting. While *The Book of* ل simply contrasts Al Mahdi's Elijah loyalism with W. D. Muhammad's upheaval of the tradition, *The Book of Lamb* celebrates Elijah but also expresses a greater interest in undermining the "classical" Nation's authority.

Simultaneously claiming and correcting the Nation, at the center of Al Mahdi's appropriation of Elijah Muhammad is a complex conspiracy theory drawing on claims that Elijah's teacher, Master Fard Muhammad, had been a white charlatan. The "white Fard" narrative had circulated since 1959, when Caribbean-born, Philadelphia-based Sunni leader Talib Dawud published a photograph of Fard in the *New Crusader* with the headline, "White Man Is God for Cult of Islam."[65] Elijah Muhammad responded with a charge that Dawud had sold out to the "pale Arab."[66] In the early 1960s, similar stories appeared in newspapers across the country, based on FBI-leaked information, alleging that Fard was a white hustler who duped ignorant and vulnerable African Americans.[67]

Al Mahdi's narrative, which underwent elaboration throughout the 1980s, posits that there were two Fards. The first and "true" Fard was a Sunni Muslim, born Abdul Wali Farrad Muhammad Ali on February 26, 1891, in Palestine. His father was of Turkish and Syrian descent. He came to America in 1913, arriving in New Jersey with the intention of causing discord within Noble Drew Ali's Canaanite Temple. One year later, Wallace Dodd Ford, the man who would become the second and more famous Fard, arrived in Los Angeles. Ford was also born in 1891. He was the son of a white British merchant marine and a Muslim woman from Fiji and had been raised Mormon in Portland, Oregon. Ford was a "notorious criminal," writes Al Mahdi, and had been arrested repeatedly for charges such as drug trafficking and false identification. Upon conviction for treason, Ford was sent to San Quentin State Prison, where he made a deal with the government to assume Abdul Wali Farrad Muhammad

Ali's identity, infiltrate the Moorish Science Temple, and undermine its leadership from within. Meanwhile, Ford was also working on behalf of the German and Japanese governments, which sought to introduce communism to Black America. As evidence, Al Mahdi compares Communist Party statements on Black self-determination from 1928 with later statements from the Nation of Islam.[68]

In 1928, Marcus Garvey was deported to Jamaica, and Faisal established his State Street Mosque in Brooklyn. The U.S. government secretly designated 1929 as the year in which important Black leaders would be assassinated. Falling victim in the conspiracy were both Noble Drew Ali and Abdul Wali Farrad Muhammad Ali, after which Wallace Dodd Ford embarked on his mission to destroy what was left of the Moorish Science Temple. He appeared in Chicago later in 1929, claiming to be Noble Drew Ali's reincarnation, and promoted factional schisms that permanently split the community.

In 1930, Ford began preaching in Detroit as W. F. Muhammad. To become believable as a Muslim leader, Ford attempted to study Islam, though he lacked an adequate grasp of Arabic. He did possess a series of questions from Abdul Wali Farrad Muhammad Ali—half of the question-answer catechism that would become the Nation's Supreme Wisdom Lessons—but could not produce his own answers, "so he just philosophied [sic] on the politics and the economics that the questions dealt with." Ford replaced much of Ali's Islamic content with communist ideology and atheist materialism.[69] The questions were then presented to Elijah Muhammad as an examination; the questions and answers thus form the Supreme Wisdom Lessons as they were then transmitted within the Nation. Within Nation discourses, therefore, we find not only Wallace Dodd Ford's economic teachings but also traces of Abdul Wali Farrad Muhammad Ali's religious material. Al Mahdi suggests that we can easily determine the sources of Elijah's ideas; when Elijah refers to historical figures and scriptures by their Arabic names (such as Yakub), we know that he is using the real Fard's material.[70] Despite Elijah's ignorance of the situation, Al Mahdi regards him as a faithful Muslim; it was because of Elijah's pure "faith in ALLAH SUBHANA WA TA'ALA" that he could build the glorious Nation of Islam, despite a sophisticated conspiracy by white devils to mislead him.[71]

As the Reformer, Al Mahdi takes it upon himself to "renew" and complete the Nation's flawed catechism. In his commentary on the Supreme Wisdom Lessons, he presents each question and offers his own answer, incorporating biblical exegesis, numerology, his theory of racial "grafting," and arguments for the superiority of his movement's six-pointed star to the five-pointed star on the Nation of Islam's flag. The first question of the Lessons' "Student Enrollment" asks, "Who is the Original Man?" Al Mahdi omits the original answer ("The Original Man is the Asiatic Black Man, the Maker, the Owner, Cream of the Planet Earth, God of the Universe") in favor of his correction: "The Asiatic Black Man. The Ruler of the earth. Made Khalifat by ALLAH SUBHANA WA TA'ALA." He then adds Qur'anic verses, his definition of the term *Khalifat*, and a breakdown of his own racial categories. The Asiatic Black Man is the "black and brown race" and the "original Ishmaelites," as opposed to other Asiatic peoples: the Edomites (the "red" and "yellow" races) and the Caucasian (Caucus-Asian) "sub-original" Amorites, "Ape Man Deteriorating Asian, Pale man." Elsewhere in the Lessons, Al Mahdi takes the statement that Africans learned of the enslaved African diaspora "approximately 60 years ago" as a reference to the Sudanese Mahdiyya: if the Lessons were composed in 1930, going back sixty years would mean 1870, the year that the Ansar were established in the Sudan, and exactly one century before the emergence of the new Ansar under the Reformer in 1970. Al Mahdi answers the Lessons' question "Why does the devil call our people 'Africans'?" with an explanation that they should instead be called "Asiatic Sudanese" in recognition of their heritage as builders of the pyramids.[72]

In 1985, Al Mahdi republished *The Book of Lamb: The Message of the Messenger is Right and Exact*, which had consisted of two pamphlets, as a single booklet, *The Book of Laam: To Whom It May Concern, Fear No Longer for I Have Arrived*. In 1989, he added material and released a 386-page *Book of Laam: The Message of the Messenger Is Right and Exact*. Al Mahdi's complex uses of Elijah Muhammad enable him to simultaneously claim Elijah as his inheritance, position himself as Elijah's true successor as the leader of Blackamerican Muslims, and authorize himself over Elijah as the master teacher who will correct his mistakes. Elijah himself saw this coming. Al Mahdi is "the one the Honorable Elijah Muhammad (HWON) prophesied . . . the true REFORMER (MUJADDID) for this era of time." Al Mahdi credits Elijah for having "carried the Nation of Islaam as far he could," but nonetheless affirms his own superior power: "The covenant of leadership was passed in 1975 to me. . . . I have come with the sole purpose to explain the teachings of the Honorable Elijah Muhammad (HWON) and to give you the meaning behind the letter (ل)."[73]

Amid the factional schism between Farrakhan and W. D. Muhammad, Al Mahdi intervenes with his own claims. Reading AAC/NIH literature diachronically, comparing works that appeared just before and just after Farrakhan's break from W. D. Muhammad's reform project, one discerns a growing imperative for Al Mahdi to locate his authority not only in the classical Muslim Blackness of the Sudan, but increasingly within the local histories of American Islam and the contested destiny of the Nation of Islam.

"HE WAS OF THE NOBLE": MALCOLM X

In 1979, as Al Mahdi presented himself as the true reformer (*mujaddid*) and challenged W. D. Muhammad's claim to that designation, contested W. D. Muhammad's rhetorical deployment of Bilal, and countered Farrakhan's Nation revival with his own reconstruction of Elijah Muhammad's mission, Malcolm X remained absent from AAC/NIH literature. Throughout the 1979 edition of Al Mahdi's *Book of Lamb*, we are reading for what goes unsaid.

In addition to the alternative histories, numerological analyses, and commentary on Nation lessons that characterized the 1979 *Book of Lamb*, the 1989 *Book of Laam* includes new discussion of Malcolm. This late emergence of Malcolm in Al Mahdi's claim upon the history and future of Black Islam points to Malcolm's growing prominence in the late 1980s as a foundational figure in that trajectory. In the 1989 *Book of Laam*, Al Mahdi extends his use of the acronym HWON ("He Was of the Noble") beyond Elijah Muhammad to honor other figures, such as Noble Drew Ali and Malcolm X. Al Mahdi's brief treatment of Malcolm begins with a celebration of Malcolm's oratorical skills and contribution to the Nation, and includes a biographical sketch, through which Al Mahdi weaves himself into Malcolm's life. Al Mahdi claims that his own mentor, Sheikh Daoud Faisal, made arrangements for Malcolm's post-Nation pilgrimage to Mecca. Through this Faisal connection, Al Mahdi himself becomes a character in Malcolm's hajj narrative.

In his *Autobiography*, Malcolm refers to a "young Arab *Mutawaf*'s aide," dressed in "skull cap, long white gown, and slippers," who attempted to teach him Sunni prayers while he was in Jedda. "I tried to do what he did," Malcolm writes. "I knew I wasn't doing it right.... When my guide was down in a posture, I tried everything I could to get down as he was, but there I was, sticking up." Malcolm recalls letting the aide perform ablutions and prayers first, watching him in order to learn the motions.[74] In the 1989 *Book of Laam*, Al Mahdi identifies himself as this aide; while representing his own mission as the divinely appointed fulfillment of Elijah Muhammad's work, he also assists Elijah's attritioned minister in his reinvention as a Sunni.[75]

The 1989 *Book of Laam* also criticizes Malcolm for overestimating Sunni Islam's transracial brotherhood. "He did not see the reality of racism in Al

Islaam," Al Mahdi writes. "He also did not learn the history of the pale Arab." Al Mahdi adds that Malcolm, having been deceived by the devil, condemned Elijah Muhammad prematurely for his extramarital affairs, failing to realize that in "Al Islaam," there was no crime in a man's having more than one wife or concubine. Malcolm, in Al Mahdi's judgment, had become "another Judas," for which he has received disproportionate praise and recognition from "the pale man." Al Mahdi concludes his treatment of Malcolm in *The Book of Laam* by affirming that Malcolm, "our beloved brother," had been tricked by the devil, and that Elijah Muhammad had no involvement with Malcolm's assassination.[76]

Between the 1979 and 1989 versions of *The Book of Lamb*, we find an escalation in Al Mahdi's hostility toward transnational Sunni networks and what he perceives as Arab interference in the lives of African American Muslim communities. Whereas in the 1979 edition, Al Mahdi engages both W. D. Muhammad's community and Farrakhan's nascent Nation revival primarily within the terms of their shared Nation tradition, by 1989 the terrain has shifted. The 1989 edition displays more focused concern with the intersection of African American Muslims and Saudi-led projects of globalizing Arabocentric Sunni hegemony. This text stands between anti-Muslim trends within Afrocentrism and the prominence of Salafi networks in African American Sunni communities, which would enjoy increasing success throughout the late 1980s and peak in the mid-1990s.[77] Responding to renewed interest in Malcolm X, the 1989 edition treats Malcolm's post-Nation reconversion as sincerely driven and as engaging a classical authenticity—Al Mahdi, after all, tries to teach him Sunni prayers—but nonetheless presents Malcolm's reinvention in Saudi Arabia as a cautionary tale about the danger that outside forces pose to Black unity. The parable of Malcolm thus privileges Al Mahdi against Black Salafi imams who favor Saudi-networked discourses over the teachings of Elijah Muhammad.

Al Mahdi's treatment of Malcolm following the 1989 *Book of Laam* continues this antagonism toward Black Sunnis. Al Mahdi elaborates on his Malcolm narrative in his 1991 volume *The Book of the Five Percenters*. Merging two characters from Malcolm's *Autobiography*, Al Mahdi maintains his previous claim that he had met Malcolm in Jedda, adding that he was also the *mutawaf* who guided Malcolm through the rites of hajj and protected him from being trampled during prostrations. In his *Autobiography*, Malcolm describes the *mutawaf* as a "short, dark-skinned Arab, named Muhammad" who spoke no English.[78] Al Mahdi remarks, "The part about me speaking no English was added in because if I did not speak to him in English I could not teach him his Shahadah. Alex Haley added many things in that book to make it sell."[79]

The Book of the Five Percenters charges that Malcolm had been brainwashed by what Al Mahdi terms the "Wahhabi Sect." The Wahhabi Sect, he writes, "had succeeded in their plan to 'set up' Malcolm by sending him to Mecca and changing his views on Al Islaam to fit theirs. In Mecca, Malcolm X was welcomed and treated royally just like they are presently doing with Wallace D. Mohammed and Siraj Wahhaj who they also employ." Al Mahdi Al Mahdi argues that Malcolm, unaware of the Wahhabi Sect's plan, surrendered to their authority and joined in the defamation of Elijah Muhammad. Once Malcolm had served his purpose, "the red Arabs then had him killed."[80] Al Mahdi adds that the Wahhabi Sect is currently engaged in a similar project with "Jamaican Negro" and Salafi convert scholar Abu Ameenah Bilal Philips, who had become Al Mahdi's chief Sunni antagonist in the 1980s through his Riyadh-published polemical tract *The Ansar Cult in America*.

Examining AAC/NIH literature from 1979 through the mid-1990s, we find a growing investment in Malcolm X that mirrors the Malcolm renaissance taking place in American popular culture. At the start of the 1980s, Malcolm does not appear in the community's arguments for its Islamic authenticity against rivals W. D. Muhammad and Louis Farrakhan. By the end of that decade, however, Al Mahdi had reworked Malcolm's life to oppose a rising Sunni triumphalist narrative, as well as to warn Black Salafi networks of the Saudi threat. Post-Mecca Malcolm finds himself rewritten by the AAC/NIH—not as having recovered true Islam but, instead, as a tragic figure. Meanwhile, Al Mahdi authorizes himself over Malcolm as a Muslim custodian, gatekeeper, and guide, teaching Malcolm not only prayers but even the *shahadah*, the testimony of faith by which Malcolm performs his Sunni reconversion. His narrative preserves an essential Blackness for Islam in Mecca, while writing against the Saudi state that sponsored Malcolm's Sunni reinvention and the American Muslim communities that may legitimize themselves in part as heirs to post-Mecca Malcolm.

"A STEPPING STONE": NOBLE DREW ALI

In a photo spread titled "At Home with the Nubians Within the Tents of Qaidhar," an AAC/NIH pamphlet from 1972 displays a photo captioned "Grand Sheik of Moorish Science Temple Visits Our Tents."[81] Apart from this caption, I could not find references to Moorish Science or Noble Drew Ali in early AAC/NIH sources. At the turn of the 1980s, Al Mahdi proclaims that, like Elijah Muhammad and Daoud Faisal, Noble Drew Ali "told his followers to expect me, and now that I am here, his followers are not with me."[82] In 1980, Al Mahdi published a pamphlet titled *Who Was Noble Drew Ali?* and devoted to refuting the Moorish Science Temple's teachings while appropriating its prophet. Al Mahdi praises Noble Drew Ali as a pioneer in the history of Black liberation and the restoration of Islam but notes that because Noble Drew Ali "had very little religious backing and . . . a limited knowledge of the Scriptures," and "did not know the language of his people which was Arabic," he could not teach Islam or inform Black people of their Ishmaelite lineage. Instead, he was "forced to deal with the people on a political level and not a spiritual one." While discussing Noble Drew Ali's plagiarism from New Thought texts, Al Mahdi asserts that Noble Drew Ali got his idea of Islam from the Shriners. According to Al Mahdi, the Shriner organization, "a fun and drinking society" known for its appropriation of an exotic Muslim "Orient," was designed by white people to undermine Islam. Noble Drew Ali, however, creatively reappropriated the appropriation; "he took this mockery of Islam from the Shriners and used it along with the teachings he learned from traveling to Egypt and came up with a concept of Islam that stopped the entire nation."[83]

While slighting his religious authority, Al Mahdi defends Noble Drew Ali against Sunni condemnations over his claim to prophethood. For Al Mahdi, Noble Drew Ali is indeed a prophet in the range of meanings of the English word, which does not completely correspond to the Arabic *nabi*. Noble Drew Ali did not know Arabic, Al Mahdi reminds us, and therefore could not have claimed *nabi* status; he only referred to himself as "prophet" in English.[84]

In 1988, Al Mahdi disseminated a revised *Who Was Noble Drew Ali?* (fig. 17), citing a "tremendous upsurge of requests for this book" from "many followers of the Moorish Science Temple philosophy." Al Mahdi laments that Noble Drew Ali's significance and the fullness of his contribution have been ignored. Al Mahdi's work on Noble Drew Ali thus seeks to repair Black historical consciousness.[85]

Al Mahdi constructs a sympathetic biography of Noble Drew Ali, highlighting the oppression and poverty he had experienced as a Nubian in America. Young Timothy Drew was intelligent, Al Mahdi writes, and a natural seeker of knowledge. He traveled to Egypt, where he visited universities, studied under "Egyptian sages," entered the "inner chambers of the pyramids," and obtained a new understanding of the slave trade. During his Egyptian sojourn, he "learned of his heritage, which laid the foundation for his becoming a pioneer of Al Islaam in the Western Hemisphere. He went to Egypt as Timothy Drew, and he returned to America with the Arabic name 'Ali.'"[86]

FIGURE 17 Advertisement for Al Haadi Al Mahdi, *Who Was Noble Drew Ali?* (1988) and *Who Was Marcus Garvey?* (1988).

Noble Drew Ali sought to improve his people's conditions. In Al Mahdi's estimation, he correctly diagnosed the problem (the devil's rule) and the solution (a collective Black return to divinely revealed scriptures) but could not deliver Islam "in its pristine purity" because of his ignorance of the Qurʾan and Arabic.[87] He "never taught his followers Arabic. He taught them in the language they had been using since slavery, English." This left his authority vulnerable in the face of Abdul Wali Farrad Muhammad Ali, who impressed Noble Drew Ali's followers with his superior command of Arabic and his presentation of Islam in "more classical form." While Farrad stole Noble Drew Ali's followers, Al Mahdi writes, Elijah Muhammad was able to attract them by integrating Noble Drew Ali's teachings into his own discourse.[88]

Unequipped to teach Islam, Noble Drew Ali drew from numerous sources, Muslim and non-Muslim, Black and white alike: the Shriners, "Eastern Moslems," and New Age writers such as Levi Dowling. Despite his lack of "authentic" Islamic credentials and the later splintering of his movement, Al Mahdi affirms Noble Drew Ali's significance in Black Islam. "He did serve as a stepping stone," Al Mahdi explains, "in introducing Al Islaam to a people who had totally lost the knowledge of their real way of life." Even if Noble Drew Ali could not complete the mission, he achieved a crucial intervention for his time and place. Al Mahdi draws Noble Drew Ali, Sheikh Daoud Faisal, Marcus Garvey, and Elijah Muhammad together for their collective contributions to Black freedom. Though they disagreed on the details, they shared one mutual understanding: Nubian redemption from Amorite oppression begins with a return to *all* of the divine scriptures. To this end, their works "laid the foundation for your true way of life," the religion of Abraham, which continues with Al Mahdi.[89]

Noble Drew Ali "tried to give the Nubian in America a link to his past through developing a nation with a code of dress, mystic symbols and a flag by borrowing from other cultures. Although his intentions were good you can now see that his information was not always correct."[90] Even if he possessed virtually no Islamic knowledge, and resorted to plagiarizing from white men for his personal *Holy Koran*, Al Mahdi draws from that very text as an authorizing discourse on behalf of his own status. *Who Was Noble Drew Ali* asserts that Moorish Science scripture itself reveals that Noble Drew Ali anticipated the future Reformer, Isa Al Haadi Al Mahdi.[91]

The final section of the revised *Who Was Noble Drew Ali* covers various leaders who came after him, with Al Mahdi's appraisals: Sweet Daddy Grace, swindler; Father Divine, false god; Abdul Wali Farrad Muhammad Ali, conspiracy victim; Wallace Dodd Ford, imposter; Sheikh Daoud Faisal, Sunni community builder whose failed dream lives on in Al Mahdi's success; and the Honorable Elijah Muhammad. Al Mahdi then examines contemporaries who appear as branches of Elijah's tree, starting with Farrakhan, a "good brother" who "means well" but lacks proper Islamic knowledge and "therefore cannot guide his followers to the truth." Al Mahdi optimistically asserts that Farrakhan has denied Fard's divinity: "Slowly, he is coming to the knowledge of true Islaam." From there, Al Mahdi examines W. D. Muhammad (responsible for "the complete destruction of all that his father created"); Silis Muhammad (whose splinter group is summarized without editorial comment); the former Clarence 13X, who taught the youth because they were "more easily influenced" and whose flag uses the same star, crescent, and number 7 as Noble Drew Ali; and Malcolm X, who was "coming to the realization of true Islaam when he was murdered." Finally, Al Mahdi himself appears as this history's conclusion—in turn the conclusion to these pioneering legacies. The truth manifests itself when one compares the failures of past leaders with his own thriving community. "The proof is in the pictures," Al Mahdi promises. "See your way to the truth and come home to your own." The book concludes with photographs of children and adults in the community's classrooms, masjids, and private campground, dressed in white *thobes* and black niqab, along with a listing of successful AAC/NIH operations, including schools, apartment buildings, various clothing businesses, farms, restaurants, buses, and media-related ventures.[92] The Moorish Science attempt to restore Black people to their true flag, nationality, economic self-sufficiency, names, prayers, health regimens, clothing, and way of life appears as an inferior prototype.

"NOW YOU KNOW WHAT IT REALLY MEANS": MARCUS GARVEY

The title page of Al Mahdi's *Who Was Marcus Garvey?* (1988) features an image of Africa that includes the Arabian Peninsula, reflecting Al Mahdi's Afro-Arabia narrative in which the two landmasses had been joined before the devil's destructive mischief caused the creation of the Red Sea. Locating the Arabian Peninsula as part of Africa resonates with Al Mahdi's larger interest in bringing the pan-Africanist leader into his genealogy of Black Islam, which he pursues not only by discussing Garvey's significance for Noble Drew Ali but also by pronouncing Garvey himself a Muslim. According to Al Mahdi, Duse Mohamed Ali had educated Garvey on points that later became AAC/NIH touchstones: that Jesus was a Black man; that the pyramids were "storehouses of knowledge which safeguarded the ancient teachings" and that the Egyptian elders had installed similar centers throughout the ancient world; that the awaited Mahdi had arrived in the Sudan, and that he carried a black, red, and green flag. Duse Mohamed Ali witnessed Garvey's performance of the *shahadah*, after which the man who had been called the "Negro Moses" renamed himself Musa and adopted the six-pointed star, the true star of Islam. Al Mahdi argues that Garvey's conversion also became evident in the dress code of women in his Universal Negro Improvement Association (UNIA).[93]

While Al Mahdi's celebration of Elijah Muhammad, Noble Drew Ali, and the former Clarence 13X deliver a sleight-of-hand polemic, *Who Was Marcus Garvey* devotes considerable space to confronting Ras Tefar I tradition, in which Garvey is regarded as a prophetic forerunner of Haile Selassie. Al Mahdi's tribute to Garvey becomes an anti-Rasta tract; Garvey "could not have been referring to Haile Selassie as the black prince to be crowned because Haile Selassie had no respect for Garvey or the United Negro Improvement Association," as Selassie had "turned his back" on Garvey and "refused to talk with him." Nor did Garvey's vision of an "Africa for Africans" assign special privilege to Ethiopia, the Zion of Rasta tradition, as Al Mahdi argues that "Ethiopia" in early pan-Africanist discourse (including the UNIA anthem) served as a generic catch-all for the entirety of Africa. Ethiopia was not Garvey's Zion any more than the rest of the continent was. Al Mahdi also argues that "many practices of the Rastafarians do not coincide with the teachings of Marcus Garvey," as Garvey did not wear dreadlocks, regard marijuana as a biblical sacrament, or claim the green, yellow, and red Ethiopian flag as a symbol of pan-Africanism. In his criticism of dreadlocks and marijuana, Al Mahdi attacks Rastas for selectively following the scriptures; in his rejection of the Ethiopian flag, he argues that Garvey's red, black, and green flag was based on the black, red, and green Mahdiyya flag. While rearranging the colors, Garvey also removed the flag's testimony of faith because he did not understand Arabic.[94]

Rejecting Rasta constructions of metaphysical Africa, Al Mahdi presents his own, charting his lineage through the Sudanese Mahdi to the Prophet. The Mahdi, who followed "the Religion of Abraham" and liberated the "real Arabs" (the Sudanese) from British oppression, is foretold in the book of Revelation, which mentions a woman who "brought forth a man child, who was to rule all nations with a rod of iron" (12:5). Al Mahdi reveals the woman to have been Fatima, daughter of Muhammad, and her son to be her distant but direct descendant, the Mahdi of the Sudan. Al Mahdi also detaches "Lion of Judah" imagery from Selassie, asserting that this title was first bestowed upon 'Ali ibn

Abu Talib and that the "prayer of Abraham" confirms the arrival of a successor from Muhammad's bloodline. Adding that one can be both Israelite and Ishmaelite, Al Mahdi claims that the line of Judah can preserve the covenant of Israel while coming from the line of Ishmael.[95]

Who Was Marcus Garvey then departs into Al Mahdi's Afrofuturist history of Salaam, the "ultra-advanced civilization ruled by 24 Elders who are called ELOHIM in Hebrew and ALLAHUMA in Arabic. They are extra-terrestrials or angels." Of particular significance to his Rasta readers, he argues that these are the elders mentioned in Revelation. In the kingdom's capital city of Mu, the elders performed their advanced scientific research, kept the universe in order, and transmitted messages from Allah to humankind; the names Mu and Salaam combined to make the title Mu-Salaam, "one who is of peace," the root of "Muslim." This utopian age ended when the devil forced the division of the Arabian Peninsula from Africa and created the Red Sea. The perception of Africa and Arabia as two separate entities speaks to the devil's work. Similarly, treating the religions of Moses and Muhammad as separate also follows the devil, since these are "actually the same way of life"; the devil divided Judaism and Islam by "reforming" both traditions away from scripture, which in Islam's case meant the replacement of the Qur'an with false hadiths and the violent suppression of the Prophet's family.[96]

Establishing distinctions between true Islam (an indigenously African and authentically Black tradition) and the reformed Islam of white devils and "pale Arabs," Al Mahdi returns to his narrative of the Black *ahl al-bayt* and explains that the Sudan is where Fatima fled from "the pale Arabs of Egypt." The wise Nubians concealed her for three and a half years, which Al Mahdi reads as a prophetic number: Fatima hiding for 1,260 days symbolizes 1,260 years of Ishmaelite bondage that will end in the year 2000. According to Al Mahdi, Fatima's exile in the Sudan is referenced in the book of Revelation: mother of the man who will rule all nations, Fatima is the woman who flees into the wilderness, where she will rest for 1,260 days (12:6) and find nourishment while hiding from the serpent (12:14). Al Mahdi asserts that many of the ancestors who came to the Americas as slaves were taken from the Sudan, and that their bondage is also referenced in Revelation. Anchoring his treatment of prophetic history in the biblical text most salient for Rasta readers, Al Mahdi turns *Who Was Marcus Garvey* into an accessible pathway for Rastas to enter his own discursive universe. Al Mahdi returns to his discussion of Garvey and reminds readers that the AAC/NIH waves a truer version of Garvey's flag, the Mahdiyya banner: "You accepted this flag when you did not know what it meant under Marcus Garvey. . . . Now you know what it really means."[97]

"A REBEL": ALLAH, THE FORMER CLARENCE 13X

The Five Percenter movement, popularly known since the 1980s as the Nation of Gods and Earths, originated in 1964 when Clarence 13X broke from the Nation of Islam's Mosque No. 7 in Harlem and began sharing the Nation of Islam's Supreme Wisdom Lessons with youths who were not registered Muslims. Signifying his mastery of the Lessons, Clarence 13X "dropped his X" and renamed himself Allah; in Nation theology, this did not mean that he was a "manifestation" of a higher supernatural power or that such a power had "incarnated" itself in his body. Rather, Clarence *was* Allah, the "best knower" of his time, supplanting Fard in that position. As Allah, the former Clarence 13X ultimately democratized the Nation's Black godhood, teaching young men to claim the divine name for themselves. The Five Percenter community took its name from references in the Lessons to those who recognized themselves as gods and sought to liberate the minds of the masses (85 percent) from the false religions imposed upon them by the ruling powers (10 percent). As Allah disseminated his teachings among teenagers, and instructed them in turn to teach younger boys, the Five Percenters spread through the 1960s significantly as a youth movement. After Allah's assassination in 1969, Five Percenters maintained their headquarters, an "Allah School" in Harlem, and held monthly assemblies ("parliaments") and rallies that dominated public parks and other spaces throughout the five boroughs. They received fairly frequent and generally sympathetic coverage in the *Amsterdam News* as a fixture of local community life, and also experienced negative attention from the NYPD, which viewed their conversion of gang members with suspicion. By the end of the 1970s, Five Percenters enjoyed such a strong presence in Black and Latino youth cultures of New York that their unique ideologies, reference points, and vocabulary became ubiquitous in hip-hop, even among artists who were not themselves Five Percenters.[98]

Though relations between the Five Percenters and the AAC/NIH were often strained, the media of both communities reveal an ongoing exchange. Al Mahdi published the Nation's lessons with his annotated commentary and disseminated them via street peddlers, having an impact on Five Percenter interpretive traditions. In Five Percenter literature and the lyrics of affiliated hip-hop artists, there are numerous concepts with AAC/NIH genealogies.

These include Al Mahdi's claim that the word "God" represents an acronym for "Gomar Oz Dubar," which he defines as "Wisdom, Strength, Beauty"; the claim appears often in Five Percenter discourse, even in hip-hop artist Rakim's 1997 lyrical masterpiece "The Mystery (Who Is God)."[99] Al Mahdi's interpretation of the word "Muslim" to mean "one of peace" echoes popular "Islam means peace" arguments found in Sunni Muslim pamphlets, though this interpretation produces different consequences in AAC/NIH and Five Percenter materials. While Five Percenter discourses use the "one of peace" argument not to deflect Islamophobic narratives but rather to distance their lessons' references to "Muslims" from formal religious identity—arguing that one can be a lowercase *muslim* as "one of peace" without making a religious or sectarian claim—the argument seems to reflect a flow of AAC/NIH media into Five Percenter currents.[100] Meanwhile, AAC/NIH literature also reflects its conversation with Five Percenter tradition. Though Al Mahdi's frequent use of numerology and lettrism by no means depends on Five Percenter influence—neither the former Clarence 13X nor any prominent builders of Five Percenter tradition after him displayed an interest in the premodern Islamic lettrism and numerology that informed Al Mahdi's work—his use of letters and numbers resonates in Five Percenter registers, and Al Mahdi sometimes couches his own alphanumerics in distinct Five Percenter terms (i.e., "Supreme Mathematics").[101] Finally, while the Five Percenters originated in Harlem and spread throughout the city (and beyond), the community boasts an especially rich history in the AAC/NIH's cradle of Brooklyn, which the Five Percenters renamed Medina (with Harlem as Mecca), "land of the righteous warriors."[102]

Despite these communities' intersections, overt references to Allah and his Five Percenter movement in AAC/NIH literature are difficult to recover, particularly in early sources. A comic strip in Al Mahdi's *Signs of 73* pamphlet depicts a Black man named Leroy who proclaims himself God before taking a punch to the face and falling at the feet of a white-garbed Ansar.[103] While a reader already familiar with Five Percenter culture could read the cartoon as a mockery of the community, the pamphlet makes no explicit reference to the former Clarence 13X or his movement. Allah remains neglected throughout 1970s AAC/NIH literature. Al Mahdi's introduction to his 1979 *Book of Lamb* mentions a host of men, Muslim and non-Muslim, alongside Elijah Muhammad as leaders in the struggle for Black liberation—Daoud Faisal, Noble Drew Ali, Marcus Garvey, and Puerto Rican independence leader Pedro Albizu Campos—but makes no mention of the former Clarence 13X. Arguing for the Qur'an as a mathematical miracle due to patterns regarding the number

19 and its multiples, Al Mahdi describes these patterns as "the Supreme Mathematics of the Holy Qurʾan"; though the argument and his specific language resonate with themes in Five Percenter tradition, Al Mahdi does not further connect his "Supreme Mathematics" to Five Percenters.[104] In the 1970s and '80s, when Al Mahdi makes reference to numerous communities in his appeal to Black universalism—"Whether you call yourself a Christian or a Jew, Israelite, Hebrew, Rasta, Muslim, Bilalian, Nation of Islaam, Sunni Muslim, Shiʿite Muslim, Black Nationalist, African, Puerto Rican, whatever name you have picked up"—he does not typically mention the Five Percenters.[105] At most, Five Percenters receive rare passing acknowledgment in earlier materials simply as one of many groups that exist but never as serious interlocutors, and Allah makes no appearance as a figure with a meaningful legacy.

The AAC/NIH literature of the 1980s, however, reveals an increasing engagement with Five Percenter tradition and its founder. The 1988 edition of *Who Was Noble Drew Ali?* marks this shift, providing a brief discussion of the Five Percenters that does not appear in the 1980 edition. In its cursory treatment, the 1988 edition offers various dismissals of the Five Percenters: the founder borrowed his "five percent" concept from the Nation of Islam and Five Percenters still rely on the Nation's flawed Lessons; it is impossible for the Five Percenters to represent 5 percent of the world's population, as this would amount to more than one million people in the United States alone; the former Clarence 13X targeted young men because they were "more easily influenced"; and finally, Five Percenters are guilty of "the unforgivable sin of binding partners with ALLAH Most Glorified and Exalted"—Al Mahdi cites the Qurʾan in Arabic and English (4:48) to support this claim. Al Mahdi includes an image of the Five Percenters' Universal Flag with the caption "Notice that they use the number seven and the five-pointed star and crescent as Noble Drew Ali (HWON) did," and a photograph of Allah among his young followers captioned "Notice the young boy smoking."[106]

Al Mahdi adds references to the Five Percenters in his 1989 *Book of Laam*, which examines Allah and his community, among other movements and leaders. Malcolm X had expelled the former Clarence 13X from the Nation of Islam, Al Mahdi asserts, for being "a rebel," after which he attracted a large following among Black youth in New York for teaching that they, as "sons of Allah," were entitled to the divine name. Citing the Qurʾan and Genesis, Al Mahdi concedes that God breathed life into Adam but argues that "man fell from grace with the very first man, the Prophet Adam (PBUH) and lost his divinity. You lost your godlike qualities." While he acknowledges a kernel of truth in Five

Percenter theologies, Al Mahdi attacks Five Percenters' immature knowledge: "You are a lost people who have no right to choose divine titles you cannot live up to. You must first be born again. Take your shahaada.... Then you can begin to work towards the perfection of your being to enable you access to the Supreme within you." Perfection cannot be attained "by standing on the corner in a 'square,' philosophizing ('building on mathematics')."[107]

In 1991, Al Mahdi produced *The Book of the Five Percenters*, a hefty 627-page volume bearing Allah's photo on the cover with a caption reading, "Clarence Jowars [Jowers] Smith, Clarence 13X (1929–1969 A.D.)." The black background and gold text evoke the Five Percenters' black and gold Universal Flag. The book's back cover displays only the black, red, and green AAC/NIH flag with accompanying Nubic text. Many readers of *The Book of the Five Percenters*, encountering the book via AAC/NIH peddlers and street vendors, might have first taken the book as an "official" Five Percenter text, perhaps even written by the former Clarence 13X himself. *The Book of the Five Percenters* corresponds to the community's rising prominence not only throughout New York but in urban centers across the country. In part because Five Percenter artists dominated Islam's representation in hip-hop, Al Mahdi's massive *Book of the Five Percenters* appears to reflect a growing recognition of the Five Percenters' significance at the turn of the 1990s.

Despite the book's title and cover design, Five Percenters are not the consistent focus of *The Book of the Five Percenters*. Asking Five Percenters for a "pow-wow" for the purpose of arriving at a shared platform, Al Mahdi appeals to them to join his AAC/NIHNIHN rather than Sunni communities or the Nation of Islam. He devotes significant space to attacking the "Wahhabi Sect" and its "world wide plot" to "kill all potential Black (Nubian) leaders and destroy all Muslim organizations which were not affiliated with them."[108] This conspiracy's victims include Al Mahdi's own father, "the Nubian President of Egypt" Anwar Sadat, and Rashad Khalifa, who claimed to have discovered the Qur'an's miraculous mathematical patterns. According to the Wahhabi Sect, Al Mahdi argues, the only authentic Islam is "that which condones 'white' superiority" (108). The Wahhabi Sect's violence against Black liberation in the United States claimed the lives of Malcolm X, Martin Luther King Jr., and Allah within the short span of four years. Malcolm, Al Mahdi writes, had fallen victim to a joint conspiracy between the Wahhabis and the U.S. government. Al Mahdi finds evidence of Saudi involvement in King's assassination because it took place in Memphis, a "Wahhabi city" owned by the Saudis. Allah's assassination was also an "Orthodox Sunni plot, funded by Red Arabs in Arabia" (67). Al Mahdi's references to Allah by his Nation name, Clarence 13X, would strike Five Percenters as an offensive slap at their patriarch; however, Al Mahdi also grants him the title of "Messenger" and includes him among the esteemed sages of Black mental resurrection. Meanwhile, Al Mahdi argues that his Sunni contemporaries, such as Siraj Wahhaj (a "'puppet' for the Orthodox Sunni pale Arabs") (74) and Abu Ameenah Bilal Philips (a "Jamaican negro" who converted to "the white man's version of Al Islaam") (108–9), have been co-opted by the Saudis, and that a similar process has already started to bring Farrakhan under their control, as evidenced by a photo of Farrakhan embracing Wahhaj and W. D. Muhammad (102). Al Mahdi alternates throughout *The Book of the Five Percenters* between respect for Farrakhan and sadness that Farrakhan has "no foundation, no doctrine, no facts," leaving Al Mahdi "alone to carry on the work of the Messenger Elijah Muhammad" (210, 217). Presenting the former Clarence 13X as a rebellious but sincere student of Elijah, Al Mahdi positions himself as more compatible with the Five Percenters' founder than the Saudi-controlled Farrakhan.

Throughout *The Book of the Five Percenters*, Al Mahdi generally treats "Messenger Clarence 13X" as a sympathetic character. Equipped with what Al Mahdi terms "the raw version of Al Islaam and the teachings of the Messenger Elijah Muhammad" (34), Messenger Clarence 13X made an important intervention in the lives of young Black men in New York. Messenger Clarence 13X, Al Mahdi writes, rejected the double-edged "genocide of the mind" (Christianity and "Orthodox Sunni Islam") that afflicted his people, and he prioritized the teaching of young men because he "believed that the older generation was too indoctrinated by the Devil's society to bring about any real change" (34). Al Mahdi credits Messenger Clarence 13X for his pedagogy: he "didn't harness or restrain the children he taught, he just gave them knowledge of the lessons he received from the Nation of Islam under the Messenger Elijah Muhammad" (58). Messenger Clarence 13X taught them to complete their education, get job training, and "build a nation"; he also understood that white people were devils (59).

The Book of the Five Percenters presents Allah in a kind of pictorial hagiography, with a painted portrait of Messenger Clarence 13X in a uniform reminiscent of the Nation's Fruit of Islam regalia, all white (resonant with the AAC/NIH's dress code), with a pillbox-style hat bearing the Five Percenters' Universal Flag. A halolike glow emanates from his head (37) (fig. 18). The image, which appears in AAC/NIH literature as early as 1989 in texts such as *The Book of Laam* and *Our Flag: The True Banner of Al Islaam*,[109] is markedly ahistorical—Allah had

FIGURE 18 AAC/NIH portrait of Allah ("Messenger Clarence 13X").

never adopted a formal Five Percenter uniform—but relocates Allah within AAC/NIH sacred history, making icons of him and his flag.

As in his treatment of Elijah Muhammad and Noble Drew Ali, Al Mahdi presents Allah as a man of good intention but limited knowledge and ability. Endowed with an intuitive sense that the Nation's platform could not fully resurrect Nubians in America, the former Clarence 13X broke away from the Nation and embarked on his own flawed project. "Messenger Clarence 13X felt that there was more to the doctrine than what the ministers of the Messenger Elijah Muhammad were revealing at that time," Al Mahdi explains, "but the time had not yet come when many truths were destined to be revealed" (38). The former Clarence 13X was "unable to give you the pure truth because he was stopped by the Devil. He took you as far as his teachings would allow" (369).

Al Mahdi draws a distinction between the historical "Messenger Clarence 13X" and contemporary Five Percenter teachings, which enables him to absorb the former into his authorizing genealogy while delegitimizing the latter. He acknowledges that the former Clarence 13X taught that Black men "should look inside themselves for the power that they looked for in the God of religion" (38). But Five Percenters have reconstructed the former Clarence 13X as an undeserving idol, just as the Nation has done in venerating Master Fard and as "Mohammedan" Sunni Muslims (18) have done in worshipping the Prophet. Further incorporating his critique of Sunnis into his discussion of the Five Percenters, Al Mahdi subjects Five Percenter oral tradition to his skepticism regarding hadiths, even referring to concepts and practices that he deems suspect as "Five Percent Hadith" (338). Five Percenter imaginaries of their founder, Al Mahdi argues, rely on fabricated reports and flimsy hearsay: "Messenger Clarence 13X didn't leave a successor, nor did he author any books. So how do you know the teachings you're following today are what Messenger Clarence 13X really taught?" (625). Al Mahdi goes so far as to employ the former Clarence 13X's distance from contemporary Five Percenters as a means of critiquing Five Percenters' disavowal of the "mystery god." Five Percenters generally espouse self-deification not as the incarnation or manifestation of a higher spirit but in a materialist rejection of belief in unseen beings. According to Al Mahdi, however, "If you are a Five Percenter and you have never seen or talked with Messenger Clarence 13X in the person, and only have a picture of him, then you're just like Christians . . . THEN YOU TOO BELIEVE IN THE UNSEEN GOD" (12). The chronological gulf between a man who was assassinated in 1969 and the community that follows him in 1991 enables Al Mahdi to assault Five Percenter tradition while preserving the founder's innocence. Had "Messenger Clarence 13X" actually claimed to be Allah? Did he teach young Black men to consider themselves creators and lords of the universe? If he had made statements with these possible implications, what did he *really* mean? According to Al Mahdi, the man's intentions had been misunderstood by those who authorized themselves as his heirs and successors: "Messenger Clarence 13X knew that he was not the Creator of all things in existence. In many ways he told his followers they were of ALLAH, not ALLAH himself" (207).

Much of Al Mahdi's critique of Five Percenters targets their lack of fluency in Arabic. Discussing Five Percenter interpretations of the word "Allah" as an acronym for "Arm Leg Leg Arm Head," signifying godhood with the human form, Al Mahdi scolds Five Percenters, "You can't take English, the language of the devil and use it as if it were divine!" (146). He discredits Five Percenter alphanumerics, their codes of Supreme Mathematics and Supreme Alphabets, in part with a display of his proficiency in classical Arabic *abjad* (342–64). Al Mahdi also addresses Supreme Mathematics and Supreme Alphabets in his 1989 *Book of Laam*, alleging that their true creator was Malcolm X.[110] Boasting in *The Book of the Five Percenters* that "we here at the Nubian Islaamic Hebrews teach about the real Supreme Mathematics," Al Mahdi refers to the Qurʾan's patterns of the number 19 as promoted by "Messenger Rashad Khalifa." He subjects what he erroneously claims was Allah's given name, Clarence

Jowars [sic] Smith,[111] to the test, digit-summing the three names to arrive at 8+6+5=19—revealing the truth of Khalifa's claims. Further connecting Five Percenter concepts to Khalifa's mathematical esotericism, Al Mahdi refers to a AAC/NIH pamphlet, *The Supreme Mathematics of the Number 19*, that is no longer extant (136–37).

Al Mahdi writes that Five Percenters, "more than any other offshoot of the Nation of Islam," used the Nation's Supreme Wisdom Lessons as their foundation (368). In the 1989 *Book of Laam*, this opens the Five Percenters to Al Mahdi's dismissal: "The members of the Five Percent Nation would do well to exert the same amount of effort towards studying the Qur'aan and Bible, so that they can find true Islaam."[112] Al Mahdi points out that not only were the Lessons flawed in their corrupted origins; owing to their circulation in Five Percenter contexts as memorized oral traditions, they have been distorted over time. Adding even more confusion, Five Percenters, unable to comprehend Elijah Muhammad's teachings or to read scriptures in their original Arabic, heap mountains of unqualified interpretation and commentary upon the Lessons (369). Five Percenters, in Al Mahdi's judgment, thus follow unreliable commentaries on inauthentic versions of texts that were never genuinely authoritative, even in their "original" form. Al Mahdi devotes most of the final two hundred pages of *The Book of the Five Percenters* to his own annotation of the Lessons, providing the "original" and "corrupted" versions, Five Percenter exegesis (which he derisively terms "hadith"), and the Lessons' "Real Meaning by the Reformer" (368–572).

While issuing challenges to Five Percenter theology and practice, Al Mahdi preserves the integrity of their intention. Writing to "salute their efforts and seek to join forces with them," he affirms the Five Percenter mission as "creating the proper cultural environment to raise sound children.... Our common goals are more important than any differences we might have!" (36). He praises Five Percenter hip-hop artists, singling out such stars as Poor Righteous Teachers, King Sun, Eric B. and Rakim, and Big Daddy Kane ("who used to be in the 5% Nation," Al Mahdi claims, "and now he is an Ansaar of the Nubian Nation") (31–34), and claims to have influenced Five Percenter artists, citing references to Nubian identity: "There is a rap group of Five Percenters who call themselves 'Brand Nubians.' Now, why didn't they call themselves 'Brand Five Percenters'?" (108).

Al Mahdi contrasts failed Five Percenter efforts at building and maintaining institutions with his own community's success. The former Clarence 13X had received his Allah School through the Urban League's "street academy" program during his work with the Lindsay administration, but the school has suffered in the decades since owing to "lack of leadership" and neglect. Likewise, "many other street academies of the Five Percent Nation have also been set up after the example of the founders. Yet, they too have been unable to survive for a variety of reasons ranging from lack of support, to lack of finances in Brooklyn, Bronx, Queens and many more" (62). Contrasting these inauthentic teachings and feeble institutions with his own superior mastery of Arabic and with photographs of AAC/NIH children enjoying life in a properly "Islamic" community, with its own masjids, schools, businesses, and entertainment, Al Mahdi pronounces the Five Percenters a sincere but failed experiment. "Let's work together," he pleads in conclusion. "United we are an undefeatable force. You'll find out the differences came about due to the opinions of men. . . . In the end, truth will prevail over all sects and all differences. But at this stage it just doesn't matter. We have to make a start by coming together" (625–27).

CONCLUSIONS

Al Mahdi ostensibly calls other communities to follow him, not as a disavowal of their founding heroes or traditions but rather in the name of Black unity against the combined forces of white supremacy and transnational Sunni hegemony, his treatment of Blackamerican Islamic histories veering between appropriation and polemic. He weaves the biographies of figures such as Noble Drew Ali and the former Clarence 13X into a masterly epic in which he stands as the conclusion. He praises Elijah Muhammad and Daoud Faisal for taking their followers as far as they could take them, but concludes that "there's more to that journey, and I, As Sayyid Issa Al Haadi Al Mahdi, am here to complete the mission" (207).

The tension in this literature finds expression in a curious AAC/NIH artifact, a poster from circa 1990 (fig. 19) depicting Al Mahdi seated at a banquet with a host of patriarchs: not only figures of Black Islam (Elijah Muhammad, Malcolm X, Noble Drew Ali, Daoud Faisal, the former Clarence 13X, and Louis Farrakhan), but also Marcus Garvey (himself a figure of Black Islam in Al Mahdi's view), Haile Selassie, Black Hebrew/Israelite leaders Ben Ammi and Yahweh Ben Yahweh, and even Martin Luther King Jr. and Puerto Rican revolutionary Pedro Campos. All of the men are dressed in white robes. The Islamic and Hebrew/Israelite figures don varieties of head covering, in some cases matching what they historically wore or displaying the emblem of their community. On the wall hangs a Mahdiyya flag; through the window, we see

FIGURE 19 "We Are Family: The Nubian Nation," AAC/NIH poster, ca. 1990. Back row, left to right: Noble Drew Ali, Pedro Albizu Campos, Allah (the former Clarence 13X), Marcus Garvey, Elijah Muhammad, Malcolm X, Yahweh Ben Yahweh, Dr. Martin Luther King Jr. Front row, left to right: Ben Ammi Carter, Haile Selassie, As Sayyid Al Imaam Isa Al Haadi Al Mahdi, Louis Farrakhan, Daoud Faisal.

a nearby masjid. The poster is captioned, "WE ARE FAMILY / THE NUBIAN NATION," and provides brief biographical notes on each figure. "All these great men are our saviors," the poster tells us, "as stepping stones towards the truth. They were all sent from ALLAH to guide us to the true Al Islaam. Let's give thanks for them."

Al Mahdi sits in the center foreground, Farrakhan on his right and Selassie on his left, seemingly the force behind this gathering that takes place entirely on his terms—as expressed in everyone's white garb and the Mahdiyya flag hanging above, as well as the masjid beyond the window. Al Mahdi, of course, embodies the truth to which his companions here were stepping-stones, and the "true Al Islaam" for which they were sent. To this end, he can viciously tear apart figures like Selassie and Farrakhan and yet still offer them up as objects of veneration within his larger narrative of Black destiny.

112 ♦ Metaphysical Africa

CHAPTER 3

"The Covenant Is Complete in Me"

Nubian Islamic Hebraism and the Religion of Abraham

> We are Africans.... Here is a significant fact, that those of us here never had a Caucasian teacher to instruct us into the principles of our faith up to the present, this alone is evidence that as regards our faith as original.... It is not customary for Caucasian (is that a nice name?) Hebrew brethren to admit that behind the African mind there are originally the roots of Hebrew culture; but this is our contention; and although in ritualism we may differ and perhaps be found wanting; in heart and in custom we are Hebraic and nothing else.
>
> —RABBI ARNOLD JOSIAH FORD

In April 1994, the *New York Times* reported that sometime in the previous year, "at least 300 members of an unusual, insular sect that blended Islamic and Jewish precepts packed up and abandoned" their Bushwick Avenue community, leaving stores, apartment buildings, and their masjid boarded up.[1] The article noted that this sect, the Holy Tabernacle of the Most High, was also known as the Children of Abraham, that it identified its "prophet" as Rabboni Y'shua Bar El Haady, and that its members identified themselves as "the true Israelites" but also "adapted Muslim modes of prayer and lifestyle, while rejecting orthodox Muslim worship." While reporting rumors of internal divisions between "one big group" that had relocated upstate and another that moved to Georgia, the article concluded, "Precisely where and why they went remains a mystery."[2]

A community poster from the era evokes Jehovah's Witness aesthetics: Al Mahdi stands in a valley in a white robe, cradling a lamb in his left arm, while a lion rests behind him (fig. 20). His hair is straight and shoulder-length, enhaloed with a misty white light. He poses his right hand in a symbolic gesture of blessing. He is surrounded by followers, mostly children whose clothes emphasize their cultural diversity. One boy wears a white yarmulka, and his shirt bears the Nubian flag on an arm patch. An older man's shirt displays the community's new crown logo. The poster declares, "Peace in the Lamb It's Truly Wonderful," and repeats these words in Arabic in the community's stylized Nubic script as *as-salam bi-l-kharuf anahu 'ajib*, "the greeting of those who follow the lamb." It calls the community "the Holy Tabernacle of the Most High" and gives an address for the "Tents of Abraham" in Atlanta. The poster features two flags: the "Nubian Nation flag," the Mahdiyya flag with the black changed to brown and *huwa* (he) in Nubic script instead of the Mahdist symbol, and the "Holy flag," bearing the six-pointed star without a crescent. The poster identifies the central figure as Al Mahdi but adds, "Now we know him as Rabboni Y'shua Bar El Haady" and gives an account from an unnamed witness: "He said with a slight smile, 'I have seen worlds come and go. Where I come from, beyond the stars, we have seen many things. Now I am sent here to a being who thinks I'm crazy, however, I will do my job.'" With its aesthetic makeover of the Lamb, its reference to the central figure as both Al Mahdi and El Haady, and its allusion to his extraterrestrial origin, the poster reads as a liminal artifact of a community between stages. Now known as the Tents of Abraham, the Ansar are apparently no longer Ansar, and they have left something behind—but to become what?

To read this poster in the context of assumptions about clear Muslim, Hebrew, or UFO-centered "stages" would be to miss its continuities with AAC/NIH materials; this circa 1992 depiction of Al Mahdi, after all, can also be found in literature from 1986.[3] Examining the significance of Hebrew identity throughout AAC/NIH history and reconsidering a 1992–93 "Jewish" period, this chapter challenges representations of the community as a kind of postmodernist "holy madness, crazy wisdom" that relish its supposed instability and portrays its disintegration of categories as a "gnostic" exercise. Certainly, AAC/NIH media from the early 1990s exhibit significant changes from previous community publications. Nonetheless, the community also maintains common, consistent elements and themes found in its ostensibly "Islamic" and "Jewish" materials.

FIGURE 20 "Peace in the Lamb," AAC/NIH poster, ca. 1992.

"The Covenant Is Complete in Me" • 115

Contrary to Susan Palmer's account of the Nuwaubian Nation, the Ansaru Allah Community had not "evolved out of the Nubian Islaamic Hebrews, gradually transforming [itself] into a Muslim group as it discarded its Hebrew themes," nor did early pamphlets feature photographs of Black Hebrew leaders such as Ben Ammi or Yahweh Ben Yahweh. Al Mahdi's movement began with Muslims at a Sunni masjid and consistently prioritized genealogical claims upon leaders who identified themselves as Muslim; moreover, Yahweh Ben Yahweh did not even start his movement until 1979.[4] The presence or absence of "Hebrew" in the community's name did not correspond to the adoption or "discarding" of "Hebrew themes" in its discourse. Instead of treating the signifiers "Hebrew" and "Islamic" as mutually repellent terms that only an irrational "syncretist" would attempt to mix, we can ask how specific materials were connected within Al Mahdi's setting. What did "Hebrew" mean for a young Muslim at State Street Mosque?

It is not unreasonable to suggest an encounter with Black Hebrew/Israelite materials. Al Mahdi's Hebraism overlaps with Ben Ammi's African Hebrew Israelites on key themes, such as his tracing the word "Hebrew" to its root meaning of "crossing over" and the act of the "first Hebrew," Abraham's crossing the river Jordan. Like African Hebrew Israelites, Al Mahdi locates Eden in Africa, includes the Arabian Peninsula as part of Africa, and envisions wars that force refugees across the continent into West Africa, meaning—depending on which narrative you read—that many of the Africans brought to the Americas as slaves were descended from either the Israelite tribe of Judah or Sudanese Muslims. While African Hebrew Israelites identify West African "Hebrewisms" that attest to Yoruba's Judahite heritage, Al Mahdi claims that Yoruba culture derives from Islam.[5]

Many of the parallels between AAC/NIH and Black Hebrew traditions, such as Al Mahdi's rejection of Christmas and Easter as European "pagan" innovations, are so widespread that Al Mahdi's Hebraic thought cannot be traced to a specific source. Palmer identifies Clarke Jenkins's 1969 work *The Black Hebrews of the Seed of Abraham, Isaac, and Jacob of the Tribe of Judah, Benjamin, and Levi, After 430 Years in America* as a possible source for several of Al Mahdi's key points, such as the attribution of white skin to leprosy, the identification of Black people with Judah, and the link between Adam and Blackness through Adam's creation from black earth (though Al Mahdi prefers Qur'anic citations to argue for Adam's creation from black mud).[6] Palmer suggests that it was in

Jenkins that Al Mahdi first encountered the argument that the book of Revelation, comparing Christ's hair to wool and his feet to molten brass, reveals him to be a Black man.[7] However, this interpretation originated much earlier than the 1960s, going back to the turn of the twentieth century or earlier: Garveyite biblical scholar James Morris Webb called attention to Christ's "woolly hair" in 1910,[8] and resistance to the whitening of Jesus dates to at least the 1830s.[9] The "woolly hair" interpretation has proliferated through so many channels that efforts to determine a "family tree" for its presence in Al Mahdi's work would not be productive. The biblical exegetes who wrote of a woolly-haired, brass-footed Christ include Muslim elders such as Elijah Muhammad and Daoud Faisal, not to mention Al Mahdi's contemporary Louis Farrakhan.[10] One recent Christian author even identifies this reading of Revelation 1:13–15 as distinctly "the Black Muslim's interpretation."[11]

Intersections between Black Hebraism and Black Islam had long preceded Al Mahdi; the two commingled before "Black Hebraism" and "Black Islam" could even stand apart as separate traditions. Black Israelite movements in America, which emerged in the nineteenth century and flourished after the Great Migration, developed amid many of the same discursive flows, including Ethiopianism, New Thought, Freemasonry, and Garveyism, that informed Black Islam. UNIA official and Beth B'nai Abraham founder Arnold Ford (1877–1935) led a synagogue in the 1920s known as the Moorish Zionist Temple, identified co-religionists as "Ethiopian Hebrews," preferred "Hebrew" and "Israelite" over "Jewish," advocated fasting during Ramadan, referred to "blessings of Allah" in correspondence with other Black Israelite rabbis, wore a turban over his Jewish skullcap, and prioritized both Hebrew and Arabic as original African languages.[12] His *Universal Ethiopian Hymnal* contained a hymn titled "Allah-Hu-Ak Bar" and lyrical references to the news of God's love ringing from "steeples and mosques." According to his son, Ford believed that perceptions of Judaism, Christianity, and Islam as separate religions were due to the "political machinations of man." If AAC/NIH media had "blended" Black Islam and Black Hebraism (fig. 21), it only reflects the unavoidable polyculturalism of what Jacob Dorman terms the "reblending of the already blended."[13]

These reblendings of the already blended were not restricted to a local "Black cultic milieu," but engaged the world. Just as Black Muslim communities developed in conversation with transnational movements, figures, and bodies of literature, we cannot discuss Black Israelite movements in the United States without touching upon the Black Atlantic, the emerging global prominence of Ethiopian Jews (Falashas/Beta Israel) in the nineteenth century, and

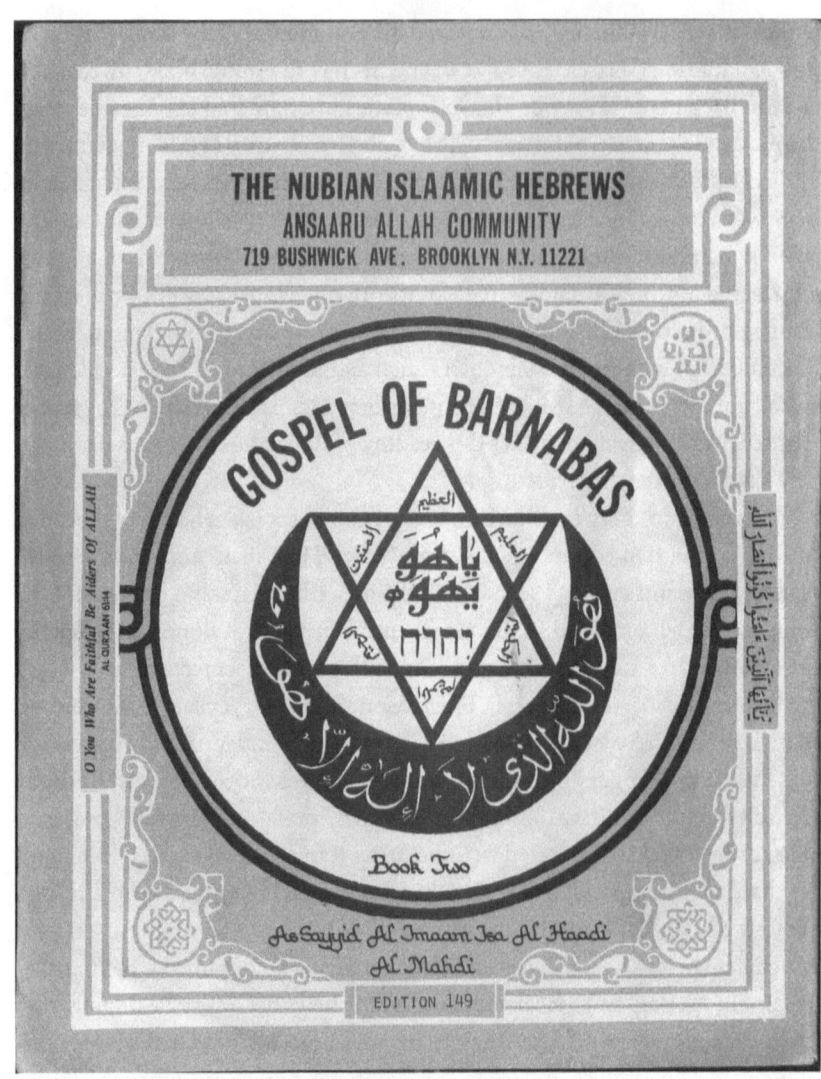

FIGURE 21 The AAC/NIH six-pointed star and crescent as it frequently appeared in community literature. The crescent bears the opening words of the Qurʾan's famed *ayat al-kursi*: "He is Allah, there is no god but him" (2:255). The center of the star contains Arabic text reading *Ya huwa Yahuwa* ("O He, YHWH") and the Hebrew YHWH. Each of the star's six points contains an attribute of Allah. Clockwise, from the top: al-Adim (the Magnificent), al-ʿAlim (the Knower), al-Karim (the Noble), al-Hakim (the Wise), al-Rahim (the Merciful), al-Matin (the Firm). From Al Haadi Al Mahdi, *Gospel of Barnabas, Book Two* (1984).

the migration of Black Hebrew communities from the United States to Israel, Ethiopia, and West Africa. Both Black Islam and Black Hebraism reflect knowledge production as formed in a "global system," Dorman explains, "that traded in ideas as much as commodities."[14]

Long before Al Mahdi's supposed acts of "borrowing" and "mixing," interest in the Hebrews' racial identity was already embedded in Black Islam. In *The Autobiography of Malcolm X*, Malcolm recalls challenging a prison Bible class teacher by asserting that the "original Hebrews were Black"; in Spike Lee's cinematic reimagining of the scene, Malcolm also stuns the teacher with an argument that Jesus was Black, based upon the "hair like wool" and "feet like brass" verses from Revelation.[15] Malcolm was not a "syncretist" who "borrowed" from Black Hebrew ideas; he articulated what he understood as an essential teaching of Islam. Nor was Hebrew Blackness only an interest for "heterodox" movements such as the Nation of Islam; it would have been part of Al Mahdi's early education as a Sunni Muslim. Daoud Faisal's first publication, *Al-Islam, the Religion of Humanity* (1950), asserts that "the White European Jews and the American Jews who have migrated to Jerusalem in the new state of Israel are not the Israelites, but Europeans who embraced the religious cult of Judea.... To be an Israelite you must be of the blood and seed of Abraham." In addition to being Black, "the Israelites were Muslims and their Religion was the Religion of Abraham, 'Islam.'"[16]

For Faisal, Abrahamic ancestry was a prerequisite to spiritual authority. While Faisal attacks white Jews as imposters, he also refers to the "seed of Abraham" in his anti-Catholic polemic. Any leader of "the Religion of God" must descend from Abraham, whether through Isaac or through Ishmael; because the pope is not descended from Abraham, "he is not an authorized leader of humanity, but a pretender and his Religion is not the Religion of Jesus and his teachings are contrary to the teachings of Jesus."[17] Al Mahdi likewise supports his religious authority with genealogical charts tracing his ancestry and conceptualizes spiritual authority as a biological inheritance. The true "Shi'as" are not "the Iranians or Ayatollah Khomeini, who is a pale Arab," but rather the immediate *ahl al-bayt* of the Prophet, who are slighted both by Sunni Muslims (who deny their rightful status) and by most Shi'i Muslims (who deny their Blackness).[18] Though legend has it that Faisal had written a manuscript designed to bring Black Israelites into Islam, which Al Mahdi allegedly stole to use as his own blueprint, we can chart Faisal's significance for Al Mahdi's "Islamic Hebrew" project without esoteric speculations upon the unread. It was at State Street Mosque—an institution that identified itself as Sunni, orthodox, mainstream, and connected to global Islam—that Al Mahdi first learned that the Hebrews were both Muslim and Black, that modern Jews were white usurpers of a Black domain, and that leadership was genealogical.

Regarding biblical Hebrews and later Jewish communities, Nathaniel Deutsch observes a complex treatment in Elijah Muhammad's work: while modern Jews are white people, and white people are devils, Jews appear to hold a higher position than other whites in Elijah's racial stratification. "They are like us," Elijah declares, because they adhere to the same dietary restrictions as Muslims and are "wiser, more skillful" than Christians. Orthodox Jews "live more closely to the Muslim way of eating," having lived among Muslims in Asia. "The Holy Quran teaches us that we can eat their food and they can eat our (the Muslims') food."[19] As with Faisal and Al Mahdi, Elijah emphasizes that major figures of the Bible were Black, Muslim, and speakers of Arabic; Moses spoke "ancient Egyptian Arabic," while Jesus spoke both Arabic and Hebrew.[20]

Elijah Muhammad, son of a Christian preacher, had grown up with the Bible, and he understood his encounter with Master Fard Muhammad through frameworks that the Bible provided. "You are the One," he exclaimed to Fard, "that the Bible prophesied would come at the end of the world under the name Son of Man and under the name The Second Coming of Jesus." Fard did not redirect Elijah to the Qur'an but affirmed his intuition. Elijah then engaged the Bible to confirm that Fard was the awaited one, and would argue for Fard as the future prophet mentioned in Deuteronomy.[21] Fard's teaching materials included biblical verses and the radio sermons of Jehovah's Witness leader Judge Rutherford, whose scriptural interpretations became resources for Elijah.[22] As the appointed Messenger after Fard's disappearance, Elijah believed that he possessed the proper exegetical key to unlock the secret knowledge of the Bible, which was otherwise "poison": "The Bible means good if you can rightly understand it. My interpretation of it is given to me from the Lord of the World. Yours is your own and from the enemies of the truth." Later in his mission, while Elijah presented the Qur'an as superior to the Bible, he still held that both scriptures should be studied, and that both would expire with the arrival of a new holy book "which no man as yet but Allah has seen."[23] Even as Elijah became an authoritative Muslim leader who drew from the Qur'an, Herbert Berg notes that in his major writings, Elijah refers to the Bible nearly twice as often. Elijah defended his emphasis: "There are many Muslims who do not care to read anything in the Bible. But those Muslims have not been given my job."[24]

Between Daoud Faisal, Elijah Muhammad, and Malcolm X, we find the most powerful voices in Blackamerican Muslim landscapes of 1960s New York affirming the importance of the Bible and the Blackness of Israel. For Al Mahdi, these were thoroughly Islamic concerns.

FROM NUBIAN ISLAMIC HEBREWS TO THE ORIGINAL TENTS OF KEDAR

At the start of the 1970s, Al Mahdi rewired the meanings of the six-pointed star, explaining that "some tribes throughout Africa tattoo the Shield of David on various parts of the body," and presenting the star's top and bottom points as diametrically opposing paths: the bottom signifies the devil, while the top signifies "Sufi," which he defines as "purity."[25] In its earliest extant material, the AAC/NIH valorizes Hebrew alongside Arabic and Swahili, privileges biblical citations over the Qurʾan and especially over hadith literature, comments on the Star of David and the biological descent from Abraham, and claims "Abrahamic" religion. "We observe the way of life of prophet Ibrahiim (Abraham PBUH)," we read in *Back to the Beginning: The Book of Names* (1972); the pamphlet also asserts that Black people in North America represent the house of Kedar and that "Rabbi" is the Hebrew word for "Arab." "We teach that there is no distinction in any way amongst the prophets," Al Mahdi writes. "We teach that all true Muslims are to observe and should observe the SABBATH. . . . We know the prophet-apostle Muhammad Al-Amin (PBUH) did not change the laws given to the prophet Musa (Moses PBUH)."[26]

Answering the question, "What is a Hebrew?" in *Arabic: The First Language* (1977), Al Mahdi explains who is *not* a Hebrew: "Jews are not Hebrews, nor are they a pure seed of Ibrahiim (Abraham PBUH). The European Jew has adopted a portion of the Hebrew doctrine (TORAH—OLD TESTAMENT), the same as did the Caucasians (Caucus-Asians) of Pakistan, India, Iraq, et cetera, with the teachings and practices of the Qurʾan." In both cases, Caucasians "are not and were not able to live according to the total sum of the commandments of ALLAH SUBHANA WA TAʾALA's scriptures" and are therefore "cursed people."[27] In *The Tribe Israel Is No More!* (1975) and *The Holy Gospel: The Revelation of Jesus the Messiah to the World, Book 3* (1979), Al Mahdi argues that the last true Israelites, the Judahites, had migrated to Ethiopia, become known as Falashans [sic], and endured persecution at the hands of Coptic Christians because they knew of the coming Ishmaelite prophet, Muhammad.[28] For Al Mahdi, Falashas are "Islamic Hebrews" in the truest sense.[29]

Al Mahdi's argument that the Ethiopian Falashas represent the *only* surviving trace of Israel serves as a polemic not only against "white" Jews but more principally against Black Israelite communities: Black people who identify with Israel have lost the knowledge of themselves. *The Tribe Israel Is No More!* features a portrait of Haile Selassie with the remark that he is "a figurehead and has absolutely no power" and a repudiation in capital letters of Ras Tefar I: "HE IS NOT THE LION OF JUDAH." Al Mahdi writes, "In recent years, we have seen an assortment of groups who claim that they are the descendants of the original Israelites . . . Nubians who believe or make-believe that they too are descendants of Israel. Israel was promised destruction on account of their going astray several times." Against Black Israelites and the Rastas, AAC/NIH literature identifies its community as the "'Lost Sheep' of Ismail [Ishmael]."³⁰

Because Nubians in the Western Hemisphere are Ishmaelites and heirs to the covenant, Al Mahdi tells us, "we follow the Millat Ibrahim." Throughout the second half of the 1970s, newsprint pamphlets like *How Many Muslims Really Follow the Holy Qur'an?* deploy biblical references against other Muslim communities and interpret the six-pointed star as symbolizing Jerusalem, the crescent moon as Mecca, and their coming together in the AAC/NIH symbol as "the totality of Islam."³¹

The designation "Nubian Islamic Hebrews" disappeared from mid-1973 through the early 1980s. In 1978, Al Mahdi recalled, "We were called 'those Nubians,' 'Zionists,' 'Jews,' and all kinds of ridiculous names," adding that his movement alone survived while rivals fell away: "There are no more Yorubas, or Black Jews, or Israelites, or Black Muslims or any of the others. There's nobody left but Ansaru Allah." Al Mahdi does not treat his community's name changes as evidence of transformed doctrines or as pivots between identities; the community was formerly known as Nubian Islamic Hebrews, he says, and "we do not deny that we still are."³²

The tag "Nubian Islamic Hebrews" returned in 1984, appearing alongside "Ansaaru Allah Community" as a name for the movement. In *Whatever Happened to the Nubian Islaamic Hebrews?* (1985), Al Mahdi clarifies that when Muslims reacted with hostility to his use of the six-pointed star and crescent ("Isn't that the star of David?"), he "put it away for awhile until they find out that David (PBUH) is a Muslim in Qur'aan." According to Al Mahdi, the Nubian Islamic Hebrews went "underground" from 1977 to 1985, choosing to grow quietly rather than entertain antagonistic Muslims.³³ The six-pointed star appears prominently from 1977 to 1980 and resurfaces on book covers in 1984. Nor did Al Mahdi's public discourse relinquish or revise his claims that

Nubians were the true Hebrews or that Muslims must adhere to all revealed scriptures. A publication of circa 1976–77, identifying the community strictly as Ansaru Allah, maintains its six-pointed star and crescent with the explanation that "we do not call ourselves Jews, since the so-called Jews are of the cursed seed of Canaan.... The only Israelites are the Falashians who reside in Ethiopia." Hebrews are not Jews. To be Hebrew is to be alien, and Nubians "are Hebrews because we are not in our own land."[34]

In its "Muslim Pledge" on the back pages of its pamphlets and newspapers in the late 1970s, the Ansaru Allah Community describes its mission as the return of Islam "to its purest form" and the raising of the 144,000 to ascend Mount Zion, as per Revelation 14:1. The Muslim pledge avows that to follow the religion of Abraham as prescribed by the Qur'an, one must follow scriptures that the Qur'an confirms: "You cannot understand Qur'an without understanding Taurat and Injil." The pledge also affirms that Black people of the Western world represent the seed of Ishmael, making them not only Hebrews but also the true Chosen People.[35] AAC/NIH publications throughout the 1970s and '80s, even when they do not explicitly identify adherents as Nubian Islamic Hebrews, argue that to follow the true religion of Abraham, Muslims must read biblical texts in their original language (Arabic) and adhere to biblical law, like Muhammad himself. A 1985 pamphlet recognizes that this position alienates popular "orthodoxy," but Al Mahdi displays no concern: "So where they make their mistake is that they associate the word Muslim with themselves.... We don't want to be classified as what you are; because as far as we are concerned you don't know what you are doing. You are wrong! You are following the religions of men." The pamphlet proclaims that Muhammad was a Hebrew and redefines its terms: "When we use the word Muslim we mean one who is of peace; but we are Hebrews foremost. We don't want to be classified with all Muslims; we are distinct."[36]

Should Muslims Observe the Sabbath? (1985) (fig. 22) accuses Muslims of ignoring divine revelation, content instead to "pick and choose from the commandments sent down to them. This is what is known to some as AL ISLAAM." Al Mahdi's objection is that Muslims do not follow *all* of the scriptures, having prioritized hadiths over revealed scriptures such as the Torah of Moses and the Gospel (*Injil*) of Jesus: "Why do the words of men rule the words of ALLAH TA'ALA?" he asks.[37] Defending the Sabbath in *Prehistoric Man and Animals—Did They Exist?* (1980), Al Mahdi presents verses from Exodus and the Qur'an alongside each other, showing that the former advocates the death penalty for transgressors of the Sabbath (31:14) and citing the latter to

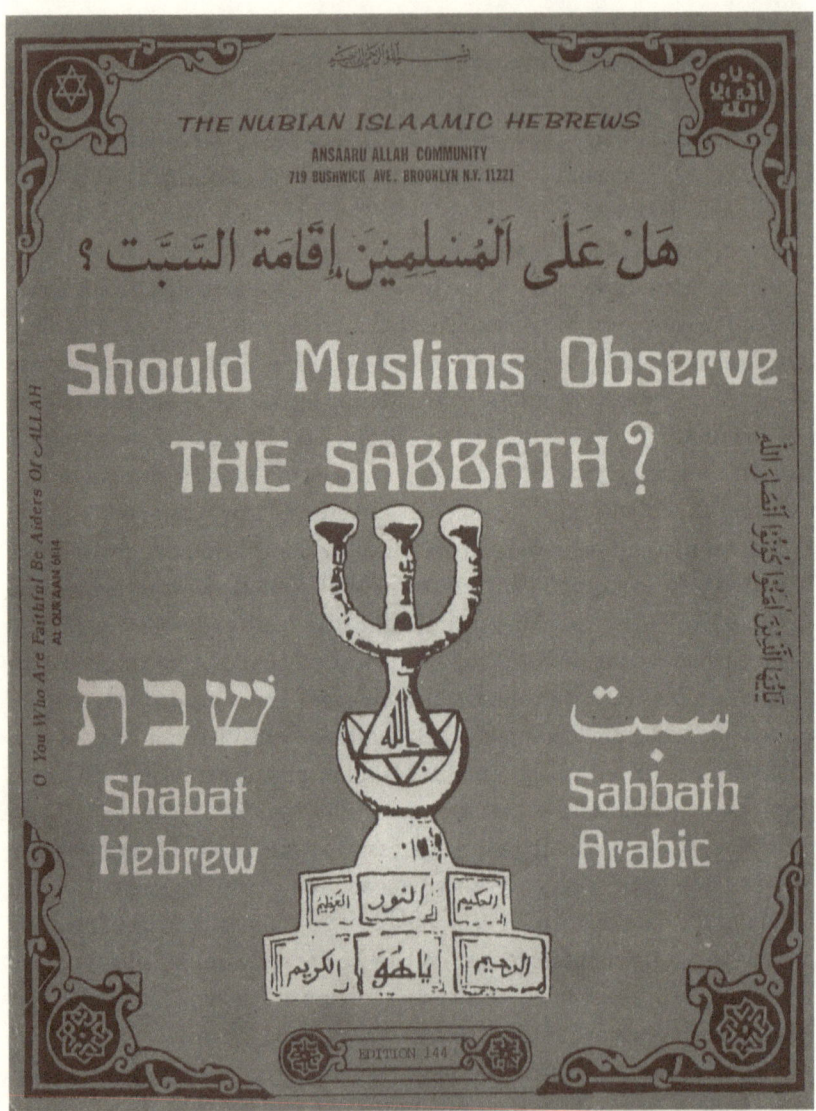

FIGURE 22 Al Haadi Al Mahdi, *Should Muslims Observe the Sabbath?* (1985), front cover.

remind readers that Allah transformed Sabbath breakers into monkeys (2:65).[38] He further supports his critique of "pale Arabs" who violate the Sabbath with two verses of the Qur'an: 2:4, which refers to belief in "what was revealed to you, and what was revealed before you," and 9:97, which calls Arabs the "strongest in disbelief and hypocrisy."[39]

Al Mahdi says that Muhammad did not "pick and choose" which commands to follow but adhered to what had been revealed before him, including the Sabbath. While many Muslims place heightened emphasis on Muhammad's illiteracy, Al Mahdi reimagines Muhammad as a scholar of Israelite knowledge: Muhammad had studied under Waraqa, uncle of his wife, Khadija, just as Moses was prepared for prophethood by studying under his priestly father-in-law, Jethro.[40] Muhammad was Nubian, Islamic, and Hebrew. Following the precedent of Elijah Muhammad, the booklet's citations of biblical passages outnumber those of the Qur'an by roughly two to one.

Al Mahdi rejects claims found "throughout the Muslim world" that the Torah of Moses, the Psalms of David, and the Gospel of Christ have been corrupted and changed over time. According to Al Mahdi, misunderstanding of the scriptures developed owing to their translation into various languages, but the Qur'an does not discredit the scriptures that preceded it. Without evidence, Muslims have fabricated the story that pre-Islamic revelations were corrupted because they do not want to follow Abraham's religion in full. In an intertextual confirmation of his sources, Al Mahdi argues that the Qur'an's affirmation of Christ's *Injil* (57:27) refers to the book of Revelation, not the entirety of the New Testament, and that Revelation in turn presents the Qur'an as the seventh seal that will be opened by the Lion of Judah (5:5). Lacking this knowledge, Christians miss Revelation's references to Muhammad: the woman "clothed with the sun, and the moon under her feet, and upon her head a crown of twelve stars" signifies Fatima and the twelve Imams, while her labor pain refers to Islam's Mahdiyya revival.[41]

Al Mahdi's charges against Muslims who deny biblical revelation stand as one half of a double critique; on the other side, Jews and Christians cannot claim to follow the religion of Abraham as long as they deny the Qur'an. Al Mahdi's comprehensive scripturalism takes aim at different communities in accordance with his changing interests. His 1978 edition of *The True Story of Noah (PBUH)* argues that Jews and Christians cannot understand Noah because they lack the Qur'an's account; the two-part 1986 revision redirects the argument toward Sunni Muslims, arguing that the Qur'an alone cannot provide the full story.[42]

Where Is the Tabernacle of the Most High? (1986) reflects Al Mahdi's developing outreach to Ras Tefar I, who Al Mahdi claims is the true "Lion of Judah." While this title holds unique meaning in Al Mahdi's exegetical universe, designating him the supreme interpreter of the Qur'an—opener of Revelation's seventh seal—it also makes a claim on the honor that Rastas reserve for Haile Selassie.

This booklet issues a "Proclamation of Redemption," common to 1985–87 publications, that collectivizes Nubians as "Abraham's seed," regardless of "whatever name you have picked up or carry or attribute to your beliefs"; "Christians, Jews, Israelites, Hebrews, Rastas, Muslims, Bilalians, Nation of Islaam, Sunni Muslim, Shiʿite Muslim, Black Nationalist, African, Puerto Rican" are all identified as those for whom he has come. The proclamation invites Rastas to "come sip with me," American Muslims to "reconsider their acceptance," and "Black Hebrews and Israelites to follow, for the covenant is complete in me."[43]

Literature of 1987–91 refers to the community as the Original Tents of Kedar, maintaining the previous identification of Nubians—"Ishmaelites, Cushites, Hebrews . . . Africans, Semites, Bedouins, Arabs, Nomads, Sudanese, and other titles"—as descended from Kedar, the Ishmaelite tribe that kept its line pure.[44] The adoption of the new name seems to reflect institutional change, as advertisements direct mail orders to Monticello rather than Brooklyn. During this time, Brooklyn was supplanted as the community's center of gravity by its Jazzir Abba property (renamed Mount Zion) in the "Borscht Belt" region of the Catskills that had once been the site of thriving summer resorts and camps catering to New York's Jewish communities and that remained home to Hasidic enclaves. In publications from this era, Original Tents of Kedar, Ansaaru Allah Community, and Nubian Islaamic Hebrews often appear interchangeably, and Original Tents of Kedar publications also contain advertisements for the community's in-house Sufi order, Sons of the Green Light.[45] While consistent with AAC/NIH doctrine since the 1970s, the Tents of Kedar rebranding—drawn from Song of Solomon 1:5, "I am Black, but comely, O Daughters of Jerusalem, as the tents of Kedar"—redistributed the weight of AAC/NIH scriptural references.[46]

In 1989, the community published an expanded *Whatever Happened to the Nubian Islaamic Hebrew Mission?* (first released as a pamphlet in 1985) as a 315-page book. Released around the same time as *The Ansaar Cult: Rebuttal to the Slanderers*, Al Mahdi's response to the anti-AAC/NIH polemic by Abu Ameenah Bilal Philips, the revised book displays growing concern with Sunni figures such as Brooklyn rival and "Wahhabi spokesman" Siraj Wahhaj and Saudi-networked organizations like the Muslim World League. The text maintains that pale Arabs worship Muhammad, pale Jews falsely claim the Star of David, and Nubian Islamic Hebrews follow Muhammad's Sunna, which is only Abraham's Sunna, which was revealed by Allah.

The inside back covers of Original Tents of Kedar pamphlets and books depict Al Mahdi in the Ansar robe and turban, holding his staff and prayer beads (fig. 23). In the heavens floats the community's flagship Brooklyn masjid; behind it a flying saucer hovers, with a beam radiating from the spaceship to the masjid. The Arabic caption reads, "I call to accept this truth as bestowed upon me by the masters who guide my pen, for of myself I could not have done the works of it," with an attribution to Al Mahdi and Yanaan,[47] who was first mentioned in AAC/NIH publications from 1983 as an extraterrestrial from the eighth galaxy who occupied Al Mahdi's body.[48] In some publications, the flying saucer is cropped out, though I could not discern a clear relationship between a book's content and the decision to show or cut the spaceship.[49]

The 1988 booklet *Who Was Marcus Garvey?* (which appears under the Tents of Kedar publishing label but with the Brooklyn address) does acknowledge a shift, as Al Mahdi explains that he needed to meet his readers where they were: "At one time we dealt strictly with Islaam; but ... because you have been indoctrinated so deeply, you still think as a Christian. It is very hard for you to change. You still try to judge Al Islaam by Christian standards."[50] Around the turn of the 1990s, "Christ Series" literature ostensibly gives renewed focus to Al Mahdi's Christology, with titles such as *The Final Messenger: Christ the Final Word*; *The Wisemen*; *Who Was Jesus Sent To?*; and *The Resurrection*. As part of this intervention, *What Laws Did Jesus Follow?* (1988) charges that Christians do not truly follow Christ but rather a false religion of "Paulism." Answering the question posed in the title, Al Mahdi argues that Jesus followed Mosaic Law. The text includes a polemic against "devil" Jews and "so-called" Muslims, both of whom have abandoned Mosaic Law for spurious texts (i.e., the Talmud and hadith corpus); to Muslims, Al Mahdi argues that Muhammad's revelation contained no knowledge "that wasn't already given."[51] Rather than provide new laws, the Qur'an only confirmed what had been sent to Israelite prophets.

"Christ Series" back covers maintain an expected AAC/NIH alignment: *The Final Messenger* displays the Nubian flag with Mahdist spear, flanked by the seal of Muhammad and AAC/NIH star-and-crescent logo, with the familiar "Duaa'a Ansaaru Allah." The front covers, absent any AAC/NIH symbols or stylistic conventions, depart from the community's previous aesthetics, displaying no Arabic text or identification with a specific group. Framed by blank white margins, the front covers' central images seem to be presented as Christian: Jesus in white robe, praying with hands clasped, a halo around his head; the Magi surrounding newborn Christ in the manger; Jesus riding a donkey, surrounded by followers of diverse complexions; and Jesus flying out of the cave in which he was buried, while Roman soldiers look on. Apart from

FIGURE 23 "As Sayyid Al Imaam Isa Al Haadi Al Mahdi (Allah preserve him), born 1945." AAC/NIH poster, ca. 1988.

minute details that convey content only if a reader already knows to look for them—a tiny six-pointed star in the distance behind the Magi on the cover of *The Wisemen*, an upward-pointing crescent on the front of *Who Was Jesus Sent To?*—the front covers give no sign that these publications came from Muslims, let alone the Ansar. Inside, readers find the usual image of Al Mahdi in turban and robe with hooked staff, a new caption indicating that the photo was taken in 1973 in the Sudan.

Apart from the new aesthetics, these materials do not break from the past. While themes of intergalactic sages receive increased focus, even this was not new or random. References to spaceships do not move the Ansar from Islam into a separate category of "UFO religion": when Al Mahdi explains that some human beings have extraterrestrial origins, he offers proof with the Qur'an's references to Allah sending Adam and Eve *down* to earth.[52] He affirms Elijah Muhammad's Mothership vision as genuine and links it to the Buraq, the steed that Muhammad rides in classical Muslim ascension narratives.[53]

These books also preserve AAC/NIH Egyptosophy, arguing that John the Baptist was trained by "Matheno, an Egyptian Israelite who was a master from the Temple of Sakkara, under the instruction of Zoser, the master healer,"[54] and that Jesus, after training at mystery schools throughout the world, entered an Egyptian pyramid for initiation in the school of Hajar, Ishmael's mother and Imhotep's daughter. Zoser's pyramid, Al Mahdi explains in *Sons of Canaan*, was "never intended to be a place of burial, but instead was intended and used for a temple of initiation into the deeper sciences of mystics."[55] When Jesus died of natural causes, the angel Gabriel (his biological father) carried his body to the top of the pyramid at Saqarra, where it disintegrated and each element returned to its place in the universe.[56] Al Mahdi expands on these themes in his revised commentary on the book of Revelation, which appears in its 1991 iteration as a series of blue books bearing the Arabic letter *lam* on the front cover and the six-pointed star and crescent on the back. In the first volume, Al Mahdi rewrites popular categories: "I am a Muslim, if it means 'One who is of peace'; I am a Jew if it means 'One who is of the Tribe of Judah, and follows the religion of the Prophet/Apostle Abraham,' and I am a Christian, if it means 'One who follows the Prophet/Messiah Jesus.'"[57]

A drastic change came in 1991 at Mount Zion, when Al Mahdi declared that his followers, the Ishmaelites, had "forfeited our Covenant with ALLAH just as the children of Israel did before us." The loss of covenant came with a new dress code. The white robes, turbans, and *khimars* disappeared: men were instructed to wear tunics, pants, and a yarmulke that Al Mahdi called a "kuwfiy," while women wore tunics, baggy pants, and a head shawl (hijab) and no longer covered their faces. For both men and women, the changes were bolstered with biblical citations from Numbers, Deuteronomy, and Genesis.[58] Al Mahdi soon added specifications to the dress prescriptions, such as a gold sash for men.[59] Meanwhile, community members abandoned their previous "Muhammadan type names" and "ridiculous names from the hadith" in favor of names exclusively from scripture.[60]

Al Mahdi also underwent a makeover, discarding his familiar turban. He now appeared in painted portraits with shoulder-length straight hair parted down the middle and backed by a glowing halo. Publications increasingly referred to him as "the Lamb," a designation that he had used throughout his career—"Shaikh Khidr (Melchisedek, SRA) at the junction of the two Niles . . . annointed me as the 'Lamb,'" he declared in 1977[61]—and eventually as Rabboni Y'shua Bar El Haady.[62] Materials also identify him as Yanuwn and Melchisedek and note that "we call him Malachi-Zodok" as well. Meanwhile, community literature switched its publishing brand from the Original Tents of Kedar (with the Monticello, New York, address) to the Tents of Abraham (with the Atlanta, Georgia, address) and then to the Tents of Nubia by the end of 1992. The community also introduced a white version of its Nubian flag featuring the Arabic pronoun *huwa* (he) in Nubic style within a six-pointed star. A community member's 1991 essay promises, "We will have our own music, our own dress, our own holy days, our own food, etc. We are on our own. No one can tell us what to be because no one understand [sic] what we have been through."[63]

Community media refer to the "19 Classes," a process of reorientation that had taken place in 1991 at Mount Zion, which included statements from Al Mahdi that his community would restore the Torah's sacraments; like Jesus, Al Mahdi had come not to change the law but to fulfill it.[64] *The Holy Tablets* (1996) says that "because of these false teachings of the so-called Arabs who deliberately mistranslated verses of the Qur'aan to confuse non-Arabic speaking Nubians in the west," Al Mahdi moved to the Catskills and "set up the nineteen tests of nineteen weeks of the faithful that would come through blizzards." These tests set forth a path to "the Mecca of Nubians, Georgia."[65]

In 1992, community publications from Mount Zion reported that billboards had been observed along Route 17 proclaiming, "Moshiach Is on the Way! Be Part of It!" The signs were placed by the Lubavitcher Hasidim, followers of Brooklyn-based Rabbi Menachem Schneerson (some of whom believed that Schneerson was the Messiah). El Haady's pamphlets suggested that the Route 17 billboards led directly to his own Mount Zion. Community media also argued that by exposing Christianity's lies and the dangers of eating pork, El Haady fulfilled Islamic expectations of Jesus's return (i.e., "breaking the cross" and killing the swine). With disclaimers that El Haady did not personally identify himself as Jesus—a charge that he had faced since the turn of the

1980s—community literature also pointed out that his birth certificate gave his parents' names as Mary and David, that he performed miracles and withstood Christlike persecution from his enemies, and that he matched Jesus's physical description in Revelation: "There are too many coincidences to be unreal."[66]

Pamphlets from 1992 proclaim, "The Nubian Islaamic Hebrews are now in a transition stage," liken the community's condition to that of a cocoon that will produce a butterfly,[67] and herald the arrival of a "very new and dynamic doctrine" of "Right Knowledge."[68] But what precisely was changing, and does this transformation correspond to later narratives of a temporary "Jewish" period in the community's history?

MUHAMMAD WAS A HEBREW

While the AAC/NIH adopted a new name, new dress codes, new ritual practices, new inventory for sale ("Shabat Cloths," "Shabat Candles," "Khallah Bread Cloths," and mezuzahs), and new theological vocabulary (replacing references to Allah with Eloh or Yahuwa)[69] that might signal a movement from Islam to Judaism, it never identified itself as a "Jewish" community. The only references to a time spent within the "school of Judaism" appear later, as retroactive comments on the early 1990s. Publications from 1992–93 identify "Jewism" as a false sect, to be counted alongside contemporary Islam ("Muhammadism") and Christianity ("Paulism") as distortions of the authentic "Religion of Abraham." El Haady maintains what had consistently been his position: that Nubian Islamic Hebrews follow all divine scriptures, affirm the Qur'an, and recognize the Qur'an's mentions of Christ's *Injil* as references to the book of Revelation.[70] When the Qur'an charged Jews with altering the Torah, AAC/NIH material argues, it was not so much wrong as simply limited by context: Medina's Jews possessed corrupted scriptures, but this did not undo the Qur'an's praise of the Torah as a light and guide, since "we as Muslims are aware of the fact that there are no contradictions in the Qur'aan."[71]

The community also preserved its claim upon Muhammad. Echoing Sunni apologetics while reaching a dramatically different conclusion, El Haady writes that Muhammad did not establish a new religion but rather confirmed the timeless religion of all the prophets. The Lamb insists in 1992 writings that his community's new dress code is not "an innovation to the sunnah of the Prophet Muhammad" but rather a reversion to true Islam, which the Qur'an calls Millatu Ibraahim (Religion of Abraham). The "real Muslims," he writes, are not the followers of an innovated heretical "Muhammadism" but rather those who follow Abraham (which includes Muhammad himself).[72] El Haady's *Muhammad Was a Hebrew* (1993) (fig. 24) in his *Truth* pamphlet series further drives this point home. Consistent with earlier AAC/NIH material, he reads "Hebrew" as meaning "to cross, to pass or traverse," and explains that the designation was first given to Abraham when he "crossed over" Mesopotamia en route to Canaan. El Haady argues that because Abraham, the first Hebrew, represents the shared foundation of Judaism, Christianity, and Islam, all of these traditions and their countless subdivisions serve as carriers—however distorted—of "some type of Hebraic teaching." God's command to follow Abraham applies to all of humankind, including those who follow the Qurʾan, since the Qurʾan itself regards Hebrew scripture as divine guidance. "Jewish-period" literature upholds the Qurʾan as a revelation for "Nubians, the true Arabs" against non-Black imposter Muslims: "All these Arabs do is lie about your heritage.... They (the Arabs) want you to believe that El Islam (The Peace) is theirs, and that they are the real Arabs. Well, El Islam is theirs now that they have tampered with the original teachings." El Haady thus uses Muhammad and maintains his agency to demarcate original and pure Islam—the religion of Abraham—as Nubian territory, while rejecting later Islamic tradition as a scheme "concocted by the Arabs of Saudi Arabia."[73]

CONCLUSIONS

It may seem intuitive to place AAC/NIH literature on a spectrum with "Hebraism" and "Islam" at opposite ends, and then chart its movement along this spectrum, as though becoming more "Hebrew" necessarily requires increasing distance from "Islam" and vice versa. Al Mahdi/El Haady, writing later as Malachi Z. York, would explain his trajectory as a succession through various "schools," including distinct "Muslim" and "Hebrew" phases, but this retroactive account is not supported by the documentary evidence. In other words, the Lamb does not treat his identity and platform at any given time as temporary markers of a school that he plans to leave, nor does he announce formal entry into a Hebrew or Jewish phase. The Lamb attributes changes in clothing to forfeiture of the divine covenant, stresses pragmatic reasons for reform—"We do not want to be mistaken for Muhammadans or pale Jews or confused Negroes saying they are Hebrew or Israelites"[74]—and insists upon continuity with the Ansar past, clarifying that the laws "have not changed. The only thing that has changed is the name."[75] Though the community obviously did undergo changes, he does not present these developments as complete reinventions

FIGURE 24 Tents of Nubia, *The Truth, Edition 16: Muhammad Was a Hebrew* (1993).

or mass conversions from one neatly bound, self-contained stage to another. Clean time lines are only offered later, in retrospective accounts.

Even if we call the early 1990s a "Jewish" period, this mass conversion remains grounded in an act of *tafsir*, Qurʾan interpretation. The community understood its reforms through Qurʾanic references to the "religion of

Abraham." In AAC/NIH exegesis, the Qur'an itself instituted the Mosaic Sabbath as a requirement for Muslims. In an intertextual confirmation underpinning the Ansar project, Al Mahdi's reading of the Qur'an identified the book of Revelation as Christ's *Injil*, and his reading of Revelation named the Qur'an as the seventh seal. During his "Jewish period" as El Haady, he still affirmed the Qur'an, and his followers still identified themselves in official community publications as "knowledge seeking Muslims" who were taught to follow the Bible.[76] It can be said that in the early 1990s El Haady intensified his long-standing interest in Israelite law, but he contextualized this move with a quotation of Jesus from the Gospel of Matthew, and then constructed an ambiguous relationship between the returning Christ and himself using Muslim hadith traditions. He does not offer a clean break from one confession and jump instantly to another. In addition to his use of Qur'an and hadith literature, he also continued to produce commentaries on a foundational text in Blackamerican Muslim history, the Nation of Islam's Supreme Wisdom Lessons.

During what is called the "Jewish" period, El Haady declared that his community still maintained the fast of Ramadan but gave the fast a new meaning. As "the last Hebrew Prophet," Muhammad fasted like the Israelites, who fasted for thirty days whenever they dropped the Torah on the ground. When the Qur'an descended from the heavens to the earth in the month of Ramadan, it was similarly desecrated, necessitating the fast. El Haady argues not as someone who has abandoned the Qur'an for Judaism but as a committed Qur'an exegete, a *mufassir*, who finds the revelation commanding adherence to "the ways of the Israelites."[77] To suggest that the community quit its Muslim school for a new Jewish school oversimplifies a complex intertextuality that has persisted throughout its journey.

CHAPTER 4

Between Zion and Mecca
Bilal as Islamic and Hebrew

> The scepter shall not depart from Judah,
> nor the ruler's staff from between his
> feet, until Shiloh comes; and to him shall
> be the obedience of the people.
>
> —GENESIS 49:10

Throughout the twentieth century, Bilal ibn Rabah, an Ethiopian companion of the Prophet, became an increasingly salient resource for American Muslims and also non-Muslims. Arguments that Islam is color-blind make frequent reference to Bilal, citing his biography to prove that a Black man could find the respect in Islamic societies that was not possible in America or Western Christianity. For non-Muslim scholars such as Edward Blyden and J. A. Rogers, the rise of a "bushy-haired Ethiopian slave" to the prestigious position of Islam's "high priest and treasurer" illustrated the possibilities for Black people in non-European, non-Euro-American, and non-Christian worlds.[1] Bilal's Ethiopian background also constructed a bridge between Muslim identities and long-standing American images of Ethiopia. "The idea of 'Ethiopia,'" writes Yvonne Chireau, "had been the locus of black American visions of destiny in the nineteenth century," nourished by the biblical verse "Princes shall come out of Egypt; Ethiopia shall soon stretch forth her hands unto God" (Psalms 68:31).[2] Muhammad's embrace of an Ethiopian among his closest companions provided a possible node of connection between Islam and Black Atlantic rhetorics of Ethiopianism, while Bilal's recognition of Muhammad in turn read as an endorsement of Islam from the true birthplace of civilization.

AAC/NIH literature depicts Bilal as a Judahite, rendering his embrace of Muhammad a unification of the lines of Isaac and Ishmael. His ancestry thus speaks to the claims of Black Israelite thinkers that Ethiopians were the true Hebrews, and that modern "white" Jews were inauthentic. As a descendant of Judah, Bilal recalls the "Lion of Judah" symbology of Ras Tefar I, engaging the Rastafarian image of Ethiopia as Zion. Trained in Mosaic Law and a leader among the first Muslims, Bilal is represented in AAC/NIH literature as the prototypical "Islamic Hebrew."

This chapter examines Bilal's significance in AAC/NIH literature. In polemics against non-Black Muslims, Al Mahdi turns Sunni treatments of Bilal against their authors, charging that their use of Bilal to prove Islam's transcendence of race ironically exposes their anti-Black racism. He also weaponizes Bilal against W. D. Muhammad, who had named his post-Nation community after Bilal and presented Bilal as a symbolic patriarch for all Blackamericans. The figure of Bilal supports AAC/NIH media on all fronts, serving to defend the community's lineages and authenticities to diverse audiences.

BILAL'S JOURNEY TO AMERICA

Bilal appears in Scottish Orientalist Sir William Muir's *Life of Mahomet* (1861), which describes him as "tall, dark, and gaunt, with negro features and bushy hair," honored by Muhammad as "the first-fruits of Abysinnia," and "to this day ... renowned throughout the Moslem world" as the first to perform the call to prayer. Muir notes that as captives from foreign lands, Mecca's slaves, including Bilal, were "generally familiar either with Judaism or Christianity" and thus open to Muhammad's message. Muir praises Bilal as the only Muslim to escape "the shame of recantation" when Mecca's polytheists tortured Muhammad's followers, but he also judges him a "heartless negro" for bringing two young women across a battlefield littered with corpses to see "their anger and their fright."[3]

Bilal enters American consciousness as evidence of Islamic antiracism through Edward Blyden (1832–1912), an ordained Presbyterian minister. Blyden appreciated Islam's potential as "an instrument of black nationalism," writes Kambiz GhaneaBassiri, "that could bolster self-reliance and 'civilizational' progress among blacks."[4] In *Christianity, Islam, and the Negro Race* (1887), Blyden compares the apparent equality among Muslims to Christian racism: "Frederick Douglass, as a Mohammedan, would have been a *walees*—a saint of the religion, an athlete of the faith; as a Christian, his orthodoxy is suspected." Islam, Blyden argues, was pro-Black from the beginning. "Mohammed not only loved the Negro," he writes, "but regarded Africa with peculiar interest and affection." Muhammad praised Africa as a "land of righteousness," echoing Homer's description of "blameless Ethiopians." Owing to Bilal's role as the first *mua'dhin* ("from those Negro lips the beautiful sentiment found utterance—'Prayer is better than sleep'"), Blyden boasts that "the forms of daily worship now used throughout the Mohammedan world were fixed by a Negro."[5]

Blyden's use of Bilal as proof of Islam's racial egalitarianism was repeated in Ahmadiyya efforts to spread Islam in the United States. A 1921 issue of the Ahmadiyya newspaper *Moslem Sunrise* quotes Muhammad declaring, "I tread under the feet the Racial prejudice" and promotes Islam as "the only religion that has ever destroyed color and race prejudices from the minds of the people." Making a comparison to the Black experience of Christianity, *Moslem Sunrise* promises that "in Islam no Church has ever had seats reserved for anybody and if a Negro enters first and takes the front seat even the Sultan if he happens to come after him never thinks of removing him from that seat."[6] Ahmadiyya literature cites "Bilal the Ethiopian" as proof that "slaves looked upon the Prophet as their greatest friend and helper, the sincerest advocate and champion of their cause." Bilal is depicted as one of the earliest converts to Islam ("deliberately and after mature thinking"), faithfully enduring torture for his beliefs and reaching such prominence that even 'Umar ibn al-Khattab, the second caliph, described him as "Chief of the Muslims." Bilal's status is reflected even in modernity at his tomb, which "attracts more pilgrims than are attracted by any other tomb in Damascus," and thus illustrates "the inestimable service that Islam rendered to the cause of slaves in raising them from the lowest depths of degradation to the highest pinnacles of social eminence."[7]

Bilal also appears in non-Muslim media, becoming an exemplar of the "great black man in history" motif in Afrocentrist discourses. Throughout the 1920s, J. A. Rogers's praise of Bilal as a "Warrior-Priest" circulated in Black newspapers like the *New York Amsterdam News*, the *Chicago Defender*, and the *Afro-American*, under headlines such as "Bilal, a Negro, Helped Found Mohammedanism," "Says Islam Faith Knows No Color Line," and "Mahomet's Chief Aid Black with Bushy Hair." Contemporary to Al Mahdi's early career, Afrocentrist scholar Yosef Ben-Jochannan discusses Bilal in his *African Origins of the Major "Western Religions"* (1970). While dismissive of Black people who regard Islam as their redemption from "Judeo-Christian religious enslavement"—exposing their "complete lack of knowledge of the history of the Jihads (Holy Wars) Islam brought to Africa"—Ben-Jochannan challenges "Moslem Arabs" who marginalize and erase Islam's "indigenous African founders." Assigning Bilal a more foundational role than Arabocentric histories allow, Ben-Jochannan celebrates Bilal as Islam's co-founder, a man whose Africanity shaped Islam. Bilal's call to prayer, which "influenced every Moslem's way of life," was rooted in "a civilization in Ethiopia where it was an established 'divine rule' for the worshippers of Koptic (Coptic) Christianity, Judaism, and other indigenous traditional African religions that demanded it—including the 'MYSTERIOUS SUN and FIRE GODS.'" Under a Black Ethiopian's tutelage, Muhammad preserved his community's veneration of a black meteorite—which itself was taken from Ethiopia. Bilal educated Muhammad in stories of the Hebrew prophets; in the Medina period, he helped Muhammad form a new government. Ben-Jochannan describes Bilal as no less than an "assistant-prophet" for his creative contributions to Islam's "original prayers and doctrines." These include depictions of paradise as a realm of limitless sexual pleasures: it was Bilal who introduced the notion of the *hur*, the dark-eyed maidens of paradise, as a reward for male believers. Aware that "the entire Arab world" fetishized "African virgins," Bilal "may have been manipulating the same people (Arabs and Persians) who had once held him in contempt as an 'African slave.' For he knew their greatest weakness at that era, their apparently unquenchable thirst for the indigenous African 'Black-eyed daughters.'" On his deathbed, Muhammad named Bilal his successor, but Bilal yielded to Abu Bakr. Even after refusing to assume official authority, Bilal remained Islam's de facto leader. The full importance of Bilal and other Black companions of the Prophet, however, has been edited out of Islamic history by Arab and Persian Muslims. Ben-Jochannan asserts that "the black color of the Africans' skin has become the sole criterion for excluding them.... Yet it was the Africans, and others of African ancestry, who were most influential in Islam's creation."[8]

Ben-Jochannan's treatment of Bilal appears to have been a significant resource for Al Mahdi. The misspelling of Bilal's father's name in AAC/NIH literature (as Rahab rather than Rabah) repeats an error in *African Origins* and thus suggests the possibility that Al Mahdi had read Ben-Jochannan's work (though one or both authors could have been repeating the earlier misspelling by J. A. Rogers).[9] The major point of resonance between Ben-Jochannan's and Al Mahdi's treatments of Bilal, however, remains the charge that non-Black

Muslims who praise Bilal actually deny his full importance and expose their own anti-Blackness.

BILAL AND THE NATION(S) OF ISLAM

In an interview the day before his assassination, Malcolm X referred to Bilal while insisting to the weekly magazine *Al-Muslimoon* that "the most fertile area for Islam in the West is the Black American." Following J. A. Rogers, Malcolm placed Bilal even before Abu Bakr, Ali, and Muhammad's wife, Khadija, in the chronology of Islamic conversion: "Was it not Bilal, who was the first to receive the seed of Islam from the prophet himself in Arabia 1,400 years ago?"[10] In 1966, the Nation of Islam sponsored a screening of an Egyptian film on Bilal, and *Muhammad Speaks* described Bilal as "the first black man to embrace the truth of Islam"—momentarily ignoring Nation doctrine that great prophets throughout the ages were Black.[11]

For the post-Elijah Nation, Bilal became a device that allowed W. D. Muhammad to uphold the Nation's claims of authentic Blackness while moving toward new constructions of authentic Islam. In October 1975, W. D. Muhammad announced that he was adopting the term "Bilialian" to signify members of his own community, African Americans at large, and even global Blackness, honoring a "beautiful and well-known man who was an ancestor of our people here in America." Bilal, he explained, "represents the old so-called African people. We have a double connection with Bilal because he was a Muslim and also a so-called African." For this Muslim Africanity that Bilal embodied, "there is no more reason to have doubt or confusion when you are asked to identify your race or your nationality. We are 'Bilalians' from this day forward."[12]

W. D. Muhammad presents Bilal's journey as analogous to that of African Americans in terms of the possibility of reconciliation between enslavers and enslaved. "Bilal was an Ethiopian and he was made a slave by Arab people," he observes. "And it was the Arab people who freed him.... We were made slaves by the Christians, Caucasians of the West.... And it was the Christian Caucasian who said, these people have to be freed." For W. D. Muhammad, the difference between white slaveowners and whites who joined in the Black freedom struggle was as substantial as the difference between the "heathen, idolatrous" Arab who held Bilal captive and the "dignified" and "righteous" Muslim Arab, Abu Bakr, who set him free. He read Bilal's words to Abu Bakr— "Have you freed me that I should be the servant of Allah, or have you freed me that I should be your servant?"—to express the same question of African

Americans: "Have you freed me that I should be your servant, or have you freed me that I can be free as all other human beings are free?" He further wove Bilal into American history with reference to Bilali Mohammed, a nineteenth-century slave at Sapelo Island, Georgia. For W. D. Muhammad, America's forgotten Muslim history is also Bilalian history. In Bilal's life, he finds a "prophetic figure resembling us—the whole people—a figure speaking to our problems and to our beautiful destiny." Bilal also connected W. D. Muhammad's community to transnational Muslim networks that shared in their love for the Prophet's companion: "When the Syrian president and the Muslim community of Syria got the news that I had named our race Bilalians, they got busy to build a new masjid, a new mausoleum for Bilal."[13]

As W. D. Muhammad deracialized the Nation's teachings, he advocated readings of his father's texts that emphasized alternative, allegorical meanings for terms such as "white people" and "black people." Bilal fueled the imam's racial esotericism, as the Prophet, "speaking to his companions, pointed to Bilal, and told them, we are all Bilal. What did he mean by that? That we are all black. . . . Human nature is a dark form. But, out of that form comes the light of intelligence and knowledge—the science in everything that lights the world."[14] While W. D. Muhammad used Bilal as a bridge for his Nation into the "Muslim world," Louis Farrakhan also made use of Bilal. Discussing the hadith in which Muhammad says that he heard Bilal's footsteps ahead of him in paradise, Farrakhan explained in 1989 that the statement held deep meanings for future Islam. Muhammad "didn't mean his own personal footsteps," Farrakhan argued. "He was white. He was an Arab. And he was saying that it is the Blacks who are going to lead the Arab world back to the faith that they had forsaken."[15]

BILAL, THE SCEPTER BEARER

Al Mahdi distributed a booklet titled *Bilal* in 1973, two years before Elijah Muhammad's death, and then in 1979 published an expanded version to confront the Nation's "Bilalian" period. The 1979 booklet opens with charges that Muslims have mistreated Bilal, reducing him to a patronizing cliché: "Every other book or article you may have read on Bilal (HWON) is written by the European or Pakistanian Moslem and tells you that he was a negro slave that called the Adhan very well or something to that effect."[16] Al Mahdi presents a new narrative in which Bilal becomes a critical piece in the divine plan. It is through Bilal's body, knowledge, and mission that Ethiopia becomes the point of connection between Israelite and Ishmaelite lines of prophecy. "Bilaal (HWON) was one of the first Nubian Islaamic Hebrews," Al Mahdi writes elsewhere, identifying Hebrew as Bilal's native tongue.[17] According to *Bilal*, Ethiopian Jews (Falasha) represent the last pure remnant of Judah, itself the last remaining Israelite tribe, which had fled Assyrian conquest. The Israelites who chose to remain in Palestine eventually fell victim to miscegenation with surrounding communities such as the Edomites and Midianites, leaving the unmixed "Falashians" in Ethiopia "the last of the chosen people on earth."[18] Arguing in *Should Muslims Observe the Sabbath?* that Muslims must follow *all* of the revealed scriptures, Al Mahdi deploys Bilal to establish that Israelite prophetic heritage remains Black territory that was stolen by white imposters.[19]

Bilal stood out from childhood for the brilliant light in his eyes. His father, Rahab (again, Al Mahdi here repeats a spelling error from Rogers and Ben-Jochannan), aware that Moses had prophesied a "Black child pure in seed" to take part in the transition of prophethood from Israel to Ishmael, named him Bilal for *bal*, meaning "water pouring forth"; the child would represent the "gushing forth of the twelve springs, and he, himself, is the unification of the twelve tribes," in order to pass prophethood to the Ishmaelites.[20] In preparation, Rahab trained Bilal in the Torah, the *Zubuwr* (Psalms) of David, and the *Injiyl* (Gospel) of Jesus, and in rabbinical jurisprudence. Rahab was also custodian of the Mihjan, the hooked scepter carried by the prophets Abraham, Ishmael, and Moses. He came to understand that his role in sacred history was to prepare his son to carry the Mihjan to the coming Ishmaelite prophet in Arabia, thereby fulfilling the divine covenant. Bilal "was not just a black slave as the pale Arabs would have you believe," writes Al Mahdi. "He was an educated man learned in the Scriptures of the Old and New Testaments . . . like the Sceptre was passed to Bilaal (HWON), so was the knowledge. Bilaal (HWON) came from a line of men who knew they were to keep the prophecy alive, and through them the prophecy was to be fulfilled." Al Mahdi interprets the promise in Genesis 49:10 that "the scepter shall not depart from Judah" prior to Shiloh's arrival as a prophecy of Bilal passing the Mihjan to Muhammad, the foretold Shiloh.[21] Bilal, "culmination of the twelve Tribes of Israel," was to safeguard the Mihjan until he could present it to Muhammad. When the time came, Bilal left home with the Mihjan in his hands and tears in his eyes.[22]

At age sixteen, Bilal left Ethiopia with his sister, Madyana, and brother, Zubir (who was "named after mount on Sinai where Moses conversed"),[23] to find the Ishmaelite prophet, crossing the Red Sea and journeying into the Arabian Peninsula, where he warned people of the messenger's imminent arrival. The close relationship of Hebrew to Arabic enabled Bilal to communicate effectively with Arabs. When Bilal arrived in Mecca and searched for the prophet, he encountered the legendary hanifs, pre-Islamic monotheists, who appreciated his knowledge of scripture. Persecuted by the people of Mecca for their rejection of idolatry, the hanifs were ultimately exiled from the holy city and took refuge in a cave at Mount Hira, the same cave in which Muhammad later received the first revelations of the Qur'an. Bilal joined the group in campfire discussions beyond Mecca's city limits, telling them of the awaited prophet.

When these hanifs insisted upon proclaiming the oneness of God in Mecca's streets with shouts of "Allahu Ahad," the local polytheists responded with violence. During these attacks, Bilal was captured and sold into slavery. The surviving hanifs kept the Mihjan hidden on Mount Hira, wrapped in a white cloth that would become Muhammad's turban. Bilal later sent word that the Mihjan was to be sent to 'Abbas, Muhammad's uncle. The staff would later demonstrate Bilal's special status among the believers; Al Mahdi argues that Bilal was respected not only for his enduring faith or beautiful voice but especially for the Mosaic knowledge signified by his custodianship of the Mihjan.

As both AAC/NIH and more popular narratives report, Bilal's cruel master tortured him for his faith until Abu Bakr purchased his freedom. Bilal joined Muhammad and rose to prominence as the first *mu'adhin*. In AAC/NIH narratives, however, Bilal becomes arguably *the* central figure in Muhammad's prophetic career. Muhammad, Al Mahdi asserts in *Bilaal, the Sceptre Bearer* (1985), merely "furnished the executive ability and generalship for the new faith," while Bilal "provided most of the inspiration." Aware of Bilal's importance, Muhammad attested—as seen in canonical hadith literature—that he heard Bilal's footsteps preceding him in paradise. Muhammad even named Bilal his official successor, though Bilal declined.[24]

Al Mahdi writes that while Bilal emigrated with the Muslims to Medina, he had not joined in the Muslims' earlier *hijra* to his homeland; upon their arrival in Ethiopia, however, Muslims found shelter with Bilal's family. Al Mahdi provides a genealogical chart to show that Bilal was a second cousin of Khadija, Muhammad's first wife; Ethiopians and Arabs, therefore, are "really one family.... This is why they were warmly welcomed to Ethiopia."[25] Al Mahdi adds that Muhammad had undergone religious instruction at the hands of Khadija's uncle, Waraqah, who was also Bilal's uncle. The familial tie between Khadija and Muhammad meant that Muhammad and Bilal were related: if "pale Arabs" admitted that Bilal was Black, then Muhammad himself was Black.[26] It was both an ancestral and a prophetic kinship that attracted Bilal to Islam: it was as a genuine Israelite and one learned in the teachings of Jesus the Messiah that Bilal could recognize Muhammad as the awaited prophet.[27]

During his reconquest of Mecca, Muhammad handed Bilal his sword, and Bilal destroyed the various statues surrounding the Ka'ba. This was not Bilal's first idol-smashing project; he had also ridden through Jerusalem after Muhammad's heavenly ascension, smashing divine icons to prepare that city for pure monotheism. Al Mahdi's pamphlet *Bilal* illustrates the purification of Mecca with an image of a sword-wielding Muhammad from Manly P. Hall's occult text *The Secret Teachings of All Ages*. The face has been retouched to portray Bilal, and Muhammad's left hand, which held pages of the Qur'an, now holds the Mihjan. After purging the Ka'ba, Bilal climbed to its roof and called the *kalima tayyiba*, the "good word," which is linked to the "Word" mentioned in John 1:1–3. Bilal then climbed down, handed the Mihjan to Muhammad, and declared him seal of the Prophets, thus fulfilling Jacob's promise and completing his mission.[28] The passing of the scepter was signified in the AAC/NIH symbol, a Star of David seated within an Islamic crescent.[29]

In 1985, the community published another revision, *Bilaal, the Sceptre Bearer*, more than doubling the size of the 1979 booklet. While the 1979 edition does not make clear reference to other communities in the AAC/NIH's contemporary landscape, the 1985 edition takes explicit aim at Sunni Muslims, specifically W. D. Muhammad's followers: "Stop calling yourselves Bilaalians.... If you call yourself a Bilaalian, why don't you name yourself an 'Alian or a Zaidian; they were great Black men in Islaam also."[30] Bilal becomes illustrative not of Islamic antiracism but of condescending tokenism and the failure of Arab and South Asian Sunni Muslims to recognize Islam as a Black religion. The 1985 edition quotes a treatment of Bilal by Pakistani scholar Qamaruddin Khan and attacks Khan for the statement "Though Bilal was black, yet his heart was pure and enlightened by faith." Khan thus exposed so-called orthodox Islam as guilty of the same racism that Sunnis deny. "Does being Black make his heart less pure?" the 1985 edition asks. "Would his heart be more pure were he not Black?"[31]

The 1985 edition reduces Sunni claims on Bilal to the creation of a Black mascot. The devil will "swear that there is no RACISM IN ISLAAM, yet he'll tell you the Prophet Mustafa Muhammad Al Amin (PBUH) was White and Bilaal (HWON) was Black before he'll tell you about the KALIMAT [Islam's declaration of faith]."[32] In *The Book of Laam*, Al Mahdi mocks Bilalian identity as a claim on "the one renowned Islaamic personality whom the pale world openly acknowledges as having been black (Ethiopian)."[33]

For Al Mahdi, Bilal's true importance remains his role as a critical link in the chain connecting Muhammad to Moses. The 1985 edition, while repeating the 1979 claim that Bilal was offered the caliphate but declined "in favor of another," names this other candidate as 'Ali (in literature from 1981, Al Mahdi reports that Bilal had "yielded in favor of Abu Bakr").[34] The 1985 edition constructs Bilal as a figure of proto-Shi'ism, reporting that while Bilal yielded to Abu Bakr's assumption of power, he also retained close ties to 'Ali. In later years, Bilal refused to pledge loyalty to 'Ali's rival, Mu'awiya. Repeating the story of Bilal's performing the *adhan* for Hasan and Husayn, the 1985 edition claims that Bilal would give the call to prayer exclusively for Shi'is.[35]

While the 1979 edition praises Abu Bakr for his sincerity, honesty, and generosity in purchasing freedom for many slaves, the 1985 edition complains that throughout Muslim literature, "Abu Bakr has been made to look so great." Celebrated for securing freedom for slaves like Bilal, Abu Bakr also appears in the 1985 edition as a trespasser who smuggled himself into a tradition that did not belong to him: "Abu Bakr was the alien, the paleman," and his historical legacy reveals "orthodox" Islam as disguised white supremacy.[36] Writing in 1989, Al Mahdi quotes Bilal's statement to Abu Bakr—"If you brought me for your own sake, keep me, but if you brought me only for Allah's sake, let me go and undertake Allah's work"—as evidence of lingering "hardness in Bilal's heart" over the "red Arab" Abu Bakr's taking advantage of Bilal and continuing to treat him as a "slave" or "client."[37]

Bilal becomes yet another discursive bridge, as his sons are depicted as emigrating to Morocco, becoming the ancestors of all Black Moors.[38] "When you say Moorish," Al Mahdi writes in *Who Was Noble Drew Ali?* (1988), "it is the same as saying Bilalians because the original Moors were descendants of Bilaal (AS)." Noble Drew Ali and his mission become absorbed into AAC/NIH thought, which both leans on Moorish Science for its own lineage and presumes to correct what Moorish Science has missed. According to Al Mahdi, descent from Bilal establishes African Americans as both true Israelites and true Arabs, since Bilal "mixed his seed" with Arab women.[39]

In *Should Muslims Observe the Sabbath*, Al Mahdi repeats the assertion that Bilal descended from Judah and that his masterly knowledge of Israelite tradition enabled him to recognize Muhammad.[40] The hooked scepter that Bilal passed to Muhammad would itself become crucial to Al Mahdi's authority, as Al Mahdi claimed that the Mihjan now rested against the minbar in his Brooklyn masjid. AAC/NIH books and pamphlets consistently include photos of Al Mahdi holding the Mihjan (fig. 25). The resemblance of its shape to the Arabic

FIGURE 25 Al Mahdi holding his Mihjan staff, an inheritance from the prophets, as typically displayed on the inside cover of AAC/NIH publications in the 1980s. This photograph was also used to depict Al Mahdi's appearance at the times when Jesus occupied his body.

letter *lam* (ل) signifies Al Mahdi's status as the fulfillment of Elijah Muhammad's mystical vision of the letter, the future teacher with knowledge of the *lam*.[41]

Coincidentally, the AAC/NIH's chief Sunni antagonist in the 1980s was also named Bilal. In 1988, Abu Ameenah Bilal Philips published his polemical assault on the movement, *The Ansar Cult in America*. Philips refers to Bilal's friendship with the Prophet, often cited in Muslim apologetics as proof that Islam is inherently antiracist, as a refutation of AAC/NIH racial consciousness.[42] Al Mahdi responded with his 607-page *The Ansaar Cult: Rebuttal to the Slanderers*, which mocks Philips as "Belial," the name of one of the two hundred angels who had fallen from grace with Lucifer, meaning "worthlessness, wickedness, restlessness, and lawlessness." Al Mahdi also uses Philips's adopted name to expose his hypocrisy and that of Arab Sunni communities. "There's basically two Black people in the Islaamic world that the desert Arabs give credit to," he writes. "One is Zayd ibn Haarith (579–629 AD) . . . whom they say was so ugly, his wife Zaynab bint Jahsh (589–642 AD) did not love him. The second is Bilaal . . . the one recognized in the Arab world as the singer or the caller of the Adhaan." Zayd and Bilal reflect the limits of Black possibilities in pale Arab imaginations: "ugly and musically inclined." Al Mahdi then suggests that Philips study AAC/NIH literature, since he has "a little trouble defining what is and is not racism in Al Islaam."[43]

CONCLUSIONS

This chapter illustrates how the figure of Bilal contributes to the community's construction of Nubian Islamic Hebraism. Bilal weaves discursive threads together within the AAC/NIH narrative universe. Perhaps most immediately, he clears a path for Al Mahdi's appeal to Black Israelite movements. With a key role in the fulfillment of prophetic history and a biography that presents Ethiopia as home to the Israelite tribe of Judah, he speaks to Ras Tefar I. His sons' migration to what is now Morocco, where they become the progenitors of modern Moors, enables an AAC/NIH claim upon Noble Drew Ali's sacred genealogies. Bilal also fuels AAC/NIH polemical attacks on Black and non-Black Sunni communities that would appropriate him as token evidence of Islamic antiracism. Bilal, like Al Mahdi himself, possesses a deep reservoir of materials that can multiply his meanings and values for diverse communities.

CHAPTER 5

The Sudan Is the Heart Chakra

The AAC/NIH as Sufi Tariqa

> If we look at the Egyptian pyramids with open hearts and illuminated souls, they speak to us of the past.... And if today or in the future, people inquire about the site that was chosen for the pyramids, they would find that it is exactly in the center of the solid part of the earth's surface.... What was the meaning of placing the pyramids in the exact center of the earth? The real human heart is the solar plexus, and that is to be found in the center of the body, which is the shrine of God.
>
> —HAZRAT INAYAT KHAN

Explaining baraka as a "positive force" that was "passed down to us from Adam," Al Mahdi writes in *The Lost Children of Mu and Atlantis* that baraka can "only be conjured or aroused by Dhikr."[1] The practice of dhikr, the recitation of divine attributes or prayer formulas, leads to spiritual and physical perfection, healing, and growth, potentially bringing the seeker to the advanced station of *al-insan al-kamil*, which Al Mahdi translates as "self-perfected man or woman." He explains that at this level, the aspirant's third eye reopens.[2] While scholars have not looked at the AAC/NIH as a Sufi order, AAC/NIH literature reflects investments in a number of phenomena that observers often link to Sufism:

sheikh-disciple relationships, formal initiation, the recitation of divine names, and interest in the esoteric properties of the Arabic alphabet.

In 1984, the AAC/NIH established an auxiliary Sufi lodge, Sons of the Green Light (SGL). The AAC/NIH thus staked an explicit claim on Sufism, and Al Mahdi presented himself as the master of a Sufi order. The question considered in this chapter is not whether Al Mahdi's Sufi ideas and practices would satisfy everyone's idea of legitimate Sufism but what Sufism meant for Al Mahdi and his community. As Carl Ernst reminds us, there is no such thing as "Sufism in general"; Sufism remains "always local."[3]

At its height, the AAC/NIH could boast thousands of followers, spread primarily throughout major cities of the northeastern United States and enjoying an especially visible presence in Brooklyn. Whatever its formal membership might have been (and I view specific estimates with skepticism), this number neglects the unaffiliated consumers of AAC/NIH books, pamphlets, and lecture tapes who extend Al Mahdi's influence in what Yusuf Nuruddin has called African American "urban mythology" exponentially.[4] That this community (and the broader circle of consumers) recognized Al Mahdi as a Sufi master renders him one of the most—if not *the* most—successful Sufi masters in the United States in the 1970s and '80s. He was certainly the American Sufi master with the highest public profile; artists did not display the flags or portraits of Frithjof Schuon or Bawa Muhaiyaddeen on *Yo! MTV Raps*. This chapter investigates the neglected Sufi dimension of AAC/NIH discourse, situating the AAC/NIH within the context of American Sufism.

THE ANSAR'S SUFI GENEALOGIES

Al Mahdi, whose life as a Muslim leader began with chanting divine names in the street with a West African drum, started his movement in 1967 under the name Ansar Pure Sufi. Sufism remained important to Al Mahdi after his movement was rebranded as the Nubian Islamic Hebrew Mission in America. His 1972 essay "Can You Be Sufi?" argues for his readers' right to claim the term. "Many Muslims are under the impression, and are indoctrinating others with the fallacy that you must be from the East in order to elevate yourself to the degree of a Sufi," he writes. A Sufi, however, is simply an advanced Muslim who has "completed the study of the Sunna (practices) and the Sharian [sic] (law) of Islam" and is inclined toward the "spiritual aspects of Islam" rather than "physical or elementary practices." This elevated station is not only the domain of Muslims in Muslim-majority societies: rather, "the Muslim in the Western world is, if anything, more so entitled to the majestic rank of Sufi because he has to strive to perfect his way of life, whereas those Muslims in Eastern countries are surrounded by Islam and given the prayer rug." Al Mahdi assures his readers, "Allah does not deny to anyone the path of a Sufi."[5]

In a poem written around the same time, "Many Questions, One Answer," from Al Mahdi's poetry collection *Was Created with One Thought: The "Key" Is Within* (ca. 1972), he presents Sufism to explain his detachment from society's expectations:

> *I came to a city, where people crowded around . . .*
> *They said: "Where are you from?"*
> *They said: "Where are you going?"*
> *They said: "In what company do you travel?"*
> *They said: "What is your pedigree?"*
> *They said: "What is your inheritance?"*
> *They said: "What is your request?"*
> *They said: "Whom do you understand?"*
> *They said: "Who understands you?"*
> *They said: "What is your doctrine?"*
> *They said: "Who has no doctrine at all?"*
> *I said to them:*
>   *"What seems to you to be many is one."*
>   *"What seems to you simple is not."*
>   *"What seems to you complex is easy."*
>   *"The answer to you all is: the Sufi."*[6]

The definition of "Sufi" as a type of advanced Muslim appears later in *Abba Island in America* (ca. 1974–77), as Al Mahdi reports his successful creation of community spaces in which children can experience proper Islamic living and education. "Our children will be our salvation," reads one photo caption, "because they are the true Muslims, the future of the Islamic World . . . it is they who will be the Hafidhs [sic] [memorizers of the Qur'an], the Maulanas, the Shaikhs and the Sufis."[7] Al Mahdi depicts Sufis as Muslim spiritual elites who were present from the very beginnings of Islam. In *Id with the Ansars* (1977), he writes that Muhammad would devote the final ten days of Ramadan to recitation of divine names with Sufis. He traces "Sufi" to *safa* (pure, serene, undisturbed), defines *tasawwuf* as "effort to gain metaphysical purity," and explains "Sufi doctrine" as living in this world as a traveler to Allah.[8]

Though "Sufi" disappeared from the community's formal self-identification around the start of the 1970s, Al Mahdi continued to authorize himself by way of Sufi attributes and practices: lineages (both biological and pedagogical), pilgrimages to holy sites, privileged receptions of secret knowledge, proficiency with talismans, intuitive and scholarly mastery over scripture, visionary encounters with transcendent figures (most notably the Sufi paragon of initiation, Khidr), and contemplation and recitation of Allah's attributes. In *The 99+1 Attributes of Allah* (1983), Al Mahdi introduces the divine names as essential to "chants of the Suwfi" and the making of talismans, and lists "aspects of Suwfi doctrine" that start with the point that "Allah is one, all things are within him and he is within everything."[9] Writing on specific divine names and the benefits of reciting them, Al Mahdi also uses verbatim uncredited material from Shems Friedlander's *Ninety-Nine Names of Allah*.[10] Al Mahdi's interest in Sufism in the 1980s was not another of his supposed breaks from the past; Sufism was always among the elements in his matrix.

Academic literature has organized American Sufism into successive waves. The first wave appears with Hazrat Inayat Khan (1882–1927), founding master of the Sufi Order in the West, who presented Sufism as a timeless "Oriental wisdom" but also as a universal spirituality beyond any particular context or religion. Promoting Sufism as an option in Western spiritual marketplaces without imposing conversion to Islam as a prerequisite, Khan met with some success.[11] The Ahmadiyya, who engaged in missionary efforts in the United States during the early twentieth century, also contributed to this first wave; while the Ahmadiyya did not present itself as "officially" a Sufi order, Adil Hussain Khan has argued for Sufism's salience in studies of the community.[12] The Ahmadiyya was led by a charismatic Muslim mystic, Mirza Ghulam Ahmad (1835–1908), who not only boasted a kind of revelatory experience that seemingly threatened the finality of prophethood but also threatened borders between Islam and Hinduism in identifying himself as Krishna.[13] In the later twentieth century, opposition to the Ahmadiyya had escalated to such a degree that Pakistan inserted a denunciation of Ghulam Ahmad's teachings into its constitution. In the United States, Ahmadiyya networks intersected with Western metaphysical religionists. This context of encounter and exchange was also the setting in which the Moorish Science Temple and the Nation of Islam developed as charismatically driven movements with initiatory lodges, narratives of secret hierarchies, and challenges to both the finality of prophethood with Muhammad and the notion of an absolute, stable division between God and the created universe.

American Sufism's "second wave" is characterized by orders that came to the United States between the 1960s and 1980s and often attracted non-Muslims who were interested in Sufism as "spirituality" independent of "religion" and could think of themselves as Sufis without necessarily identifying as Muslims. In addition to these newly arrived orders, this wave includes the continuation of Hazrat Inayat Khan's community under his son, Pir Vilayat Khan, who formed Sufi Order International in 1968. At the Abode, his order's commune in downstate New York, Vilayat presented a Sufism in harmony with the dharmic traditions—"what Sufism is saying and what Buddhism is saying is exactly the same"—that enjoyed great resonance with New Age seekers.[14] One Inayat Khan follower, "Sufi Sam" Lewis, was both an initiated Sufi and a Zen Buddhist, and developed his "universal dances of peace" in conversation with Hare Krishna practices. One of the most significant figures of the second wave, Sri Lankan mystic Bawa Muhaiyaddeen, was head of an order centered in Philadelphia, a major Ansar city, and attracted disciples through multiple routes: while some were Muslims who sought spirituality within definitively Islamic frameworks, others came to him via yoga and Hinduism. In Bawa's community, as Gisela Webb has observed, we find followers who identify as Sufi Muslims, non-Sufi Muslims, and universalists.[15] This period also saw the development in the United States of the Maryamiyya led by Swiss-born master Frithjof Schuon and named for his visionary encounters with the Virgin Mary. Schuon presented himself as the mystical climax of a perennial wisdom uniting the world's great religious traditions.[16]

Following the 1979 Islamic Revolution, the Nimatullahi Order's leadership fled Iran and reoriented itself in cities such as New York and San Francisco as an order in Western exile, advocating an image of Sufism as universal rather than specific to Islam and Muslims. The order's master, Javad Nurbakhsh (1926–2008), was also a psychiatrist who joined Sufi traditions with modern psychiatric science. Through the Nimatullahi publishing house, Nurbakhsh disseminated a considerable body of literature, positioning Nurbakhsh as a leading producer of Sufi knowledge in North America.[17]

Al Mahdi's establishment of Ansar Pure Sufi in the 1960s marks his participation in American Sufism's "second wave." In the 1970s, advertisements for his Opening of the Seventh Seal class featured Sufism among "uncovered secrets" that also included the book of Revelation and "mystics of Tibet."[18] Even when criticizing other traditions, AAC/NIH literature also advances themes of esoteric perennialism that had flourished throughout twentieth-century American spiritual traditions, including Muslim communities like Noble Drew Ali's

Moorish Science Temple and Schuon's Maryamiyya. While the late-1970s publication *Id with the Ansars* reads as an explicitly Muslim-coded artifact—its front page celebrating the Muslim Eid al-Fitr holiday (marking the end of the Ramadan fast) with elegant Arabic calligraphy and a photo of Daoud Faisal, the Sunni imam whom Al Mahdi calls the "Founding Father of Orthodox Islam in the West"—Al Mahdi espouses a somewhat perennialist view of difference inside the publication. *Id with the Ansars* presents a diagram of a menorah (the caption calls it both a menorah and the Arabic *manaraat*), its seven candles representing different traditions and corresponding to verses in Revelation that contain messages for specific "congregations": Buddhism (3:14), Islam (3:7), Judaism (3:1), Hinduism (2:18), "Mythology" (2:12), Christianity (2:8), and Zoroastrianism (2:1). Al Mahdi breaks down the meanings of the menorah with reference to the Qur'an's famed "Verse of Light" (24:35), which has been privileged in Sufi interpretive traditions as a reservoir of esoteric meaning. While asserting that all religions must bear witness to the truth of Muhammad, Al Mahdi also treats each religion as a unique illumination. Atop each candle is a six-pointed star signifying the tradition's respective angel, read in the Verse of Light's imagery as its "brightly shining star." In reference to the Verse of Light's description of a lamp lit with the oil of a tree "neither east nor west," Al Mahdi explains, "the oil that these Candlesticks are lit from give the Light, the Spirit of Truth, which is neither eastern nor western, but UNIVERSAL." The returning Jesus will be confined neither to East (Judaism) nor West (Christianity).[19]

"Why is there such a separation amongst religions of the world?" Al Mahdi asks in *Ahmad, Jesus' Khalifat (Successor)* (1980). His answer: "As religious stories were interpreted and translated into different languages, the essential meanings were lost." To Al Mahdi's eyes, traces of these shared essential meanings remain observable. Asserting that "all religions depict the same things esoterically," Al Mahdi finds the notion of a singular creator across religions, citing evidence in Islam, Judaism, Christianity, Zoroastrianism, Hinduism, Buddhism, Sikhism, Confucianism, and Taoism. He describes "spiritual guidance" as a universal human need, and affirms scriptures such as the Tao Te Ching, Bhagavad Gita, Upanishads, and Zend Avesta as "sacred guidance from the Creator."[20]

Beyond its resonance with universalism and perennialism in American Sufism, AAC/NIH literature also engaged Sufism as a growing phenomenon among African American and African immigrant Muslim communities. Leading figures in the Dar—which had developed from the Ya-Sin Mosque (which itself had broken away from the State Street Mosque at which Al Mahdi became a Muslim)—pledged themselves to a Pakistani Qadiriyya sheikh, Syed Jilani, who connected with the Dar while leading Thursday-night dhikr circles in New Jersey. Disagreement over Sufism's legitimacy led to a factional splintering of the Dar, with the pro-Jilani circle establishing Jamaat al-Fuqra—described by Robert Dannin as "Sufi-mysticism combined with radical Islam"—in 1980.[21] Abu Ameenah Bilal Philips claims that the Dar's redirection by a "Pakistani Sufi extremist" into the Qadiriyya led Al Mahdi to reintegrate Sufism into his own brand.[22]

Sufism's significance for Al Mahdi's metaphysical Africa could also have been affected by growing diasporic communities, for his Sudan-centered vision of African Islamic spirituality shared space with popular Sufi traditions from Senegal and throughout West Africa. The Tijaniyya Order's membership was estimated at 80 percent African immigrants and 20 percent African Americans,[23] and the Muridiyya Order was recognized in New York with the institution of a "Bamba Day" parade in honor of Sheikh Ahmadou Bamba (1853–1927) in 1988. Apparently in response, AAC/NIH media advertised June 26, 1988 (Al Mahdi's birthday), as its own "Banner Day for Nubians."[24]

Al Mahdi's first access to Sufism probably came from the Sudanese community at State Street Mosque, and his writings on the Sudanese Mahdi regularly highlighted the Mahdi's Sufism. Muhammad Ahmad—"more interested in the spiritual aspect of life, rather than the social or political," Al Mahdi explains—was initiated into the Sammaniyya Order at age sixteen.[25] After breaking with the order over what he regarded as its poor discipline, Ahmad experienced a vision of Khidr at the junction of the two Niles. In 1870, "after his refusal to join any Order," he "began the life of a Sufi" and became a wandering preacher. His popularity as a Sufi leader enabled his revolution against British and Egyptian oppressors.[26]

Africa's significance as a Sufi archive (and Sufism's significance as an expression of metaphysical Africa) developed further in Al Mahdi's 1973 adventure, when he not only received initiation into an earthly order, the Khalwatiyya, but also went to the junction of the White and Blue Niles and experienced his own encounter with Khidr.[27] AAC/NIH Sufism becomes Egyptosophic in a photo of Al Mahdi at the Step Pyramid in Saqqara, captioned "the Temple of Initiation in Egypt." Al Mahdi calls attention to the "aura" visible around him: "This is the manifestation of the light which resides within me. This is what you are up against."[28]

When the AAC/NIH established its Sufi order in the 1980s,[29] it stood at the intersection of various forces, both local and transnational, including perennialist and universalist Sufi orders, the increasingly visible Sufi tariqas linked to transnational African Muslim communities, New Age, Afrocentric, and Egyptosophic spirituality movements, and overlapping conversations about global Blackness and global Islam.

KHIDR: TEACHER OF THE MASTER TEACHER

The Qur'an tells the story of Moses meeting his unnamed teacher, identified as Khidr in the tradition, at the "junction of the two seas" (Al Mahdi renders this "junction of the two rivers" and identifies the rivers as the White and Blue Niles, making the story resonate with his own experience).[30] Khidr demands that Moses ask no questions and they go on their way. Moses is repeatedly shocked as Khidr engages in bewildering acts, even murdering a child. When Moses loses patience and demands explanations, Khidr ends their time together. In Muslim intellectual traditions, particularly Sufi literature, Khidr and Moses appear as signifiers not only of masters and disciples but also of mystics and jurists and the superiority of the transrational esoteric sage over the purely textualist, exoteric scholar. For these readings of their encounter, Hugh Talat Halman has argued that the Khidr-Moses story remains "essential to understanding Sufism."[31] Throughout Sufi traditions, Khidr appears as an immortal guide who can visit aspiring saints. As Halman writes, "almost every saint (wali) receives a visit from al-Khidr at least once during his lifetime"; the roster of those who experienced Khidr visions includes premodern sages such as 'Abd al-Qadir al-Jilani (d. 874) and Ibn al-'Arabi (d. 1240), but also Al Mahdi's contemporaries in American Sufism Schuon and Lewis.[32]

For Al Mahdi, Khidr is more than a master teacher; he is no less than a cosmological principle. Al Mahdi envisions Khidr's "green essence" as the stuff from which Allah creates; from Khidr's light came the souls of "people of the right hand"—that is, prophets and holy figures. From Khidr's fire came Jann, "father of the jinn, a race of evil angels."[33] Khidr continues to function as a conduit for "all the energy generated into and around the Ka'ba"[34] and as the vessel through whom "all Muslims receive spiritual energy to strengthen the soul during the times of worship ... it was through him that the Prophets received their teachings.[35] In his reading of Khidr as Melchizedek, the King of Salem and immortal priest, from Genesis 14:18–20, Al Mahdi speaks from popular American Muslim discourses: in his widely disseminated Qur'an translation, Yusuf Ali also connects the two figures.[36] Frithjof Schuon likewise treats Khidr as a parallel to Melchizedek in his *Understanding Islam* (1963).[37] Both figures, Schuon contends in a 1978 article, represent "supraformal, universal, and primordial spirituality."[38] Al Mahdi's presentation of Khidr and Melchizedek as the same being does not amount to "syncretism" or a "bricolage" of disparate materials from separate traditions; it was already accessible to him as Islam.

Beyond the Melchizedek connection, Al Mahdi's Khidr narrative resonates with a prominent theme in Western metaphysical religion of the nineteenth and twentieth centuries, namely, the existence of superior beings that nurture humanity's spiritual development by sharing secrets. In his survey of theosophical and New Age epistemological strategies, Olav Hammer describes a recurring trope of ascended Masters who guide human progress from hidden locations on earth or even other planets and dimensions.[39] Helena Blavatsky (1831–1891) had claimed revelation from figures known as "Mahatmas," "Brothers," "Adepts," and "Masters," among other designations, including Egyptian teachers bearing such names as Tuitit Bey and Serapis Bey. Writers like Charles Leadbetter, Edgar Cayce, and Alice Bailey provided their own treatments of the masters. These invisible guides constituted a formal brotherhood and were capable of occupying human bodies as their vessels. They communicated with special individuals to intervene in human consciousness and usher in a more enlightened age. In some cases, Jesus appeared among the masters' ranks. Tibet and the Himalayas featured prominently as possible locations for the brotherhood, and writers such as George Adamski (1891–1965) claimed guidance from extraterrestrial teachers.[40]

Theosophical concepts of ascended masters, secret lodges, and occult hierarchies flourished in the Moorish Science Temple and Nation of Islam. Noble Drew Ali appropriated material from *The Aquarian Gospel of Jesus the Christ*, which author Levi Dowling presented as a direct transcription from the Akashic records. Dowling's work portrays Jesus's "lost years," during which Jesus studied under Egyptian, Indian, and Tibetan masters and realized his own divinity— not as the incarnation of a transcendent spirit but as a mortal being whose path remains accessible to all humans.[41] Ali reproduces these narratives in his *Holy Koran* and authorizes his own status as an Islamic prophet with an account of training at the Great Pyramid, where he joined the same secret priesthood that trained Jesus.[42]

Elijah Muhammad's theology features a council of twenty-four god-scientists, corresponding to the twenty-four elders referenced in Revelation, who predetermined world history for the next twenty-five thousand years. One god on the council, best knower of his time, carries special status as Allah. Writing each twenty-five-thousand-year period falls to a different council, each council with its own Allah.[43] The god-scientists are not immaterial spirits but Black men. In this system, Allah is not a spirit that becomes "incarnated" in a succession of bodies, because there is no spirit to incarnate; rather, "Allah" signifies a succession of mortal men who earn the title by way of superior knowledge and self-perfection.

With interest in the Nation of Islam and his own biblical exegesis, Al Mahdi constructs an AAC/NIH theory of the council. He identifies these elders as the "Sons of Allah" mentioned in Genesis, "mental giants" who descended to earth and established an "ultra-advanced civilization" prior to the separation of Africa and Arabia. They constituted "a special people of high order" sent to "bring about a people who would teach men, once again, the path of righteousness. Thereby keeping man from total destruction." They lived in Mu, the capital city of their empire of Salaam; from *Mu-Salaam*, "One of Peace," comes *Muslim*, "the highest title within all of the universe."[44] As with the Nation's construction of Allah as the god who leads the council of scientists, Khidr appears in AAC/NIH literature as head of an order in which the elders serve as priests. While Khidr's leadership remains consistent, Al Mahdi's Khidr narratives occasionally appear in tension with one another. In *Ancient Egypt and the Pharaohs* (1980), Al Mahdi writes that Khidr was the first of the "Sons of Allah" who descended to earth to procreate with the daughters of men.[45] In *Science of Healing* (1985), however, Al Mahdi claims that when these "sons of Allah" and "mental giants" married the "daughters of men," they enabled Khidr/Melchizedek to become physically manifest.[46]

These elders established mystery schools across the globe at sites such as Tibet, Persia, India, Easter Island, Mexico, the lost lands of Mu and Atlantis, and the Sudan. The most important mystery school was located in Egypt, where Jesus spent the last thirty years of his life inside the Great Pyramid training directly under Khidr, passing a series of tests for his scroll and title as a high priest in Khidr's order.[47] Echoing the Nation's association of Ezekiel's vision with advanced spacecraft, Al Mahdi writes that the mothership of Ezekiel's wheel represents a "high order" in which Jesus is prince and Khidr is king.[48]

In *The Man of Miracles in This Day and Time* (1983), Al Mahdi places Khidr among eight figures ("avatars") who occupy his body and work through him, producing effects in him that become visible to others. His avatars are Shaikh Al Qutb (disciple of Idris/Enoch); Isa al-Masih (Jesus, "merely a student of very great learnt men"); Yanaan (whose home civilization in "the eighth galaxy" is "100,000 years more advanced than this planet"); Zoser ("great Egyptian healer," builder of pyramids, and teacher of Imhotep); the Sudanese Mahdi (Al Mahdi's great-grandfather); Rahmah (an incarnation of Vishnu who came to earth among the "sons of Allah" in Genesis 6:4); and Khidr, "an angelic being" who is not only Melchizedek but also the angel Michael "when in the heavens." Al Mahdi writes that when these avatars work upon him, he can "manifest a flow of pure and inexhaustible love, a special grace that transcends all condition of karma (fate). In the Arabic language, this is called QADR." In one account, Al Mahdi asked whether human poets can match the eloquence of the Qur'an; as he gave his stunning answer ("We can"), his eyes changed color to a "piercing green."[49]

As a child, Al Mahdi's possession by these beings took the form of multiple personalities ("When I was a little kid, I was thought to be crazy") and strange powers, such as the ability to make candy materialize with a wave of his hand or fix broken radios and televisions without even touching them. Khidr first clearly manifested himself to Al Mahdi in 1970, at which point Al Mahdi began to learn of his "special assignments." Al Mahdi says that he is not exactly Khidr but a vessel through whom Khidr works and speaks in the world. *The Man of Miracles* includes photographs of Al Mahdi while in the possession of each of the avatars, demonstrating that when possessed by a particular avatar, corporeal features such as skin tone and the shape of his face change in correspondence to that avatar's attributes. Both volumes caption the image of Al Mahdi that often graced his booklets, showing him with his hooked staff, as "Isa al-Masih." The representation of Al Mahdi as Khidr shows him standing outside by a tree.[50] Al Mahdi writes of a ninth personality, "which is me. The person being utilized. Why? ... Only ALLAHU SUBHAANAHU WA TA'ALA, the Supreme Creator of all things knows."[51] Nor is Al Mahdi the only person who serves this function; Indian spiritual teacher Sai Baba was himself "an incarnation in the flesh."[52] These human vehicles are not to be conflated with Khidr or the other avatars; they remain passive sites at which these forces enact divine interventions.

Al Mahdi's connection to Khidr is marked by his possession of the Mihjan, the hooked staff that was carried by Abraham, Ishmael, Moses, and Muhammad. "The staff has great significance among Muslims," Al Mahdi explains, "and if a man is one of the relatively few who has acquired one (Mihjan) through the thousands of years, then men of all nations can respect him and rely on him for knowledge, truth, and guidance." Possession of the Mihjan also signifies membership in the ancient order of Khidr. Initiates into Khidr's order train in numerous schools and pass a sequence of tests before receiving their staffs.[53] Al Mahdi writes that along with gifts of frankincense, myrrh, and gold, the newborn Jesus also received the Mihjan (in advance of his training); the Three Wise Men were "Nubian mystics" and members of an ancient mystery school. After Jesus "passed on to a higher life," the staff remained in the custody of the Judahites; Bilal's father passed it to Bilal, who in turn delivered the staff to Muhammad.[54] In the 1970s, the Mihjan passed into the hands of Al Mahdi himself, who kept it in his Brooklyn masjid. Another staff that appears in photos and paintings of Al Mahdi, the *shuwba*, consists of a forked head (with the fork representing the junction of the two Niles) and is likewise "only awarded to those who receive the teachings from the Ancient Order of Melchisedek."[55] Calling attention to the similarity between the Mihjan's hook and the Arabic letter *lam*, Al Mahdi connects Khidr to Elijah Muhammad's 1967 vision of the *lam*. The letter signifies "lamb," as in the Lamb mentioned in the book of Revelation; this Lamb is not Jesus, however, but Khidr,[56] with whom Al Mahdi identifies his own spirit.[57] Al Mahdi's "76 trillion years" of Khidriyya knowledge reflects the entire knowledge of the material universe.[58]

This connection between Al Mahdi and Khidr/Melchizedek remained a prominent theme throughout Al Mahdi's career. Although the AAC/NIH's discursive and aesthetic makeovers caused the community to appear unstable and incoherent to outsiders, the figure of Khidr/Melchizedek preserved a consistent center.

SONS OF THE GREEN LIGHT

Halman observes that "the New Age Movement and Islam have intersected whenever Sufism has been introduced to the Euro-American baby-boomer, hippie, and yuppie generations."[59] The New Age–Sufism encounter developed not only as a white Orientalist appropriation of the "spiritual East" that inherited from movements such as the Theosophical Society, but also through globally interconnected esotericist networks in which figures like Inayat Khan creatively reconstructed Sufism for their transnational audiences. Moreover, Sufism as it appears in AAC/NIH discourse resists the image of "New Age Sufism" as essentially a liberal white domain. *Science of Healing* (1985, revised from the 1979 edition) depicts Al Mahdi sitting in meditation, his hands in mudra position. The pamphlet offers prescriptions for enhancing dhikr with breathing exercises and correct posture, and conceptualizes Muslim prayer movements as activators of energy flows from the crown seat to the third eye. Al Mahdi treats the Arabic *nafs* and *ruh* as equivalents of the Sanskrit *prana*, which he in turn defines as the substance of material creation, thereby presenting the soul and the entire universe in a microcosm-macrocosm relation. The recitation of divine names, accompanied by physical discipline and visualization, becomes a technology by which the green light that flows from Allah to Khidr can undergo channeling into one's crown chakra. Al Mahdi explains that he learned these techniques from his visionary teacher at the junction of the Niles: "One night, I became aware of a majestic being. My inspirational impression indicated that he was concerned with HEALING WORK.... I immediately identified him as the GUARDIAN OF THE EARTH."[60]

Science of Healing and *The Man of Miracles in This Day and Time* include an advertisement for the Sons of the Green Light, identifying Al Mahdi as "the formless in form" and "a temple of the incarnated divinity" that appears with human embodiment in order to teach humans to heal themselves "with pure mind" and to save the planet in accordance with its karma. "Ye are gods, not merely men," the ad proclaims. "The time has come again for the sons of God to be born in the pure light.... Now you can find your real self.... Are you earth born or are you born of the holy spirit?" Al Mahdi calls the prospective initiate to "attune yourself. Stimulate the latent centers within you. Open your third eye to new worlds of truth."[61] The advertisement includes a cut-out mail-in form in which the prospective initiate is to sign the statement, "I affirm with all sincerity that I wish to become a member of the Sufi Order of the Sons of the Green Light."[62] Al Mahdi promises, "Any questions that you have, can and will be answered if you are accepted into the Order," and offers training in extrasensory perception (ESP), astral projection, travel between dimensions, and communication with "the Masters of Awe."[63]

Readers find advertisements for the SGL in Al Mahdi's *The Travels of a Sufi* (1987), which tells the story of Shams ad-Din al-Tabrizi (transliterated as Shamsud Diyn), whose search for a master teacher caused him to become a master himself and the teacher of Rumi. The small tract includes images of Al Mahdi, with the Ansar masjid and a spaceship behind him. Throughout *The Travels of a Sufi*, Al Mahdi appeals to his readers to join him on the path: one ad invites the reader, "Don't walk alone.... The Sons of the Green Light welcome you. Remove the veil from your hearts and eyes and learn the discipline of the Sufi." Another ad presents the SGL's official "Meditation Mat," along with "An Nuwr," a glow stick that "radiates a soothing green light that will illuminate throughout your house. To activate the light stick, just bend it in half."[64]

Al Mahdi's Sufism intersects in his 1980s discourse with an increasingly salient theme in his work, often taken by observers as a later phase from the

1990s: Al Mahdi's intimate connection to technologically advanced extraterrestrial civilizations that have intervened in human history. Angels, he writes, are "masters from other galaxies." The twenty-four elders (including Yanaan, who occupies Al Mahdi's body and "arrived to this planet Earth" on March 16, 1970) travel by chakra-powered ships, which Al Mahdi presents as Sufi technology: "Raising the 'Self' being done together made it a 'mothership.'... Join the Sons of the Green Light and you will learn all about the masters and the hows and whys."[65]

The SGL emblem consisted of the Arabic masculine pronoun *huwa* inside a six-pointed star, itself inside an inverted heart ("'ISHQ, Divine Love of the Omnipotent"), in turn inside a seven-pointed star and crescent, often surrounded by a sixteen-petaled lotus flower (fig. 26). Al Mahdi writes that the shape of the star and crescent resembles the Arabic letter *nun*, which signifies *nur* (light), and he breaks down the meanings of the word's n-w-r root into *nur*/light, *wahy*/inspiration, and *ruh*/spirit. The lotus petals, Al Mahdi explains, represent the avatar's sixteen principles. "Each petal emits a revitalizing green light that emanates from the hands of the Master Al Khidr."[66] Advertisements for the SGL feature the Christian cross, Sikh khanda, Hindu Aum, Taoist taijitu and bagua, Egyptian ankh, and other symbols emanating as rays from the lotus.[67] In harmony with popular discourses in American Sufism, the SGL offers a "universal" order with a mission of "spreading divine love across the world." Al Mahdi writes, "all religions are good dogmas but... man corrupted the essence of these dogmas" and abandoned the universal heart of the matter, producing a multiplicity of competing sects instead. Recovering the "spiritual essence," the SGL "separates the religious people from the spiritual people"[68] and enables its initiates to "blossom and make the vertical contact, the contact with the heavens."[69]

Much like the Nation of Islam, the SGL trained its neophytes through sequences of initiatory lessons. The first lesson prepares them for initiation into the order. After forty-eight hours of abstinence from intoxicants, the initiate follows a detailed script for meditation and posture: "Imagine that you [are] in a great temple of a higher plane," the lesson reads, "and that you are being guided by the Master: AL QUTB, into the initiation chamber." "Sending love and vitality through it, unto the Spiritual Guide so that he may help you on your way," the initiate copies out the oath by hand: "I _____ having undergone a self initiation, hereby affirm that I have the sincerity and integrity to meet the requirements of the steps that are to come. Therefore, I solemnly vow to keep secret and uphold all of the tenants [*sic*] established by the Sufi Order of the Sons of the Green Light and to maintain a state of absolute purity and Divine Love."[70]

While most SGL literature was regarded as privileged information strictly for initiates of the order, Al Mahdi produced a more public pamphlet, *You and the Sons of the Green Light*, which initiates could use to educate their family and friends. The pamphlet's opening pages explain the significance of green as the "most divine" color, a powerful "healing force" controlled by al-Khidr/Melchizedek. The pure green light provides healing against diseases of both mind and body.[71]

While centering his Sufi order (and much of his broader authorization) on Khidr, Al Mahdi sometimes attributes his words to Al Qutb, another of his avatars and the name under he which he published several pamphlets during this period. Al Qutb speaks through Al Mahdi's pen as "an incarnation of the Spirit of Truth, a high priest after the Order of Melchizedek."[72] In the SGL's *Secret Document: The Second Step of the Sufi*, intended for neophytes, "Al Qutb" articulates his mission: "I descend to this plane, the formless in form, a temple of the incarnated divinity to guide you.... Revolve around me, feel my love and feed off my wisdom, for in me you will find understanding."[73] Every Sufi order, Al Qutb explains, is grounded in a lineage (*silsila*), and the SGL *silsila* traces through 'Ali to Muhammad, who himself is described as a descendant of the Essenes, whose roots trace to al-Awwaliyna, "children of the men of renown." Ultimately, the chain of SGL authority extends to "the original spark of creation called 'Adh-Dhaat.'"[74]

The SGL articulates its Sufism in recognizably "classical" Sufi concepts such as the *silsila*, Al Mahdi's embodiment of Al Qutb, and terms such as *'ishq* (divine love, excessive love, spiritual love, and complete devotion), while also promising future pamphlets "for the enlightenment of your spirit, and for the advancement of your soul" on such topics as telepathy, clairvoyance, metaphysics, reincarnation, meditation, the human aura, and exercises that will help initiates develop the third eye.[75]

Just as Al Mahdi turns his various rhetorical dials up or down when targeting different audiences, the SGL's Sufi universalism downplays Al Mahdi's emphasis on Nubian heritage. Throughout AAC/NIH literature, as we have seen, Al Mahdi portrays Nubians as possessing a capacity for spiritual connection and insight that distinguishes them from Amorites, demonstrated in Nubians' heightened sensitivity to music and recitation of divine names (dhikr). He may hint at this genetic predisposition to mysticism in the SGL pamphlet *Celestial Being or Terrestrial Being . . . Which One Are You?*, in which he tells the reader, "You have a very prophetic descendancy," but he leaves the explicit significance of race unspoken.[76] In contrast to the AAC/NIH's extensive engagements with Elijah Muhammad's teachings, white demonologies, and the stated mission to uplift global Nubian consciousness, SGL literature tends to disavow racial identities altogether: "You have no color or race. You are love not merely flesh."[77] While ostensibly moving away from metaphysical Africa, however, SGL theology resonates not only with the Nation's idea of Allah as a self-perfected man, but also with non-Muslim Afrocentrists such as Maulana Karenga, who argues that African spiritualities locate God within the human being, and Molefi Asante, who claims that in Yoruba and ancient Egyptian religions, God is immanent (as opposed to the absolute transcendence of God in "Abrahamic" monotheisms).[78] SGL literature also plays down Muslim jurisprudence (*fiqh*) and the patriarchal discipline of gendered interactions common in AAC/NIH media.

In the fifth study of the first degree, Al Mahdi (writing as Al Qutb) provides the hidden hierarchy of orders: beneath six celestial orders there are six terrestrial orders, which are divided into higher orders that have taken "secret abode" (located in the polar regions, the Gobi Desert, and the Bermuda Triangle) and lower orders that are more accessible to humanity (the orders of the Essenes, Brahamic orders, and Sufi orders). The Essene orders include the Persian magi, the Egyptian schools, Tibetan Lamaism, and Solomon's Masonic Lodge. The Brahamic orders are known by their famous graduates, among them Buddha, Confucius, Zoroaster, and "true" swamis and gurus. Al Qutb's roster of Sufis features an eclectic assemblage, including the poet Omar Khayyam, ninth-century polymath al-Jahiz, astrologer and philosopher al-Kindi, medieval historian Ibn Khaldun, and even twentieth-century mystical poet Khalil Gibran. All six terrestrial orders remain under the protection of Khidr, who emits a "healing Green Light" that in turn informs and empowers Al Qutb. Khidr, Al Qutb explains, "dedicates his time to the Sufi Order of the Sons of the Green Light and is not associated with any other spiritual school or organization here in the West." Al Qutb then names various ascended mystics, such as the prophets Enoch/Idris, Jesus, and Muhammad, noting that Moses was a member of the Order of Sheikh Khidr who failed to become a high priest because he failed Khidr's test of patience.[79]

While SGL lessons were intended only for members of the order, the SGL's themes resonated with broader AAC/NIH literature. Throughout AAC/NIH writings, Al Mahdi expounds upon the meanings and powers linked to specific letters of the Arabic alphabet, most prominently in his commentary on *lam*. "Each letter," Al Mahdi writes (under the name Isa Muhammad) in *Talisman* (1979), "has a magical power and a single letter might be developed into a design which could in itself be effective as a talisman."[80] Writing while occupied by the extraterrestrial teacher Yanaan in 1986, Al Mahdi breaks down Yanaan's name using classical Arabic *abjad*, which he presents in Five Percenter vocabulary as "Supreme Mathematics," and again interprets the name's Arabic letter *nun* (ن) for its visual resemblance to the community's six-pointed star and upright crescent. Yanaan's descent to earth corresponds to the dot (*nuqta*) over the *nun* descending to make the letter *ba* (ب), which stood for both Bennett (the comet that became visible from earth on March 16, 1970) and the sons (*bani*) of Allah.[81] SGL literature also elaborates on Al Mahdi's letter esotericism as a science of healing. We are told that the Arabic letter *thal* (ذ), for example, appears 4,677 times in the Qurʾan, "one for each of the 4,677 nerves and vessels which help to make up the human body and which make the pores of the skin vibrate and wake up in inner intelligence." These are the channels through which "ether power" becomes accessible to the "19,000 universes that lie within your being."[82]

As the 1980s progressed and the AAC/NIH's long-standing antagonism with Sunni communities intensified, Al Mahdi's Sufi project faced harsh criticism from Salafis who regarded Sufism in general as heretical. Philips's *Ansar Cult* polemic of 1988, which contextualized the AAC/NIH as one of "many movements" throughout Muslim history "bent on fighting Islaam, and destroying its values and teachings," weaponized the historical anti-Sufi/anti-Shiʾi slur of "Baatinite" (literally "esotericist") against the movement. In his attack against the AAC/NIH's "pagan roots" and "heretical" theology, Philips charges that Al Mahdi had identified himself as "God Incarnate" and formed the SGL to exploit a growing interest in Sufism among African American Muslims.[83] At this specific point in the feud between Philips and Al Mahdi, their mutual hostility echoes controversies between Saudi-networked Salafis and Muslims who embrace what could be termed "Sufi" phenomena, such as ecstatic vocal dhikr, scriptural esotericism, visionary encounters, and veneration of masters. Al Mahdi himself treats the issue as such. While references to Sufi concepts and practices might not satisfy an author of Philips's sectarian orientation, Al Mahdi responds in his massive *Rebuttal to the Slanderers* by contextualizing his lodge within "traditional" Sufism: "I was the Qutb (Axis) of the Sufi Order. . . . All devotees revolve around the center when we have our dhikr circles. If you disagree with that, go visit the 'Halvati Order' in Turkey and attack them, or the whirling Dervishes." *Rebuttal to the Slanderers* also defends the SGL by

FIGURE 26 Advertisement for the Sons of the Green Light, 1985.

demonstrating that Al Mahdi embraced Sufism long before any observable rise in Sufism's popularity among African American Muslims. As Al Mahdi argues in *Rebuttal*, the AAC/NIH was *always* a functional Sufi order where members followed the dervish path: he asserts that he only established the SGL because members of his community were *already* reaching the advanced spiritual rank of "complete human," *al-insan al-kamil*.[84]

CONCLUSIONS

Secret Document offers detailed prescriptions for dhikr, instructing the initiate on proper formulas as well as posture and breath, leading the practitioner to "feel invigorated, revitalized. . . . Practice this step until you receive the next sacred document which will contain step three of the Sufi way to the pure light."[85] Advancing through the lessons, the initiate ultimately seeks to reopen the third eye and attain the level of *al-insan al-kamil*: the seeker can "become a hospital within yourself, a MASHAFA'A . . . you seek to cure yourself and others by excelling in your mental powers."[86]

Moreover, Al Mahdi's Sufism offers a return to what the Nation of Islam and Five Percenter traditions term "knowledge of self": "you are a heavenly being and with the right guidance, you can become a god again."[87] As with the Nation and Five Percenters, the history of American Sufism cannot be isolated from histories of American metaphysical religion, including discourses that emphasize personal spirituality, intuition, esotericism, and the mind's capacity for accessing higher flows of energy and achieving union with a divine consciousness.[88]

American metaphysical traditions flourish throughout AAC/NIH media, in which Al Mahdi often discusses healing and spirituality in New Age vocabulary, making references to auras, ethers, chakras, kundalini, the third eye, the pineal gland, astral influence and projection, mindfulness meditation, and visualization. These references appear throughout the AAC/NIH archive with a consistency that belies the assumption that a "New Age" phase replaced his earlier commitments. Resonant with theosophical narratives, Al Mahdi's writings present these concepts as reflecting a universal wisdom found throughout the premodern world, principally in secret "mystery schools." This wisdom was suppressed by Christianity but had begun to resurface in the modern Age of Aquarius.[89] Does any of this "count" as Sufism, and if so, how does it get there? For Al Mahdi, such vocabularies and narratives do not require the work of "reconciliation" with Islam or "synthesis" with Sufism; rather, he engages Sufism as it already appears in a local dialect. He was not the first Sufi master in the United States to use such terms as "avatar" or to link Khidr to Melchizedek, nor does he simply move from one family tree to another and then concoct a relationship between them. To treat AAC/NIH Sufism as though the community stands before a buffet, picking from naturally and obviously separate categories, fails to engage the historical relationships between these categories and the instability of their borders.

CHAPTER 6

Islam Is Hotep
Ansar Egyptosophy

> I began thinking on the symbolic meaning of the pyramid in the religious world.... At the base of this pyramid we have four corners.... They saw creation as being composed of four fundamental or basic elements. The elements of man: solid, water, air and fire. Man in his nature is characteristic of these elements.... They built the pyramids because they had this knowledge and they built it showing as its base these four elements.... Not only that, a study of Ancient Egypt will reveal that circumcision didn't start with the Jews, it started with the Africans of Egypt. The belief in the soul and resurrection didn't start with Israel, it started with Egypt.
>
> —W. D. MUHAMMAD
>
> And there was Dr. Malachi Z. York ... / Called himself the Lamb ... / Built his own Egypt on the top of the sand.
>
> —KILLAH PRIEST

It is easy to imagine the AAC/NIH movement making a sudden sharp turn during the 1990s from Islam into a completely disconnected Egyptosophy.[1] Al Mahdi seemingly erased his Muslim past and embraced a new discursive universe of ancient Egyptian mysteries, expressed in the landmarks of the community's Georgia property, in photos of himself in community literature dressed as a pharaoh, and in his use of the name Amunnubi Rooakptah. The assumption that Egyptian motifs were not significant in earlier AAC/NIH materials, which fails to recognize the linkages between ancient Egypt and Islam in the AAC/NIH's multiple genealogies, supports a troubled image of the community as an experiment in random eclecticism. This chapter challenges that assumption, resisting the compartmentalization of AAC/NIH history into distinct "Egyptian," "Jewish," and "Muslim" phases.

Certainly, the post-1993 images of Amunnubi Rooakptah dressed in ancient Egyptian regalia depart from Al Imaam Isa Al Haadi Al Mahdi's white turban and robe. Beyond sartorial choices, one could also envision tensions between an identity grounded in Islam and another based on ancient Egypt, considering not only the question of Egypt's pre-Islamic polytheism but also the fact that Pharaoh appears in the Qur'an as the paradigmatic example of human wickedness. Nonetheless, I aim in this chapter to demonstrate that pharaonic Egypt was significant in various ways throughout the community's history. First, I introduce Egyptosophy as a tradition within American metaphysical religion, and specifically as a resource for African American Muslim movements, especially the Moorish Science Temple and Nation of Islam. Both communities intersect with Egyptosophy, incorporating pharaonic Egypt into their visions of Islam as an eternal Black tradition, and both construct Jesus as a trained initiate in timeless Egyptian—which also means *Islamic*—knowledge. I then trace the development of an AAC/NIH Egyptosophy that weaves into a singular narrative web stories of Abraham's family, pharaonic Egypt as a supremely advanced civilization of fantastic technological wonders, the persecution of Muhammad's family after his death, and the role of the Sudan in human salvation. Long before the community left Brooklyn to build its Egypt in the West, Egypt had been a significant part of its rhetorical nexus. Finally, I address the importance of Jesus as a student of Egyptian mystery schools, a thread running through the community's writings both before and after its Nuwaubian turn. This chapter situates Al Mahdi's Egyptosophy within American Muslim discourses and his own metaphysical Africa, highlighting continuity and coherence in its pharaonic imaginary.

OCCULT EGYPT AND ISLAMIC PHARAOHS

In Western fascination with the wisdom of ancient civilizations, Olav Hammer writes, "Egypt, especially, was a long-standing focus of projection."[2] Untranslated hieroglyphs had been seen as endowed with hidden mystical symbolism since late Hellenism. The notion of a secret, advanced Egyptian wisdom persisted through early Christianity to the Renaissance and reached a new level of "Egyptomania" after Napoleon's Egyptian campaign (1798–1801). Despite early colonial representations of Egypt as an Enlightenment project, a "blank slate" upon which Europeans could fashion a society of reason after the removal of Islamic despotism, a counterimage persisted of Egypt as a land of timeless occult wisdom.[3] Philosophical or symbolic Freemasonry, which emerged in the late seventeenth century, bolstered its authority with claims of ancient origins among the Israelites, identifying its founder as Hiram, the builder of Solomon's Temple. While early Freemasons did not claim Egyptian origins, preferring their biblical genealogies and forged connection to Solomon, the figure of Moses—recoded as a proto-Masonic "Grand Master" and known to have studied "all the lore of the Egyptians"—became a point of connection between Israel and Egypt.[4] In the next chapter, as the AAC/NIH tradition becomes Nuwaubu and expands upon its Egyptosophy, while also reconstructing itself in Masonic terms, these Egypt-Israel-Freemasonry connections become exceedingly potent.

Though the deciphering of hieroglyphs, starting with Jean-François Champollion's project in 1822, softened the image of Egypt as a fount of secret knowledge, Egyptian mysteries continued to fascinate seekers and would-be prophets. The golden plates of Joseph Smith's *Book of Mormon*, which offered the text in "Reformed Egyptian" hieroglyphs, resonated with contemporary imaginations of magical languages and of Egypt as the birthplace of civilization.[5] In 1859, the British publisher John Taylor argued in *The Great Pyramid: Why Was It Built? And Who Built It?* that the ancient architect must have been Noah, and that the Great Pyramid was a model of the earth. Later writers attribute the pyramid's design to Melchizedek, and the science of "pyramidology," the prediction of future events using measurements of the Great Pyramid, entered into the practices of several Christian denominations in the late nineteenth century.[6]

Egyptosophy enjoyed some prominence in the discourses of the Theosophical Society, which had grown out of the Hermetic Brotherhood of Luxor, an occult secret lodge that marked its publications with the ankh. Luxor initiate and Theosophical Society founder Helena Blavatsky, who was largely responsible for the Western popularization of the Egyptian *Book of the Dead*, claimed that ancient Egyptians were descended from the inhabitants of Atlantis and built the pyramids seventy-three thousand years earlier than their conventional dating.[7] She also claimed that her first book, *Isis Unveiled* (1877), came from the advanced masters who were apparently based in Egypt and included such unseen figures as Serapis Bey and Tuitit Bey.[8]

Blavatsky and other white esotericists who appropriated Egyptian mysteries were not necessarily interested in Egypt as part of continental Africa; instead, they took the ancient Egyptians' whiteness for granted and reprocessed Egyptian wisdom in harmony with assumptions of their own racial supremacy.[9] Confident that the ancient Egyptians belonged to "the Caucasian type of mankind," Blavatsky went further, suggesting, "If they were less copper-colored than the Aethiopians of our modern day, the Aethiopians themselves might have had a lighter complexion in days of old."[10]

Contemporary with a rising Aryanism that envisioned meaningful racial and spiritual links between ancient India and modern Europe, the Theosophical Society and other Western esotericists ultimately lost interest in Egypt and shifted their attention to India and Tibet. As racial anxieties and debates contributed to white seekers' favoring (Aryan) Indic civilization over (Semitic and/or possibly Black) Egypt as the privileged site for recovering universal spiritual truths, Blavatsky relocated her Beys from the Nile to the Himalayas, where the masters became mahatmas. Meanwhile, Afrocentric Egyptologists reimagined the pharaonic heritage, presenting Egypt either as a Black civilization or as a white civilization that remained indebted to its Black parent cultures in Nubia and Ethiopia.[11]

Even if many early producers of Western Egyptosophy were Aryan supremacists, the Egyptosophic tradition found new power in African American metaphysical religion. Streams of esotericist literature concerning Egypt as the original fount of all wisdom and spirituality intersected with Black intellectuals' argument for ancient Egypt's Africanity, leading to a privileged status for Egyptian esotericism among Afrocentrist metaphysical thinkers. In this fantasy image of the "Orient," sensational representations of pharaonic Egypt and Islamic tradition often blurred into one another. Noble Drew Ali (known as "Professor Drew, Egyptian Adept Student" early in his prophetic career) claimed that his *Holy Koran* (often cited as the *Circle Seven Koran*) was revealed to him when he encountered the last priest of a lost mystery school, who took him to the Pyramid of Cheops.[12] Noble Drew Ali privileged Egypt as the point of origin for African Americans, constructing a mythic history in which the biblical Moabites expanded from Egypt across all of Africa and founded the "Moroccan Empire" (the territory of which included Atlantis).[13] A major source text for Noble Drew Ali, *Unto Thee I Grant*, was published by the Ancient Mystical Order Rosae Crucis, the San José–based American branch of the Rosicrucians, which was founded in 1915 but imagined itself as originating from a secret order established in 1500 BCE, which built the pyramids not as tombs but as "places of study and mystical intuition" and inspired the religious reforms of Akhenaten.[14] Noble Drew Ali's Moorish Science was informed by a romantic Black Orientalism that had grown popular in Chicago. At the 1893 World's Columbian Exposition in Chicago (which had famously included a "parliament of world religions"), the most successful attraction was the "Street of Cairo," which featured a mosque and market at which attendees could purchase fezzes and other exotic imports. Just one month after the exposition, John George Jones established what would become the "Black Shriners," the Ancient Egyptian Arabic Order, Nobles of the Mystic Shrine, claiming that a figure known as Noble Rofelt Pasha had conferred degrees upon him.[15]

Gnostic priesthoods and modern Sunni revivalisms could conceivably blend together without challenge. While receiving initiation in Egyptian mysteries, Noble Drew Ali is also said to have encountered Ibn Sa'ud, future king of Saudi Arabia, who gave the new prophet his name. While some Muslims perceived an irreconcilable contradiction between celebrations of Egypt's pre-Islamic and Islamic heritage, Noble Drew Ali regarded one civilization's esoteric gravitas as bolstering the other's exoteric religion, holding Islam in higher esteem than Christianity in part because of Islam's association with the land of the pharaohs. At least according to some sources in Moorish Science circles, Noble Drew Ali could simultaneously boast credentials from both an ancient priesthood of Egyptian high magic and the founding monarch of a modern "Wahhabi" state.[16]

In his vision of a metaphysical Africa in which Islam and ancient Egyptian wisdom could coexist within a singular coherent tradition, Noble Drew Ali was not alone. The Fahamme movement, also known as the Ethiopian Temples of Islam and Culture, was founded by a Black convert named Paul Nathaniel Johnson, who took the name Ahmad Din when he joined the Ahmadiyya. Patrick Bowen writes that Johnson became a prominent Ahmadi missionary but experienced friction with Sufi Bengalee, who arrived from India in 1928.[17] Bengalee reportedly arranged Sufi practices exclusively for white converts but denied access to Sufism for Black converts on the grounds that they were not ready.[18]

By the early 1930s, Bowen writes, Johnson left the Ahmadiyya and started his own movement as Paul J. Achamad, "noble prophet" of the Ethiopian Temples of Islam, teaching that "African people, their culture, and their religion all originally came from Ethiopia, where their true religious culture was Islamic and their original language was Arabic."[19] Claiming distinctions such as the Ra Rasool, the "Culture Prophet," "Prophet of Amun-Ra," "Successor to the Gods of Kem," and "spiritually the King of the Negroes," he described his "science of Islam" as Fahamme, drawn from the Arabic triconsonantal root for "understanding."[20] Johnson regarded Islam as the original religion of humankind, but he also understood Islam, "son of Ancient Aethiopia, a child of Africa, Kem or Ham," to include ancestor worship, its name an amalgamation of the Egyptian deities Isis, El, and Amun. Johnson increasingly prioritized his Egyptosophic orientation, moving the community away from its earlier Muslim ritual practices, Qur'an readings, and Arabic studies. "Negroes are the only people in the world who have no God, no heaven, no hell, except those whom other races have taught him," Johnson writes in his *Holy Fahamme Gospel*.[21] Declaring that "Negro culture need not be Jewish nor Mohammedan, but a creed and a system unto itself," he had removed "Islam" from the movement's name by 1937.[22]

Though an exegete of the Qur'an and Bible who identified with Moses rather than Pharaoh and understood the pharaonic regime to have earned divine wrath for its oppression of the Hebrews, Elijah Muhammad held Egypt in high esteem as one of two centers of Black civilization first established by the tribe of Shabazz (the other being Mecca). The valorization of pre-Islamic Egypt continued in Nation of Islam tradition, expressed in Louis Farrakhan's sermon at the Million Man March when—facing the Washington Monument, an obelisk echoing Black Egyptian civilization—he spoke of the pharaoh Akhenaten destroying Egypt's pantheon to promote monotheism.[23] In *Black Muslim Religion in the Nation of Islam, 1960–1975*, Edward E. Curtis IV provides the example of a Nation family that appears in a 1965 issue of *Muhammad Speaks*. In their home, a statue of a guard of King Tut's tomb stands below a wall hanging of the opening words of the Qur'an—*bismillah ar-rahman ar-rahim* (in the Name of Allah, ar-Rahman, the Merciful)—in Arabic script. As Curtis notes, the pairing of such items could appear "odd or even heretical" to many Muslims, but for this Nation family they were "complementary symbols."[24] Links between esoteric Egyptosophy and Islam did not expire with the Nation's post-1975 turn to "orthodoxy," as W. D. Muhammad gave his own esoteric reading of the pyramids.[25] Yusuf Ali's commentary to his Qur'an translation also includes an essay titled "Egyptian Religion and Its Steps Towards Islam," which portrays ancient Egyptian intellectuals as achieving a rationalist grasp of monotheism, exemplified in Akhenaten's worship of the "One Supreme God."[26]

While Noble Drew Ali and Elijah Muhammad framed Egypt as timelessly Islamic, complicating what might appear as a commonsense boundary between the categories "Islam" and "Egyptosophy," non-Muslim Egyptosophists also informed Al Mahdi's Egyptian imaginary. In 1970s Brooklyn, a local contemporary of Al Mahdi's movement, Ra Un Nefer Amen (b. 1944), established the Ausar Auset Society as a project to revive Egyptian (Kemitic) wisdom. While drawing from its own eclectic blend of sources, including pre-Aryan Indic cultures and Kabbalah, the Ausar Auset Society argued that all of these traditions originated in Egypt. In its reconstruction of the Egyptian mystery school, the Ausar Auset Society offered the necessary training for human beings to unlock their inherent divinity. Afrocentrist authors such as Maulana Karenga (b. 1941) and Molefi Asante (b. 1942) also prioritized Egypt in their visions of African spirituality, both arguing that a truly African theology favors concepts of immanent divinity over the remote, transcendent god of "Abrahamic" monotheism. Both Karenga and Asante brought Egyptosophy further into encounter with Afrocentrism, the former by presenting Ethiopia as the origin of Egyptian civilization, which in turn becomes the source for Christian myths of virgin births and resurrected gods, and the latter by centering Egypt alongside Yoruba within his "African Cultural System."[27] In conversation with Egyptosophic Afrocentrists, Al Mahdi exposes and condemns "the Paleman" who "tries to make you think that Misr [Egypt] is separate from Africa."[28]

Over the course of AAC/NIH history, from the 1960s to its 1990s "Nuwaubian turn," we find diverse articulations of the relationship between Islam and pre-Islamic Egypt, enabling imaginaries of both naturally harmonious Black traditions and irreconcilable antitheses—whether these reflect the division between pre-Islamic *jahiliyya* (ignorance) and divinely revealed Islam or between indigenous Black wisdom and Arab invader culture.

AL MAHDI'S EGYPT

At least as early as 1972, Al Mahdi taught that Hajar, mother of Ishmael, was also the daughter of Imhotep (an "understudy of Zoser the master healer"), and it was from the pharaonic regime that Abraham learned how to genetically engineer pigs to provide food for white people.[29] Images of pyramids and ankhs appear in the earliest extant AAC/NIH literature.[30] The cover of *Eternal Life After Death* (1977) bears an image of Allah's name in Arabic, shaped to match the outline of a six-pointed star, placed inside the loop of an Egyptian ankh, itself within an Islamic crescent—remarkably similar to Nuwaubian logos of the 1990s (fig. 27). Inside the pamphlet, Al Mahdi displays a photograph of himself astride a camel in front of a pyramid with the caption "I, myself, was in the Great Pyramids reading the hidden words of truth." Al Mahdi asserts that "the pyramid draws magnetism and energy from the center of the earth as well as the poles" and charges that "the Amorite mind" cannot comprehend the magnitude of the pyramid architects' knowledge and sophistication; the pyramids indeed contain "the secrets of life and death." Al Mahdi writes that the "pyramid fields" of Egypt and the Sudan were first designed as "storehouses of universal knowledge" and "temples as well as tombs," adding that Jesus had studied in the pyramids under Melchizedek to become one of the twenty-four scientists mentioned in Revelation. This 1977 pamphlet does not provide the developed Egyptosophy that we will find beginning in 1980. Moreover, *Eternal Life After Death* also *blames* the pharaohs for misunderstanding the afterlife, as evidenced by their hoarding material possessions and employing the ankh as a guarantor of immortality. In a polemic against neo-Kemetic communities that appropriated the ankh, Al Mahdi scoffs, "The ankh is an ancient symbol worn by many youths today. Do you desire the life of this world to be everlasting?"[31]

Throughout the 1970s, AAC/NIH discourse engaged metaphysical Africa chiefly through connections to the Sudanese Mahdiyya and historical Nubia. Community literature around the turn of the 1980s shows an increased emphasis on both the Blackness and Islam of ancient Egyptians. "We refer to ourselves as Nubians," Al Mahdi writes in 1983, "knowing our origin comes from across the pyramids."[32] It was through the connection to Nubia that Al Mahdi and his community recognized themselves as the authors of civilization: "The land of our ancestors is the origin of all Sciences, mathematics, the mysteries."[33]

The site of Al Mahdi's visionary encounter with Khidr in the early 1970s was also the birthplace of humankind; Allah created Adam in the Sudan, fashioning his body from black mud found at the junction of the two Niles, after which Adam was placed in the Garden of Eden at present-day Mecca.[34] After his death, Adam's body was preserved in heaven, until descending in Abraham's time as the Black Stone that would be placed in the Ka'ba.[35] The kissing of the stone by pilgrims becomes a sacralization of both the Sudan and Black people themselves.

Ancient Egypt and the Pharaohs (1980) introduces a complex set of materials into the AAC/NIH corpus, portraying pharaonic Egypt as a technologically and spiritually advanced Islamic civilization. The booklet focuses on the figure

FIGURE 27 Al Mahdi, *Eternal Life After Death* (1977), front cover, incorporating an ankh into its star-and-crescent symbol. References to ancient Egypt are often assumed to represent the community's "post-Muslim" Nuwaubian era.

of Zoser/Abdul Quddus, a high priest in the Order of Melchizedek (and named in the 1983 pamphlet *The Man of Miracles* as one of the avatars that occasionally occupy Al Mahdi's body as a vehicle). Trained by Khidr/Melchizedek, Zoser became a scientist (writing works on alchemy and mastering the arts of healing), mathematician (whose formulas were later stolen by Pythagoras), artist (originator of hieroglyphics), and architect (developing lasers and methods of levitation by which the pyramids were constructed).[36] Zoser was known and worshipped under numerous names across the world; in Egypt he was Thoth, god of knowledge; in ancient Mexico he was identified as the gods Quetzalcoatl and Huehueteotl. The worshippers of Zoser failed to recognize that he was only a messenger of Allah.[37]

In *Ancient Egypt and the Pharaohs* and his later *Science of the Pyramids* (1983), Al Mahdi explains that the pyramids were not only tombs but, more important, archival centers in which the elders of Khidr's order preserved the "necessary knowledge" for humans to maintain their position as Allah's earthly *khalifah*.[38] These elders had once inhabited the city of Mu in their kingdom of Salaam, a land now covered by the Red Sea. When warmongering descendants of Cain shifted the earth's axis and forced a global disturbance, they successfully parted the Arabian Peninsula from Africa, creating the Red Sea and destroying Mu, along with much of what had once been the Garden of Eden. As Mu was submerged, the elders fled in their chakra-powered mothership. They first headed northwest to Egypt, where they built the pyramids with their knowledge of lasers and levitation.[39] The pyramids became home to mystery schools in which "the knowledge was locked away from mortal man so it would not be destroyed or stolen to be used by the Devil (paleman)." The pyramids' secret chambers housed libraries in which one could find the "Archaic Records," the collected scriptures of Allah's prophets.[40] The elders used the same powers that drove their spaceships to lock up their libraries: "When a pyramid is sealed," Al Mahdi explains, "the only possible means of getting into the interior of a pyramid is by mental means."[41]

The Great Pyramid of Giza was built at the center point of the earth's surface. "This was not a coincidence," Al Mahdi argues, as "the Elders knew science, astronomy and geography of each continent on earth. It was their fields so that they could construct similar schools of learning like this around the world," as evidenced by the appearance of pyramidal structures in various ancient cultures.[42] Traces of the mystery schools can be found at locations as diverse as Easter Island (where Zoser was revered in local mythologies as a birdman), the Americas, Tibet, India, and Yugoslavia. These scattered pyramids acted as broadcasting stations through which elders could send messages to one another, enabling communication between sites such as the Nile valley and Central America.[43] AAC/NIH literature describes their technology in terms of both advanced physical science and esoteric metaphysical knowledge. "These men had the intelligence to communicate back and forth from pyramid to pyramid by using their six and seventh senses," Al Mahdi writes. "The Amorite (physical Devil) calls this Telepathy." When explaining the use of such advanced technology in the distant past, Al Mahdi draws connections between these elders and Islamic revelation; the science of the atom had been made known to Muhammad by the angel Gabriel.[44]

Another member of the council of elders, Imhotep, was trained by Zoser, and the two of them guided Abraham, who journeyed to Egypt for help in his mission: the civilizing of white people. Imhotep informed Abraham "that these lepers are not Asiatic Black men, but Caucasus-Asians," meaning "deteriorating Asians."[45] While Al Mahdi calls the white people of Canaan "clean" lepers for their having been "civilized," Abraham's project targeted "unclean" lepers, covered in sores, who walked on all fours, ate uncooked meat, engaged in bestiality, and bred themselves to become "literally half animal and half man." In the Caucasus Mountains, these animalized lepers were so overtaken by their divine curse of leprosy that the carcasses of their dead piled up, further spreading disease and famine. To solve the health crisis, Zoser decided that white people needed a new animal, "something that was just as nasty as these creatures," to consume the dead bodies. This new animal would also curb cannibalism by providing meat for the Caucasians, who were otherwise willing to eat their own dead. The creature had to be filthy enough to resist disease and smart enough to outwit the lepers, yet stupid enough not to feel disgusted by the squalor in which it would live. Imhotep gave Abraham a symbol—a downward-pointing triangle inside a larger triangle—as instructions for Abraham to give to Zoser, who understood: the three points of the external triangle signified dog, cat, and rat, the animals that would be grafted together to make the Caucasians' new animal, the inner triangle. Just as Elijah Muhammad had taught that the pig had been grafted from dog, cat, and rat in a narrative that resonates with his account of the white race (which itself was created by an ancient geneticist), Al Mahdi reformulates the pig's origin story as a tale of white depravity, the marvels of ancient Egyptian science, and harmony between pharaonic Egypt and Abraham's religion.[46] After engineering the pig, Imhotep gave Abraham his daughter, Hajar, saying that although Hajar would have been a queen in Egypt, it was better for her to be Abraham's slave. Imhotep understood the future greatness of the lineage that would come from Abraham's first-born son, and he wanted Egypt to share in that legacy.[47]

In *Ancient Egypt and the Pharaohs*, the story of Abraham's developing the pig under pharaonic guidance provides a segue for Al Mahdi's focus on the Ishmaelite prophetic heritage. Expounding upon monotheism and polytheism, he presents the former as evidenced in ancient Egyptian worship of Aton, and the latter as a fabrication of Greeks and Babylonians.[48] Al Mahdi writes that just as Imhotep trained Abraham, Abraham educated the Hotep dynasty in monotheism. Al Mahdi asserts that Queen Tiye, mother of the famously monotheist pharaoh Akhenaten, was descended from the Sudanese peoples that had been the original settlers of Mesopotamia, and that she passed Abraham's religion to her son. Akhenaten's attempted reform of Egyptian religion, therefore, is integrated into Al Mahdi's system as a return to the Hoteps' pure Islam.

Al Mahdi stakes diverse claims upon Egypt. In *Egypt and the Pharaohs* and *Science of the Pyramids*, he emphasizes pharaonic Egypt as a scientific/mystical marvel while weaving Islam into the narrative; elsewhere, he gives priority to Egypt as a Muslim civilization, while also celebrating Egypt's pre-Islamic wonders. The AAC/NIH publication *Al Imaam Isa Visits Egypt 1981* (fig. 28), presenting photographs and narratives from Al Mahdi's travels, operates primarily as a demonstration of Al Mahdi's transnational Muslim credentials. It prioritizes Egypt as a site of authoritative and classical Islamic tradition rather than of pre-Islamic pharaonic heritage, providing photos of Al Mahdi visiting masjids, sitting in minbars, and meeting Muslim scholars; only in the back pages does the reader encounter photos of Al Mahdi at the pyramids. The opening pages report an interview between Al Mahdi and Egyptian Muslims in which Al Mahdi speaks as a representative of American Muslims. One interviewer asks, "Do many people of your community in the West speak Arabic classical and read Qur'an as well as yourself?"—to which Al Mahdi answers that no Muslim community in the West can match the AAC/NIH in its devotion to raising children fluent in Arabic. The first reference to pre-Islamic Egypt confronts tensions between Al Mahdi's Islamocentrism and anti-Muslim Egyptocentrism: the interviewer asks whether Muslims can claim polytheistic civilizations as part of their heritage. Should the AAC/NIH define pre-Islamic Egypt as a Black glory or an age of ignorance (*jahiliyya*)? Al Mahdi answers that ancient Egyptians were not polytheists at all, but Muslims. Blaming white devils for stealing and distorting Egyptian knowledge, Al Mahdi singles out "a Negro called Dr. Yosef Ben J." (Ben-Jochannan), who makes unfounded assertions

FIGURE 28 Ansaru Allah Community, *Al Imaam Isa Visits Egypt 1981* (1981), front cover.

Islam Is Hotep • 179

without ever having trained in hieroglyphics, Hebrew, or Arabic, or even spending extended time in Egypt. The devils have misunderstood the hieroglyphics and denied ancient Egypt's actual religion. A photo of Al Mahdi touching hieroglyphic carvings bears a caption explaining that Egyptians used hieroglyphics to communicate "belief in tawhiyd (Oneness of Allah)."[49]

In its concluding pages, *Al Imaam Isa Visits Egypt* shows Al Mahdi at various ancient sites, including a photo of him hunched over in a low-ceilinged tunnel, apparently entering one of the great pyramids. Al Mahdi marvels at the technological achievement of the pyramids and elaborates on Zoser/Abdul Quddus but does not advance the full mythology that he offers in other works. He does, however, proclaim that "Egypt is the birthplace of hidden wisdom and mystic teachings," and he argues that Egyptosophy does not conflict with Islam: "What the Europeans try to hide from the Nubian (Black Man) is that all things come from Allah and all great civilizations stem from Islaam."[50]

Al Mahdi connects pharaonic Egypt to the heroes of Islam in his 1988 revised edition of *Who Was Noble Drew Ali?* with an account of the *Suhuf* (pure pages), the revelations of Adam, Seth, and Enoch. Before Abraham cast out Hajar and Ishmael, he gave Hajar the *Suhuf* to pass on to their son when he matured. Hajar and Ishmael first journeyed to the land that would become Mecca, but Hajar later took the child to her homeland of Egypt for the purpose of finding him a wife. In Egypt they reunited with her family, who became custodians of the *Suhuf* for centuries, until 'Ali and Fatima, fleeing A'isha's persecution, sought refuge in Egypt. 'Ali and Fatima continued south into the Sudan, where the texts had become "dormant amongst the mystics" and accessible only to "beings of higher knowledge." Al Mahdi's teacher and imam at the great masjid in Khartoum, As Sayyid Mahmuwd, guarded the *Suhuf* and passed them to Al Mahdi, who made them public for the first time.[51] Given that AAC/NIH genealogies present all Nubians as descended from the union of Abraham and Imhotep's daughter, Hajar becomes an important node of connection. The Imhotep priesthood in turn becomes crucial to the preservation of Islamic knowledge, keeping these artifacts safe for the *ahl al-bayt*. In Al Mahdi's metaphysical Africa, Islam and Egyptosophy are not separate traditions.

Crucial to Al Mahdi's imaginary of pharaonic Egypt is the notion that ancient Egyptians were Muslims, even performing ritual prayer in postures and movements similar to Muslim salat. In AAC/NIH literature, harmony between Islam and ancient Egypt does not reflect a bricolage of unrelated ingredients; they relate under the rubric of a universalizing Black perennialism. The Nubian, Sudanese, Asiatic Black Man suffers no contradiction in claiming both Islamic and pre-Islamic Egypt. AAC/NIH literature does maintain a disconnection, however, between imaginaries of classical Egypt as a Black Islamic civilization and its present reality as a nation dominated by pale Arabs. Al Mahdi concludes *Science of the Pyramids* with condemnations of modern Egypt for having turned its back on the Sunna, becoming a haven of alcohol, drugs, and Western fashions. Al Mahdi charges that only his own followers recognize the nature of the pale devil and raise their children in truly Islamic environments.[52]

JESUS IN EGYPT

In the late nineteenth century, multiple narratives claimed that Jesus had traveled to India and studied in "the school of the Brahmans." The notion of Jesus as an initiate of Indic wisdom, Simon J. Joseph observes, "emerged within a European fascination with the 'mystic East' and the 'ancient wisdom' of India." European interest in Indian spirituality developed alongside ideas of race that saw Aryan and Semitic peoples as racial and spiritual opposites; "Jesus in India" narratives thus helped to Aryanize a Jewish prophet. The narratives also helped to forge connections between Jesus and the Buddha, nourished perennialist themes of a singular esoteric core that connected all religions, and supported New Age reconstructions of Jesus as an exemplar of hard-earned personal growth—an adept who became one with the divine by virtue of a path accessible to everyone, rather than via the privilege of supernatural incarnation. In the second half of the twentieth century, New Age seekers increasingly embraced the image of Jesus as a wandering student of Buddhist monks and Brahmin yogis.[53]

In the alternative religious discourses of the period, writes Susan Nance, "many perceived Jesus as a profound example of a degree of perfection that all men and women could strive for through examination of the wisdom of mystical brotherhoods which dated back to the ancient Holy Land and Egypt."[54] The text from which Noble Drew Ali extracted the first half of his *Holy Koran*, Levi Dowling's 1907 work *The Aquarian Gospel of Jesus the Christ*, depicts Jesus wandering the world to study not only with Buddhists and Brahmins but also with Greek philosophers, Persian sages, and Egyptian adepts. Dowling claimed transcendent authority for his own work, having accessed the supernal Akashic records. Dowling's Jesus expresses various themes that would resonate with Noble Drew Ali: the realization of one's "higher self," secret brotherhoods, and the existence of a *sophia perennis* that encompasses diverse cultures of the ancient world. Islam, as Noble Drew Ali understood it, honored Buddha,

Confucius, and Zoroaster in addition to Muhammad and the Israelite prophets. Noble Drew Ali's Jesus, when teaching God's unity to the Hindus, argues that despite the differences in names, it is the same God; Allah is equivalent to Zeus, Jehovah, and the Egyptian god Thoth. Jesus also travels to Heliopolis and undergoes initiation into the "temple of the sacred brotherhood," which bears witness to his resurrection from the dead.⁵⁵

Noble Drew Ali's construction of Jesus in Egypt comprises a tangled multiplicity of genealogies, a series of rhizomatic connections between popular New Age discourses of the early twentieth century, Black Egyptocentrism and Egyptosophy, Freemasonry, and even—insofar as the Ahmadiyya would have been positioned within Noble Drew Ali's milieu of Chicago after the Great Migration—transnational "mainstream Islam." In the contexts of colonial India and postmigration cities such as Chicago, accounts of Jesus as a traveling initiate of mystery schools circulated in global Muslim currents. The Ahmadiyya held that Jesus was buried in Kashmir⁵⁶ and published a photo of Jesus's reported tomb in a 1923 issue of *Moslem Sunrise*.⁵⁷ Noble Drew Ali's entering an Egyptian pyramid in order to become an Islamic prophet would not have been a contradiction or paradox; Jesus Christ was himself a Muslim prophet who learned Islam in the pyramids. Echoing Noble Drew Ali's narrative of Jesus as an initiate of Egyptian wisdom, Elijah Muhammad asserts that Jesus "was a well learned man," evidenced by his training in Egypt. In Elijah Muhammad's narrative, Jesus graduated from the Islamic university of al-Azhar and then walked six hundred miles "from Cairo University in Al-Azhar into the land of Israel" to start his mission.⁵⁸ With ahistorical reference to Christ studying at a Muslim university established nine centuries after his lifetime, the distinction between Egypt's "pre-Islamic" and "Islamic" traditions dissolves.

Al Mahdi portrays Jesus as a student of wisdom traditions and schools throughout the ancient world, with special focus on Egypt. While the Jesus-in-India narrative had served to Aryanize the Israelite Jesus, Al Mahdi's depiction of Jesus in the pyramid affirms a Black perennialism in which pharaonic and Abrahamic lineages are intertwined. AAC/NIH literature presents Jesus as learning from sages in every locale that he visited (with the exception of Athens, where he *taught* sages). Jesus entered the Essene brotherhood at a temple near Jordan where the Dead Sea Scrolls were housed, received knowledge from Jains at their temple in Palian, mastered Vedic literature under a Brahmin priest, studied with Tibetan adepts and accessed their vast archive in Lhasa, stopped at Persepolis ("the great spiritual center of that time"), and studied under his own Judahite tribe in Rashidim, Ethiopia. In Medina, seemingly an "Islamic" city centuries before Muhammad, he encountered the Wise Men who had visited him at birth and learned from them the history of the ancient masters. In Mecca, he learned of the future comforter, Muhammad.[59]

In Egypt, Jesus attended an annual meeting of Sufis and mystics at the Great Pyramid of Giza[60] and entered the mystery school that Hajar had attended, where he passed seven tests to earn "the highest degree any man would ever receive."[61] His first test was in sincerity: "For many days, he remained alone in a room in which the light was faint and mellow like the light of early dawn. He read the sacred texts, and studied the hieroglyphics." When a priest tried to convince Jesus that the other priests had grown jealous of him, and that he must save Jesus's life, Jesus rejected the deception and thus passed the first test. He passed his second test, in justice, after spending many days locked in a chamber and seeing through the trickery of two men who came to him in priests' garb and offered to help him escape. For his third test, in faith, Jesus was placed in a "Hall of Fame" filled with shelves of "books by the master minds." A priest came to Jesus and offered the hall of fame as a worthy achievement in itself: "Why seek for further mystic lights within these dens?" Jesus then entered the "Hall of Mirth"; rejecting its carnal pleasures to instead help the hungry and poor who had been turned away, he passed the test for his fourth scroll, in philanthropy. He passed his fifth test, in heroism, when priests bound him in chains and Jesus's superior force of will revealed the chains to be "merely worthless cords that parted at his touch." His sixth scroll, in love divine, was won when he resisted the temptations of a beautiful woman who played music and sang "songs of Israel." At this stage, Jesus established himself as a "wiser student of Al Khidr."[62]

Passing the seventh test required that Jesus work in the "Chamber of the Dead." Jesus first completed a "senior course" focused on "the secrets of mystic lore of Egypt," and then entered this chamber, where he encountered a small girl and learned from her that "grief and hopes and fears are reflexes from the lower self and that all emotions are prayers that arise from human loves, hopes, and fears; that perfect bliss cannot be ours until we have conquered these." Having passed the seventh test, Jesus stood before the high priest (Melchizedek) and received the final scroll, Ruhu Allah (spirit of Allah). Melchizedek told him, "Allah will confirm your title and degree," after which a white dove entered the temple and Jesus heard a voice declare, "This is Ruhu Allah." At this station, Jesus became a priest in Melchizedek's order and joined the council of elders, occupying the twenty-fourth seat (available to the prophet of the age). At the age of 120, Jesus passed away. His biological father, the angel Gabriel, brought

FIGURE 29 Al Haadi Al Mahdi, *Gospel of John, Chapter One* (1984), front cover, displaying the crescent with six-pointed star containing an ankh, reflecting the significance of ancient Egypt in AAC/NIH Christology and anticipating the Nuwaubian symbology of the 1990s.

his body to the top of the Step Pyramid so that it could dematerialize, each element of his body returning to its place in the universe. His spirit ascended to the second heaven, where he would remain with John the Baptist.[63]

This story, which appears in *Was Christ Really Crucified?* (1980) and *Science of the Pyramids* (1983), can also be found in the 364-page Original Tents of Kedar volume *The Final Messenger: Christ the Final Word* (1991). Al Mahdi reproduces the narrative of the seven tests, essentially copied verbatim from *Was Christ Really Crucified?* He adds a postscript in which Allah summons "Angelic beings, Extra-terrestrials," to claim Jesus's soul. To prevent human beings from worshipping Jesus's grave, Gabriel brings Jesus's body back to the pyramid so that it can properly rejoin the universe.[64] Regardless of how one categorizes the community's changing discourses, its story of Jesus in Egypt remains consistent in iterations roughly a decade apart. Later, after the Nuwaubian turn and the migration to Georgia, Al Mahdi—now Malachi Z. York—published *Jesus Found in Egipt* (1996), which recalibrates connections between traditions, positioning "Abrahamic" religions as derivative offshoots of an Egyptosophic perennialism. Nonetheless, *Jesus Found in Egipt* preserves the Ansar vision of Jesus—who in this work appears as the third of three distinct Jesuses—as a student of Indian and Egyptian mystery schools, whose postmortem remains were carried atop a pyramid "to decompose naturally with the elements of nature."[65] The post-Brooklyn community did not build its Egyptosophic archive from scratch (fig. 29).

CONCLUSIONS

Noble Drew Ali exhibited no fear of contradiction in his drawing from Islam and pharaonic Egypt; he became a Muslim prophet inside a pyramid. Elijah Muhammad looked to Egyptian civilization as evidence of timeless Black greatness, which by definition meant timeless Muslim greatness. AAC/NIH accounts of the pyramids' relationship to Islam cannot be reduced to "syncretic" hodgepodges compiled from naturally unrelated materials. In the context of the AAC/NIH—as natural a state as any—the connections were already established. AAC/NIH material built upon these connections with an image of Islam eternally anchored in Nubia and Al Mahdi's visionary experience of Khidr at the junction of the two Niles. Incorporating ankhs alongside stars and crescents in its earliest media, Al Mahdi's Islam always possessed a built-in Egyptosophy.

While it is not my aim to claim "orthodox" or "classical" credentials for the AAC/NIH by finding precedents or similarities in broader Islamic tradition,

AAC/NIH treatments of the pyramids are not dramatically different from the ways in which Muslims in other contexts have imagined pharaonic Egypt. Premodern Muslim commentators offered a variety of interpretations of pre-Islamic Egypt, including praise of the ancient Egyptians' scientific and occult sophistication (even claiming that ancient Egyptians, informed in part by astrology, could make "pictures that moved" and give birth to babies who could already speak), identification of a particular pharaoh with the prophet Idris/Enoch, and the belief that pyramids were tombs of prophets, which reinscribed the pyramids as worthy *Islamic* sites of Muslim pilgrimage and ritual veneration.[66] Medieval scholars such as al-Idrisi (d. 1165) and al-Maqrizi (d. 1442) held that the occult figure of Hermes—identified in numerous Islamic traditions as the ascended prophet Enoch/Idris—had built Egypt's temples to store documents after the Flood; al-Maqrizi notes that "all the Egyptians' knowledge of alchemy, magic, talismans, medicine, astronomy, and geometry were set down" on the temple walls of Akhmim.[67] Al Mahdi (repeating the claims of Ivan van Sertima and other Afrocentrist intellectuals) asserts that the Sphinx lost its nose to Napoleon's army in an act of racial insecurity meant to erase its Nubian features, but the nose was actually destroyed by a fourteenth-century Sufi, Muhammad Sa'im al-Dahr, who was horrified to see that other Muslims made votive offerings to the Sphinx. Al-Dahr perceived a clear boundary between *jahiliyya* polytheism and authentic Islam, but some of his Muslim contemporaries drew their boundaries differently. Like other Muslims throughout history, the AAC/NIH made its own decisions about what counted as Islamic.

CHAPTER 7

The Pyramidal Kaʿba
Malachi Z. York and the Nuwaubian Turn

> God taught me that he has pictures of the Martian people.... You have people on Mars! Think how great you are. Ask the white man if he has any out there. We have life on other planets, but he don't.
>
> —ELIJAH MUHAMMAD

The community's migration to Georgia as the Tents of Abraham and its eventual reconstruction as the United Nuwaubian Nation of Moors (UNNM) could mark the point at which Al Mahdi (thereafter known as Dr. Malachi Z. York) becomes especially challenging terrain for unfamiliar readers.[1] In UNNM media, he presents himself as a metaphysical Egyptologist, intergalactic master teacher, Native American tribal leader, and Freemason. He appears in the garb of an ancient pharaoh in one photo, wears a feather war bonnet in another, and in a third wears a Masonic fez and apron. Meanwhile, he still claims to embody the ultimate fulfillment of Black Islam, having inherited, decoded, and refined the teachings of those who came before him, among them Elijah Muhammad, Daoud Faisal, Noble Drew Ali, and Allah (the former Clarence 13X), though he simultaneously disparages Islam as "poison."

While 1993 saw dramatic transformations in the community, Nuwaubian literature still echoes earlier sources, repeating key themes and maintaining claims from the Bushwick era. This chapter covers the community's physical migration to Georgia, which corresponds to its ideological relocation from Muslim identity to Nuwaubu. Though York vehemently distanced himself from Muslim identity, I focus on the continued presence of Islam as an important resource in Nuwaubu's "post-Islamic" materials. This chapter also demonstrates that the resources meaningful to the community, while seemingly "eclectic" or even "random" and "incoherent" to some observers, were deeply intertwined in genealogies of metaphysical Africa.

ESCAPE FROM NEW YORK

At least as far back as the 1973 confrontation with Mosque of Islamic Brotherhood members in Harlem, the AAC/NIH experienced hostility and threats from other Muslim groups that would escalate in the late 1980s.[2] While we cannot measure the damage of Abu Ameenah Bilal Philips's 1988 anti-Ansar polemic with concrete data, the book enjoyed strong distribution and the gravitas of endorsement from formal authorities in Saudi Arabia. Philips's work appears to have been devastating not only in its Salafi-informed critiques and its testimony from a member of the Mahdi family that Al Mahdi had fabricated his lineage, but also—and perhaps primarily—in its interviews with former members, who attested to Al Mahdi's hypocrisy, greed, and financial and sexual exploitation of his followers. Al Mahdi's writings from Monticello as El Haady, condemning estranged followers who had left the community owing to "Shaytaanic whispers and suggestions," suggests that Philips was effective. Philips at least concerned Al Mahdi enough to warrant a 315-page counterpolemic, *The Ansaar Cult: Rebuttal to the Slanderers* (1989), and frequent demonizations of Philips throughout AAC/NIH literature and tape-recorded lectures. Al Mahdi was also motivated to launch a six-hundred-page attack against Sunni Muslims at large, his *360 Questions to Ask the Orthodox Sunni Muslims*, which makes frequent mention of Philips and warns that Islam will "perish" under the "fake Islam being pushed by the Wahhabis of Saudi Arabia and the Ikhwani Muslims of Egypt." The book is attributed to "Reverend Dwight York" with explanations that he was indeed trained as a minister, and that since Philips and Siraj Wahhaj mockingly referred to Al Mahdi by his birth name, he decided to counter them with "the kind of book a 'Dwight York' would write."[3]

In 1990, sectarian violence confronted Al Mahdi with his personal vulnerability. Rashad Khalifa, whose findings of a "mathematical miracle" regarding the number nineteen in the Qur'an were embraced by figures as diverse as

Al Mahdi, Louis Farrakhan, leading Nation intellectual Tynetta Muhammad, W. D. Muhammad, Ahmed Deedat, and even officials at Al-Azhar University, was assassinated in January, stabbed to death in his Tucson masjid. The murder was immediately linked to theological controversies; though Khalifa's mathematical analysis of the Qur'an had once been given the stamp of approval by "orthodox" authorities, his anti-hadith positions alienated him from Sunni communities in the 1980s.[4] The Lamb described Khalifa as "a wise man and an extremely intelligent man" and a "Nubian messenger," and wrote that Sunni Muslims (who had embraced the miracle of the number nineteen until Khalifa began criticizing hadiths) killed Khalifa because "he no longer complied with their mythology of Islam."[5] Responsibility was ultimately attributed to Jamaat al-Fuqra, the mystical jihadist organization that had grown from the splintering of the Dar ul-Islam in 1980 and bombed a Portland hotel owned by spiritual leader Rajneesh in 1983.[6]

On April 22, Sayyid El Nosair, a Sunni Muslim later convicted for his involvement in the 1993 World Trade Center bombing, reportedly walked into a class at the AAC/NIH Bushwick Avenue masjid and asked to see Al Mahdi. According to Al Mahdi, Nosair had planned to assassinate him but was stopped by Al Mahdi's Swords of Islam security force. In November, Nosair assassinated New York–based Jewish Defense League leader Meir Kahane with a .357 caliber pistol.[7] While antagonisms with Sunnis intensified, Al Mahdi attempted to smooth over relations with Farrakhan's Nation by recanting his claims on its founder. In *An Apology to the Nation of Islam, the True Followers of the Honorable Elijah Muhammad* (1990), Al Mahdi disavows his conspiracy theories surrounding Fard Muhammad, insists that unidentified "people of Chicago" had misled him, and reveals that he was personally corrected by Elijah Muhammad in a dream. In an unprecedented departure from his usual confidence, Al Mahdi promises that his followers have been ordered to burn all copies of *The Book of Laam*. Al Mahdi and a number of followers began to spend less time in Brooklyn, favoring their Jazzir Abba property in the Catskills. Jazzir Abba had long been a refuge from the city's chaos: Al Mahdi purchased the land in 1983 after an attritioned follower, disguising himself in Ansar women's *khimar*, stormed an afternoon class at the Bushwick masjid, stabbing four men (seriously or critically injuring three of them), starting a fire, and brandishing a pistol before he was subdued.[8]

Beyond the threat of physical violence, Al Mahdi was also legally vulnerable. In her memoir of life as one of Al Mahdi's wives, Ruby S. Garnett recalls that shortly after the move from Brooklyn to Jazzir Abba, Sullivan County officials "started to harass him and started hitting him with all sorts of taxes and violations of one thing or another. We were probably there less than 2 years when Doc started making plans to re-locate to Georgia."[9] But Al Mahdi's legal troubles extended beyond county tax and zoning issues. A 1992 FBI memo, categorizing the community as a "domestic security/terrorism" concern, observes, "More recently, information has been received . . . of criminal activity taking place within the AAC and at the direction of its leadership."[10] This included word from multiple informants connecting Al Mahdi to the 1979 murder of Horace Green, a Bushwick community leader who had spoken out against Al Mahdi's expansion in the neighborhood. During its initial investigation, the NYPD had interviewed Al Mahdi, who explained that he had always gotten along well with Green and had no idea why anyone would harm him. Al Mahdi also offered the NYPD his bodyguard's assistance in case men were needed to fill a lineup.[11] In 1991, the FBI learned from several sources that a former AAC/NIH member and enforcer for Al Mahdi, Hashim Muhammad (a.k.a. "Hashim the Warrior"), had reportedly murdered Green.[12] In addition, the FBI memo alleges an extensive criminal history, implicating the community in homicide, arson, extortion, bank robberies, welfare and credit card fraud, prostitution, drug trafficking, the use of AAC/NIH locations as contact points for criminal operations, and even possible connections to 1990's Islamist coup attempt in Trinidad.

Al Mahdi had been on the FBI's radar at least since 1972, when his literature was found in a fugitive Black Panther's apartment; investigators at the time came to believe that Al Mahdi himself was a former Panther. In 1976, two former AAC/NIH members came to the FBI's Buffalo office to report that Al Mahdi was leading a criminal enterprise and that they feared for their lives. In 1987, Al Mahdi was arrested after applying for a passport with false identification, for which he ultimately received probation.[13] The 1992 memo calls for continued investigation of Al Mahdi and the community, noting that the New York office "anticipates placement of a source within the AAC to monitor present ongoing criminal activity" and was in contact with a former member who would talk. Additionally, "two female individuals have recently been identified as having primary responsibilities for finances within the AAC. New York anticipates interviewing and debriefing these individuals within the next 180 days." Given the delegation of responsibilities within the AAC/NIH, these women were probably Al Mahdi's wives. The FBI's Atlanta and Baltimore offices also planned to pursue possible informants. In Philadelphia, where the Nation of Islam's Mosque No. 12 had essentially merged with the Black Mafia Family,[14] the FBI developed a strong source of information about AAC/NIH criminal activity and was "also pursuing potential ties between leadership of the Philadelphia AAC and leaders of the Junior Black Mafia based on allegations through source information and telephone toll records."[15] According to Robert Rohan, an attritioned former member, York was well aware that the federal agents had infiltrated his community and "would speak indirectly to them in class to justify his earnings and speak about how we have over a thousand stores making $1000 or more each month and what we can do with this type money."[16] If Al Mahdi, like Elijah Muhammad before him,[17] knew of the FBI's growing interest and presence in his masjids—a probable scenario, given the FBI's multicity investigation, which included nearly twenty documented informants and the pursuit of Al Mahdi's wives—the retreats to Sullivan County and then rural Georgia could be read as a survival strategy.

Whether the threat came from sectarian rivals or law enforcement, whatever drove Al Mahdi from Brooklyn might have been the force that pushed him to rebrand himself, for the Catskills camp witnessed his new identity as Rabboni Y'shua Bar El Haady. During this time, he also changed the property's name from Jazzir Abba to Mount Zion and redesigned the community's aesthetic and ritual dimensions, leading to popular treatments of the early 1990s as his "Jewish phase." The Lamb ceased using Islam-coded terms such as "masjid" (replaced by *Manzilur Rab*, "House of the Lord") and removed Muhammad's name from community prayers and the call to prayer ("your pagan Adhan") on the grounds that "Orthodox Sunni Muslims" had taken to worshipping Muhammad as a false idol just as Christians had done with Jesus.[18] He increasingly attacked sexism in Muslim communities, condemning "fundamentalists and religious fanatics" who erased women from their traditions and erroneously masculinized their genderless god.[19] On December 22, 1991, at five community chapters on the East Coast, women taught their own classes for the first time. Community pamphlets announced that women, "now unveiled," will "no longer be expected to shut up and sit down."[20] On a 1992 lecture cassette, the Lamb affirms that "women should be able to pray alongside of us or even in front of us . . . lead prayer, call to prayer," citing the hadith in which Muhammad authorizes Umm Waraqa to act as imam.[21]

Between feuds with various Muslim groups and possible legal peril, community sources and former members' accounts alike report that around 1992 at Mount Zion, the Lamb announced that a coming surge of anti-Islamic prejudice would render Muslim identity unsustainable. Garnett mentions a moment at which the Lamb intimated that the community must pursue a non-Muslim future for its survival: "He'd called a meeting and asked us to come up with ideas on what kind of clothing we wanted to start wearing. He said we'd eventually end up being targeted if we didn't start to appear more western. He told us that the world would eventually start to target Muslims and it was imperative that we not be associated with anything related to Islam."[22]

While Garnett writes as an attritioned former member, her account is corroborated by the community's narrative. A 1993 pamphlet explains that a year earlier in the Catskills, the Lamb "predicted we would stop living the life of a Muslim," promising that Islam would soon come to be associated with violent extremism and that "your so-called Arab brothers are leading you down the road of destruction.... So to all of you Siraj Wahhaj's and Louis Farrakhan's you better disassociate yourselves with these Arabs or you will just be another thing of the past."[23]

Around the same time that Al Mahdi battled local adversaries in Blackamerican Islam, links to his metaphysical Africa's Islamic center began to break down. Philips's *Ansar Cult* included a statement from Muhammad Ahmad's grandson, Is-haaq Khaleefah, who had met Al Mahdi in the Sudan in 1973, attesting that Al Mahdi's claim of Mahdiyya lineage was a complete fraud.[24] Meanwhile, Al Mahdi's dream of the Sudan as an Afrocentric alternative to Saudi-centered Sunni revivalism—briefly rejuvenated with the return of his alleged cousin Sadiq al-Mahdi to power in 1986—disintegrated with a 1989 Islamist military coup. The new government, led by 'Umar Hasan Ahmad al-Bashir, with Hasan al-Turabi as its ideological architect, envisioned itself as the vanguard of a new global pan-Islamism and aspired to a pure Islamic state, which included the criminalization of apostasy and the persecution of non-Muslim minorities.[25] By 1993, Al Mahdi had returned to his birth name (York) and severed what had been his primary tether to transnational Muslim networks, condemning the Sudan's economic and ideological relationships to Saudi Arabia: "We don't want any association, in any form or fashion with the so-called Muslim world, not even with our own brothers of Sudan! Many of the Mahdiyya are beginning to surrender to the Islamic world for money."[26] In 1996, after a Maryland group called Majma Al-Bahrayn circulated flyers that identified Sadiq al-Mahdi as the true imam of the Ansar against "those who misuse and misrepresent Islam," York blamed Sadiq for the Ansar's decline in the Sudan, even attributing Al-Hadi's assassination to Sadiq's founding of the Umma Party in the 1970s (the party had actually been established by Sadiq's grandfather, 'Abd ar-Rahman, in the 1940s). York deflects questions of his Mahdiyya credentials with the implication of a greater claim: "We Don't Need ... Any Ties To Sudan Or

The Mahdi Family. Our Facts Stand For Themselves. I Am Linked To The Stars And BEYOND."[27]

BECOMING NUWAUBIAN

From its new 476-acre commune in Eatonton, the community produced a stream of pamphlets that placed increasing emphasis on Christ's imminent return for the chosen 144,000 and York's pivotal role in that event—a prominent theme of earlier AAC/NIH works such as *Christ Is the Answer* (1977) and *I Don't Claim to Be . . .* (1981), in which he rejects accusations that he had personally identified himself as Christ. In his new pamphlets, the Lamb treats Islam as a wayward Christian sect, calls on Muslims to recognize Christ as Allah's son ("not by conception, but by spirit"),[28] imagines Christ returning with twelve spaceships from the Mothership Nibiru (the "Crystal City" of Revelation 21:10–11),[29] identifies himself as the reverend and founder of an "Egiptian Church of Karast,"[30] and presents ancient Egyptian and Sumerian systems as the obscured roots of biblical and Islamic traditions. Resonant with the community's shifts at Mount Zion, pamphlets increasingly targeted various Black Hebraisms, as in *360 Questions to Ask the Israeli Church*, *360 Questions to Ask a Hebrew Israelite*, and *Is Haile Selassie the Christ?* (1994). Mirroring his Muslim genealogy as the twelve-year-old mentored by Daoud Faisal in Brooklyn, he claimed to have received his bar mitzvah with Rabbi Wentworth Arthur Matthew in Harlem at age thirteen.[31]

Early pamphlets from Georgia identified the community as Holy Tabernacle Ministries and presented its new symbol as a crown topped by the familiar upright crescent and six-pointed star (the star now containing an Egyptian ankh) (fig. 30). On the front of the crown appears a subtle *huwa*, the Arabic masculine pronoun, in Nubic script. The origins of the star and crescent were now traced to images of ancient Egyptian deities such as Isis, Hathor, and Djehuti/Thoth, and the *huwa* became a reference to the Egyptian god Hu, representing "the creative force of will," the divine presence, and "the love of our people the Nuwaubian race." The symbol also appears with a new version in which the crescent points downward and is accompanied by Zulfikar, the famous double-bladed sword of 'Ali. This redesigned emblem "symbolizes the teeth of the noble african lion, who roams the jungle of mother Africa, as the king, proudly dominating his crown."[32]

As noted above, Al Mahdi changed his own name, becoming Dr. Malachi Z. York, sometimes presented as Malachi Zodok York-El or Malachizodok-El.

FIGURE 30 "The Savior," Dr. Malachi Z. York, 1993.

The new name was not entirely new: as we shall see in the next chapter, York had maintained a well-known double life since the late 1970s as simultaneously Al Imaam Isa Al Haadi Al Mahdi and aspiring R&B singer-producer-mogul "Dr. York."

Upon their arrival in Georgia, community members briefly adopted a dress code that included cowboy hats, cowboy boots, large belt buckles, and blue jeans. The dominant visual presentations and visual culture, however, increasingly drew from Egyptosophy. York named his commune Tama Re and ornamented it with ritual spaces that emphasized pharaonic glories, including sphinxes, a large image of Jesus in a Plains Indian war bonnet crucified on an ankh, and multiple pyramids, including a central black structure with gold trim that could look to Muslim eyes like a pyramidal Kaʿba. Community literature explains that the pyramids were constructed for "connection with our spiritual elders through meditation," but also as "preparation for the alignment of the inner planets which according to scientific calendars is to take place May 5, 2000."[33] Framing Tama Re as his "Egypt in the West," York declared, "We no longer need those pyramids out there where them Pale Arabs are at, that dry desert. We don't belong out there."[34] He prescribed specific acts for pilgrimage to Tama Re, including instructions for recitations in his new Arabic-derived language, Nuwaupic; bathing (*ghasul*); fasting (*el saawum*); and ritual movements around the pyramids.[35] In a departure from earlier literature, York identifies various Muslim practices as plagiarisms from pharaonic Egypt: using ancient art as evidence, he argues that the hijab and the fez were inspired by Egyptian queens[36] and kings,[37] and that the pharaoh Amenemhat III had erected a large granite cube for worship to the sun god Amun, which influenced Muslim veneration of the Kaʿba.[38] Even the Qurʾan "supposedly revealed to Muhammad" amounted to Gabriel's sharing scriptures that were already written by the Neteraat,[39] and York's career as a Muslim leader amounted to just one station on his followers' path to divine *neter* status.[40]

York's material from the 1990s onward elaborated his 1983 claim to serve as corporeal vessel for transcendent masters. Of these "avatars," he increasingly identified with "the Green One," Khidr/Melchizedek,[41] as well as with Yanaan, who had come from the eighth galaxy. He sometimes referred to his extraterrestrial identity with coy intimations. In 1991's *Book of the Five Percenters*, when acknowledging Elijah Muhammad's vision of the Mothership's pilots as having large heads and slanted eyes, he identifies them as extraterrestrials and says, "Of course all of us don't look like this."[42] After the migration to Georgia, York revised and developed his extraterrestrial narrative, naming Yanaan/Yaanuwn's galaxy (now the nineteenth galaxy, not the eighth) as Illyuwn (recalling *'Illiyun*, mentioned in the Qurʾan 83:18–21 as a place in paradise where the records of the righteous are held) and designating his home planet Rizq (from the Arabic word for provision, which appears more than fifty times in the Qurʾan).

While York turned up his Egyptosophic and extraterrestrial dials, he also added entirely new dials to his discursive control panel. These new resources include the pantheons and mythologies of ancient Sumerian civilizations as presented through the lens of "ancient astronauts" theorist Zecharia Sitchin, who argued that alien "gods" came to earth from an undiscovered "Planet X" (Nibiru) and attributed humanity's development to their intervention as genetic engineers.[43] In his reading of Sumerian pantheons, York understands Anu as Allah, Marduk as Khidr/Melchizedek, and the Anunnaqi deities as extraterrestrials equivalent to the "angelic beings," the Eloheem. York also claims this status for himself: "I, YAANUWN, Am An ANNUNAQI Or What You Would Call an Extra-Terrestrial... What You Call An Angelic Being, An Eloheem," who arrived in human form to save "The Children Of The ELOHEEM (ANUNNAQI), The Banaat... The Chosen 144,000."[44] While York's Sumerian material is uniquely post-1993, he had identified himself with the extraterrestrial Yanaan/Yaanuwn at least a decade earlier, and throughout the 1980s had developed his ideas of angels as intergalactic travelers from whom some humans were descended.[45]

York's elaborations on "ancient astronaut" themes overlap with the "reptoid thesis" of David Icke, who argued that the Anunnaqi engineered the human race to mine mono-atomic gold. Icke's "533-page Rosetta stone for conspiracy junkies," *The Biggest Secret* (1999) expresses Icke's "totalizing ambition to weave numerous sub-theories into an extraordinary narrative that is both all-inclusive and all-accounting." Icke racializes his narrative of alien lizard imperialism: Icke's Anunnaqi (or Anunnaki), having created human beings to work as mining slaves, then produced the "super-hybrid" Aryan peoples to rule humanity on the Anunnaqi's behalf. A "Babylonian Brotherhood" of Aryan lizard overseers, more popularly known as the Illuminati, have reigned across human history from the pharaohs to modern presidents and prime ministers, and are responsible for the wars, oppression, authoritarianism, and ideologies of racism that have plagued the species.[46] To more effectively control human societies and serve the interests of their Anunnaqi lords, the Illuminati have also produced and promoted the false religions of Judaism, Christianity, and Islam.[47] York's own intergalactic mythology departs from the Sitchin/Icke construction in that it does not read the Anunnaqi as oppressive alien imperialists but as benevolent angelic forces, and offers a theodicy rooted in the earlier AAC/NIH demonology of two hundred fallen angels descending to earth.[48]

In works such as *The Melanin-ite Children* (1995), York provides detailed intergalactic genealogies of various races and species and their respective habitats (including communities under the earth's surface in Shamballah, a popular theme in Western occult literature). His narrative of human origins reads as an Afrocentric reworking of these "ancient astronauts" narratives. He also incorporates popular melanin theories that had spawned a "small publishing industry" of Afrocentrist writers, including Frances Cress Welsing, who envisioned melanin-loaded pineal glands as the reason why the Dogon could access vibrations from Sirius B and thereby obtain their advanced astronomical knowledge.[49] In his own melanin theory, York asserts that Nubians received abundant melanin from the Anunnaqi, in whose likeness they were created.[50] Returning to his AAC/NIH writings on Amorites, York writes that white people fell into their animalistic condition thanks to the impact of the mountain climate on their iodine levels, which deprived them of melanin, causing their mental instability.[51] York's account of white racial origins, while preserving and revising his earlier "cursed seed of Canaan" narrative, also speaks to the Nation of Islam in new ways; in addition to Amorites, York now writes of Flugelrods, a subterranean species grafted by Yaaquub, who became the ancestors of modern Nordic peoples.[52]

Nubian spirituality remains biologically advantaged. "You Are The Original Descendants Of The WOOLY-HAIRED BEINGS, The Deities Bearing Nine Ether," he writes in *The Melanin-ite Children*, "THE ANUNNAQI, ELOHEEM Who In Our Cream History Were Created 76 Trillion Years Ago By Etherians, Coming By Way Of Nibiru, From The 8th Planet RIZQ, Of The 19th Galaxy ILLYUWN."[53] He scolds his readers for the internalized oppression that causes them to hate the way they look: because they were created in the image of the Anunnaqi/Eloheem, who themselves have "9 Ether hair" (in contrast to the "6 Ether" hair of white people), this amounts to hatred of the gods.[54]

Despite these divine origins, Nubians lost their Barathary gland, a pea-sized gland in the hippocampus that enabled telepathy, clairvoyance, intuition, and psychometry, meaning that they can no longer communicate with the Anunnaqi.[55] York's brain was repaired for his mission; while still in the womb, his body underwent neurological modifications to enable an "intellect higher than other normal Earth Beings who have had their Barathary Glands removed."[56] The radio silence between Nubians and their extraterrestrial ancestors/creators, a "spell" lasting six thousand years, is to be broken by York via a process that will start in the year 2000. In the year 2030, the spacecraft Nibiru will dispatch its smaller "sham" ships to earth to retrieve the 144,000 "worthy passengers," whose Barathary glands will be restored.[57]

York's ostensible departure from Islam and embrace of extraterrestrial mythologies does not mean that he erased his Islamic archive; rather, he locates Sumerian pantheons and "ancient astronauts" narratives within the Qurʾan. According to York, humanity's origin from angelic alien scientists is the secret of the very first verse that Muhammad received (96:1, which becomes 1:1 in

York's chronological arrangement of the Qur'an). The verse commands, "Recite in the name of your lord who created"; for York, "your lord" (*rabbuka*) is not Allah/Anu, but rather Allah/Anu's son Enqi, who is responsible for the genetic engineering of humanity.[58] The angels' objection to Adam's creation in 2:30 (8:30 in York's order), their questioning whether Allah would create one who causes mischief and bloodshed on the earth, becomes a debate between Enqi ("your lord") and the "angelic messengers," identified as Eloheem/Anunnaqi.[59]

To read York's trajectory as moving between separate discursive matrices of "Islam" and "UFO religion" neglects not only the connections within his thought but also the ways in which UFO narratives were established as Islamic resources prior to York's project and among his contemporaries. Spaceships visiting earth were already thinkable as Islamic, constructed as such most famously in Elijah Muhammad's Mothership and Louis Farrakhan's account of his visionary ascension aboard the Mothership in 1985.[60] UFO themes also appeared in the Hebrew Israelite discourses of Yahweh Ben Yahweh, whose biblical exegesis argued that God traveled in spaceships,[61] and who included images of flying saucers in his illustrated Bible and in the murals on his Nation of Yahweh temple walls. Between the Nation of Islam and the Nation of Yahweh, York would have been an outlier had he *not* adopted UFO narratives. York's exegesis of Revelation reads the "New Jerusalem, coming down from God out of heaven" in 21:2 as a "Mothership." He repeats Elijah Muhammad's view of the Mothership as a carrier for smaller vehicles: "Nibiru holds 2,088 shams, which are passenger crafts, that can hold 50 passenger crafts each totaling 144,000; these are those prepared just like a bride adorned for her mate." York identifies this Mothership as "the same craft that Muhammad was taken up in a craft called a Buraaq."[62]

Nation sources report that Farrakhan boarded the Mothership in 1985 while visiting the ruins of an Aztec temple dedicated to feathered serpent-god Quetzlcoatl in Tepoztlan, Mexico. The location was neither random nor insignificant. "For Farrakhan," writes Michael Lieb, "Quetzlcoatl is a very important figure" with whom Farrakhan partially identifies; Farrakhan's narration of his ascension also presents Elijah Muhammad's inclusion of the Aztecs in his vision of Blackness. The Aztecs were "dark-skinned beings, pyramid builders: our ancient forefathers."[63] Shortly after Farrakhan's vision, his *Final Call* newspaper included an editorial from Wauneta Lone Wolf titled "The Mothership on Big Mountain," which reads Hopi traditions through a lens informed by the Mothership narrative. Lone Wolf interprets petroglyphs to signify flying saucers, claims that the Hopi have "called down" UFOs, and recalls a personal communication that she experienced with the Mothership.[64]

From the early 1990s onward, York took a growing interest in the indigenous peoples of the Americas. A 1991 pamphlet refers to a forthcoming Al Mahdi volume, *History of the Black Indians*, promising to demonstrate "how the Native Americans (Indians) and Nubians (Blacks) are one and the same family of the tribe of the Prophet Abraham's covenant." It was also in 1991, around the start of what is typically termed his "Jewish period," that Al Mahdi first modified his family tree to claim descent from Ben York (1779–1893), "a Nubian slave who mixed with the Seminole Indians" and guided the Lewis and Clark expeditions.[65]

Newsletters from 1997 assert that York's mother, Mary C. Williams, was the daughter of an "Egyptian Moor who wore a fez" and was descended from Yamassee, Massachuset, and Moorish heritages. Through his maternal grandmother, York then traces his descent to Ben York (a.k.a. Ibn Ali), whom he depicts as both Native American (Yamassee) and Moorish. Ben York was in turn the son of "Old York," Yusef Ben Ali (1756–1861), a "Malian Moor" who came to the Americas on a slave ship. York clarifies here that Yusef Ben Ali was not himself a slave but a "crew member and an Arabic translator who spoke 19 languages." Yusef Ben Ali was also descended from the Idrisid dynasty, the "first Arab rulers of the whole of Southern Morocco" and direct descendants of Muhammad's Ethiopian companion, Bilal b. Rabah. In addition, York traces a genealogy for David P. York, the man named as his father on his birth certificate, identifying David as another descendant of Old York. However, York does not explicitly concede that David was his biological father, thus preserving his patrilineal connection to the Sudanese Mahdiyya.[66] Though Mary happened to have married a man named York, it was from her ancestors that he claims the York name. "The line of descendancy among American Indians is through the mother," a community staff writer explains, "unlike your Biblical and Koranic Beliefs, where it passes through the father." For this reason, Malachi York had previously ignored his matrilineal name, living instead under the name Al Mahdi and the tribal name Dongolawi. He reclaimed Black Eagle, his matrilineal Native American name, after a chance encounter with a bald eagle at Jazzir Abba/Mount Zion in the Catskills: "there was no doubt in his mind that this was a sign from the ancient ones."[67]

Dominic Montserrat writes that in the 1990s, "Native American belief systems compete with Egypt for the title of pre-eminently spiritual."[68] These competing brands in the New Age marketplace blend seamlessly together within York's metaphysical Africa. Since the early 1980s, York had taught that Zoser, master healer and teacher of Imhotep, was venerated as Quetzlcoatl in the Americas, and that the elders of Khidr's order built pyramids all over the world as archives and broadcast towers for advanced global communication. Still writing as Al Hajj Imam Isa Al Haadi Al Mahdi in 1990's *The Paleman*, he explains that Nubians from the lost city of Atlantis came to South America's eastern coastline, commingled with the Edomites (East Asians) there to produce the "so-called American Indian," and "influenced the culture of the Inca, Aztec, and Maya civilizations."[69] York's Native American discourse speaks from and to a narrative that had become virtually canonical among Afrocentrist thinkers, in which ancient Africans had come to the Americas circa 700 BCE and influenced the flowering of Olmec civilization in what is now Mexico. The theory that ancient Egypt and the Americas shared a mutual heritage, which developed as an answer to the problem of pyramids on opposite sides of the Atlantic, dates to the nineteenth century; the argument appears in Ignatius Donnelly's *Atlantis: The Antediluvian World* (1882), which still circulates as a prominent New Age text. Donnelly argued that similarities between ancient civilizations separated by a vast ocean proved the existence of the lost continent Atlantis. Later literature argued that ancient Africans did not need a land mass to enable travel between hemispheres but had in fact crossed the Atlantic nearly two millennia before Europeans; after them, the next ships to reach the Americas came not from Spain but from the African Muslim Empire of Mali. Disseminated most widely by Ivan van Sertima's *They Came Before Columbus* (1976), this narrative was endorsed by such Afrocentrist luminaries as Molefi Asante and Maulana Karenga in the late 1980s and early 1990s.[70] York refers to his followers as Yamassee Indians and identifies Yamassee as the "tribal name of the Olmecs, the original Nuwbuns 'African people' from Nuwba, the original name of 'Africa.'"[71] His metaphysical Africa thus includes indigenous American cultures and forges a link between his followers and their adopted home. "When we arrived in Eatonton, Georgia from New York back in 1993 A.D.," York writes, "many people from town assumed that we were part of some militant, Islamic organization."[72] Instead, York says, the Yamassee, who had been "chased off their land" in the seventeenth and eighteenth centuries by Spanish and British settlers, were now returning to their "sacred land."[73] As their leader, York appeared in community newsletters wearing a large Native American war bonnet and seated on a throne that featured ankhs and his six-pointed star in an upright crescent, identifying him as "Chief Black Eagle" (fig. 31).[74] York presents himself as president of a "Sovereign Nation," the Yamassee Tribe of Native Americans,[75] with the power to issue passports, identification cards, reclamation forms, and birth certificates.[76]

York's Yamassee claims place him in a new relationship with questions of indigenous peoples' rights and a growing Moorish Science discourse regarding

FIGURE 31 York as Chief Black Eagle, head of the Yamassee Nation. From York-El, *The Constitution of U.N.N.M.: "The United Nuwaubian Nation of Moors"* (1992).

legal sovereignty, particularly their intersection at claims that Black people (Moors) are indigenous Americans.[77] From the beginnings of Noble Drew Ali's prophetic career in Chicago in the 1920s, themes of nationality and citizenship had been integral to the Moorish Science mission. Incidentally, Moorish Science legends claimed that Noble Drew Ali was born to a Moroccan father and a Cherokee mother, both of whom had joined the teaching circle of famous Muslim reformer Jamal ad-Din al-Afghani.[78] The 1980s saw an important encounter between these discourses in the Washitaw de Dughdahmoundyah movement, led by Empress Verdiacee "Tiari" Washitaw-Turner Goston El-Bey and articulated in her *Return of the Ancient Ones* and in various booklets by Dr. R. A. Umar Shabazz Bey. According to the Washitaw, the empress remains the rightful owner of the entire domain covered in the Louisiana Purchase. Washitaw adherents hold that the Washitaw Muurs [sic] were a "highly civilized society of technically and spiritually advanced, woolly-haired Blacks who were INDIGENOUS (Native) to North America," settled in the Americas contemporary to Moses,[79] and built pyramids all over the premodern world.[80] For evidence of Nile-Mississippi trading relationships lasting thousands of years, Washitaw point to ancient ceremonial mounds in Louisiana, the work of their ancestors. Examining the decentralization and diversity that characterize Washitaw discourse, Spencer Dew observes that Washitaw narratives draw from numerous religious orientations, including Native American spirituality, Christianity, Islam (including Moorish Science),

The Pyramidal Ka'ba • 201

and "ancestor-based spirituality rooted in African symbolism."[81] York endowed his community's land in Eatonton with significance through his own Washitaw Moorish narrative. Moving to Eatonton, home of the Rock Eagle Mound, signified a move to "our ancestors," the Washitaw mound builders, who themselves were descended from the Olmecs and "Malian Moors."[82]

York's Nuwaubian community also developed as an assemblage of Masonic orders. York established numerous lodges, including the Brotherhood of Imhotep, Sacred Society of Anubis; the Daughters of Zoser, Sisters of Isis; the Ancient Egyptian Order; and the Ancient and Mystic Order of Melchizedek (AMOM), Lodge 19, which succeeded York's Islamic lodge. While the AMOM fraternity was founded in Georgia in 1995, "our spiritual order was incorporated in 1984 A.D. in Brooklyn, New York, as the Universal Order of Love—Sufi Order, Sons of the Green Light."[83] Rohan suggests in his memoir of his time as a Nuwaubian that Freemasonry was "the last school of thought" that York adopted prior to his arrest, and that this rebranding was contemporary with York's move to Athens, Georgia, to avoid criminal investigations of Tama Re.[84]

Freemasonry, like other resources that are accentuated or marginalized at various points, was present in York's imaginary throughout his work—including not only his anti-Masonic polemics but also his breakdown of the word "God" as "Gomar Oz Dubar," meaning "Wisdom, Strength, Beauty," derived from Masonic texts.[85] York's Freemasonry does not exist in an intellectual universe separate from his Egyptosophy or Islam. Black Freemasonry boasts a long tradition as a leading force in Black social, political, spiritual, and philosophical uplift, and Black Freemasons were pioneers in the intellectual reconstruction of African diasporic consciousness. Prince Hall (1738?–1807), founder of the African Lodge of Boston in 1787, creatively reinterpreted Psalms 68:31 ("Princes shall come out of Egypt; Ethiopia shall soon stretch out her hands unto God"), which had previously been employed to encourage subservience and obedience among slaves, to call instead for active struggle toward a divinely promised redemption.[86] Hall's redirection of the verse's consequences would turn Psalms 68:31 into a powerful resource—"the most quoted verse in black religious history," as Albert Raboteau observes[87]—for later Ethiopianism and a range of thinkers and communities, including Ras Tefar I, numerous Muslim writers, and York. Black Freemasons such as Hall and African Lodge chaplain John Marrant (1755–1791), in arguing for the legitimacy of Black Freemasonry, challenged and rewrote popular narratives of the African role in human progress and enlightenment. Contemporary with the beginnings of Black Freemasonry, discourses tracing Freemasonry's origins to Egypt enabled Masonic lodges to become compelling sites for the reclaiming of African civilizational legacies, which also opened new windows into biblical knowledge and the place of Black people in sacred history, as Moses—"educated in all of the wisdom of the Egyptians" (Acts 7:22)—became a student of Black knowledge.[88] Martin Robison Delany's *Origin and Objects of Ancient Freemasonry* (1853) locates Freemasonry's beginnings in the "earliest period of the Egyptian and Ethiopian dynasties," and asserts that "the Egyptians and Ethiopians were the first who came to the conclusion that man was created in the similitude of God." For Delany, as Scott Trafton summarizes, "Africa produced Egypt, Egypt produced Masonic knowledge, and Masonic knowledge produced the world."[89] Black and white Masonic historiographies, while often overlapping in their content, thus differed in their consequences. As Maurice O. Wallace observes, "While white Freemasons have claimed descent from ancient Egyptian stock and style as consistently as their black counterparts, only those histories authored by black Freemasons record the ancestral Egyptians as black."[90]

The imagined Egypt-Freemasonry linkage was even connected to York's Native American discourse; in the Afrocentrist classic *Stolen Legacy: The Egyptian Origins of Western Philosophy* (1954), a work called "as much a mystic-ritualistic, and more specifically Masonic, work as it is an Afrocentric one,"[91] George G. M. James argues that the Grand Lodge of Luxor established branch lodges all over the ancient world, including lodges "among the American Indians and among the Mayas, Aztecs and Incas of Mexico."[92] This foundational Afrocentrist work was among the volumes reprinted by the African Islamic Mission under York's brother, Al Imam Obaba Oyo.

By the 1920s and '30s, which produced Moorish Science and the Nation of Islam, Black Freemasonry had become the most powerful window through which many African Americans understood Islam and Muslims. In 1921, Punjabi Ahmadiyya missionary Muhammad Sadiq sent five hundred letters to Masonic lodges across the country, inviting them to Islam. The next year, Abdul Hamid Suleiman reached out to the "Black Shriners" (Ancient Egyptian Arabic Order, Nobles of the Mystic Shrine), presenting himself as having come from "the city of Khartum [sic], Sudan, Egypt," and as "a Mohammadan by birth, Master of the Koran, having pilgrimaged to Mecca three times and thus become an Eminent High Priest and head of all Masonic degrees in Mecca, from the first to the ninety-sixth degree." He invited them to place themselves under the jurisdiction of a "Mecca-Medina Temple" in Arabia. The Black Shriners declined his offer.[93]

The significance of Freemasonry for Noble Drew Ali's Moorish Science Temple—and as a node in the Moorish Science reading of Egyptosophy as Islamic—has been extensively documented. Susan Nance, who dismisses Noble

Drew Ali's credentials as a Muslim leader, writes, "Moorish Science is most accurately described as a black Spiritualist-style religion steeped in the philosophies of mystical Freemasonry."⁹⁴ As discussed in the preceding chapter, Noble Drew Ali's sources for his own *Holy Koran* included *Unto Thee I Grant*, distributed by the Rosicrucians and attributed to a Tibetan translation of a book by the pharaoh Akhenaten, "famous in Western mystical and Masonic folklore as the founder of the first great school of mysticism."⁹⁵ For Noble Drew Ali, the mysteries of Freemasonry, Islam, and pharaonic Egypt would have been inseparably triangulated.

E. D. Beynon, author of the earliest scholarly work on the Nation of Islam, wrote in the 1930s that Fard's sources for teaching his followers included numerous books on "Freemasonry and its symbolism."⁹⁶ In Nation literature, Islam is treated as Freemasonry's guarded secret. Prior to his conversion, Elijah Muhammad was a Freemason. Writing immediately after Fard's disappearance in 1934, Elijah upholds Solomon as an exemplar of Islamic knowledge and charges that Masons have exploited the Solomonic Islamic tradition for their personal wealth and power: "They changed the name Moslem to Mason and no one must be called Moslem under the Masonic law until he pays a great sum of money for the 32nd Degree."⁹⁷ Writing in later decades, Elijah declares, "A Mason cannot be a good Mason unless he knows the Holy Qur'an and follows its teaching. This book is the only book that will make a true Mason. . . . I say, if you are a true Moslem friend, then alright, lets have it in the open and not in the secret."⁹⁸ The Nation's Supreme Wisdom Lessons seem to refer to Shriners in their discussion of "Muslim Sons" who must add a sword to the flag of Islam as symbolic of their oath of secrecy.⁹⁹ Nation tradition also reads Masons as the "ten percent" mentioned in the Lessons, who actively conceal knowledge of God so as to maintain their control over the 85 percent, the "slaves to mental death and power."¹⁰⁰ Confronting the historically permeable boundaries between Muslim identity and Masonic initiation, York had devoted some resources in his AAC/NIH years to highlighting and decoding popular appearances of Masonic symbols (such as the Egyptian pyramid and the all-seeing eye on one-dollar bills), and to circulating anti-Freemason polemics, such as his *Opening of the Seventh Seal: Secret Societies Unmasked* in both its mid-1970s and 1984 editions. York additionally seeks to decode the apparent references to Freemasonry in the Supreme Wisdom Lessons.¹⁰¹ These permeable boundaries and shared connections to Egyptosophy also enabled York to present his Masonic lodge as a logical continuation of his Sufi lodge.

As a resource for both the Moorish Science Temple and the Moorish Zionist Temple, Freemasonry enriched the overlap between York's archive of

Blackamerican Islam and his Hebrew commitments. As Freemasonry's legends made claims upon the architects of Solomon's Temple and the pyramids, finding their intersection in Moses as both Hebrew lawgiver-prophet and initiated student of secret Egyptian knowledge, Freemasons came to imagine themselves as heirs simultaneously of Israel and Egypt. In a parallel to the significance of Freemasonry for pioneers of Black Islam, Jacob Dorman observes that "all of the founders of Black Israelite faiths" in the United States had been Masonic initiates.[102] To the historical triangulation of Islam, ancient Egypt, and Freemasonry in York's context, we should add Israel and make a square.

Labeling his assemblage of resources "Nuwaubu" (often written as Nuwaupu), York renamed his community the United Nuwaubian Nation of Moors (UNNM). He presents Nuwaubu as an "ancient Nubian word" that he defines with the Arabic n-w-b root, using Lane's *Arabic-English Lexicon*, as "of color inclining to Black." York also employs the classical Islamic sciences of lettrism and numerology (*abjad*) to break down the Arabic n-w-b root letters for their numerical values and correspondence to divine attributes: the letter *nun* signifies the fiftieth attribute of Allah, Ash Shahiydu, "the Witness"; the *waw* signifies the sixth attribute, Al Mu'minu, "the Believer"; the *ba* signifies the second attribute, Al Rahiymu, "the Merciful." With the declaration that "This Is Supreme Mathematics Unfolding Right In Front Of You," York then digit-sums the three letters to get fifty-eight, which leads him to Allah's fifty-eighth attribute, Al Mubdiyu, "the Beginner," signifying Nuwaubu as a point of renewal in the community's shared journey.[103]

The term was not York's own invention. References to Nuwaupu appear in a series of pamphlets that appeared under the publisher name "Those Who Care" between 1966 and 1972, including *Bible Interpretations and Explanations*, a two-part booklet by Amunubi Rahkaptah, and *The Nine Ball*, a four-part work attributed to Wu Nupu, Asa Nupu, and Naba Nupu (Rahkaptah and two collaborators). After adopting the name Amunnubi Rooakhptah (with occasional variations in spelling), York would insist that he was in fact the original Amunubi Rahkaptah and the true author of these works. Rahkaptah, however, was born Johnnie Eugene Brown in 1926, moved from Savannah, Georgia, to New York as a young man, and for years operated a novelty store in Brooklyn.[104] Writing for the salvation of the Ethiopian race, which appears in these works as a comprehensive term for all "Wooly-Haired People by Nature," Rahkaptah and his coauthors present Nuwaupu as "Ethiopian science" and "the Ethiopian's equalizer" against white supremacy on both physical and metaphysical levels. The pamphlets express themes that would resonate with readers of AAC/NIH literature: a belief that "Wooly-Haired People by Nature" possess a racial predisposition to spiritual insight and harmony with the universe; white power's use of religion as a means of cutting Black people off from consciousness of their true selves; the narrative, prominent in Nation of Islam tradition, that white people were allotted six thousand years, a tenure that has expired; advocacy of "right racism" to prevent racial dilution through intermarriage; the debt of ancient Greek intellectuals to Egyptian mystery schools; Caucasian persecution and destruction of ancient Egyptian religion; the connection of transhistorical white supremacy to the biblical Leviathan; and "Nine Ether." "The root of the word Ethiopian is ETHER," Rahkaptah explains, "and Ether is the Creative Power that the Sun and other True Stars produce and emanate. Nine Ether is the celestial origin of all Ethiopians." Because the term "Ethiopia" had once signified all of Africa, and the Atlantic Ocean was called the Ethiopian Sea, "Ethiopian is the best all around name-identification for mentally resurrected Wooly-Haired People, until Nuwaupu by power of Nine Ether gives us Ethiopians our new-cycle name."[105] Before the Greeks referred to woolly-haired people as Ethiopians, "we were called NUBUNS by the Ancients. The words Ethiopian and Nubun are the same in meaning. They both mean ETHER—the life-giving, light-giving burning energies that the Sun produces called PROMINENCES and SUNSHINE."[106] It is difficult to find much evidence of Rahkaptah's work circulating in Brooklyn or elsewhere, though in 1974 a Jamaican reggae band or artist curiously performed under the name Nuwaupu and released a song titled "Marcus Garvey."[107]

Having boasted for years of his followers' superior rigor in the study of the Arabic language over other Muslim communities, York marked his Nuwaubian era with Nuwaupic, which he presented as an "Egyptian mystery language," the "secret tongue of tones" and language of the celestial Neteraat—the deities known elsewhere as Eloheem, Alihaat, Nephilians, or Anunnaqi—that had been secretly passed down through the centuries by the Ancient Egiptian Order.[108] Nuwaupic was written in a hieroglyphic script, and the spoken language was reportedly based on a unique Arabic dialect that young members of the community had developed among themselves in New York.[109] Comparatives and superlatives appear as Arabic-English hybrids: as the Nuwaupic word for "big" is *kabur*, "bigger" becomes *akbar*, and "biggest" would be *kaburist*.[110]

While appropriating the term Nuwaubu/Nuwaupu in the second half of the 1990s, York presented his Nuwaubian platform not as a traumatic rupture or sharp turn from what had been his community's past experience of Muslim life, but rather as an organic continuation of the AAC/NIH message and the fulfillment of what had always been its mission. AAC/NIH literature had consistently reflected upon changes in the community's dress codes and intellectual activity, but only after the 1993 migration does York retroactively describe the community as having passed through a succession of clearly separate Christian, Jewish, and Islamic schools. He also repositions his post-Islamic African spirituality, placing it at the beginning of the movement's history. In *Does Dr. Malachi Z. York Try to Hide The Fact That He Was Imaam Issa?*, York writes that he was an Afrocentrist as far back as the 1960s but felt a need to present his message as Islamic in harmony with the era's trends. Even as Islam dominated Afrocentrism, York persisted and "Wore African Garbs.... We Played African Drums And Our Women Wore African Clothes, But As The Islaamic Craze Grew, Again I Had 'To Give You What You Wanted, So That You Would Learn To Want What I Have To Give.'"[111]

Relocating Nuwaubu/Nuwaupu at the origins of his mission, York rebranded himself as Amunnubi Rooakhptah—which, like Black Eagle, supplemented rather than replaced his primary identity as Malachi Z. York—and claimed that he was the same Amunubi Rahkaptah who had written *Bible Interpretations and Explanations* (1968) and *The Nine Ball* (1971).[112] Just as W. D. Muhammad had insisted that movement away from the Nation's teachings in favor of "orthodox" Islam had been the master plan of his father and Master Fard Muhammad all along, York reveals that what appears to be a departure is in fact a return.

EL'S HOLY SCRIPTURES

From his earliest published works to the 1993 exodus, York based his authority as a Muslim leader on his mastery of revealed scriptures, emphasizing three key points: (1) he was the only Muslim intellectual to recognize the Qurʾan's command to follow *all* of the scriptures; (2) he alone possessed the command of all required languages to translate and interpret the scriptures correctly; and (3) he had been blessed with "Furqaan," which Allah had previously given only to the prophets, apostles, imamate, and the Mahdi, enabling York to "differentiate between the allegorical and decisive portions of the Scriptures."[113] Though he ostensibly marginalized biblical tradition in favor of Egyptosophy, ancient Sumerian mythology, Freemasonry, Washitaw Moorish ideology, and UFO religion, this did not mean that York abandoned more than three decades' worth of scriptural exegesis as obsolete. Rather, he continued to present himself as the master decoder of the texts and as uniquely qualified to recover truth from revelations that had been polluted and corrupted by human editors, forgers, plagiarists, and unqualified translators. York's literature promised to clear a path through the lies and distortions of false religions toward a fuller comprehension of the scriptures and their secrets.

In the 1990s, York produced new scriptural translations in attractive hardcover volumes: *El's Holy Qur'aan*, *El's Holy Injiyl* (the book of Revelation), *El's Holy Torah*, and *El's Holy Tehillim (Zabuwr)* (the Psalms). Each volume includes color images of the prophetic "Receiver" for that particular scripture (Muhammad; John; Moses, Aaron, and Joshua; David) and names York as "the Translator," along with pages for charting one's personal genealogy, as in family heirloom Bibles. He followed this template for his translation of the Egyptian *Book of the Dead*, again presenting himself as "the Translator" and naming the text's "Receiver" as the pharaoh Akhenaten, whom York had recognized as an Islamic prophet in his Ansar years (fig. 32). In the El scripture series, York continues to stand as the master teacher who can properly decipher the revelations and expose the false religions that have distorted their meanings.

El's Holy Injiyl frequently repeats York's AAC/NIH-era exegetical work, in terms of both his conceptualization of Christ's *injil*, as equivalent to the book of Revelation, and his commentary on its verses. The woman described in Rev. 12:1, with "the moon underneath her feet, and upon her head a crown of twelve stars," remains Fatima, "symbolic of the re-establishment of Al Islaam in its pristine purity as was practiced by the Ansaaru Allah Community, then in the world." Her labor pains in Rev. 12:2 connect the birth of her sons to the emergence of York's mission. In his commentary on Rev. 12:5, York reads the "man child, who was to rule all nations with a rod of iron," as the Sudanese Mahdi. Reading Rev. 12:6—"And the woman fled into the wilderness, where she hath a place prepared of God, that they should feed her there a thousand two hundred and threescore days"—York returns to his account of Fatima, who fled with her family "from the pale Arabs of Arabia to Egypt then down to Sudan."[114]

El's Holy Qur'aan is a difficult text to penetrate, in part because York reorganizes the Qur'an's suras into what Rashad Khalifa regarded as the chronological order of their revelation, rather than their order in the 'Uthmanic codex.[115] York also loads the translated verses with parenthetical explanations, and terms left untranslated sometimes become new concepts. The sixth verse of *al-Tariq*, historically the eighty-sixth sura (twenty-third in *El's Holy Qur'aan*), for example, could read straightforwardly, "One of soundness, and he rose." In *El's Holy Qur'aan*, the verse appears as "The source of strength—(the wisdom of the Qur'aan); then He, (Gabriel) took a Faastawa 'Physical Form From An Etherian To A Mortal Man'; (Gabriel appeared to Ahmad and taught the Qur'aan to him)."[116] The sura's forty-ninth verse, which could read, "And surely,

FIGURE 32 Pharaoh Akhenaten, regarded by York as a prophet to whom the Egyptian *Book of the Dead* was sent as a revelation. Note the Arabic *huwa* ("him") at the top of the image. At Akhenaten's forehead, his headdress bears the first half of the Islamic testimony of faith, *la ilaha illa Allah* (there is no god but Allah), beneath the familiar crescent and six-pointed star. From York, *El Katub Shil el Mawut (The Book of the Dead): Coming Forth by Day* (1990s).

he is the lord of Sirius," undergoes profound elaboration: "And sure, He is the Rabb 'Sustainer' of Al Shi'raa—Sirius (Sirius A Is Called Pototolo 'Tiny Grain,' Which Has A Satellite, Sirius B Called White Dwarf; Sirius also called the Dog Star with an active planet called Nirvana, home of the original Hindu, in the Canis Major star constellation; the home of the Dogon Star And Nommos)."[117]

The second verse in the 'Uthmanic codex's thirty-fourth sura (fifty-eighth sura in *El's Holy Qur'aan*)—"He knows what penetrates into the earth and what emerges from it and what descends from the heaven and what ascends in it; and he is the merciful, the forgiving"—becomes another portal for York's extraterrestrial narratives: "He (He Not We) knows that which Yaliju 'Penetrates' (passes) into the Ard/Qi (crafts that go into Shamballah the Inner World), the planet 'Earth' and that which Yukhruju 'Comes Out' of it (crafts that come out of Shamballah), and that which Yunzilu 'Comes Down' from Al-Samaa-i 'The Sky' (crafts that leaves); and He is Al Rahiymu 'The Most Yielding,' Al Ghafuwru 'The Forgiving.'"[118]

York's introduction to *El's Holy Qur'aan* charges Muslims with corrupting the revelation by dropping some verses and adding others (partly in their effort to worship Muhammad as an idol), and with developing schools of grammar and modifying the Arabic script (by, for example, adding dots to letters). These "demonic strategies" divided the children of Abraham by producing "Islam" as a separate religion. York maintains that the original Qur'an remained with Muhammad's "true descendants" in the Sudan; while York himself has access to this original Qur'an, *El's Holy Qur'aan* is a translation of the popular corrupted Qur'an.

Despite his anti-Muslim polemics, York affirms Muhammad's experience of revelation, upholds the Qur'an's mathematical miracle as presented by Rashad Khalifa, and contrasts the innocence of true Islam "in its pristine purity" with the "Pale Arabs Way of Islaam." He laments that W. D. Muhammad could only find acceptance from Arabs by saying bad things about his father, while Siraj Wahhaj "has to talk bad about any other Muslim leader, who doesn't agree with Saudi Arabian concepts on racism." As much as York has distanced himself from Muslim identity, *El's Holy Qur'aan* remains tethered to its Ansar heritage.

This complex engagement of Islam continues in *The Holy Tablets* (1996), York's original revelation (as marked by York's portrait on the first page, captioned "The Receiver" rather than "The Translator"), which has been reproduced in numerous editions and prompted a variety of study guides and classes to guide readers through its more than sixteen hundred pages. The text appears in a format reminiscent of the Bible, printed on scritta paper, the material organized into chapters, subchapters ("tablets"), and verses. York acknowledges in his introduction to a revised edition that he has made improvements to the text and corrected changes made by the Christian printers, who imposed their own edits. The original text's references to "Nubians in the Western hemisphere" thus become "Nuwaubians in the Western hemisphere" in the revised edition.[119] While scholarly discussions of Nuwaubu emphasize York's abandonment of Islam, *The Holy Tablets* does not erase Ansar history. Instead, it reflects its AAC/NIH background in several ways, beginning with its chapter titles, which draw upon the Arabic vocabulary that had defined not only AAC/NIH media but the community's lived experience: the first two chapters, for example, bear the respective titles "El Khalqu, the Creation" and "El Abd, the Slaves"; the fourteenth chapter is titled, "Qisa Nuwh, The Story of Noah." Preserving its investment in the theological significance of the number nineteen, informed by Rashad Khalifa's arguments, the sum of the numbered verses in each "tablet" equals a multiple of nineteen. Throughout the text, readers encounter narratives and references that could read as "Islamic." The character of Lucifer/Ibliys, objecting to the creation of humankind, offers an argument that echoes his words in the Qur'an: "How can mortals, created of dust, claim to be a being of superiority and I am created before him, of fire?" Likewise, the angelic beings (Anunnaqi) ask El Eloh a question that echoes the angels' concern in the Qur'an: "Will you make a mischief maker in it, one who shall shed blood?"[120] The second chapter, "El Abd, the Slaves," traces a history of Black Islam in the United States through the twentieth century, providing discussions of Duse Ali (described as a follower of the Sudanese Ansar), Noble Drew Ali (who "came from Cherokee" and was a student of Duse Ali) (2.1.3), Elijah Muhammad, Daoud Faisal, Allah (the former Clarence 13X), and Master Fard Muhammad (depicted here as a Venusian "'god' from Saudi Arabia" who sought the lost tribe of Shabazz) (2.1.1–4).

York takes the reader through a series of epic narratives that include spaceship battles and interstellar genealogies. The Dogon appear as a human-alien hybrid descended from the Nommos—a reptilian species with "dark green scaly skin" that fled the Sirius B system after Nibiru drained the star's energy and caused it to collapse—and Egyptians who had migrated to Mali (3.5.114–30). The nineteenth and final chapter of *The Holy Tablets* ("Al Khidr, Murdoq") traces the history of Islam, starting from seventh-century Arabia and culminating in the AAC/NIH's trajectory from 1960s Brooklyn through the 1990s and its collective migration to Georgia. In this "post-Islamic" text, the community remains deeply invested in Islamic tradition and its own Muslim history. The chapter's second tablet initially appears to offer a conventional *sira* (biography) of the seventh-century Muhammad, starting with an account of the "Army of the Elephant" that had attempted to destroy the Kaʿba in the year of his birth. However, the tablet then says that the devil (Shaytaan) had "given birth to his own prophet Muhammad," whom the chapter connects to the famed imposter prophet Musaylimat. This "fake Muhammad" would grow up to establish the inauthentic religion of "Muhammadism," characterized by a "corrupted set of laws called shariya, laws made by man, not found in the real Al Quraan," a "system called Fiqh, rules and regulations," and guidance from "the demon Al Hadith." With the help of Khadija's uncle Waraqa, Musaylimat composed a false "Koran" and formed a "secret brotherhood," the Ikhwaani Muslimuwn (Muslim Brothers) (19.2.31–71). Repeating and reconstructing popular anti-Islamic tropes, York asserts that a Jewish-Catholic conspiracy enabled Musaylimat to produce this false Koran, facilitate the assassination of Muhammad by a Jewish woman, and take over the Prophet's movement, seducing all of his followers throughout history—with the exception of "Al Mukhlisina, the Purified Ones," the Ansaaru Allah, who would emerge as followers of the true Mahdi in the Sudan, "protected from the touch of this worldwide deception called Muhammadism." But the text laments that even the Ansar themselves would fall, as a "political egotist" in the "bloodline" formed an "Ummah party," departed from the original Mahdiyya teachings, and allowed intermarriage between Ansar and Ikhwaani Muslims (19.2.31–71).

Musaylimat's fraudulent Koran triumphed with the support of his installed caliphs Abu Bakr, ʿUmar, and ʿUthman. The true and original Qurʾan survived only with Muhammad's daughter Fatima, who passed the singular handwritten copy to her husband, ʿAli, who in turn sent it to Kufa for secret reproduction in Kufic script. The Fatima codex was then disseminated through Egypt into the Sudan, "where it was protected and never translated into any foreign language until now," with *El's Holy Qurʾaan* (19.2.52–66).

Abu Bakr, a "red Arab," becomes suspect here for arranging a marriage between Muhammad and his young daughter A'isha. Elsewhere, York suggests that Abu Bakr was so consumed with taking over Islam that he arranged for Muhammad to marry his daughter as a child;[121] *The Holy Tablets* asserts that he set up the marriage to depict Muhammad as a pedophile, and that A'isha grew up to become a "very disloyal and evil woman" who caused chaos and brought Muhammad "much unhappiness and unrest" (19.2.157–60). Though Abu Bakr eventually came to recognize Musaylimat's threat and ordered his assassination, Musaylimat's followers had already won control of Islam. ʿAli and his family were slaughtered, "but not before their seed was well planted in the

Sudan," eventually giving rise to the Sudanese Mahdi—empowered through both his biological descent from the *ahl al-bayt* and his possession of the original written copy (*mushaf*) of the Qurʾan (19.2.67–68).

> We are the Ansaaru Allah, the Ahlil Bayt.
> This fake Muhammad that is responsible for Islaam as you know it today,
> Be it Sunni, Shiʿite, Ahmadiyya, Wahabbiy, Ikhwaaniy Muslim, Nation of Islam, World Muslim Community,
> And the many other sects that the Prophet Muhammad, peace and blessings of Allah be upon, said would raise in the last day and oppose his nation the Ansaaru Allah,
> For as the real Qur'aan said: "oh you who are of the Faithful, be Ansaaru Allah."
> And again it says, "oh you who is of the faithful, if you help Allah, Allah will help and plant firm your feet."
> They plan a plan and Allah plans a plan,
> And Allah is the best of planners. (19.2.74–81)

From there, the nineteenth chapter returns to the familiar theme of Bilal and his role as a bridge between Israelite and Ishmaelite prophetic traditions. Bilal's great-great-grandfather Abdul Uzza was "keeper of the original Torah"; as a member of Judah, the last remaining Israelite tribe, Bilal became custodian of the Mihjan. The text also notes that Bilal came from the members of Judah who would later become the Dongolawi tribe from which Al Mahdi himself claimed descent. The chapter makes the critical point that when Bilal passed the scepter to his cousin Muhammad, it did not correspond to a change in Bilal's religious identity:

> Al Islaam was Bilaal's way of life.
> He was not converted; he was born into the law of Moses,
> For as a Judahite of royal bloodline,
> He was raised in Mosaic law,
> Thus, he was always a Muslim and adhere[d] to Al Islaam.
> He did not subtract or add to this divine way of life. (19.3.105–10)

This section seems to have been written in the early 1990s, perhaps speaking to the anxieties of a community amid changes in its names, practices, and aesthetics. Furthermore, while the 1996 edition of the book is attributed to Malachi Z. York, this chapter refers to York as Rabboni Y'shua Bar El Haady (19.6.60), perhaps pointing to 1992–93 as its time of composition.

Amid markers of the "Jewish period," the chapter also identifies the community as the Ancient and Mystic Order of Melchizedek (AMOM), which is described here as a Sufi order (19.6.311–21). York's treatment of Sufism remains consistent throughout the community's history. According to the nineteenth chapter, York began publishing material in the late 1960s under the name Amunnubi Rooakhptah, "an unknown writer in the science of Nuwaubu," and soon took on his identity as Imaam Isa thanks to Islam's prominence in Black political and religious consciousness in the 1960s (19.6.219–23). The chapter traces the progression from Ansaar Pure Sufi (1967) to the Nubian Islaamic Hebrews (1969) and York's journeys through the 1970s, walking the streets of New York and other cities, he writes, "as I propagated Sufi Islaam." He provides details of the clothing that community members wore in various periods ("Our code of dress changed from time to time, to suit the time we were in") and the sequence of addresses at which they established headquarters (19.6.225–78). As Ansar, community members adhered to strict dress codes of turbans, *thobes*, and *khimars*, lived in accordance with the Qur'an, and raised their children to master classical Arabic. However, the outward performance of Islam proved inadequate to the mission:

> *Our children were raised speaking fluent classical Arabic, reading the Qur'aan in Arabic,*
> *Yet the Qur'aan is a fourteen hundred year old book,*
> *And Islam is a fourteen hundred year old religion the way they practiced it.*
> *And was doing absolutely nothing to change the condition of the Nubian in the Western hemisphere.*
> *They may put on a taggiyah, grow a beard, or shave their beard, put on oils from the east or robes from the east, prayer beads in their hands,*
> *And carry an English translation of the Qur'aan but the condition and state of mind did not change. (19.6.293–98)*

At this point in the text, lamenting the damage done by "false teachings of the so-called Arabs who deliberately mistranslated verses of the Qur'aan," York proclaims, "it is my job to reform all the false teachings that had been taught to Nubians in the west and restore Islaam to its pristine purity" (19.6.299–300).

He then describes a period in which the community relocated to its Jazzir Abba camp in the Catskills, during which time he subjected followers to "the nineteen tests of nineteen weeks," followed by their collective migration "to the Mecca of Nubians, Georgia" (19.6.302–4). Nearing its final pages, *The Holy Tablets* presents the community as having undergone a progressive evolution and completed a "full circle" return to its roots: the community began as Ansaar Pure Sufi, "and so we are at the beginning again with Sufi and fezzes. Only now we are Sufi under the A.M.O.M. the Ancient Mystic Order of Malchizedek" (19.6.321). *The Holy Tablets* claims Sufism as both the community's past and its future, and Islam as simultaneously a master teacher's pedagogical strategy to reach his students and a corrupted tradition that he will restore to its "pristine purity."

ISLAM AND METAPHYSICAL AFRICA: RENEWING THE LESSONS

While York expressed disillusionment with the condition of Mahdism in the contemporary Sudan and modified his family tree, he also preserved his status as the Mahdi's great-grandson. It was through his connection to the Mahdi, now termed "Mahdi of the East," that York elevated his own position to the "One and Only Mahdi of the West." He published a Nuwaubian edition of the *Ratib*, the Mahdi's prayer book, titled *The Raatib for Shriners*, in which he reframes the text, the Mahdiyya tradition, and his own authorization from it in terms of Freemasonry. The advertisements in the back of the book focus on Freemasonry-related materials, including *The Secret Rituals of the Sisters of Fatimah (Lady Shriners)* and *The Noble Koran for Shriners*, a translation of the Qurʾan that promises to demonstrate that the Qurʾan recognizes Jesus as the son of God and that "Islam is really a form of Christianity. All true Christians are Muslims and all true Muslims are Christians."

The Raatib for Shriners names York as "The Translator," the Prophet as "The Inspirer," and Muhammad Ahmad as "The Inscriber." York introduces the text with an elaborate account of his initiation at the junction of the Niles. While studying at the University of Khartoum, he says, he received a visit from Khidr, who revealed that York would become his vessel to communicate a "message of the green light" and intervene for "lost sheep of the House of Israel." Khidr explained that York would be summoned back to the Sudan when the time came for his initiation. Khidr then referred York to the verses in the Qurʾan detailing Khidr's encounter with Moses ("in Chapter 69, which was changed to Chapter 18 verses 60–82").[122]

It was in 1973 that York received the call. "I knew then," he writes in *The Raatib for Shriners*, that "I was not always to be a Muslim, but it was just one degree in my studies" (16). He returned to the Sudan and journeyed to the Grand Temple in Khartoum, the "Grand Lodge in true Egypt," where he encountered the "Grand Master Mahmuwd." York is thus faithful to his earlier narrative about obtaining Islamic credentials in the Sudan—in texts from the 1970s and '80s, Mahmuwd is described as imam at the Great Masjid in Khartoum and is credited with teaching York the *fiqh* of ritual prayer—while rewriting it in Masonic terms.[123] Mahmuwd belonged to the "final part of the three letters miyms (م م م) of the name Muhammad," the first being preprophetic Ahmad, followed by the Prophet, followed in turn by "Mahmuwd in the end." Mahmuwd took York through "a whirlpool of information, a rainbow of colors, a spectrum of light and octaves of sound. He filled my soul with so much information.... Once I was cleansed, I felt as if I were 7 feet tall" (18).

This experience did not complete his training. York then traveled to the junction of the two Niles, where he observed small huts "used by mystics for Khalwa or initiation" (20). A man appeared and told York to take one step; York complied and suddenly found himself standing before a beautiful temple with marble floors and a long hallway of doors. His guide led him down a "majestic corridor" to a door that opened into a huge room. "The walls of the room were white and they appeared to emit a soft flowing light," York writes. "The room was bare, except for twelve rugs, which were arranged in such a manner that they formed a large circle. In the center of the circle were three rugs." York was told to sit on the middle rug in the center of the circle. Then Khidr materialized and faced him, followed by other men who materialized and introduced themselves, each occupying a rug. The final rugs at York's left and right were occupied by his great-grandfather, the Mahdi (Aluhum Al Mahdi Zodoq), and his distant ancestor, the Prophet (Aluhum Muhammad Zodoq), emanating scents of musk and rose, respectively (20–22).

Each man's forehead emitted a light beam of a unique color: "All around my body I could feel this energy surging through my being" (22). After the initiation, Mahmuwd signaled to the heavens, where York witnessed a lotus with a seven-pointed star in a crescent moon, the star containing an inverted heart and the Arabic *huwa*, the symbol surrounded by a "green light wavering brighter and brighter against the dark violet hue of the sky." The symbol, Mahmuwd explained, would represent the Sufi order, Sons of the Green Light, for which York would serve as the Qutb (Axis) (22–23).

York then ventured to Egypt for another initiation, "the test of men," at the Great Pyramid of Giza. York entered into a room and immediately heard a voice announce, "You have now failed the first test." York asked, "What do we do now?" and was then told that he had failed the second test. As a wall appeared in front of him, York was told, "All that you seek to know, and will ever need to know about man, is on the other side of this wall." When York asked how he could reach the other side, the voice told him, "You have failed the third test." York's choices repeatedly resulted in failure until he found a "speck of light" and ran to it until he found himself outside the pyramid. The Master told him, "you failed the seventh test. . . . In failing the seventh test, you have passed the first test, for you now know what it feels like to be a man" (25–26).

Writing as both the "third Khalifah," after his father Al Haadi and grandfather Abdur Rahman, succeeding his great-grandfather as "Grand Mufti of world-wide Shrinedom," York offers his great-grandfather's Islamic prayer book as a spiritual manual for Freemasons and Shriners (49). He traces the Shriners' origins to Sufis under the leadership of Bilal, who led their flight out of Arabia during the oppressive regime of Abu Bakr. While the Prophet's family fled into the Sudan and became the Dongolawi tribe, the Sufi-Shriners moved across northern Africa and settled in the Moroccan city of Fez. Their order spread across Algeria, Tunisia, Libya, Egypt, Ethiopia, and even to Spain and France, where "Euro-Shriners gradually transformed into a pseudo-Christian sect after pressures in Christian countries that called them a Muslim cult" (58). Later Europeans who observed Sufi practices would form various brotherhoods and lodges as their own distorted imitations (59–60). When Shriners reached the Sudan in the nineteenth century as a result of the Turko-Egyptian occupation, they formed the Khalwatiyya order. A Khalwatiyya dervish named As-Sammani then formed the suborder from which the Mahdi arose (61–62). In answer to the question "Why isn't The Mahdi of the East recognized by Muslims around the world?" York explains that the Mahdi would have been recognized if he were a white man, but to revere a Black man as the Mahdi would "lower the Indo Arab's superiority in the Islaamic world . . . they can't lower their pride to obey one who they've been calling a slave" (69–70).

Even if no longer a self-identified Muslim, York remained "Mahdi in the West," the prophetic conclusion to Black Islam and master of its sacred sources. York's Nuwaubian-era discourse presented Black Muslim leaders as steps on a ladder that set the stage for York's mission. Consistent with York's pre-Nuwaubian treatments of Black Islamic histories, Nuwaubu appears in this literature as the transcendent post-Islamic culmination of Black Islam, as well as an umbrella tradition in which Moorish Science Temple members, Nation members, and Five Percenters could all find their familiar symbols, figures, and texts.

Some of the most notable artifacts from this project were York's publications of other communities' sources. He produced his own reprint of Noble Drew Ali's *Holy Koran*, along with *The Problem Book*, a Nation of Islam text that became particularly important to Five Percenters. Both publications are attractively produced, with imitation-leather covers that display their respective communities' symbols: the "circle 7" and Moroccan flag for *The Holy Koran*, the Five Percenters' Universal Flag for *The Problem Book*. They are higher-quality products than any produced at the time by the Moorish Science Temple of America (MSTA) or the Five Percenters, and York presented them as benevolent acts; as his preface to *The Holy Koran* states, he printed the edition with cooperation from an MSTA member "in an effort to further uplift my Moorish American brothers and sisters who continue their spread of truth and unity amongst my Nubian brothers and sisters."[124] Inside these books, one finds full-color images of the community leaders (Noble Drew Ali and Allah) and of York himself. Nuwaubian publications advertising these texts offer them free to members of the respective communities: *The Holy Koran* costs $15 for non-Moors, but MSTA members can receive it just by sending York a copy of their MSTA credentials.[125]

York continued to engage in polemics against other Muslim communities. He published *Shaikh Daoud vs. W. D. Fard*, which returns to his narrative of multiple Fards and withdraws his apology to the Nation on the grounds that he had received his earlier information on Fard from Faisal, and that he has since confirmed Faisal's account. In *Shaikh Daoud vs. W. D. Fard*, Faisal takes an expanded role in the story; Al Mahdi asserts that while Elijah Muhammad had known only the imposter Fard, Faisal knew both men. Faisal had met Abdul Wali Farrad Muhammad Ali at a Moorish Science assembly in New Jersey, and decades later encountered Wallace Dodd Ford, who appeared at State Street Mosque while claiming Ali's identity. Having known the true Fard, Faisal was not fooled. Faisal also understood that Ford was not only a communist and U.S. agent who had been sent to sabotage the Black freedom struggle, but that he was also working as a double agent on behalf of the Nazis to destroy Islam in America.[126]

Despite his conspiracy theories regarding Fard Muhammad, his rejection of W. D. Muhammad, and his intensifying hostility toward Louis Farrakhan, York's Nuwaubian-era writings maintain affection for Elijah Muhammad. In *The Holy Tablets*, York proclaims that Elijah Muhammad was the third incarnation of

Elijah—the first having been Elijah the Tishbite, the second, John the Baptist—sent to prepare the world for York's own arrival as Malachi and making explicit the biblical parallels that he had implied since the late 1970s (19.6.177–82). York disseminated small booklets of transcribed Elijah Muhammad sermons, bearing Elijah's photo on the covers.[127] And he continued to treat the Nation as a primary interlocutor. In 1996 he published *Post Graduate: The Renewal of the Lessons*, in which he offered an extensive commentary on the Nation's initiatory text.

The text of *The Holy Tablets* itself, while signifying a graduation from Islam, also represents the fulfilled promise of Elijah Muhammad. York reminds readers in a 1996 pamphlet that Elijah had spoken of a future scripture that would replace both the Bible and the Qur'an. Drawing from the Supreme Wisdom Lessons, York declares that the arrival of Elijah Muhammad signaled Islam's expiration at the end of a twenty-five-thousand-year cycle, requiring its renewal. "Elijah Muhammad Upgraded The Outdated Teachings of Orthodox Islam To Suit What He Referred To As The 'Lost-Found' Which Are The Nubians," York writes. "We Are The Re-Newers Of That History." With the publication of *The Holy Tablets* in 1996, Elijah's promise of a future book was fulfilled. York thus offers an alternative "second resurrection" to that of rival *mujaddid* W. D. Muhammad, calling "For All Of True Followers Of The Honorable Elijah Muhammad To Come Under Nuwaubu."[128]

CONCLUSIONS

"Islam is poison to your body, heart and soul," York writes in a Nuwaubian pamphlet. "It is made up of stuff which Desert Arabs borrowed, added to and took away from us, as the Nuwbuns who are the true Egyptians and Olmec."[129] But even in his most virulent "post-Islamic" writing, York still presents himself as a restorer of Islam in its "pristine purity," a phrase that he had used since the early 1970s. In spite of and apart from the "poison" of historical Islamic tradition, something remains real. As evidence that Islam had become uniquely oppressive against women, he presents Fatima as a genuine "messiah" figure, a master teacher and healer whose miracles were erased by Muslim tradition.[130] While he refutes Nation of Islam doctrines, he does so as Elijah Muhammad's true heir, who can communicate with Elijah in his dreams, and he still claims guidance from the Sudanese Mahdi and the Prophet via transcendent visions. In his *Sacred Records of Neter: Aaferti Atum-Re* (1998), he still self-identifies as Al Qutb, "spiritual guide of the pure Sufi."[131]

The Holy Tablets depicts York's journey as coming full circle to end where it started, as a teacher of Sufism wearing a fez. For all of its ruptures, Nuwaubu also represents continuity. It may be tempting to imagine Nuwaubu as a gnostic trickster's exercise in postmodernist challenges to rationality, but these are not the terms in which York authorizes his claims. In her discussion of York's presentation style, Susan Palmer writes, "His discourse is riveting—but not what one might expect from a conventional religious leader. He does not formulate doctrines, relate moral parables or explain ideas in a coherent fashion. Rather, he shakes the very foundations of belief."[132] Palmer's analysis of York as a charismatic clown and his followers as embracing him without concern for what he actually says is belied by accounts that she provides—both from her own interviews and from Abu Ameenah Bilal Philips's earlier work—of community members who were attracted to the rationally compelling arguments they found in York's writings.[133] York did of course "formulate doctrines"; he did not "shake the very foundations of belief" but rather made assertions of fact and provided evidence that persuaded many readers to believe his arguments and purchase more of his work, endeavor to convince others of his claims, and sometimes even dedicate their lives to his mission.

The community's literature maintains that its master teacher holds the key to distinguishing absolute truth from subjective falsehood. The Nuwaubian publishing industry takes it as a given that scriptures exist to convey real meanings, and that scriptural exegetes' claims on those meanings can be proved factually correct or incorrect through philology and hard science. There's nothing "postmodernist" about that. My point is not to suggest that the entirety of York's written output "really" holds together perfectly or that his vast corpus contains no inconsistencies or contradictions, but at the very least, *The Holy Tablets* seeks to provide a coherent narrative of his community's journey. His Nuwaubian writings tell us that while different lessons were learned at different stages, Nuwaubu—a *science* of "factology" supported by rationally verifiable evidence—had been the consistent core all along.

CHAPTER 8

Nuwaubian Ether
Ansar Legacies in Hip-Hop

> I talk like Dr. Malachi York played the sidewalk.
>
> —NAS, "TRIPLE THREAT"

> Amorites just can't understand the groove we're in.
>
> —JAY-Z, "THE ORIGINATORS"

One of the more fascinating artifacts of the AAC/NIH's later years appears in a 1990 music video of a song titled "The Originators," by The Jaz and his protégé, a young Jay-Z.[1] The video features scenes from the Ansar heartland of Bushwick and contains numerous visual and aural references to the community, including such landmarks as the masjid and the Nubian Laundromat. Several Ansar men appear in the video, wearing kufis, *thobes*, and jackets covered in AAC/NIH symbols and the phrase "Nubian Nation." The Jaz wears various articles of Ansar garb, and Jay-Z wears a medallion bearing the outline of Africa with what appears to be a Mahdiyya flag. Al Mahdi/York himself appears indirectly, via a painted portrait held by his followers and audio excerpts from his sermons.

The video's short glimpses of community spaces are entirely male; there are no Ansar women in *khimars* with their faces veiled. The studio portions of the "Originators" video do include women: the keyboardist is female and so are the dancers behind The Jaz and Jay-Z; they do not wear Ansar clothing but follow the contemporary fashions of the early 1990s. The video is bookended by appearances of a woman who does not cover her hair or face. Appearing in silhouette at the start of the video, she proclaims, "It is indeed a pleasure to see so many Nubian faces, so many original faces, here tonight." She reappears in two contexts at the video's end. First, her earlier statement and silhouette are repeated. She also looks directly into the camera and recites the Arabic greeting of peace, *as-salamu alaikum*. Her image, juxtaposed with quick cuts to the Bushwick scenes, simultaneously presents a woman as an embodiment of proud Nubian Muslim identity and imagines the community's public spaces as entirely empty of women.

Observers familiar with AAC/NIH narratives might perceive a tension between the content of this video and Al Mahdi's usual discourses on music and gender. Al Mahdi, after all, routinely condemns American popular culture and advocates the creation of alternative Muslim spaces in which children are raised with Nubian and Islamic social norms and "traditional" modes of musical expression. He also denigrates Muslim-majority societies for failing to uphold what he regards as nonnegotiable rules for women's dress and gendered interactions. Although it is full of references to Al Mahdi and his movement, even showing his portrait and sampling his voice, "The Originators" was released on a mainstream label and received exposure on *Yo! MTV Raps*, taking part in the corporate pop culture that Al Mahdi rejects as a plot against Nubian consciousness. In an apparent compromise with Amorite demands, women are shown playing Western instruments and dancing in American style, their bodies, by Ansar standards, improperly exposed.

"The Originators" might provoke a momentary impression of dissonance, but Al Mahdi himself embodies what would appear to many observers as a paradox. While leading a morally conservative Islamic revival movement that prescribed rigidly policed gender roles and sexual norms, notions of modesty that included full niqab and resistance against a "Satanic" music industry, Al Mahdi was also an aspiring pop star and recording mogul (see figs. 33–34). Under the name "Dr. York," he performed as the lead vocalist for the band Passion, released solo albums, and managed his studio and record label with a roster of artists such as the group Petite ("The female version of 'NEW EDITION,'" boasts his full-page ad in the May 4, 1985, issue of *Billboard*) and Christian gospel singer Doc McKenzie. In his music videos, Dr. York does not wear Sudanese robes and turbans but flashy suits and gold jewelry. While Al Mahdi publishes tracts against pop music and Christian holidays, Dr. York sings romantic ballads such as "Let Me Be the One on Christmas." Dr. York's *Billboard* ad names Ronald Reagan as his "favorite American," describes himself as a "sexual

FIGURE 33 Dr. York publicity photo, 1986.

FIGURE 34 Dr. York, "You Can't Hide," twelve-inch vinyl (1986).

person" who "enjoys those who express their love of love," and indulges in astrology ("As a Scorpio he is hot").

While Dr. York and Al Mahdi operated as officially separate personas, their relationship was public knowledge. A November 1990 issue of *SPIN* magazine reported, "Posters recently appeared all over New York's Times Square announcing a new line of rap and R&B records produced by Dr. York," whom it identified as both "the dopest disco impressario since Barry White" and "As Sayyid Issa Al Haadi Al Mahdi ... the last Redeemer before Armageddon."[2] In his presentation as Dr. York, Al Mahdi never acknowledges his career as a Muslim leader, but he seems to wink at those in the know. The 1985 *Billboard* ad mentions that he has traveled internationally, adding, "if you listen closely, you will hear his accent which is Semetic [*sic*]." Only an initiated viewer would notice that in his video for "It's on Me," Dr. York wears a jewel-encrusted AAC/NIH symbol, the upward-pointing crescent and six-pointed star, on his gold necklace, or read possible meanings into the spaceship decorations behind him.

Community literature, whether in official publications or the work of affiliated writers, establishes that Al Mahdi's followers were fully aware of his Dr. York persona, apparently without feeling discomfort or tension over his apparent double life. Al Mahdi's alter ego never amounted to a scandal or "secret knowledge" that undermined his function as imam; some members even encountered Al Mahdi first as Dr. York, having heard his songs on the radio *before* discovering that he was also a Muslim leader.[3] In KMD's "Peach Fuzz," when Zev Love X (the future MF Doom) asks, "I eat no pork, so why can't I be as smooth as my man Dr. York?," he's referring not to extraterrestrial master teacher Dr. Malachi Z. York—Al Mahdi had not yet used this name in his writings—but rather to pop star Dr. York, playfully acknowledging his imam's other identity.

This chapter explores the AAC/NIH's complex relationship to music, particularly hip-hop. While a growing body of scholarship on hip-hop and American Muslims has neglected Al Mahdi and his community, the existing literature provides theoretical insights that could prove helpful to including them. In her examination of hip-hop's significance in Black Muslim experience, Su'ad Abdul Khabeer describes a phenomenon of "Muslim Cool," a construction of religious and racial identity "forged at the intersection of Islam and hip hop." Muslim Cool represents "a way of being Muslim that draws on Blackness to contest two overlapping systems of racial norms: the hegemonic ethnoreligious norms of Arab and South Asian US American Muslim communities on the one hand, and White American normativity on the other." In this sense,

AAC/NIH engagements of hip-hop answer Abdul Khabeer's rhetorical question: "What would U.S. American Muslim communities be like if they loved Black people as much as they love Black culture?" Abdul Khabeer's answer—"a community that binds itself to the Islamic tradition by binding itself to Blackness"—finds one of its many possibilities in AAC/NIH approaches to popular musical forms and expressions.[4]

In her book *Muslim Cool*, Abdul Khabeer discusses American Muslim debates on music with attention to the ways in which policing music, while "typically regarded as theological and thus 'unraced,'" ultimately enforces a "racialized notion of the Islamic tradition." In other words, American Muslim conversations about music's relationship to Islam intersect with multiple relationships to Blackness. The privileging of non-Black Muslims as proper custodians of "correct" Islamic knowledge (and parallel marginalizing narratives of Black Muslims as dependent upon the tutelage of transnational Muslim experts) happens to resonate with particular interpretive frameworks that would prohibit most or all music. As Blackamerican culture often appears to lack resources for "natal claims" upon the "Islamic East," Abdul Khabeer explains—noting also the common "elision of Africa from the Islamic East"—Black music becomes positioned as inescapably "un-Islamic" and as vulnerable to condemnation from non-Black authorities. She quotes poet Amir Sulaiman's criticism of Muslim anti-Blackness in the documentary film *Deen Tight*: "What makes you Black and American is haram."[5] In both its polemics against Salafism's rise in African American Muslim communities and the embodied performances of its leader, AAC/NIH media make their own interventions in the debate.

In order to examine these ostensible tensions and locate music's significance in Al Mahdi's metaphysical Africa, I first introduce what I call "Ansar musical theory," in which Al Mahdi creatively rewires tropes of innate Black musicality in the service of his double resistance, confronting both white supremacy and transnational Sunni hegemony. Ansar musical theory speaks to a U.S. context in which Black musical traditions have been stolen, corrupted, and exploited by white artists and institutions, but also one in which Blackamerican Muslims face pressures from Sunni revivalist networks to disavow those same traditions on the grounds that Islam prohibits music (either in most forms or altogether). Al Mahdi's metaphysics of race, which imagines music as key to Nubian spirituality, accounts for the racial histories of American music while also indicting Islamic condemnations of music for its implicit anti-Blackness. I then turn to an examination of the community's presence in hip-hop culture, discussing artists (both insiders and outsiders in relation to the community) who engage Al Mahdi's material in their work up to and beyond the Nuwaubian turn. This chapter extends the notion of AAC/NIH discourse beyond official community publications to include affiliated artists and their collaborators, demonstrating that the Ansar influence on hip-hop reflects Al Mahdi's vision of metaphysical Africa in its simultaneous resistance to American white supremacy and Muslim anti-Blackness. I also highlight the ways in which the permeability of borders between religious identities, so often treated as the AAC/NIH's definitive feature, can be found throughout Islamic hip-hop.

ANSAR MUSICAL THEORY

During one of Al Mahdi's question-and-answer sessions at his Hall of Knowledge on Hart Street, open to the public and recorded for his *True Light* cassette series, a Christian woman states that she likes singing in church but knows that "you don't do those things." Al Mahdi replies, "Yes, we do," and explains that Americans misunderstand music's importance in Islam because "what has happened here in America is Muslims don't have Islam as it was taught by *the Africans*." He tells the woman about dhikr and the Black origin of the piano, adding that while his community avoids certain instruments that "stimulate negative energy," nonetheless "gospel is part of us."[6]

On another *True Light* tape, Al Mahdi presents the Amorites' inability to dance—their lack of "soul"—as evidence that they literally lack souls.[7] As in *Disco Music: The Universal Language of Good or Evil?* (1979), Al Mahdi rewires tropes of innate Black musicality to present facility with music as a Nubian spiritual gift. Nubians remain in tune with the vibrations of the universe, which affect them in physical and emotional ways and endow them with an enhanced sensitivity to sound. Nubian music thus expresses "spiritual influence" that cannot be found in music from Amorites, who remain "physically bound." Unable to match Nubians' musical power, Amorites sought to erase it. In the American context, this meant the denial of access to musical training. Despite enslavers' attempts to erase music from the lives of the enslaved, however, the Amorite "could not suppress what came natural to you: that which Allah subhana wa ta'ala bestowed the Black man with. The Black man always finds ways to become involved with instruments and become masters of them." As enslaved Africans developed new musical forms in the Americas, they used songs to pass secret messages without detection by slaveowners; according to Al Mahdi, this is the origin of the blues. Amorites then manipulated Nubian music for their own purposes, reinscribing the blues as "spirituals" to indoctrinate Nubians with Christianity.[8]

The twentieth century saw an acceleration of Black musical development, again prompting Amorites to intervene, seeking Black performers who were unknown outside Black communities and emulating or outright stealing their work. The Amorite, deprived of Nubian sensitivities to "vibrations, frequencies, and amplitude effects," can only make music using technological resources as a "master thief." Al Mahdi explains that "only Allah subhana wa ta'ala has the power to bestow creative ability upon whom he pleases." It is the devil's nature and power "to take peace (Islam) from the earth, so when Black men find peace in anything, the Devil devises a plan to eliminate it and him." Amorites weaponized Nubians' vulnerability to cosmic vibrations, using it against them, developing new forms of poisonous music that brought Nubian consciousness under their control. While Black people were traditionally moved by "real and pure music, performed on naturally made instruments," the Amorites warped this experience by "creating unreal sounds with electronic devices." The Amorite has "stepped into the field of music and stripped it of all emotions and beauty. Now music is lifeless, emotionless and empty of any positiveness. Music is a tool of Shaytan's used against the Nubian man."[9]

The Amorite project culminates in the discotheque, home to loud music at harmful volumes, strobe lights, and "overall abusive activities." Among the threats of the discotheque, Al Mahdi lists exposure to dangerous radiation, nerve damage, brain tissue damage, accelerated heart rate, pitch-based mind control, and subliminal messages. The "high shrilling sounds" of disco music reflect the language of the jinn, a "race of evil angels" whose nature finds physical expression in pale Amorite peoples. Disco clubs brainwash Black women into wearing immodest dress—including high-heeled shoes that affect "the chromosomes of all those who wear them"—and immoral behavior, including sex with white men. In contrast to the disco club, AAC/NIH newspapers present photos of an all-woman Ansaru Allah dance troupe in traditional pantomimic dances. Some dances are better than others: "The Amorite has never known how to dance, because he has no rhythm or soul," but he teaches Nubians to perform dances that "imitate animals." In the dances of popular culture, Al Mahdi decodes hidden narratives that the Amorite tells about the Nubian. The Robot, for example, offers a lesson about Muslims who fall to the devil and adopt a "robot-like way of life."[10] The most severe musical proof of white "negative seed" nature would appear in white youth cultures such as heavy metal and punk rock, which Al Mahdi charges with promoting outrageous hairstyles and clothing, drug use, Satanism, witchcraft, and offerings of blood sacrifice.[11]

As an alternative to contemporary Amorite music, AAC/NIH newspapers advertise recordings by internationally renowned Nubian Egyptian composer, oud player, and vocalist Hamza El Din (1929–2006). In *Disco Music*, Al Mahdi explains that El Din became interested in music as a young man, which caused him to neglect "the Nubian language and other aspects of the country's culture." As an adult, El Din "took a sharp turn" and "became aware of how important it was to write songs in the Nubian language, affirming the bond between his art and his people." Al Mahdi identifies El Din as a member of the Ansaru Allah Community[12] and claims that El Din accompanied Al Mahdi's mother to the United States from Egypt during her pregnancy.[13] In 1988, Mahdi Records (the AAC/NIH-specific auxiliary of York's Records) released *Hamza El Din Live at the Ansaaru Allah Community in America*, with cover art depicting El Din in the Ansar's white turban and robe, playing the oud while surrounded by an Ansar audience in matching garb.

El Din serves the AAC/NIH's double resistance against a white supremacist music industry and "pale Arab" Sunni hegemony. While Amorites in the West use music to control Nubian minds, Muslim "pale Arabs"—themselves being white people and incompatible with Nubian vibrations—condemn music with claims that singing, dancing, and playing stringed instruments are prohibited in Islam. Al Mahdi's vision of Nubian music thus becomes a defense against what he perceives as the anti-Blackness of Sunni revivalism. At least as far back as the early 1970s, Al Mahdi upheld music as Islamically valid, explaining that "the prayers in Islam are actually song," and describing the "lack of soul" in pale Arabs' music as a means of distinguishing between them and true Black people in cases of uncertainty. While most of the only extant copy of *Is Music and Dance Lawful for Muslims?* (ca. 1972) is unreadable, it does defend music's legitimacy and provides drawings of instruments such as the duff, Egyptian harps, sistrum, and oud. *Islamic Music* (1977) elaborates the argument. "As the sun dances across the sky," Al Mahdi muses, "the birds sing a song in the praise of Allah subhana wa ta'ala." Music is essential to Muslim spirituality, specifically for Nubian Muslims: "Through music, stories of life are told and in the past the Blacks in Sudan told stories on the drum which told their family lineage."[14] In *Abba Island in America*, he explains that "dancing is an Islamic tradition" and that "the duff is an important part of a ceremony in Islam."[15]

Conversion to Islam, Al Mahdi assures his readers, "will not deprive you of music as some Muslims have misunderstood"; rather, "it will only put music in its rightful place." Noting that "some American Muslims think it is unlawful to participate in music and dance," he dismisses this position as a misinterpretation derived from inauthentic hadiths. Rejecting antimusic hadiths, Al Mahdi instead offers Qur'anic and biblical evidence to present music as essential to the religion of Abraham. The angels sing, and the Qur'an itself was revealed via angelic vocal performances. Citing the Bible, Al Mahdi refers to angels and Israelites alike using trumpets, and to the prophet David organizing musical performances in the Temple. He also points out that the Bible provides ample endorsements of women participating in singing, dancing, and playing musical instruments.[16]

Against the combined Euro-American and pale Arab Sunni hegemonies, Al Mahdi advocates local musical expression: "The folk-songs of a nation or a people are a part of its cultural heritage and every effort should be made to preserve them, especially in this era of swift adaptation to other cultures and other art forms." Dancing is also part of Islamic tradition, though Al Mahdi observes that many American Muslims assume otherwise. "Contrary to what a number of American Muslims think," he writes, "dancing among Muslims is not only ceremonial and ritualistic, but a practice of joy seen amongst every Muslim festival and ceremony from weddings to feasts." He argues that the Qur'an expresses no disapproval of dancing, and he supplements his case with reference to the hadith of Muhammad that permits dancing on festival days, as well as to the famous "whirling dervishes" of Sufism.[17]

Al Mahdi's discourse on sound and music informs his performance of the call to prayer (which, while typically melodic, arguably becomes more of a song when he delivers it), his recitation of the Qur'an, and his recorded reading of the Sudanese Mahdiyya's *Ratib* with musical accompaniment and background vocals. Recognizing and properly using the powers of sound remains a critical concern in Al Mahdi's Sufism, as he attests in Sons of the Green Light lessons, where he says that collective dhikr—performed under the proper conditions and with the guidance of the murshid—can merge the physical world with the unseen, enabling travel to other dimensions.[18] Al Mahdi also treats "the right type of music" as a medical cure. "We find proof of this in the very Scriptures that we follow," he writes in his *Wadhiyfah: The Science of Sound Healing* pamphlet series, which operates as a manual for reciting divine names and the corresponding bodily movements. Treating Allah's "99+1 names" as a "talisman," Al Mahdi provides instructions for chanting each name, along with the name's respective benefits and rewards. "So often," he observes, "a dhikr is accomplished by the rhythmic beating of a drum or by music either vocal or instrumental." By training the ear and soul together, one can access higher octaves, "which produce emotional and mental waves up to the sound HUWA which is the pure green light of energy.... As you can see, there are many mysteries I have yet to reveal to you!!!"[19] While Al Mahdi maintains that music is a racially exclusive portal into secrets of the unseen, Dr. York's full-page ad in the May 4, 1985, edition of *Billboard* promises that he "believes music crosses all boundaries and communicates to everyone regardless of race or nationality."

The imam's musical gifts do not contradict his claims of spiritual gifts but are symptomatic of them. *Humazah* (ca. 1979) provides a photograph of Al Mahdi wearing a white kufi and the AAC/NIH star and crescent on his jacket's shoulder patch, sitting at a piano or keyboard, with the caption "Imam Isa getting into some heavy Islamic music."[20] The photo expresses a vision of "Islamic music," which might have been unthinkable or at least controversial for many of *Humazah*'s readers, as legitimate and possible. In AAC/NIH literature, the question of music's relationship to Islam, which is simultaneously a question of Islam's relationship to Blackness, becomes a site at which Al Mahdi's metaphysical Africa meets Muslim Cool. For Al Mahdi, music and Islam remain as deeply intertwined with each other as they are innately bound to Blackness.

FROM ANSAR COOL TO THE INTERGALACTIC SUDAN

In the rare instances in which AAC/NIH publications address Al Mahdi as Dr. York, Al Mahdi defends his music as a "starting point of communication to a trouble world," a means of giving the *da'wa* and reaching "all types of people, so that they too might bear witness to the TRUTH and be saved." Not everyone was willing to learn from Muslims "gowned in sunnah: white jalabiyyah, immamah, etc., and the editions in our hand"; therefore, Al Mahdi wrote, "we must relate to them on their level. This is why the group Passion was formed and is now successfully reaching these people." Despite his critiques of the U.S. music industry, Al Mahdi would also embrace hip-hop culture as another vehicle for his mission. AAC/NIH literature from the late 1980s and early '90s gives favorable attention to artists who are either claimed as members of the community (such as Intelligent Hoodlum, later known as Tragedy Khadafi) or unaffiliated but sympathetic (such as Queen Latifah, who wears a Mahdiyya flag pin in her "Dance for Me" video).[21]

The AAC/NIH's embrace of hip-hop artists as voices of Black consciousness corresponds to hip-hop's broad embrace of Islam. Sohail Daulatzai observes a 1986–94 "golden age" in which many premier emcees treated Islam as crucial to a "history of Black radicalism and internationalism."[22] The Islam of "golden age" hip-hop was most powerfully informed by the Five Percenter tradition, which claims such past and present affiliates as the Wu Tang Clan, Rakim, Brand Nubian, Big Daddy Kane, Erykah Badu, Common, Gang Starr, Poor Righteous Teachers, Lakim Shabazz, and more. The Five Percenters' prominence in Black and Latino youth cultures of 1970s–80s New York contributed to the wide circulation of the tradition's vocabulary and references; as a result, artists who did not overtly claim membership in the Five Percenters, such as Nas, still incorporated Five Percenter concepts and vocabulary. In contrast to the widely acknowledged Five Percenter contribution to hip-hop,[23] academic discussions of hip-hop and Islam have entirely neglected the Ansar presence. I would argue that Ansar hip-hop makes a unique and compelling contribution to what Daulatzai calls "the Muslim international," the ways in which hip-hop artists conceptualized "an internationalism in relation to Africa and the Muslim Third World that challenges U.S. power in those regions."[24] In the case of Al Mahdi's community, this Muslim international—overlapping with already present Islamic spaceship narratives and Afrofuturist themes in popular music—transcends earthly bounds to become intergalactic.

The AAC/NIH's metaphysical Africa finds expression in hip-hop artifacts such as *To Your Soul* (1990), the EMI-released album of The Jaz, Jay-Z's mentor. The album's cover art presents The Jaz against a black background with red and green stripes, recalling the colors of pan-Africanism and specifically the flag of the Mahdi. "The Flag of the Mahdi" is the title of a spoken-word interlude on the record, in which The Jaz explains the meanings of the Mahdiyya flag, reciting its Arabic *kalimah* with careful pronunciation and English translation and explaining that Muhammad Ahmad was a direct descendant of the Prophet Muhammad who "fought against the Egyptian empire *and* the British empire and defeated them in his own homeland of the Sudan, using primitive weapons, as opposed to their more advanced arsenal of weapons." The Jaz credits the Ansaru Allah Community as the source of his flag, and closes with what sounds like the conclusion to a scripted infomercial: "To receive more information about it, you should check out the bookstore on Bushwick Ave." Some hip-hop references are less overt. Melle Mel wears the Mahdiyya flag in the video for "What's the Matter with Your World?," but apart from the pan-African connotations of its color scheme, its precise meanings are left to the viewer's guess. Intelligent Hoodlum would offer subtle hints of his AAC/NIH leanings in his eponymous 1990 debut album. While his song "Black and Proud" warns of white evil in very Ansar-specific terms—"Beware, the cursed seed is out there"—the lyrics give shout-outs by name not to Al Mahdi but to Louis Farrakhan and Malcolm X.

In another video from the same period, KMD's "Peach Fuzz," from the group's debut album *Mr. Hood* (1991), presents an Ansar youth culture at the intersection of Al Mahdi's African Muslim imaginaries and the community's original home of Brooklyn, New York. The video opens with a shot of the group's young members as Ansar peddlers wearing *thobes*, turbans, kufis, and nose rings. As an elder AAC/NIH member prepares to leave them at their table of pamphlets and other products, he warns, "No rappin' to the girls." The young men laughingly deny any such intention and exchange greetings of *as-salamu alaikum* with the man as he departs. The scene that follows features a cameo from white artist D-Nice of the group 3rd Bass and shows KMD talking about girls while flipping through a hip-hop magazine—carefully hidden inside a booklet from Al Mahdi's *tafsir* (Qur'anic exegesis) series, *As Sayyid Al Imaam Isa Al Haadi Al Mahdi Explains the Secret Meaning of Qur'aan to the A'immah of Ansaaru Allah*. As a group of young women approach their table, the KMD members indeed start trying to impress them. The song's lyrics offer humorous self-deprecation, as the group's young members lament their lack of facial hair while also resisting masculinist pressures (and Ansar expectations) to grow full beards.[25]

KMD's *Mr. Hood* also reflects the fluidity between archives characteristic not only of Al Mahdi's metaphysical Africa but of hip-hop's Islamic expressions at large. As Zaheer Ali has noted, the Islam of "golden age" hip-hop is historically nonsectarian. No distinction is made between Nation-era Malcolm X and Malcolm after his Sunni conversion; speeches from Louis Farrakhan and Malcolm X can both be sampled in the same song; and artists of varying communal identities and theological orientations collaborate with one another, sharing in a mutual sense of Islam that transcends doctrinal particulars.[26] "Nitty Gritty," KMD's collaboration with Brand Nubian on *Mr. Hood*, begins with the exclamation "The Five Percent and the Ansar together?" and includes references to Five Percenter concepts.

Writing under the name El Haady from his Mount Zion camp in 1992, Al Mahdi claimed that numerous struggling artists—including KMD, Melle Mel, Kenny Gamble, X-Clan, and Afrika Bambaataa—became stars or rejuvenated their careers by physically touching the hem of his garment.[27] These claims might be contested, but his material did inform the lyrics of artists beyond his own community. Professor Griff, a former Nation of Islam member and leader of the hip-hop group Professor Griff and the Last Asiatic Disciples, draws from Al Mahdi's treatment of the word "God" as an acronym for Gomar Oz Dubar ("Wisdom, Strength, Beauty") in the song "Pawns in the Game."[28] In "Living for the City," Rakim identifies himself as "Gomar Oz Dubar, which is God."[29] And in "The Mystery (Who Is God)," on his debut solo album *The 18th Letter*, Rakim incorporates Al Mahdi's analysis of the word "God" to further his Five Percenter message that he is God and Allah, naming the attributes as equivalent to those of Gomar Oz Dubar.[30]

Through his studio and label, Al Mahdi collaborated with Afrika Bambaataa, whose Zulu Nation movement—itself an intellectual platform that, while not expressly Muslim, included faith in the Qurʾan as a primary tenet—has been described as "the founding ideological movement in hip-hop culture."[31] Bambaataa recorded his 1989 album *Return to Planet Rock* at York's Studios and released the LP on York's Records. The album's cover art speaks to those already versed in Ansar symbolic vocabulary (fig. 35): Bambaataa and the Jungle Brothers appear in outer space, within the beam of green light trailing behind the Crystal City, the new Jerusalem as it is regularly depicted in the community's literature of that period; Bambaataa wears a bandana bearing the Sudanese Mahdiyya emblem; he wields Zulfikar, the famous double-bladed sword of ʿAli. In the lower left corner, we find the black, red, and green Nubian flag, complete with Mahdiyya emblem and *kalimah* in Arabic script. The album jacket's back side names Dr. York as executive producer and credits him for remixing the recordings, giving a separate acknowledgment to As Sayyid Isa Al Haadi Al Mahdi. Bambaataa also praises Louis Farrakhan ("May ALLAH always bless you both") and both the Ansar and the Nation of Islam.

The text on *Return to Planet Rock*'s jacket engages Al Mahdi's Ansar musical theory and cosmic mythology with a narrative that positions the album within a history of extraterrestrial intervention in human destiny. In 1970, the earth was visited by "space beings" who came first to Africa and discovered that, despite "lots of problems," music played a big role in keeping the people together on that continent. These beings traveled the world and found that problems existed everywhere, but they also observed that "it was music in some ways that broke social barriers." The text explains that the United States had received numerous "messengers in music" sent by the Supreme One, among them James Brown, Sly Stone, and George Clinton, to "teach and spread the word through music, but the evil ones help to delude and destroy what they have built." The Supreme One then sent DJ Kool Herc, along with a team of "space beings" who became known as Afrika Bambaataa and the Soulsonic Force. After attempts by the

FIGURE 35 Afrika Bambaataa and the Soulsonic Force, *Return to Planet Rock* (1989).

"evil ones" to suppress hip-hop's potential to create a "new world order," "the Supreme One has sent Afrika Bambaataa and the Soulsonic Force back by the Mothership." In addition, according to Ansar sacred history, 1970 was the year in which the seventh seal was opened, initiating the end times, which would culminate in the rising of a righteous nation of 144,000 and the establishment of the new City of Peace.[32] On March 16, 1970, "the year of the Opening," Al Mahdi writes in *The True Story of Noah* (1986), "we arrived to this planet Earth. Astronomers knew little of our natures and out of their ignorance, called us Comets."[33] In later years, Afrika Bambaataa donated a Moroccan fez bearing the UNNM flag and the words "PROUD NUWAUBIAN" to the Smithsonian.[34]

Al Mahdi's community entered its "post-Islamic" Nuwaubian stage in the early and mid-1990s, which roughly parallels the declining presence of "Muslim international" imaginaries in hip-hop. In 1993 Al Mahdi relocated to Georgia and became Dr. Malachi Z. York, a name that emphasized his new platform and also recalled his career in music as Dr. York. Though the exodus from Brooklyn left behind a fledgling music empire on Bushwick Avenue, the community remained a citable source for hip-hop. References to Nuwaubu appear in the lyrics of Jedi Mind Tricks artist Vinnie Paz, who describes Philadelphia as the city where "the Moors, Nuwaubians, Five Percenters will build."[35] In "Eye Is the King," Vinnie Paz and his group Heavy Metal Kings declare that York is "ahead of his time"; Paz insists, "Support Dr. York, don't believe what's said about him."[36] In "Kill Devil Hills," Paz calls himself a "United Nuwaubian Nation of Moors rhymer."[37] Not all references come from admirers, as evidenced in Talib Kweli's advice to inferior artists that they should give up music and perhaps sell drugs or "start speakin' Nuwaubian and followin' Malachi."[38]

Tragedy Khadafi's "Eloheem" includes a reference to "the Kedar."[39] In his "Allumaniti," Khadafi again offers layers of meaning for listeners who are already versed in the Nuwaubian archive, with mentions of Canaanites, Amorites, and Gomar Oz Dubar.[40]

The Nuwaubian era spawned a musical subgenre, "Nu-wop," characterized by its readings of Malachi Z. York. Nu-wop does not compartmentalize its references as either "Islamic" or "Egyptosophic." The group Lost Children of Babylon draws from the full wealth of the Nuwaubian archive in songs such as "Distant Traveller," in which member Richard Raw, "guided by the pineal gland," calls his mind "a replica of Mecca," identifies with the "order of the Sufi, understudy of Tehuti," commands that we heed 'Ali's "voice of the two edge sword," and escapes "Shamballah to follow the scholars to the Ka'ba," where he will then be transformed into a chupacabra and "stand on my altar on which I offer to the flying saucers."[41] In "The Rising Force" and "Duel of the Fates," from its *Words from the Duat—The Book of Anubis* album, the group (recording this album as the Lost Children of Egypt, rather than Babylon, reportedly at York's direction) weaves *Star Wars* references into Nuwaubian discourse, making lyrical connections between the falcon-headed god Horus and the *Millennium Falcon*, and name-dropping Anakin Skywalker and Darth Maul alongside Akhenaten and the Lion of Judah. Audio samples from the *Star Wars* film soundtracks contribute to the recoding of Jedi mythology within Nuwaubian Afrofuturism: "The Force rises within me because the kingdom of ANU is within me; it takes me from the planet earth to the nineteenth galaxy instantaneously."[42] Nu-wop lyrics constitute a body of esoteric poetry that gradually becomes accessible as one learns the vast lexicon of Nuwaubian references.

CONCLUSIONS

Al Mahdi's career as R&B singer Dr. York, while seemingly at odds with his prescriptions for embodied Muslim practice, nonetheless reflects AAC/NIH imaginaries of music and sound. Ansar musical theory reinscribes new values on worn tropes of Black musicality: Black people are innately musical, he argues, for the same reasons that they are innately Muslim, and there is no conflict between the two. Nubian musical and spiritual gifts alike are suppressed and exploited by the enemies of Black people, whether Euro-American or "pale Arab," Christian or Muslim.

While Al Mahdi officially opposes Western musical forms and electronically derived music as the devil's tools, used by whites to brainwash and rule Black people, AAC/NIH literature supports Al Mahdi's musical pursuits and hip-hop culture as positive forces for the resurrection of Black consciousness. Al Mahdi argues that his "secular" music attracts audiences that would never learn of Islam otherwise. In the case of hip-hop, AAC/NIH writings praise artists whose work expresses connections to Black liberation and Islam, including not only AAC/NIH-affiliated artists but also artists committed to the Nation of Islam and the Five Percenters. Confronting both American white supremacy and a new American Islam defined increasingly by transnational Salafiyya networks that became prime voices of antimusic perspectives, Al Mahdi's metaphysical Africa affirms music, Islam, and Blackness not only as mutually compatible but as embedded in one another as a fact of nature.

Coda

The View from Illyuwn

> Fools among the people will say:
> "What turned them from their
> *qiblah* that they were on?"
>
> —QUR'AN 2:142

On June 26, 1997, his fifty-second birthday, Malachi Z. York reinstituted a ceremony that had not been practiced for ten thousand years: El Maguraj (fig. 36). He called upon his followers, newly renamed Nuwaubians, to visit Tama Re for realignment with "your etheric parents, the elders, the ancient ones ... who are trying to reach you." While the rites around Tama Re's El Aswud Mir (Black Pyramid) might have reminded former Ansar of pilgrimage to Mecca, York tells his readers that "all Islam comes from us." The branch cannot charge the root with theft or appropriation. Even Moses, before becoming a god in his own right, was a student of Tehuti/Thoth, Egyptian god of knowledge and wisdom.[1]

In his Afrofuturist perennialism, York explains that the specific practices of El Maguraj came from the rites of Amun-Ra in the city of Karnak, but the spiritual technologies of pyramids—constructed as antennas and "electrical capacitors" that provide balance in the earth's magnetic fields and help humans to change their *halut* (auras) to more positive frequencies—existed throughout the ancient world, evidenced in Mayan and Sumerian pyramids. The Ark of the Covenant operated as a similar device and as a "portable communication center" that enabled dispatches between the extraterrestrial Eloheem and the earthly Levitical priesthood. The broader principles at work can also be found among Yoruba practices, Sufi whirling and dhikr, and the rain dance of the Hopi, who had learned the concept from their "true father," the Dogon of Mali, who in turn were taught by extraterrestrial visitors.[2] The great wisdom traditions of the world are but expressions of a singular tradition, the wisdom of a timeless and interstellar Blackness most perfectly expressed in the science of Nuwaubu as revived by the master teacher.

El Maguraj ceremonies at Tama Re included a "procession of Osiris," in which York, escorted by the Brotherhood of the Night, became Osiris's incarnation in order to properly fulfill the role of pharaoh. The procession featured the wealth of the community's symbolic reservoir: two costumed participants embodied the gods Horus and Anubis; the Brotherhood of the Green Light carried an Anubis statue; the Sisters of Isis led a Mother Isis procession; men dressed in the familiar white robes and turbans of the Ansaru Allah carried the Ark of the Covenant and a candlestick of seven candles, recalling Revelation 1:12–13; priests leading the Osiris procession blew the shofar, beat drums, and carried the sword of Solomon.[3]

Academic and popular treatments of AAC/NIH media have emphasized the community's eclectic pool of resources, taking for granted that the community haphazardly pinballed between confessional identities with no regard for stability or coherence. Describing Tama Re's "most startling artifact of all"—a "black Jesus crucified on an Ankh crowned with the feathered headdress of the Plains Indian"—Susan Palmer marvels at the Nuwaubians' "syncretistic creativity."[4] Many observers regard this new Jesus as a random assemblage of parts from otherwise separate systems. When they see the Nuwaubian Christ, they are most struck by the ways in which Nuwaubians have apparently forged inorganic connections between unrelated bodies. To designate Tama Re's Christ as an example of syncretism, however, does not merely explain what is happening in the image but actively creates and imposes new meanings on the work.

The label of "syncretism" invents categories, measures their limits, and names their violators. When we think of Tama Re's Christ as syncretic, we have suddenly created Christianity, Egyptosophy, and Native American religion for ourselves, determining where each territory ends and the others begin, with an assumption of firmly policed borders that would normally protect them from mixture; they are not *really* meant to go together. If Christ's being crucified on an Egyptian ankh means that Christianity has been transformed by its encounters with non-Christian traditions, this forces the question of what Christianity

FIGURE 36 *El Maguraj*, Nuwaubian pilgrimage manual, 1990s.

should look like "as it is," prior to all acts of blending. But as Joseph Murphy has noted in a discussion of Afro-Cuban religion, mixture remains "present in every historical religious expression."[5] Carl Ernst similarly asks, "Where shall we find this historically untouched religion? Is there any religious tradition untouched by other religious cultures? Has any religion sprung into existence fully formed without reference to any previously existing religion?"[6] While mixture happens everywhere, Murphy observes that some religious expressions become defined by mixture more than others; European Christian traditions emerged from their own blended histories, but they are not typically subjected to the same analysis of "syncretism" that African Christian traditions are; instead, Europe becomes privileged as Christianity's default setting.[7] The notion that Africans "mixed" an otherwise self-contained Christianity with their local traditions and bodies of knowledge suggests that Christianity's truest and most generic form is European. Since the "pure and unmixed" Christianity is presumed to exist outside Africa, contact with Africa means a pollution and corruption of the imported "real" Christianity. In Islamic studies, notions of syncretic exchange and mixture between "Islamic" and "indigenous" likewise threaten to racialize Islam as an Arab phenomenon that inevitably becomes less of itself when appropriated in non-Arab societies.

In the case of the AAC/NIH, my concern with resisting framing the material as syncretism relates in part to the master narrative of Al Mahdi/York as an unstable trickster who changes costumes seemingly at random and freestyles his way into power via pure charisma. For its denial of the locally specific, this model leads to an unfortunate "holy madness, crazy wisdom" framework, which would never ask that we consider how the community produces a persuasive discourse or understands relationships between its various moving parts.

Murphy suggests that if mixture is inevitable in all traditions, the fact of mixture itself is less interesting than "the way in which the mixture is organized."[8] Looking at the AAC/NIH, this means attending to a local tradition in which Muslim thinkers can code materials such as Akhenaten, Freemasonry, and the book of Revelation as Islamic resources. In Louis Farrakhan's address at his Million Man March in 1995, we find reflections on the esoteric meanings of the number nineteen ("And when you have a one standing by the nine, it means that there's something secret that has to be unfolded"), references to "secret Masonic ritual" and "our great historic past, Egypt," and more citations of the Bible than of the Qur'an. Al Mahdi did not need to venture beyond his local masjid to learn about the Blackness of the original Hebrews; he would have learned this from his Sunni mentor, Sheikh Daoud Faisal, as an essential

FIGURE 37 Extraterrestrial wearing Ancient and Mystic Order of Melchizedek fez, from an advertisement for Ancient and Mystic Order of Melchizedek and Holy Tabernacle Ministries merchandise, in Holy Tabernacle Ministries, *Savior's Day 1996: Man of Many Faces Brings Us One Message* (1996).

truth of what it means to be Muslim. Nor did his mythos of redemptive apocalyptic spaceships betray Islam's boundaries as a category. Many who came to his community, familiar to varying degrees with Elijah Muhammad's vision of the Mothership, were already prepared to think of extraterrestrial civilizations through Islamic lenses (fig. 37).

Surveying the literature at a Nuwaubian bookstore, Palmer notes the "seemingly incompatible sources" on display.[9] But Islam, Black Hebrews/Israelites, Freemasonry, pharaonic Egypt, Native American wisdom traditions, New Age esotericism, and UFOs were already organically linked in the imaginaries of metaphysical Africa long before Dwight York, Isa Al Haadi Al Mahdi, Y'shua Bar El Haady, Chief Black Eagle, Yanaan/Yaanuwn, Al Qutb, Amunnubi Rooakhptah, or Malachi Zodok York-El ever touched them. If the oral traditions are correct, young Dwight York might have first learned about the connections between Islam and Africa from his mother's participation at both State Street Mosque and Yoruba Temple: these mixtures precede him.

The Nuwaubian Christ would not have been a "startling" hodgepodge of disconnected motifs to everyone. The Ansar were not deconstructionists engaged in a postmodern dissolution of categories. They certainly made categories of their own. They drew borders and cared about policing them. Equipped with taxonomies of religion that made sense for them and armed with hard facts from their master teacher, they condemned other communities for concealing what they regarded as the objective and universal truth.

In addition to resisting the "holy madness, crazy wisdom" model, I have also challenged the popular narrative of serial reinvention that characterizes most accounts of this community. This book calls attention to the surprising degree of stability and consistency in AAC/NIH discourse from the 1970s through the early '90s and even beyond, into the Nuwaubian era. This is not to deny the community's observable transformations, nor do I claim that community literature never makes contradictory claims or violates its own continuities. Of course, I am not the ultimate judge of whether Nuwaubu makes compelling arguments. Nonetheless, I do insist that compelling arguments, rather than just bewildering charisma, be acknowledged as valuable in AAC/NIH literature—much of which was written for the express purpose of supporting rational, evidence-based debate against followers of other movements and traditions.

The community's media make frequent reference to its various changes, giving retroactive accounts of having passed through successive "schools" to reach its present truth. "I never intended for my people to remain Mohammedans," York writes;[10] Islam was merely "one of the schools we passed through on our way to godhood, Neteraat."[11] But as I demonstrated in my discussion of the Nuwaubian turn, York's "post-Islamic" arguments continued to rely on past Ansar citations, symbols, and themes, the scripts that his readers already knew as true and important. Given the field of relations within York's discursive universe, moving from the Sudanese Mahdiyya to Egyptosophy, shifting emphasis from his *ahl al-bayt* lineage to an origin in the nineteenth galaxy, or turning a Sufi order into a Masonic lodge did not require that he burn down his system to rebuild from scratch. A careful look at books, pamphlets, newspapers, and lecture cassettes over the decades reveals that amid these seemingly radical reorientations, the community maintained a sense of its own trajectory.

One of the sites at Tama Re that has generally been ignored in outsider coverage was its "Mahdi shrine," found along the road leading to the pyramids. Established through the efforts of a community elder, the Mahdi shrine was ornamented with pious formulas in Arabic script, Ansar flags, the Mahdiyya spear-and-crescent symbol, and the AAC/NIH's six-pointed star and crescent from its Brooklyn era, and it featured a small, roofless masjid painted in green and gold, complete with mihrab indicating the direction of Mecca. A younger generation of Nuwaubians, born years after the community graduated from its "Muslim school," might not have shared the elders' personal attachment to Islamic ritual spaces or Sudanese Mahdiyya references. Community members from the Bushwick Avenue days, however, could have found comfort in the through lines and visions of continuity that a Tama Re masjid offered. Even as statues of ibis-headed gods and the crucified Christ shared space with Arabic testimonies to God's unity and the prophethood of Muhammad, Nuwaubu found its own coherence, on its own terms, in its own galaxy.

Notes

INTRODUCTION

1. When referring to its members in the plural, AAC/NIH community literature has used both "Ansar," the Arabic plural, and the anglicized plural "Ansars" (while also varying its vowels, sometimes spelling the word Ansaar or Ansaars). For the sake of consistency, I refer to community members in the plural as Ansar, reflecting the Arabic plural, unless directly quoting from the community's references to itself.
2. Philips, *Ansar Cult in America*, 128–29.
3. Ibid., i.
4. Ibid., 14–18, 27–33.
5. Baer and Singer, "Toward a Typology"; Palmer and Luxton, "Ansaaru Allah Community."
6. Gabriel, "United Nuwaubian Nation of Moors"; McCloud, *African American Islam*, 61–64.
7. Smith, *Islam in America*, 100–101.
8. Haddad and Smith, *Mission to America*, 105–36.
9. Ahmed, "Muslim Organizations in the United States."
10. Smith, *Islam in America*, 100–101.
11. Gardell, *Name of Elijah Muhammad*, 205–31.
12. Gabriel, "United Nuwaubian Nation of Moors."
13. Ibid.; Smith, *Islam in America*, 100–101.
14. For an example of this treatment, see Palmer, *Nuwaubian Nation*.
15. Albanese, *Republic of Mind and Spirit*, 17; see also 330–93.
16. Ernst, "Situating Sufism and Yoga."
17. Palmer, *Nuwaubian Nation*, 11.
18. See Dorman, "'True Moslem Is a True Spiritualist.'"
19. Howe, *Afrocentrism*, 266–70.
20. Moses, *Afrotopia*, 6.
21. Hornung, *Secret Lore of Egypt*, 1–2.
22. Moses, *Afrotopia*, 5.
23. Bruder and Parfitt, "Introduction."
24. Amen, "Oyotunji: Oyo Rises Again."
25. GhaneaBassiri, *History of Islam in America*, 197–99.
26. Aydin, *Idea of the Muslim World*, 81.
27. "Mrs. Besant, Sir Harry Johnston and Sir Charles Bruce," *African Times and Orient Review* (September 1912): 79–80.
28. Knight, *Magic in Islam*, 163–93.
29. Curtis, *Black Muslim Religion*, 92.
30. Quoted in Deutsch, "'Asiatic Black Man,'" 203.
31. Jackson, *Islam and the Blackamerican*, 18.
32. Abdul Khabeer, *Muslim Cool*, 96–97.
33. Elmasry, "Salafis in America."
34. Bowen, "Search for 'Islam.'"
35. GhaneaBassiri, *History of Islam in America*, 249–51.
36. Philips, *Ansar Cult in America*, 1.
37. York, *Shaikh Daoud vs. W. D. Fard*, 116.
38. Paul Greenhouse, conversation with author, May 2018, New York, N.Y.
39. On receiving her new name from Faisal, see Javid, *Constructing Life Narratives*, 49. On Jameelah's friendship with Faisal's wife, see Bowen, "Search for 'Islam.'"
40. Abusharaf, *Wanderings*, 41, 17–32, 35–36.
41. Abusharaf, "Structural Adaptations," 242.
42. Quoted in Warburg, *Islam, Sectarianism, and Politics*, 171–75.
43. Hucks, "From Cuban Santeria to African Yoruba," 339.
44. Ibid., 345.

45. Adefunmi, *Tribal Origins of African-Americans*, unnumbered page.
46. Minor Roberts, "Malcolm X: An Image Fades," *Pittsburgh Courier*, June 11, 1966, 2.
47. Adefunmi, *Tribal Origins of African-Americans*, unnumbered page.
48. Philips, *Ansar Cult in America*, 140–41.
49. Memorandum, "The Ansaru Allah Community, Also Known as the Nubian Islamic Hebrews, the Tents of Kedar; Domestic Security/Terrorism," n.d. [1992], U.S. Department of Justice, Federal Bureau of Investigation, New York, N.Y., unnumbered page.
50. NIHMA, *What Law Says the Veil*, 6.
51. NIHMA, *Look at the Muslim Man*, 7–8.
52. NIHMA, *Back to the Beginning*, 11, 20.
53. NIHMA, *Spell of the Blacks Was Broken*, unpaginated.
54. NIHMA, *Was Christ Really Crucified*, 4.
55. NIHMA, *Spell of the Blacks Was Broken*, unpaginated.
56. NIHMA, *Nubian Islamic Hebrew Mission*, 5th ed., unnumbered page.
57. NIHMA, *From Allah to Man*, ads, unnumbered pages; "Flemington's Earthy Crafts Fair Offers Bright Rainbow of Talent," *Pocono Record*, July 28, 1973, 38; "Black Culture Week in Miami," *Pittsburgh Courier*, May 27, 1973, 5.
58. Obaba, *Some Things Concerning Blacks*, 2.
59. Incidentally, Oyo's son, Kedar Massenburg, would run Motown Records from 1997 to 2004, during which time he coined the term "neo-soul" and gave Erykah Badu her first national stage.
60. NIHMA, *Nubian Islamic Hebrew Mission*, 3rd ed., unpaginated.
61. NIHMA, *Learn the Importance of Muslim Prayer*, unpaginated.
62. NIHMA, *From Allah to Man*, unpaginated.
63. NIHMA, *Nubian Islamic Hebrew Mission*, 4th ed., unpaginated.
64. NIHMA, *Founding Father of Islam in America*, 6. To contest Philips's charge of a late Mahdiyya claim, Al Mahdi's 1989 counterpolemic, *The Ansaar Cult: Rebuttal to the Slanderers*, reproduces a 1971 pamphlet, *The Mahdi*, affirming that "the Imam Isa is of the house of Al Mahdi (PBUH), the khalifa (successor) of the Prophet Muhammad Mustafa Al-Amin (PBUH)." Al Haadi Al Mahdi, *Rebuttal to the Slanderers*, 124.
65. Al Mahdi, *Bilal*, unnumbered page.
66. NIHMA, *Imam Isa*, unpaginated.
67. Special Agent in Charge to FBI Director, memorandum, "K. Ahmed Tawfiq, Mosque of Islamic Brotherhood, Inc.," September 20, 1973, file on Mosque of Islamic Brotherhood, U.S. Department of Justice, Federal Bureau of Investigation, New York, N.Y.
68. "The History of the Mosque of Islamic Brotherhood," *Western Sunrise*, September–October 1973, 5, 14.
69. Ansaru Allah Masgid, *Fallacy of Christmas*, 6.
70. Ibid.
71. AAC, "Blessings of the Festival and Goodness for You All Year," in *Id with the Ansars*, 7–9.
72. New York Police Department, 77th precinct, Herkimer Place Mosque case file, report dated February 18, 1974.
73. Al Mahdi, *Bilal*, unnumbered page.
74. AAC, *Signs of 73*, unnumbered page.
75. Ansaru Allah Masgid, *Fallacy of Christmas*, unnumbered page.
76. NIHMA, *Imam Isa*, unpaginated.
77. Al Mahdi, *What Is a Muslim*, 25.
78. AAC, "What Happened to All the Muslims, and Other Cultured People?," in *Man of Our Time*, 14.
79. AAC, "Blessings of the Festival," in *Id with the Ansars*, 7–9.
80. Ibid.
81. Philips, *Ansar Cult in America*, 141.
82. AAC, "Blessings of the Festival," in *Id with the Ansars*, 7–9.
83. Philips charges that Al Mahdi was actually born in 1935 but later claimed to have been born in 1945 to enhance his connection to Muhammad Ahmad. Philips observes that in a 1974 pamphlet, Al Mahdi's signature over his photo gave his birth year as 1935, while in sources after 1975—the point at which, according to Philips, Al Mahdi claimed to be the Mahdi's descendant and heir—his autograph on the same photo was revised to provide a birth year of 1945. Philips, *Ansar Cult in America*, 185–86. While Philips is right to point out the discrepancy, his reading of its significance is not accurate. In sources from 1972–73, Al Mahdi is identified as the Mahdi's grandson and is given a birthdate in 1945.

NIHMA, *Founding Father of Islam in America*, 6; AAC, *Signs of 73*, 2. Moreover, I found a version of the autographed photo from the Bushwick period in which the year is neither 1935 nor 1945 but 1925. Al Mahdi, *Opening of the Seventh Seal* (ca. 1974–77), unpaginated. Finally, in a mid- to late 1970s pamphlet, Al Mahdi states that he was born exactly one hundred years after the Mahdi, while on the same page we encounter the photo with 1925 written as his birth year. AAC, *Abba Island in America* (ca. 1974–77), unnumbered page. In my view, the explanation for these different years is not that Al Mahdi falsified his age for purposes of eschatological symbolism but the fact that these years are written in Arabic. For a novice student of Arabic, confusing the numerals 3 and 4 could be a reflexive mistake, since the Arabic numeral 4 looks like a reverse of the "European" (itself technically Arabic) numeral 3, while the stems of the Arabic 2 and 3 more closely resemble the shape of a "European" 4. The inconsistencies in Al Mahdi's birth years appear only in handwritten Arabic; nowhere in his English-language writings or use of "European" numerals does Al Mahdi claim a birth year other than 1945. It would appear that Al Mahdi (or whoever signed his name) simply wrote the wrong number.

84. Al Mahdi, *Muhammad Ahmad*, 40–44.
85. Al Mahdi, *I Don't Claim to Be*, 8–28.
86. Al Haadi Al Mahdi, "Unity Is a Must," in *Book of ل: To Whom It May Concern*, 2.
87. AAC, *Are the Ansars . . . a Self-Made Sect*, 19.
88. Mosque of Islamic Brotherhood, "Black, Red, and Green: The Sequence of Creation," *Western Sunrise*, July 1979–October 1980, 6, 17.
89. Al Haadi Al Mahdi, *Our Flag*.
90. Al Haadi Al Mahdi, *Hadrat Faatimah . . . Part 2*.
91. Al Haadi Al Mahdi, *True Light Tapes 2*.
92. Al Haadi Al Mahdi, *Book of Revelation, Chapter 1*, 94–95.
93. Ibid., 161–65.
94. See also AAC, *Humazah*, 10.
95. Tents of Nubia, *Truth*, Edition 15, 1.
96. York, *Does Dr. Malachi Z. York Try to Hide*.
97. York, *El's Holy Qur'aan*, unnumbered page.
98. Garnett, *Soul Sacrifice*, 103.

CHAPTER 1

1. The epigraphs to this chapter are from Houston, *Wonderful Ethiopians*, 111, and Rogers, *Negro-Caucasian Mixing*, 95–96, respectively.
2. Grewal, *Islam Is a Foreign Country*, 119.
3. Houston, *Wonderful Ethiopians*, 28, 126, 57, 60, 111, 115–16, 136, 150–51.
4. Gardell, *Name of Elijah Muhammad*, 37.
5. Nash, "Muhammad Ezaldeen"; Nash, "Addeynu Allahe Universal Arabic Association."
6. GhaneaBassiri, *History of Islam in America*, 222.
7. Muhammad, "Warning to the Black Man."
8. Gomez, *Black Crescent*, 316, 300, 317.
9. Muhammad, "Warning to the MGT and GCC."
10. Curtis, *Black Muslim Religion*, 86–92.
11. Muhammad, *Supreme Wisdom*, 18.
12. Berg, *Elijah Muhammad and Islam*, 11.
13. Quoted in Diamant, "Engagement and Resistance," 76–77; Clegg, *Original Man*, 183.
14. Diamant, "Engagement and Resistance," 137.
15. Gomez, *Black Crescent*, 367.
16. Hucks, "From Cuban Santeria to African Yoruba."
17. Clarke, *Mapping Yoruba Networks*, 72.
18. Hucks, "From Cuban Santeria to African Yoruba."
19. Adefunmi, *Tribal Origins of African-Americans*, 1.
20. Ibid.
21. Curtis, "Urban Muslims."
22. "The History of the Mosque of Islamic Brotherhood," *Western Sunrise*, September–October 1973, 5.
23. GhaneaBassiri, *History of Islam in America*, 292–93.
24. wadud, "American Muslim Identity."
25. Quoted in el-Amin, *Afrocentricity, Malcolm X, and al-Islam*, 115–17.
26. Quoted in Diamant, "Engagement and Resistance," 1.
27. Quoted in el-Amin, *Afrocentricity, Malcolm X, and al-Islam*, 115–17.
28. Quoted in Diamant, "Engagement and Resistance," 108, 109.
29. Ibid., 104, 124–26, 16, 131–33.
30. Ibid., 83, 127.
31. McCloud, *African American Islam*, 64–65.

32. Carter, "Islamic Party of North America."
33. "Oust Rauf—Heresy Condemned," *Al-Islam* 1, no. 2 (1972): 1.
34. "Islamic Worker's Response," editorial, *Al-Islam* 4, no. 6 (1976): 10, 12; "Elijah and Fard Must Go!," editorial, ibid., 11.
35. Elmasry, "Salafis in America."
36. Ben-Jochannan, *African Origins*, 195.
37. Williams, *Destruction of Black Civilization*, 34–35, 56–58, 135, 207, 23, 34, 208–9, 153.
38. Ibid., 23.
39. "Slaves: 'Set Them Free as a Favor,'" editorial, *Al-Islam* 5, no. 3 (1976): 2.
40. "Islam in Africa," editorial, *Al-Islam* 1, no. 2 (1972): 3–5, 9, 14.
41. Van Sertima, *They Came Before Columbus*, 102–3.
42. Asante, *Afrocentricity*, 5, 8–11.
43. Al Mahdi, *Polytheism*, 3.
44. Collins, *History of Modern Sudan*, 4.
45. Al Mahdi, *Tribal Encyclopedia*, 12.
46. Al Mahdi, *Muhammad Ahmad*, 7.
47. Al Haadi Al Mahdi, *You Are Adam's Descendants*, 8–20.
48. Al Mahdi, *Forgotten Tribe Kedar*, 25.
49. Al Mahdi, *Tribal Encyclopedia*, 11.
50. Al Haadi Al Mahdi, *Sons of Canaan*, 7.
51. Al Mahdi, *Tribal Encyclopedia*, 11.
52. Al Mahdi, *Lost Children of Mu and Atlantis*, 50–52.
53. Al Haadi Al Mahdi, *Sons of Canaan*, 7–8; see also Al Mahdi, *True Story of Noah* (1978 ed.), 13–14.
54. Al Haadi Al Mahdi, *True Story of Noah (PBUH), Part One* (1986 ed.), 59.
55. See Johnson, *Myth of Ham*.
56. Al Haadi Al Mahdi, *You Are Adam's Descendants*, 36–38.
57. Al Mahdi, *Book of Lamb 1*, unpaginated.
58. Al Mahdi, *Tribal Encyclopedia*, 15.
59. Ibid., 17.
60. Al Haadi Al Mahdi, *Paleman*, 71–78.
61. Al Mahdi, *Tribal Encyclopedia*, 17–19.
62. Al Haadi Al Mahdi, *Paleman*, 72.
63. The Supreme Wisdom Lessons, Lost-Found Muslim Lesson No. 1, http://www.ciphertheory.net/supremewisdom.pdf.
64. Hornung, *Secret Lore of Egypt*, 49–50.
65. Al Haadi Al Mahdi, *You Are Adam's Descendants*, 44.
66. Ibid., 58.
67. Al Haadi Al Mahdi, *Tabernacle of the Most High? Part 2*, 104–5.
68. Al Mahdi, *Tribal Encyclopedia*, 43–44.
69. Al Mahdi, *Polytheism*, 1.
70. Ibid., 9–13, 19, 23, 22, 25, 26.
71. Ibid., 27–28, 30, 33–35.
72. Al Mahdi, *Forgotten Tribe Kedar*, 19.
73. Al Mahdi, *Muhammad Ahmad*, 5.
74. Al Haadi Al Mahdi, *Sons of Canaan*, 7.
75. Al Haadi Al Mahdi, *True Light Tapes 1*.
76. Al Haadi Al Mahdi, *Sons of Canaan*, 6.
77. Al Haadi Al Mahdi, *Tabernacle of the Most High? Part 1*, 68.
78. Al Haadi Al Mahdi, *Sons of Canaan*, 6.
79. Al Haadi Al Mahdi, *You Are Adam's Descendants*, 59.
80. Abdul Khabeer, "Black Arabic," 171, 179.
81. Al Mahdi, *What Is a Muslim*, 11.
82. Al Haadi Al Mahdi, *Rebuttal to the Slanderers*, 115, 576.
83. NIHMA, *Back to the Beginning*, 1, 31, 32.
84. Al Mahdi, *Arabic: The First Language*, unnumbered page.
85. Al Mahdi, *The 99+1 Attributes of Allah*, 4.
86. Al Mahdi, *Arabic: The First Language*, 3, 4.
87. Al Haadi Al Mahdi, *Al Mahdi Explains . . . Degree of the Pure Faith*, 72–73.
88. Al Haadi Al Mahdi, *Nubic*, 1, 2, 8.
89. The subheading for this section is from Al Haadi Al Mahdi, *True Light Tapes 77*.
90. Al Mahdi, *Who Was the Prophet Muhammad*, 1, 17.
91. Al Mahdi, *Prehistoric Man and Animals*, 39–40.
92. AAC, *Man of Our Time*, 4, 15.
93. Al Mahdi, *Muhammad Ahmad*, 6, 3.
94. United Muslims in Exile, *Ansaar Village Bulletin*, March 26–April 24, 1982, unpaginated.
95. Al Haadi Al Mahdi, *Holy Gospel . . . Book 4*, 6–7, 14–15.
96. Ibid., 12, 27–32, 34–35.
97. Ibid., 100–102, 108.
98. Al Haadi Al Mahdi, *Tabernacle of the Most High? Part 1*, 127.
99. Rogers, *Negro-Caucasian Mixing*, 95–96.
100. Chandler, "Ebony and Bronze," 288, 295, 302.
101. For one example, see Al Haadi Al Mahdi, *Al Mahdi Explains . . . Degree of the Opening*.
102. Al Haadi Al Mahdi, *Santa or Satan*, unpaginated.

103. Al Haadi Al Mahdi, *Hadrat Faatimah . . . Part 1*, 45, 63.
104. Al Haadi Al Mahdi, *Hadrat Faatimah . . . Part 2*, 47.
105. Al Haadi Al Mahdi, *Hadrat Faatimah . . . Part 1*, 101–2.
106. Al Haadi Al Mahdi, *Hadrat Faatimah . . . Part 2*, 112.
107. Ibid., 55.
108. Al Mahdi, *Hadith: Allah's Scripture Comes First*, 28.
109. Al Haadi Al Mahdi, *Hadrat Faatimah . . . Part 2*, 111–17, 56.
110. Collins, *History of Modern Sudan*, 17–22 (quotation on 22).
111. Fluehr-Lobban, "Islamization in Sudan."
112. See Layish, *Shari'a and the Islamic State*.
113. Karrar, *Sufi Brotherhoods in the Sudan*, 42–47.
114. Holt and Daly, *History of the Sudan*, 21–32.
115. Warburg, *Islam, Sectarianism, and Politics*, 3–4.
116. Ibid., 31.
117. Sirriyeh, *Sufis and Anti-Sufis*, 37.
118. Fluehr-Lobban, "Islamization in Sudan," 615.
119. Layish, *Shari'a and the Islamic State*, 17–29.
120. Mahmoud, "Sufism and Islamism in the Sudan."
121. Fluehr-Lobban, "Islamization in Sudan."
122. Layish, *Shari'a and the Islamic State*, 115.
123. Jameelah, *Three Great Islamic Movements*, 44.
124. Salomon, "Undoing the Mahdiyya."
125. Collins, *History of Modern Sudan*, 33–36.
126. Ibrahim, *Sayyid 'Abd al-Rahman al-Mahdi*, 75.
127. Warburg, "Islam and State in Numayri's Sudan," 401.
128. Abusharaf, *Wanderings*, 33–34, 39–41.
129. AAC, *Final Link*, 2–3.
130. AAC, "What Happened to All the Muslims, and Other Cultured People?," in *Man of Our Time*, 14.
131. AAC, *Final Link*, 2–3.
132. Al Mahdi, *Holy Gospel . . . Book 4*, 108; Al Mahdi, *Muhammad Ahmad*, 38.
133. AAC, *Are the Ansars . . . a Self-Made Sect*, 7.
134. Warburg, "Islam and State in Numayri's Sudan."
135. AAC, *Are the Ansars . . . a Self-Made Sect*, 7, 8.
136. AAC, *Final Link*, 6–7.
137. Ibid.
138. AAC, *Are the Ansars . . . a Self-Made Sect*, 7, 14.
139. Ibrahim, *Sayyid 'Abd al-Rahman al-Mahdi*, 70, 78.
140. AAC, *Final Link*, 6–7.
141. Al Mahdi, *Our Symbol*.
142. Al Mahdi, *Yoruba*, unpaginated.
143. Al Mahdi, *Raatib (Unshakable)*, 15.
144. Ibid., 145.
145. Al Haadi Al Mahdi, *Our Flag*, 34–35.
146. Al Haadi Al Mahdi, *About the Raatib*, 20, 57, 58.
147. Ibid., 59.
148. Al Haadi Al Mahdi, *Our Flag*, 88, 89.
149. Curtis, *Black Muslim Religion*, 129.
150. Al Haadi Al Mahdi, *Why the Nosering*, 1–8.
151. Curtis, *Black Muslim Religion*, 110.
152. AAC, *Al Imaam Isa Visits Egypt*, 16.
153. AAC, *Disco Music*, 16.
154. AAC, *Al Imaam Isa Visits Egypt*, 16–17.
155. Al Haadi Al Mahdi, *Why Do Muslim Women Wear the Face Covering* (1989), 166.
156. Al Haadi Al Mahdi, *Why the Nosering*, 1, 5, 15, 8.
157. Al Haadi Al Mahdi, *Santa or Satan*, unpaginated.
158. NIHMA, *Nubian Islamic Hebrew Mission*, 5th ed., 9.
159. See United Muslims in Exile, *Ansaar Village Bulletin*, March–April 1982, unpaginated.
160. Al Mahdi, *Yoruba*, 1.
161. NIHMA, *Nubian Islamic Hebrew Mission*, 5th ed., unnumbered page.
162. Al Mahdi, *Yoruba*, 1, 2–4, 7–8.
163. Ibid., 16, 19.
164. Al Haadi Al Mahdi, *Tabernacle of the Most High? Part 1*, 117.
165. Al Mahdi, *Yoruba*, 19.
166. Ibid., 24.
167. *Original Tents of Kedar*, 12 *Spiritual Disciples*.
168. Al Haadi Al Mahdi, *True Light Tapes* 77.

CHAPTER 2

1. The epigraph to this chapter is from Al Haadi Al Mahdi, *Who Was Noble Drew Ali* (1988 ed.), 13.
2. Al Haadi Al Mahdi, *Ahmad, Jesus' Khalifat*, 1–6.

3. Al Haadi Al Mahdi, *Who Was Noble Drew Ali*, 13.
4. Curtis, "Urban Muslims."
5. Melton, "Daoud Ahmed."
6. Faisal, *Islam, the True Faith*.
7. Philips, *Ansar Cult in America*, unnumbered page.
8. Paul Greenhouse, conversation with author, May 2018, New York, N.Y.
9. See Al Haadi Al Mahdi, *Rebuttal to the Slanderers*.
10. NIHMA, *Spell of the Blacks Was Broken*, unpaginated.
11. AAC, *Bilal*, unnumbered page.
12. AAC, *Breaking the Fast*, unpaginated.
13. Ansaru Allah Masgid, *Fallacy of Christmas*, 6.
14. AAC, *Breaking the Fast*, unpaginated.
15. Ansaru Allah Masgid, *Fallacy of Christmas*, 6.
16. Ibid.
17. Islam, *Sunni Islam in the African American Experience*, 301–2.
18. AAC, *Id with the Ansars*, 7–8, 10, 16.
19. AAC, "Our Founding Father," in *Id-ul-Fitr with the Ansars*, 2, 3.
20. Al Mahdi, *Islam the True Faith*, 5.
21. Al Haadi Al Mahdi, *Tabernacle of the Most High? Part 2*, 58.
22. Al Haadi Al Mahdi, *Whatever Happened to the Nubian Islaamic Hebrew Mission*, 314.
23. Al Haadi Al Mahdi, *Book of Laam*, 23.
24. Al Haadi Al Mahdi, *Tabernacle of the Most High? Part 2*, 37, 58.
25. Ibid., 58, 70.
26. NIHMA, *Imam Isa*, unpaginated.
27. Philips, *Ansar Cult in America*, 140–41.
28. See, for example, NIHMA, *Spell of the Blacks Was Broken*.
29. Ansaru Allah Masgid, *Fallacy of Christmas*, 1.
30. NIHMA, *Nubian Islamic Hebrew Mission*, 3rd ed., unpaginated.
31. Al Mahdi, *Our Symbol*, 8.
32. Al Mahdi, *Christ Is the Answer*, 31–33.
33. Al Mahdi, *Khutbat's of Al Hajj Al Imam . . . Book Two*, 22–23.
34. The first part of this two-volume booklet series mentions September 1978 in a photo caption. The pamphlet's book catalog lists eighty-one titles, demonstrating a release of 1977 or later. Al Mahdi, *Khutbat's of Al Hajj Al Imam . . . Book One*, 5.
35. Al Mahdi, *Khutbat's of Al Hajj Al Imam . . . Book Two*, 35.
36. Al Mahdi, *Khutbat's of Al Hajj Al Imam . . . Book One*, 35–40.
37. AAC, "Read the Evidence: The Holy Qurʾan," in *Man of Our Time*, 13.
38. Muhammad, *Theology of Time*, 198.
39. Ibid., 281–82.
40. Muhammad, "New Flag for the Nation."
41. Gardell, *Name of Elijah Muhammad*, 112.
42. AAC, "Unity Is a Must," in *Book of ل: To Whom It May Concern*, 3.
43. Al Mahdi, *Book of Lamb 1*, unpaginated.
44. Al Mahdi, *Book of Lamb 2*, unpaginated.
45. Al Haadi Al Mahdi, *Tabernacle of the Most High? Part 2*, 52.
46. Knight, *Why I Am a Five Percenter*, 154–55.
47. Al Haadi Al Mahdi, *Why the Nosering*, 29.
48. Al Haadi Al Mahdi, *Tabernacle of the Most High? Part 2*, 2.
49. AAC, *American Muslims*, 5.
50. Ibid., 2.
51. Al Mahdi, *Book of Lamb 1*, unpaginated.
52. Ibid.
53. Al Mahdi, *Book of Lamb 2*, unpaginated.
54. Al Mahdi, *Book of Lamb 1*, unpaginated.
55. Al Haadi Al Mahdi, *You Must Be Born Again, Part One*, 13.
56. Al Haadi Al Mahdi, *Tabernacle of the Most High? Part 2*, 1.
57. Ibid., 60.
58. Al Mahdi, *Book of Lamb 2*, unpaginated.
59. Al Haadi Al Mahdi, *Book of Laam*, 3.
60. Al Mahdi, *Book of Lamb 2*, unpaginated.
61. Al Haadi Al Mahdi, *Book of Laam*, 102.
62. AAC, "What We Must Do," in *Book of ل: To Whom It May Concern*, back cover.
63. AAC, "What Happened to All the Muslims, and Other Cultured People?," in *Man of Our Time*, 14.
64. Ibid.
65. DeCaro, *Religious Life of Malcolm X*, 147.
66. GhaneaBassiri, *History of Islam in America*, 249.
67. Clegg, *Original Man*, 197–98.
68. Al Haadi Al Mahdi, *Book of Laam*, 119.
69. Al Mahdi, *Book of Lamb 1*, unpaginated.
70. Al Haadi Al Mahdi, *Book of Laam*, 102, 104.
71. Al Mahdi, *Book of Lamb 2*, unpaginated.
72. Al Mahdi, *Book of Lamb 1*, unpaginated.

73. Al Haadi Al Mahdi, *Book of Laam*, 5.
74. *Autobiography of Malcolm X*, 332–33, 335.
75. Al Haadi Al Mahdi, *Book of Laam*, 293.
76. Ibid., 294, 295.
77. Elmasry, "Salafis in America."
78. *Autobiography of Malcolm X*, 343–44.
79. Al Haadi Al Mahdi, *Book of the Five Percenters*, 107–8.
80. Ibid.
81. NIHMA, *Thou Shalt Not KILL*, unpaginated.
82. Al Haadi Al Mahdi, *Ahmad, Jesus' Khalifat*, 4.
83. Al Mahdi, *Who Was Noble Drew Ali* (1980 ed.), 5–6, 39.
84. Ibid., 39.
85. Al Haadi aadiAl Mahdi, *Who Was Noble Drew Ali* (1988 ed.), 1–2.
86. Ibid., 5.
87. Ibid., 1–2.
88. Al Haadi Al Mahdi, *Book of the Five Percenters*, 256.
89. Al Haadi Al Mahdi, *Who Was Noble Drew Ali* (1988 ed.), 1–2, 13.
90. Ibid., 95; see also Al Haadi Al Mahdi, *Book of the Five Percenters*, 256.
91. Al Haadi Al Mahdi, *Who Was Noble Drew Ali* (1988 ed.), 71.
92. Ibid., 113, 114–20, 122, 123–25.
93. Al Haadi Al Mahdi, *Who Was Marcus Garvey*, 25–34.
94. Ibid., 56–58, 45.
95. Ibid., 63, 65.
96. Ibid., 68, 67, 75.
97. Ibid., 71–75, 97.
98. Ibid., 97, 177–86.
99. Rakim, "The Mystery (Who Is God)," from the album *The 18th Letter* (Universal/MCA Records, 1997).
100. Knight, *Why I Am a Five Percenter*, 17–18.
101. Al Mahdi, *Book of Lamb 1*, first page.
102. Knight, *Why I Am a Five Percenter*, 142–43.
103. AAC, *Signs of 73*, 4.
104. Al Mahdi, *Book of Lamb 1*, unpaginated.
105. Al Haadi Al Mahdi, *Whatever Happened to the Nubian Islaamic Hebrews*, 4.
106. Al Haadi Al Mahdi, *Who Was Noble Drew Ali* (1988 ed.), 116–17.
107. Al Haadi Al Mahdi, *Book of Laam*, 276–77.
108. Al Haadi Al Mahdi, *Book of the Five Percenters*, 1 (hereafter cited parenthetically in the text).
109. Al Haadi Al Mahdi, *Book of Laam*, 278; Al Haadi Al Mahdi, *Our Flag*, 126.
110. Al Haadi Al Mahdi, *Book of Laam*, 291.
111. Allah was born Clarence Edward Smith but was frequently misidentified as Clarence Jowars (or Jowers) Smith. Willieen Jowers was the mother of two of his children.
112. Al Haadi Al Mahdi, *Book of Laam*, 279.

CHAPTER 3

1. The epigraph to this chapter is quoted in Dorman, *Chosen People*, 189.
2. Hevesi, "Muslims Leave Bushwick."
3. An earlier version of the image appears in 1986 pamphlets such as *You Must Be Born Again, Part One*; *True Story of Noah* (both parts); and *What and Where Is Hell?*
4. Palmer, *Nuwaubian Nation*, 46, 13.
5. See Könighofer, *New Ship of Zion*, 68–70.
6. Maulana Muhammad Ali, whose translation of the Qurʾan was used at State Street Mosque, translates sura 15:28–29: "And when thy Lord said to the angels: I am going to create a mortal of sounding clay, of black mud fashioned into shape. So when I have made him complete and breathed into him of My spirit, fall down making obeisance to him." Al Mahdi translates the passage: "And when the Lord said to the angels: Surely I am going to create black human skin from sound baked clay from shaped mud. So when I have completed and breathed in him of my spirit, so fall down to him prostrating." Al Mahdi, *Tribal Encyclopedia*, 10.
7. Palmer, *Nuwaubian Nation*, 15. Palmer identifies Jenkins alongside Father Hurley as "two obscure Black Hebrew prophets who wrote in the 1920s," though Jenkins published *The Black Hebrews of the Seed of Abraham* in 1969. Landing, *Black Judaism*, 373.
8. Webb, *Black Man, the Father of Civilization*, 8.
9. The earliest critique of "white Jesus" that I've seen comes from the Pequot author and son of a slave William Apess, "An Indian's Looking-Glass for the White Man" (1833). See Blum and Harvey, "From Light to White."
10. Lieb, *Children of Ezekiel*, 218.
11. Vaughan, *Preeminence of Christ*, 180.
12. Dorman, *Chosen People*, 184, 121, 130–31.

13. Ibid., 130–31, 186.
14. Ibid., 80.
15. *Autobiography of Malcolm X*, 219.
16. Faisal, *Islam, the True Faith*, 77.
17. Ibid., 78, 76.
18. Philips, *Ansar Cult in America*, 32.
19. Deutsch, "Proximate Other."
20. Muhammad, *Message to the Black Man*, 93.
21. Berg, *Elijah Muhammad and Islam*, 33, 36.
22. Clegg, *Original Man*, 72–73. Clegg notes that because of their religious objections to war, Elijah Muhammad and Judge Rutherford both chose prison over compliance with the draft during the Second World War. Elijah makes sympathetic reference to Rutherford's anti-Catholicism in *Message to the Black Man*, 323.
23. Muhammad, *Message to the Black Man*, 88, 97.
24. Berg, *Elijah Muhammad and Islam*, 59, 157.
25. NIHMA, *Nubian Islamic Hebrew Mission*, 3rd ed., unpaginated.
26. NIHMA, *Back to the Beginning*, unnumbered page.
27. Al Mahdi, *Arabic: The First Language*, 26.
28. Al Mahdi, *Holy Gospel . . . Book 3*, 120.
29. Al Mahdi, *Tribe Israel Is No More*, unnumbered page.
30. Ibid., 1, 59.
31. Ibid., 120, 6.
32. AAC, "What Happened to All the Muslims, and Other Cultured People?," in *Man of Our Time*.
33. Al Haadi Al Mahdi, *Whatever Happened to the Nubian Islaamic Hebrews*, 1.
34. AAC, "Ansaru Allah Community," in *Muhammad (PBUH) and Makkah*, back cover.
35. AAC, "Goals and Purposes of the Ansaru Allah Community," in *Disco Music*, back cover.
36. Al Haadi Al Mahdi, *Whatever Happened to the Nubian Islaamic Hebrews*, 14–18, 19–20.
37. Al Haadi Al Mahdi, *Should Muslims Observe the Sabbath*, 1, 39.
38. Al Mahdi, *Prehistoric Man and Animals*, 35.
39. Al Haadi Al Mahdi, *True Light Tapes 1*.
40. Al Haadi Al Mahdi, *Should Muslims Observe the Sabbath*, 1, 29.
41. Al Haadi Al Mahdi, *Tabernacle of the Most High? Part 2*, 13–16.
42. Al Mahdi, *True Story of Noah* (1978 ed.), 37; Al Haadi Al Mahdi, *True Story of Noah, Part One* (1986 ed.), 18.
43. Al Haadi Al Mahdi, *Tabernacle of the Most High? Part 2*, 62–63.
44. Al Mahdi, *Forgotten Tribe Kedar*, 3.
45. Al Haadi Al Mahdi, *Travels of a Sufi*, 41.
46. Al Haadi Al Mahdi, *Tabernacle of the Most High? Part 1*, 68.
47. Al Haadi Al Mahdi, *Whatever Happened to the Nubian Islaamic Hebrew Mission*, 20–24, 15, 40, 2–8.
48. Al Haadi Al Mahdi, *Man of Miracles . . . Part 2*, 24.
49. In *Whatever Happened to the Nubian Islaamic Hebrew Mission*, the image is cropped to exclude the spaceship, but the full image appears in the 1988 editions of *Who Was Noble Drew Ali* and *What Laws Did Jesus Follow*.
50. Al Haadi Al Mahdi, *Who Was Marcus Garvey*, 27.
51. Al Haadi Al Mahdi, *What Laws Did Jesus Follow*, 45, 40, 51.
52. Al Haadi Al Mahdi, *True Light Tapes*, 2.
53. Al Haadi Al Mahdi, *Wisemen*, 39–63.
54. Ibid., 129.
55. Al Haadi Al Mahdi, *Sons of Canaan*, 42.
56. Al Haadi Al Mahdi, *Resurrection*, 79–82.
57. Al Haadi Al Mahdi, *Book of Revelation*, Chapter 1, 5.
58. As Siid Nafiys, "Clothing of the Lost Covenant," *Nubian Village Bulletin*, no. 1 (1991), 4.
59. "The New Dress of the Children of Abraham (Bani Ibraahim)," *Nubian Village Bulletin*, no. 2 (1992), 2.
60. As Sitt Maryam waalidat Nuwh Waliuddiyn, "Whatever Happened to the Name Abdullah Muhammad?," *Nubian Village Bulletin*, no. 1 (1991), 9.
61. Al Mahdi, *Christ Is the Answer*, 54.
62. Tents of Abraham, *Truth, Edition 3*, 8.
63. Tents of Abraham, *Truth, Edition 9*, 2.
64. Tents of Nubia, *Truth, Special Edition*, 21–22.
65. York, *Holy Tablets*, 19.6.301–4.
66. Tents of Nubia, *Truth, Special Edition*, 4, 11–19, 21.
67. "New Dress of the Children of Abraham," 2.
68. Tents of Nubia, *Truth, Special Edition*, 4.
69. O'Connor, "Nubian Islaamic Hebrews."
70. Tents of Abraham, *True Light Tape . . . People of the Sun*.
71. Brother Taalib, "The Truth of the Scriptures," *Nubian Village Bulletin*, no. 4 (1992), 3, 9.

72. "New Dress of the Children of Abraham," 2.
73. Tents of Nubia, *Truth, Edition 16*, 1, 2, 22, 3.
74. "New Dress of the Children of Abraham," 2.
75. "Do We Still Observe Ramadaan," *Nubian Truth Bulletin*, no. 4 (1992), 4–5.
76. Brother Taalib, "Truth of the Scriptures."
77. "Do We Still Observe Ramadaan."

CHAPTER 4

1. Rogers, *World's Great Men of Color*, 1:143.
2. Chireau, "Black Culture and Black Zion," 25; Moses, *Afrotopia*, 26.
3. Muir, *Life of Mahomet*, 107, 108, 365.
4. GhaneaBassiri, *History of Islam in America*, 56–57.
5. Blyden, *Christianity, Islam, and the Negro Race*, 328, 230–31, 327.
6. Quoted in Howell, *Old Islam in Detroit*, 74.
7. "Two Slave-Leaders of Islam—Bilal and Zaid," *Moslem Sunrise*, October 1932–January 1933, 31.
8. Ben-Jochannan, *African Origins*, 195–97, 204, 212–14, 199–201, 205, 217.
9. Rogers, *World's Great Men of Color*, 1:143; Rogers, "Bilal Ibn Rahab—Warrior Priest."
10. Malcolm X, "Interview with *Al-Muslimoon*," 102.
11. Curtis, *Black Muslim Religion*, 82.
12. Muhammad, "Bilalian."
13. Muhammad, *As the Light Shineth*, 100–102.
14. Ibid., 152–53.
15. Quoted in Gardell, *Name of Elijah Muhammad*, 196.
16. Al Mahdi, *Bilal*, unnumbered page.
17. Al Mahdi, *You Must Be Born Again, Part One*, 118.
18. Al Mahdi, *Bilal*, 4.
19. Al Haadi Al Mahdi, *Should Muslims Observe the Sabbath*, 78.
20. Al Mahdi, *Bilal*, 1–2.
21. Al Haadi Al Mahdi, *Should Muslims Observe the Sabbath*, 29–31.
22. Al Haadi Al Mahdi, *Bilaal, the Sceptre Bearer*, 8, 2.
23. Al Haadi Al Mahdi, *Should Muslims Observe the Sabbath*, 29–31.
24. Al Haadi Al Mahdi, *Bilaal, the Sceptre Bearer*, 16, 24.
25. Al Haadi Al Mahdi, *Should Muslims Observe the Sabbath*, 29–31.
26. Al Haadi Al Mahdi, *Bilaal, the Sceptre Bearer*, 14, 20.
27. Al Haadi Al Mahdi, *Should Muslims Observe the Sabbath*, 29–31.
28. Al Mahdi, *Bilal*, 24, 19, 21.
29. Al Mahdi, *Our Symbol*, 35.
30. Al Haadi Al Mahdi, *Bilaal, the Sceptre Bearer*, 1.
31. Ibid., 17–18.
32. Ibid., 18.
33. Al Haadi Al Mahdi, *Book of Laam*, 248–49.
34. Al Mahdi, *I Don't Claim to Be*, 42.
35. Al Haadi Al Mahdi, *Bilaal, the Sceptre Bearer*, 77–78.
36. Ibid., 19.
37. Al Haadi Al Mahdi, *Rebuttal to the Slanderers*, 390–91.
38. Al Haadi Al Mahdi, *Bilaal, the Sceptre Bearer*, 19.
39. Al Haadi Al Mahdi, *Who Was Noble Drew Ali* (1988 ed.), 27, 32.
40. Al Haadi Al Mahdi, *Should Muslims Observe the Sabbath*, 29–31.
41. Al Mahdi, *Book of Lamb*, 2.
42. Philips, *Ansar Cult in America*, 39–40.
43. Al Haadi Al Mahdi, *Rebuttal to the Slanderers*, 1–2, 69–70.

CHAPTER 5

1. Al Mahdi, *Lost Children of Mu and Atlantis*, 13. The epigraph to this chapter is from Khan, *Sufi Message of Hazrat Inayat Khan*, 10:202–3.
2. Al Haadi Al Mahdi, *Wadhiyfah*, book 2, 18.
3. Ernst, "Situating Sufism and Yoga," 22.
4. Nuruddin, "Ancient Black Astronauts," 128.
5. Isa Abd Allah ibn Abu Bakr Muhammad, "Can You Be Sufi?," in NIHMA, *Nubian Islamic Hebrew Mission*, 3rd ed., unpaginated.
6. NIHMA, *Was Created with One Thought*, 18.
7. AAC, *Abba Island in America*, 5.
8. AAC, *Id with the Ansars*, 3.
9. Al Mahdi, *99+1 Attributes of Allah*, 1, 11.
10. Muhammad, *Talisman*, 9.

11. See Webb, "Negotiating Boundaries: American Sufis."
12. Khan, *From Sufism to Ahmadiyya*, 6–8.
13. GhaneaBassiri, *History of Islam in America*, 208.
14. Sedgwick, *Western Sufism*, 222–35.
15. Webb, "Negotiating Boundaries: American Sufis."
16. Sedgwick, *Against the Modern World*, 147–60, 161–78.
17. Dickson, *Living Sufism in North America*, 100–102.
18. Muhammad, *Science of Creation*, 61.
19. AAC, *Id with the Ansars*, 9–10.
20. Al Haadi Al Mahdi, *Ahmad, Jesus' Khalifat*, 112–13.
21. Dannin, *Black Pilgrimage to Islam*, 74–77.
22. Philips, *Ansar Cult in America*, 17–18.
23. Hermansen, "Hybrid Identity Formations in Muslim America," 172.
24. Al Haadi Al Mahdi, *About the Raatib*, unnumbered page.
25. Ibid.
26. Al Mahdi, *Muhammad Ahmad*, 11–13.
27. Gardell, *Name of Elijah Muhammad*, 226, 244.
28. Al Haadi Al Mahdi, *Rebuttal to the Slanderers*, 607.
29. Ibid.
30. AAC, *Humazah*, 5.
31. Halman, *Where the Two Seas Meet*, 4.
32. Ibid., 243–46.
33. Al Mahdi, *Ancient Egypt and the Pharaohs*, 101.
34. Al Haadi Al Mahdi, *Science of Healing*, 21.
35. Al Haadi Al Mahdi, *From Allah to Man*, 56.
36. Halman, *Where the Two Seas Meet*, 50.
37. Schuon, *Understanding Islam*, 144.
38. Schuon, "Paradoxical Aspects of Sufism," n. 9.
39. Hammer, *Claiming Knowledge*, 109–393.
40. Ibid., 380–93.
41. See Nance, "Mystery of the Moorish Science Temple."
42. Gomez, *Black Crescent*, 206.
43. Ibid., 299–300.
44. Al Haadi Al Mahdi, *Science of Healing*, 14–15.
45. Al Mahdi, *Ancient Egypt and the Pharaohs*, 56.
46. Al Haadi Al Mahdi, *Science of Healing*, 14–15.
47. Al Mahdi, *Ancient Egypt and the Pharaohs*, 82.
48. Al Haadi Al Mahdi, *Science of Healing*, 21.
49. Al Haadi Al Mahdi, *Man of Miracles . . . Part 1*, 24, 19, 119.
50. Al Haadi Al Mahdi, *Man of Miracles . . . Part 2*, 27, 25, 122.
51. Al Haadi Al Mahdi, *Man of Miracles . . . Part 1*, 24.
52. Al Haadi Al Mahdi, *Man of Miracles . . . Part 2*, 28.
53. Al Haadi Al Mahdi, *Bilaal, the Sceptre Bearer*, 7–8.
54. Al Haadi Al Mahdi, *Wisemen*, 17–18.
55. Al Haadi Al Mahdi, *Muslim Prayer Book, Part One* (1987 ed.), 195.
56. Al Haadi Al Mahdi, *You Must Be Born Again, Part One*, 13.
57. Al Haadi Al Mahdi, *Tabernacle of the Most High? Part 2*, 1.
58. AAC, *Are the Ansars . . . a Self-Made Sect*, 1.
59. Halman, "Sufism in the West," 193.
60. Al Haadi Al Mahdi, *Science of Healing*, 120–25, 128–29.
61. Al Haadi Al Mahdi, *Man of Miracles . . . Part 1*, 129.
62. Al Haadi Al Mahdi, *Science of Healing*, 129.
63. Al Haadi Al Mahdi, *Muslim Prayer Book, Part One* (1987 ed.), unnumbered page.
64. Al Haadi Al Mahdi, *Travels of a Sufi*, 48, 40, 41.
65. Al Haadi Al Mahdi, *True Story of Noah (PBUH), Part One*, 69, 64.
66. Al Qutb, *Sons of the Green Light . . . Study Three*, 33, 13.
67. Al Mahdi, *Muslim Prayer Book, Part One* (1983 ed.), 36, 252.
68. Al Qutb, *You and the Sons of the Green Light*, 29, 24.
69. Al Qutb, *Celestial Being or Terrestrial Being*, 21–22.
70. Al Qutb, *Sons of the Green Light . . . Study One*, 18, 21–22.
71. Al Qutb, *You and the Sons of the Green Light*, 1, 6.
72. Ibid., 17, 1.
73. Al Qutb, *Secret Document*, 1.
74. Al Qutb, *You and the Sons of the Green Light*, 1.

75. Ibid., 5, 11.
76. Al Qutb, *Celestial Being or Terrestrial Being*, unnumbered page.
77. Al Haadi Al Mahdi, *Science of Healing*, 129.
78. See Gregorius, "Inventing Africa."
79. Al Qutb, *Sons of the Green Light . . . Study Five*, 15–17.
80. Muhammad, *Talisman*, 21.
81. Al Haadi Al Mahdi, *True Story of Noah (PBUH), Part One*, 1, 70.
82. Al Qutb, *Secret Document*, 2.
83. Philips, *Ansar Cult in America*, iii, 17–18.
84. Al Haadi Al Mahdi, *Rebuttal to the Slanderers*, 168, 167.
85. Al Qutb, *Secret Document*, 10.
86. Al Qutb, *Sons of the Green Light . . . Study One*, 8–9, 16.
87. Ibid., 16.
88. Albanese, *Republic of Mind and Spirit*, 6–7.
89. Al Haadi Al Mahdi, *Science of Healing*, 96.

CHAPTER 6

1. The epigraphs to this chapter are from W. D. Muhammad, quoted in el-Amin, *Freemasonry, Ancient Egypt*, 39–40, and Killah Priest, "Looking Glass," from the album *Behind the Stained Glass* (Good Hands Records/Proverb Records, 2008).
2. Hammer, *Claiming Knowledge*, 109.
3. Spieth, *Napoleon's Sorcerers*, 17, 50.
4. Hornung, *Secret Lore of Egypt*, 116–21.
5. Bushman, *Joseph Smith: Rough Stone Rolling*, 288.
6. Hammer, *Claiming Knowledge*, 244–45.
7. Montserrat, *Akhenaten*, 134.
8. Hammer, *Claiming Knowledge*, 380.
9. Montserrat, *Akhenaten*, 134–35.
10. Quoted in Trafton, *Egypt Land*, 30–31.
11. Ibid., 238–39.
12. Ibid.
13. Gomez, *Black Crescent*, 246.
14. Hornung, *Secret Lore of Egypt*, 112.
15. Gomez, *Black Crescent*, 246.
16. Ibid., 206.
17. Bowen, *African American Islamic Renaissance*, 327.
18. Dannin, *Black Pilgrimage to Islam*, 102.
19. Bowen, *African American Islamic Renaissance*, 342.
20. Ibid.; Johnson, *Holy Fahamme Gospel*, 1, 58.
21. Johnson, *Holy Fahamme Gospel*, 69, 58.
22. Bowen, *African American Islamic Renaissance*, 345.
23. Lieb, *Children of Ezekiel*.
24. Curtis, *Black Muslim Religion*, 88.
25. El-Amin, *Freemasonry, Ancient Egypt*, 32, 39–40.
26. Yusuf Ali, *Holy Qur'an*, 408–13.
27. Gregorius, "Inventing Africa."
28. Al Haadi Al Mahdi, *Paleman*, 5.
29. Al Haadi Al Mahdi, *Why the Nosering*; NIHMA, *Imam Isa*; see also the ca. 1972 edition of Al Mahdi, *Did the Hog Come for Mankind*, which is mostly unreadable in the copy I accessed but appears to share material with the later NIHMA version (ca. 1975–77).
30. See, for example, NIHMA, *Back to the Beginning*.
31. Al Mahdi, *Eternal Life After Death*, 33–34.
32. Quoted in Haddad and Smith, *Mission to America*, 105–36.
33. Al Mahdi, *Science of the Pyramids*, 18–19.
34. Muhammad, *Science of Creation*, 59.
35. Al Haadi Al Mahdi, *True Story of Cain and Abel*, 34.
36. Al Mahdi, *Ancient Egypt and the Pharaohs*, 32–34.
37. Al Mahdi, *Science of the Pyramids*, 61.
38. Ibid., 75.
39. Al Haadi Al Mahdi, *True Story of Cain and Abel*, 51.
40. Al Mahdi, *Science of the Pyramids*, 1–3, 75.
41. Al Haadi Al Mahdi, *Sons of Canaan*, 42.
42. Ibid., 2–3, 21.
43. Al Mahdi, *Ancient Egypt and the Pharaohs*, 83.
44. Al Mahdi, *Science of the Pyramids*, 7, 24.
45. Al Mahdi, *Ancient Egypt and the Pharaohs*, 41–44.
46. Al Haadi Al Mahdi, *Sons of Canaan*, 42–44.
47. Al Mahdi, *Ancient Egypt and the Pharaohs*, 51–52; Al Mahdi, *Science of the Pyramids*, 80.
48. Al Mahdi, *Ancient Egypt and the Pharaohs*, 55–58.
49. AAC, *Al Imaam Isa Visits Egypt*, 1–2, 15.
50. Ibid., 22.
51. Al Haadi Al Mahdi, *Who Was Noble Drew Ali* (1988 ed.), 37–38.

52. Al Mahdi, *Science of the Pyramids*, 1–2, 100, 102.

53. Joseph, "Jesus in India" (quotation on 53).

54. Nance, "Mystery of the Moorish Science Temple," 127.

55. Ali, *Holy Koran Circle Seven*, chaps. 10 and 13.

56. Khan, *From Sufism to Ahmadiyya*, 44–47.

57. *Moslem Sunrise*, January 1923, 16.

58. Muhammad, *Theology of Time*, 66–67.

59. Al Haadi Al Mahdi, *You Are Adam's Descendants*, 108–9; Al Haadi Al Mahdi, *Gospel of John*, 90–92.

60. Al Haadi Al Mahdi, *Gospel of John*, 90–92.

61. Al Mahdi, *Science of the Pyramids*, 91.

62. Al Mahdi, *Was Christ Really Crucified*, 68–69.

63. Al Mahdi, *Science of the Pyramids*, 91; Al Mahdi, *Was Christ Really Crucified*, 69.

64. Al Haadi Al Mahdi, *Final Messenger*, 332–35.

65. York, *Jesus Found in Egipt*, 425.

66. Colla, *Conflicted Antiquities*, 85–86.

67. Hornung, *Secret Lore of Egypt*, 53.

CHAPTER 7

1. The chapter epigraph is from Muhammad, *True History of Master Fard Muhammad*, 109.

2. Special Agent in Charge to FBI Director, memorandum, "K. Ahmed Tawfiq, Mosque of Islamic Brotherhood, Inc.," September 20, 1973, file on Mosque of Islamic Brotherhood, U.S. Department of Justice, Federal Bureau of Investigation, New York, N.Y.

3. York, *360 Questions to Ask the Orthodox*, 4.

4. Musa, *Hadith as Scripture*, 87.

5. Tents of Nubia, "Who Killed Dr. Rashad Khalifa?," in *Truth, Edition 12*, 5–7.

6. Carmen Duarte and Kristen Cook, "Tucson Mosque Slaying May Be Linked to Sect," *Arizona Daily Star*, October 12, 1992.

7. Al Haadi Al Mahdi, *Leviathan: 666*, 674; for Jacob York's account, see Palmer, *Nuwaubian Nation*, 68.

8. "Man Stabs Four People in Mosque in Brooklyn," *New York Times*, January 24, 1983; "4 Stabbed at Muslim Mosque," *Newsday*, January 24, 1983.

9. Garnett, *Soul Sacrifice*, 164.

10. Memorandum, "The Ansaru Allah Community, Also Known as the Nubian Islamic Hebrews, the Tents of Kedar; Domestic Security/Terrorism," n.d. [1992], U.S. Department of Justice, Federal Bureau of Investigation, New York, N.Y., unpaginated.

11. New York Police Department, 83rd Precinct, Horace Green homicide case file.

12. FBI memorandum, "Ansaru Allah Community."

13. Ibid.

14. Griffin, *Black Brothers, Inc.*, 43.

15. FBI memorandum, "Ansaru Allah Community."

16. Rohan, *Holding York Responsible*, 77.

17. Clegg, *Original Man*, 259–60.

18. As Siit Musa, "As Salaat—The Worship," *Nubian Village Bulletin*, no. 1 (1992), 3.

19. Tents of Abraham, "Were There Female Messiah-Types?," in *Truth, Edition 5*, 1.

20. Muna waliidat Sauda, "History in the Making: Ansaar Women Teach New Comers Class," *Nubian Village Bulletin*, no. 2 (1992), 4.

21. Tents of Abraham, *True Light Tape . . . Nubian Woman*.

22. Garnett, *Soul Sacrifice*, 10.

23. Tents of Nubia, "Prophecy Fulfilled," in *Truth, Edition 15*, 1–8.

24. Philips, *Ansar Cult in America*, 124–25.

25. Collins, *History of Modern Sudan*, 185–217.

26. Tents of Nubia, *Truth, Edition 15*, 1.

27. York-El, *Nuwaubu and Amunnubi Rooakhptah*, 23–31.

28. York, *Is Jesus the God of the Koran*, 116.

29. York, *Glory of Jesus the Messiah*, 116.

30. York-El, *What and Where Is Hell*, unpaginated.

31. Ibid.; York-El, *Is It Black Man's Christianity*.

32. York, *Post Graduate*, 170–73.

33. Staff Writer, "Thousands Flock to Make Pilgrimage, Not in Mecca but in Egypt of the West—Eatonton, GA, U.S.A." *Nuwaubian Moors Newsletter*, August 3, 1997, 1–2.

34. "Listen to the Supreme Grandmaster!," *Nuwaubian Moors Newsletter*, August 17, 1997, 7.

35. Malachizodok York-El, *It's Alignment Time*.

36. "Why Do People Call You All a Cult?," *Nuwaubian Moors Newsletter*, August 24, 1997, 5.
37. "So Why the Fez?," *Nuwaubian Moors Newsletter*, August 31, 1997, 3–4.
38. Staff Writer, "Thousands Flock to Make Pilgrimage."
39. Raakhptah, *Egiptian Magic*, 67.
40. Ruakhptah, *Sacred Records of Neter*.
41. Ibid., 71.
42. Al Haadi Al Mahdi, *Book of the Five Percenters*, 486.
43. Calavito, *Cult of Alien Gods*, 263–82.
44. York, *Man from Planet Rizq*, 23.
45. Al Haadi Al Mahdi, *True Light Tapes* 42.
46. Lewis and Kahn, "Reptoid Hypothesis," 46.
47. See Dyrendal, "Hidden Knowledge, Hidden Powers."
48. Nuruddin, "Ancient Black Astronauts."
49. Howe, *Afrocentrism*, 269.
50. York, *Melanin-ite Children*, 11.
51. Malachizodok-El, *People of the Sun*, 4–7.
52. York, *Melanin-ite Children*, 75.
53. Ibid., 1.
54. York, *Shamballah and Aghaarta*, 40.
55. Malachizodok-El, *People of the Sun*, 10.
56. York, *Holy Tablets*, 19.6.
57. Malachizodok-El, *People of the Sun*, 51.
58. York, *El's Holy Qur'aan*, 1.
59. Ibid., 700.
60. Lieb, *Children of Ezekiel*, 205–12.
61. Ben Yahweh, *Yahweh Judges America*, 58.
62. York, *El's Holy Injiyl*, 887–88.
63. Lieb, *Children of Ezekiel*, 205.
64. Wauneta Lone Wolf, "The Mothership on Big Mountain," *Final Call*, September 30, 1986, 30.
65. As Siit Adiylah, "How About the History of the Black Indians," *Nubian Village Bulletin*, no. 1 (1991), 7.
66. "The Supreme Grandmaster—'Nayya: Malachi Zodok York-El' Speaks at Savior's Day 1997 A.D," *Nuwaubian Moors Newsletter*, August 17, 1997, 2.
67. Staff Writer, "Black Eagle, Prophecy Fulfilled," *Nuwaubian Moors Newsletter*, September 28, 1997, 1.
68. Montserrat, *Akhenaten*, 124.
69. Al Haadi Al Mahdi, *Paleman*, 287.
70. See Haslip-Viera, Montellano, and Barbour, "Robbing Native American Cultures."
71. Staff Writer, "Inside the Temple of Imhotep," *Nuwaubian Moors Newsletter*, August 24, 1997, 2.
72. Staff Writer, "Are the Pyramid People Muslims?," *Nuwaubian Moors Newsletter*, August 31, 1997, 1.
73. Staff Writer, "Thousands Flock to Make Pilgrimage."
74. Staff Writer, "Man from Another Planet, He's Nuts!," *Nuwaubian Moors Newsletter*, June 26, 1997, 1.
75. Staff Writer, "Black Eagle, Prophecy Fulfilled."
76. York-El, *Constitution of U.N.N.M.*, 116.
77. See Dew, "'Moors Know the Law.'"
78. Gardell, *Name of Elijah Muhammad*, 37.
79. See Dew, "Washitaw de Dugdahmoundyah."
80. Bey, *We Are the Washitaw*, back cover.
81. Dew, "Washitaw de Dugdahmoundyah," 68.
82. Holy Tabernacle Ministries, "The Birth of the Holy Tabernacle Ministries in the South," in *HTM, Edition 1: The Savior*, 4.
83. Staff Writer," "Inside the Temple of Imhotep," *Nuwaubian Moors Newsletter*, August 24, 1997, 2.
84. Rohan, *Holding York Responsible*, 76.
85. MacKey and Hughan, *Encyclopedia of Freemasonry*, 301.
86. See Sesay, "Dialectic of Representation."
87. Raboteau quoted in Trafton, *Egypt Land*, 258.
88. Maffly-Kipp, *Setting Down the Sacred Past*, 40.
89. Trafton, *Egypt Land*, 69–71 (quotations on 71).
90. Wallace, *Constructing the Black Masculine*, 68.
91. Howe, *Afrocentrism*, 66.
92. James, *Stolen Legacy*, 127.
93. Bowen, "Abdul Hamid Suleiman," 6.
94. Nance, "Mystery of the Moorish Science Temple," 125.
95. Berman, *American Arabesque*, 145.
96. Beynon, "Voodoo Cult Among Negro Migrants," 900.
97. Muhammad, "Warning to the Black Man."
98. Muhammad, *Secrets of Freemasonry*, 3.
99. Supreme Wisdom Lessons, Lost Found Muslim Lesson No. 1, English Lesson C-1,

http://www.ciphertheory.net/supremewisdom.pdf.

100. Lost Found Muslim Lesson No. 2, ibid. See also Farrakhan's treatment of Masons in Gardell, *Name of Elijah Muhammad*, 149.

101. York, *Post Graduate*, 84, 150–61.

102. Dorman, *Chosen People*, 74–75.

103. York-El, *Nuwaubu and Amunnubi Rooakhptah*, 4–6.

104. See noponoone.com, "Who Is the Writer of This Presentation?," at https://noponoone.wixsite.com/noponoone/afroo-oonoo.

105. Rahkaptah, *Bible Interpretations and Explanations*, unpaginated.

106. Nupu, Nupu, and Nupu, *Nine Ball, Count 1*, 7.

107. For the song, visit https://www.youtube.com/watch?v=YusqJKsXDkY.

108. Raakhptah, *Nuwaupic*, 2–9.

109. The extensively researched "anti-cult" site Nuwaupianism: 360 Questions to Ask Nuwaupians, run by a former member of the community, provides a survey of Nuwaupic's development and also claims access to sealed transcripts from York's trial, during which a witness explained Nuwaupic's origins. See "Ask a Nuwaupian, Is Nuwaubic/Nuwaupic an actual language that was spoken by Extraterrestrials, Sumerians and Egyptians?," at Nuwaupianism.com.

110. Raakhptah, *Nuwaupic*, 2.

111. York, *Does Dr. Malachi Z. York Try to Hide*, 77–85, 70–72 (quotation on 71–72).

112. York-El, *Nuwaubu and Amunnubi Rooakhptah*, 1–4.

113. Al Mahdi, *Opening of the Seventh Seal* (ca. 1974–77), 1.

114. York, *El's Holy Injiyl*, 469, 485, 491, 493.

115. Khalifa, *Quran: The Final Testament*, appendix 23.

116. York, *El's Holy Qur'aan*, 37.

117. Ibid., 45.

118. Ibid., 454.

119. The term "Nuwaubians" appears in place of "Nubians" several times in York-El, *Holy Tablets* (rev. ed.), 19.6.296–312.

120. Ibid., 1.2.108–9, hereafter cited parenthetically in the text by chapter, subchapter (what York calls "tablet"), and verse number.

121. York, *Post Graduate*, 88.

122. York-El, *Raatib for Shriners*, 4–14 (hereafter cited parenthetically in the text).

123. See Al Mahdi, *Who Was the Prophet Muhammad*; Al Haadi Al Mahdi, *Rebuttal to the Slanderers*, 121.

124. Ali, *Holy Koran Circle Seven*, iv.

125. See advertisement in York, *Post Graduate*, unnumbered page.

126. York, *Shaikh Daoud vs. W. D. Fard*, 150, 114.

127. See, e.g., York, *Malachi: I Will Send You Elijah* (both parts).

128. York-El, *Nuwaubu and Amunnubi Rooakhptah*, 109–14 (quotations on 112 and 113).

129. "So Why the Fez?," *Nuwaubian Moors Newsletter*, August 31, 1997.

130. Holy Tabernacle Ministries, *HTM, Edition 5*, 10.

131. Ruakhptah, *Sacred Records of Neter*, 71.

132. Palmer, *Nuwaubian Nation*, 2.

133. Ibid., 59–64.

CHAPTER 8

1. The epigraphs to this chapter are from, respectively, the song "Triple Threat" by hip-hop artists Nature, Nas, and Noreaga (unreleased but available at https://www.youtube.com/watch?v--9eqcX5gh08), and a song called "The Originators," from the album *To Your Soul*, by the hip-hop artist The Jaz and featuring Jay-Z (available at https://www.youtube.com/watch?v-tzzwb8p8D4k).

2. Charles Ahearn, "Planet Rock Revisited," *SPIN*, November 1990, 20.

3. Garnett, *Soul Sacrifice*, 98–99.

4. Abdul Khabeer, *Muslim Cool*, 2, 226.

5. Ibid., 79, 101, 80, 107.

6. Al Haadi Al Mahdi, *True Light Tapes 9*.

7. Al Haadi Al Mahdi, *True Light Tapes 4*.

8. AAC, *Disco Music*, 2–4.

9. Ibid., 4, 5, 13.

10. Ibid., 6–8, 12, 17.

11. Al Haadi Al Mahdi, *Paleman*, 205–7.

12. AAC, *Disco Music*, 2–4, 16.

13. "The Reformer," poster (Brooklyn: Committee of Ansaar Affairs, n.d.).

14. Al Mahdi, *Islamic Music*, 1.

15. AAC, *Abba Island in America*, 9.

16. Al Mahdi, *Islamic Music*, 14–15, 10.

17. AAC, "Khanaas Encircles All of the Meanings of the Devil (Shaytan)," in *Disco Music*, 16.
18. Al Qutb, *Sons of the Green Light . . . Study Nine*, 20.
19. Al Haadi Al Mahdi, *Wadhiyfah*, book 4, and book 2, 6–7, 17.
20. AAC, *Humazah*, 9.
21. AAC, "Passion: The Sufferings of Christ," in *American Muslims*, 12–13.
22. Daulatzai, *Black Star, Crescent Moon*, 109–20 (quotation on 109).
23. See Miyakawa, *Five Percenter Rap*.
24. Daulatzai, *Black Star, Crescent Moon*, 110.
25. For KMD's "Peach Fuzz" video, see https://www.youtube.com/watch?v-Q_3GgAALPkQ.
26. Zaheer Ali, "Malcolm X Mixtape Project," presentation at the Duke-UNC "Legacy of Malcolm X" conference, Duke University, February 20, 2015.
27. Tents of Nubia, *Truth, Special Edition*, 28.
28. For the song, see https://www.youtube.com/watch?v-MU64e037DvA.
29. Rakim's "Living for the City" is available at https://www.youtube.com/watch?v-IrLluCOOE1Y.
30. Available at https://www.youtube.com/watch?v-XJ8g4FCNYtQ.
31. Daulatzai, *Black Star, Crescent Moon*, 113.
32. Al Haadi Al Mahdi, *True Story of Noah (PBUH), Part Two*, 93.
33. Al Haadi Al Mahdi, *True Story of Noah (PBUH), Part One*, 69.
34. See "Proud Nuwaubian Fez," National Museum of American History, Smithsonian Institution, http://americanhistory.si.edu/collections/search/object/nmah_1317248.
35. Vinnie Paz, "Righteous Kill," from the album *Season of the Assassin*, available at https://www.youtube.com/watch?v-ZRTgWG77Fg0.
36. Heavy Metal Kings, "Eye Is the King," from the album *Heavy Metal Kings*, available at https://www.youtube.com/watch?v-eIj6P_8vT4Y.
37. DJ Muggs and Ill Bill, featuring B-Real and Vinnie Paz, "Kill Devil Hills," from the album *DJ Muggs vs. Ill Bill: Kill Devil Hills*, available at https://www.youtube.com/watch?v-ZwNrK7sIcfc.

38. Consequence, Common, Kanye West, and Talib Kweli, "Wack Niggaz," from the album *Train of Thought: Lost Lyrics, Rare Releases, and Beautiful B-Sides, Volume One*, https://www.youtube.com/watch?v-MuuqzNIm7Xo.
39. Tragedy Khadafi, "Eloheem," from the album *Still Reportin*, https://www.youtube.com/watch?v-FQ0GVpdevSY.
40. Tragedy Khadafi, featuring Imam T.H.U.G., a.k.a. Iron Sheiks, "Allumaniti," https://www.youtube.com/watch?v-Qt8rMMZIK1I
41. Lost Children of Babylon (recording here as the Lost Children of Egypt), "Distant Traveller," from the album *Words from the Duat: The Book of Anubis*, https://www.youtube.com/watch?v-FkxcBDPcTsg.
42. Lost Children of Babylon (Lost Children of Egypt), featuring Luminous Flux, "The Rising Force," ibid., https://www.youtube.com/watch?v-C7f5gqeCj-Q.

CODA

1. York-El, *Maguraj: The Pilgrimage*, 2, 4, 41.
2. Ibid., 15–16.
3. Ibid., 104–21.
4. Palmer, *Nuwaubian Nation*, 71–72.
5. Murphy, "Santa Barbara Africana," 160.
6. Ernst, "Situating Sufism and Yoga," 17.
7. Murphy, "Santa Barbara Africana."
8. Ibid., 160.
9. Palmer, *Nuwaubian Nation*, 1.
10. Tents of Nubia, "El's Qur'aan 18:60–82: What it Means Today," in *Truth, Edition 14*, 11.
11. Ruakhptah, *Sacred Records of Neter*, 135.

Bibliography

AAC/NIH PRIMARY SOURCES

AAC (Ansaru Allah Community). *Abba Island in America*. Brooklyn: Ansaru Allah Community, n.d. [ca. 1974–77].
———. *Al Imaam Isa Visits Egypt 1981*. Brooklyn: Ansaru Allah Community, 1981.
———. *American Muslims: Muslims in America*. Brooklyn: Ansaru Allah Community, n.d. [1980].
———. *Are the Ansars (in the West) a Self-Made Sect?* Brooklyn: Ansaru Allah Community, n.d.
———. *Bilal*. Brooklyn: Ansaru Allah Community, n.d. [1973].
———. *The Book of ป: To Whom It May Concern: Fear No Longer for I Have Arrived*. Brooklyn: Ansaru Allah Community, n.d. [ca. 1978–79].
———. *Breaking the Fast*. Brooklyn: Ansaru Allah Community, 1973.
———. *Disco Music: The Universal Language of Good or Evil?* Brooklyn: Ansaru Allah Community, n.d. [1979].
———. *The Final Link*. Brooklyn: Ansaru Allah Community, n.d. [1978].
———. *Halloween: The Devil's Sabbat!* Brooklyn: Ansaru Allah Community, n.d.
———. *How Many Muslims Really Follow the Holy Qur'an?* Brooklyn: Ansaru Allah Community, n.d. [ca. 1975–79].
———. *Humazah*. Brooklyn: Ansaru Allah Community, n.d. [1979].
———. *Id-ul-Fitr with the Ansars 1979*. Brooklyn: Ansaru Allah Community, 1979.
———. *Id with the Ansars*. Brooklyn: Ansaru Allah Community, n.d. [1977].
———. *The Man of Our Time*. Brooklyn: Ansaru Allah Community, n.d. [1978].
———. *Muhammad (PBUH) and Makkah*. Brooklyn: Ansaru Allah Community, n.d. [ca. 1976–77].
———. *People Call Him the "Son of God."* Brooklyn: Ansaru Allah Community, n.d.
———. *Signs of 73*. Brooklyn: Ansaru Allah Community, n.d.
———. *Will Send "Elijah" Before the Coming of the Great and Dreadful Day of the Lord*. Brooklyn: Ansaru Allah Community, n.d. [1973].
Ansaar Village. *Inside Ansaar Village*. Brooklyn: Ansaar Village, n.d.
Ansaru Allah Masgid of the Nubians. *The Fallacy of Christmas/Our Symbol*. Brooklyn: Ansaru Allah Masgid of the Nubians, n.d. [1973].
Atum-Rayay, Qamamtat Mut Ptah Warat. *My Brother the Extra-Terrestrial*. N.p., n.d.
Bar El Haady, Rabboni: Y'shua. *The Real Messiah*. N.p., n.d.
Al Haadi Al Mahdi, Al Hajj Imam Isa. *About the Raatib: The Book of the Mahdi*. Brooklyn: Original Tents of Kedar, 1987.
———. *Ahmad, Jesus' Khalifat (Successor)*. Brooklyn: Nubian Islaamic Hebrews, Ansaaru Allah Community, 1980 [1984?].
———. *The Ansaar Cult: Rebuttal to the Slanderers*. Brooklyn: Original Tents of Kedar, 1989.
———. *Ansaar's Guide Through the Scriptures for Better Living: Ceremonies for Boys*. Brooklyn: Original Tents of Kedar, 1989.
———. *Ansaar's Guide Through the Scriptures for Better Living: Maintenance of*

———. *Health*. Brooklyn: Original Tents of Kedar, 1988.

———. *Ansaar's Guide Through the Scriptures for Better Living: Purity and Neatness*. Brooklyn: Original Tents of Kedar, 1988.

———. *An Apology to the Nation of Islam, the True Followers of the Honorable Elijah Muhammad*. Brooklyn: Ansaarullah Community, 1990.

———. *As Sayyid Al Imaam Isa Al Haadi Al Mahdi Explains the Secret Meaning of Qur'aan to the A'immah of Ansaaru Allah: Degree of the Opening, Chapter 1*. Brooklyn: Nubian Islaamic Hebrews, Ansaaru Allah Community, 1985.

———. *As Sayyid Al Imaam Isa Al Haadi Al Mahdi Explains the Secret Meaning of Qur'aan to the A'immah of Ansaaru Allah: Degree of the Pure Faith, Chapter 112*. Brooklyn: Nubian Islaamic Hebrews, Ansaaru Allah Community, 1985.

———. *Beginner's Arabic: Simplified Arabic Reading*. Brooklyn: Nubian Islaamic Hebrews, Ansaaru Allah Community, 1986.

———. *Bilaal, the Sceptre Bearer*. Brooklyn: Nubian Islaamic Hebrews, Ansaaru Allah Community, 1985.

———. *The Book of the Five Percenters*. Monticello, N.Y.: Original Tents of Kedar, 1991.

———. *The Book of ل: To Whom It May Concern, Fear No Longer for I Have Arrived*. Brooklyn: Nubian Islaamic Hebrews, Ansaaru Allah Community, 1985.

———. *The Book of Laam: The Message of the Messenger Is Right and Exact*. 2nd rev. ed. Brooklyn: Original Tents of Kedar, 1989.

———. *The Book of Revelation, Chapter 1, Verses 1–20*. 2nd rev. ed. Monticello, N.Y.: Original Tents of Kedar, 1991.

———. *The Book of Revelation, Chapter 13, Verses 1–18*. 2nd rev. ed. Monticello, N.Y.: Original Tents of Kedar, 1991.

———. *The Call of the Mahdi in America*. Brooklyn: Original Tents of Kedar, 1987.

———. *The Day of the Pentecost*. Brooklyn: Original Tents of Kedar, 1988.

———. *Fast of Ramadaan*. Brooklyn: Nubian Islaamic Hebrews, Ansaaru Allah Community, 1986.

———. *Fast of Ramadaan*. 2nd rev. ed. Brooklyn: Original Tents of Kedar, 1990.

———. *The Final Messenger: Christ the Final Word*. Monticello, N.Y.: Original Tents of Kedar, 1991.

———. *From Allah to Man*. Brooklyn: Nubian Islaamic Hebrews, Ansaaru Allah Community, 1984.

———. *Gospel of Barnabas, Book Three*. Brooklyn: Nubian Islaamic Hebrews, Ansaaru Allah Community, 1984.

———. *Gospel of Barnabas, Book Two*. Brooklyn: Nubian Islaamic Hebrews, Ansaaru Allah Community, 1984.

———. *Gospel of John, Chapter One*. Brooklyn: Nubian Islaamic Hebrews, Ansaaru Allah Community, 1984.

———. *Hadrat Faatimah (AS): The Daughter of the Prophet Muhammad (PBUH), Part 1*. Brooklyn: Original Tents of Kedar, 1988.

———. *Hadrat Faatimah (AS): The Daughter of the Prophet Muhammad (PBUH), Part 2*. Brooklyn: Original Tents of Kedar, 1988.

———. *Hal suliba al-masih haqqan?* Brooklyn: Original Tents of Kedar, 1988.

———. *The Holy Gospel: The Revelation of Jesus the Messiah to the World, Book 4*. Brooklyn: Nubian Islaamic Hebrews, Ansaaru Allah Community, 1984.

———. *How the Prophet Muhammad (PBUH) Read the Qur'aan*. Brooklyn: Nubian Islaamic Hebrews, Ansaaru Allah Community, 1983.

———. *Is Valentine's Day a Christian Holiday?* Monticello, N.Y.: Original Tents of Kedar, 1992.

———. *Kitab al-Nur*. N.p., n.d.

———. *Leviathan: 666*. Brooklyn: Nubian Islaamic Hebrews, Ansaaru Allah Community, 1984.

———. *Man huwa aladhi fi-l-ard?* Brooklyn: Original Tents of Kedar, n.d.

———. *The Man of Miracles in This Day and Time, Part 1*. Brooklyn: Nubian

———. *The Man of Miracles in This Day and Time, Part 2.* Brooklyn: Nubian Islaamic Hebrews, Ansaaru Allah Community, 1983.

———. *Muslim Prayer Book, Part One.* Brooklyn: Original Tents of Kedar, 1987.

———. *Nubic Calendar: The Light of Your Life.* Monticello, N.Y.: Original Tents of Kedar, 1992.

———. *Nubic: The Language of the Nubian Americans.* Brooklyn: Original Tents of Kedar, 1989.

———. *Opening of the Seventh Seal: Secret Societies Unmasked.* 1st rev. ed. Brooklyn: Nubian Islaamic Hebrews, Ansaaru Allah Community, 1984.

———. *Our Flag: The True Banner of al Islaam.* Brooklyn: Original Tents of Kedar, 1989.

———. *The Paleman.* Brooklyn: Original Tents of Kedar, 1990.

———. *Qur'aanic Arabic Lessons for the Nubian Islaamic Hebrews.* Brooklyn: Nubian Islaamic Hebrews, Ansaaru Allah Community, 1986.

———. *Al Qur'aan, Part Two: From Suwratu'l Baqarah Verses 142–252.* Brooklyn: Original Tents of Kedar, 1981.

———. *The Raatib, Chapter 1.* Monticello, N.Y.: Original Tents of Kedar, n.d.

———. *Racism in Islaam.* Brooklyn: Nubian Islaamic Hebrews, Ansaaru Allah Community, 1986.

———. *The Resurrection.* Monticello, N.Y.: Original Tents of Kedar, 1991.

———. *Santa or Satan? The Fallacy of Christmas.* Brooklyn: Nubian Islaamic Hebrews, Ansaaru Allah Community, 1986.

———. *Science of Creation.* Brooklyn: Nubian Islaamic Hebrews, Ansaaru Allah Community, 1984.

———. *Science of Healing.* Rev. ed. Brooklyn: Nubian Islaamic Hebrews, Ansaaru Allah Community, 1985.

———. *Sex Life of a Muslim.* Brooklyn: Original Tents of Kedar, 1989.

———. *Should Muslims Observe the Sabbath?* Brooklyn: Nubian Islaamic Hebrews, Ansaaru Allah Community, 1985.

———. *Sons of Canaan.* Brooklyn: Nubian Islaamic Hebrews, Ansaaru Allah Community, 1987.

———. *Teach Your Children to Write Arabic.* Brooklyn: Original Tents of Kedar, 1988.

———. *The Travels of a Sufi.* Brooklyn: Original Tents of Kedar, 1987.

———. *True Light Tapes 1: Who Are the Real Arabs?* Brooklyn: Original Tents of Kedar, n.d.

———. *True Light Tapes 2: Who and What Are You?* Brooklyn: Original Tents of Kedar, n.d.

———. *True Light Tapes 4: What Are Human Beings?* Brooklyn: Original Tents of Kedar, n.d.

———. *True Light Tapes 9: Let's Trap the Devil.* Brooklyn: Original Tents of Kedar, n.d.

———. *True Light Tapes 11: Signs of the End of the World and Matthew 24.* Brooklyn: Nubian Islaamic Hebrews, Ansaaru Allah Community, n.d.

———. *True Light Tapes 14: Know Your Language.* Brooklyn: Original Tents of Kedar, n.d.

———. *True Light Tapes 19: Who Was Jesus Praying To?* Brooklyn: Original Tents of Kedar, n.d.

———. *True Light Tapes 27: Why Use the Books of the New Testament?* Brooklyn: Original Tents of Kedar, n.d.

———. *True Light Tapes 28: Who Is the Comforter?* Brooklyn: Original Tents of Kedar, n.d.

———. *True Light Tapes 29: Are the Edomites the Pale Race?* Brooklyn: Original Tents of Kedar, n.d.

———. *True Light Tapes 37: Persecution of the Leaders.* Brooklyn: Original Tents of Kedar, n.d.

———. *True Light Tapes 39: The Nine Spirits of Messiah.* Brooklyn: Original Tents of Kedar, n.d.

———. *True Light Tapes 40: Are There Human Devils?* Brooklyn: Original Tents of Kedar, n.d.

———. *True Light Tapes 42: Angelic Descendants on Earth*. Brooklyn: Nubian Islaamic Hebrews, Ansaaru Allah Community, n.d.

———. *True Light Tapes 46: Laws and Marriage*. Brooklyn: Original Tents of Kedar, n.d.

———. *True Light Tapes 47: What Laws Did Jesus Follow?* Brooklyn: Original Tents of Kedar, n.d.

———. *True Light Tapes 50: Aiders of ALLAH*. Brooklyn: Original Tents of Kedar, n.d.

———. *True Light Tapes 55: Is Nature Man's Worst Enemy?* Brooklyn: Original Tents of Kedar, n.d.

———. *True Light Tapes 56: Polygamy*. Brooklyn: Original Tents of Kedar, n.d.

———. *True Light Tapes 57: What Is Man's Purpose?* Brooklyn: Original Tents of Kedar, n.d.

———. *True Light Tapes 61: Dinosaurs and Evolution*. Brooklyn: Original Tents of Kedar, n.d.

———. *True Light Tapes 74: The Crucifixion of David*. Brooklyn: Original Tents of Kedar, n.d.

———. *True Light Tapes 77: We Are Not Like You (Sunni Moslems)*. Brooklyn: Original Tents of Kedar, n.d.

———. *The True Story of Cain and Abel*. Brooklyn: Nubian Islaamic Hebrews, Ansaaru Allah Community, 1986.

———. *The True Story of Noah (PBUH), Part One*. Brooklyn: Nubian Islaamic Hebrews, Ansaaru Allah Community, 1986.

———. *The True Story of Noah (PBUH), Part Two*. Brooklyn: Nubian Islaamic Hebrews, Ansaaru Allah Community, 1986.

———. *Wadhiyfah: The Science of Sound Healing*. Books 2 and 4. Brooklyn: Original Tents of Kedar, 1988.

———. *What and Where Is Hell?* Brooklyn: Nubian Islaamic Hebrews, Ansaaru Allah Community, 1986.

———. *Whatever Happened to the Nubian Islaamic Hebrew Mission?* Brooklyn: Original Tents of Kedar, 1989.

———. *Whatever Happened to the Nubian Islaamic Hebrews?* Brooklyn: Nubian Islaamic Hebrews, Ansaaru Allah Community, 1985.

———. *What Laws Did Jesus Follow?* Brooklyn: Original Tents of Kedar, 1988.

———. *Where Is the Tabernacle of the Most High? Part 1*. Brooklyn: Nubian Islaamic Hebrews, Ansaaru Allah Community, 1986.

———. *Where Is the Tabernacle of the Most High? Part 2*. Brooklyn: Nubian Islaamic Hebrews, Ansaaru Allah Community, 1986.

———. *Who Was Jesus Sent To?* Monticello, N.Y.: Original Tents of Kedar, 1991.

———. *Who Was Marcus Garvey?* Brooklyn: Original Tents of Kedar, 1988.

———. *Who Was Noble Drew Ali?* Brooklyn: Original Tents of Kedar, 1988.

———. *Why Do Muslim Women Wear the Face Covering, the Veil?* 6th rev. ed. Brooklyn: Original Tents of Kedar, 1989.

———. *Why Do Muslim Women Wear the Face Covering (Veil)?* Brooklyn: Nubian Islaamic Hebrews, Ansaaru Allah Community, 1984.

———. *Why the Nosering?* Brooklyn: Nubian Islaamic Hebrews, Ansaaru Allah Community, 1986.

———. *The Wisemen*. Monticello, N.Y.: Original Tents of Kedar, 1991.

———. *Women Who Have Changed the Course of History*. Brooklyn: Nubian Islaamic Hebrews, Ansaaru Allah Community, 1985.

———. *You Are Adam's Descendants*. Brooklyn: Nubian Islaamic Hebrews, Ansaaru Allah Community, 1985.

———. *You Must Be Born Again, Part One*. Brooklyn: Nubian Islaamic Hebrews, Ansaaru Allah Community, 1986.

———. *You Must Be Born Again, Part Two*. Brooklyn: Nubian Islaamic Hebrews, Ansaaru Allah Community, 1986.

Holy Tabernacle Ministries. *HTM, Edition 1 (Revised): The Savior*. Eatonton: Holy Tabernacle Ministries, n.d.

———. *HTM, Edition 1: The Savior*. Eatonton: Holy Tabernacle Ministries, n.d.

———. *HTM, Edition 2: Women of the Scriptures*. Eatonton: Holy Tabernacle Ministries, n.d.

———. *HTM, Edition 3*. Eatonton: Holy Tabernacle Ministries, n.d.

———. *HTM, Edition 5: The True Faces of the Men of the Scriptures*. Eatonton: Holy Tabernacle Ministries, n.d.

———. *HTM, Edition 6*. Eatonton: Holy Tabernacle Ministries, n.d.

———. *Savior's Day 1996: Man of Many Faces Brings Us One Message*. Eatonton: Holy Tabernacle Ministries, 1996.

Al Mahdi, Al Hajj Imam Isa. *Ancient Egypt and the Pharaohs*. Brooklyn: Ansaru Allah Community, 1980.

———. *Arabic: The First Language*. Brooklyn: Ansaru Allah Community, 1977.

———. *Are the Scriptures Tampered With?* Brooklyn: Ansaru Allah Community, 1982.

———. *As Sayyid Al Imaam Isa Al Mahdi Explains the Secret Meaning of Qur'aan to the Imaams of Ansaaru Allah: Degree of the Night of Power, Chapter 67*. Brooklyn: Ansaaru Allah Community, 1982.

———. *Bilal*. Brooklyn: Ansaru Allah Community, n.d. [1979].

———. *The Book of Lamb 1: The Message of the Messenger Is Right and Exact*. Brooklyn: Ansaru Allah Community, 1979.

———. *The Book of Lamb 2: The Message of the Messenger Is Right and Exact*. Brooklyn: Ansaru Allah Community, 1979.

———. *Christ Is the Answer*. Brooklyn: Ansaru Allah Community, 1977.

———. *Contradictions of the Disciples*. Brooklyn: Ansaru Allah Community, 1981.

———. *Did the Hog Come for Mankind?* Brooklyn: Ansaru Allah Community, n.d. [ca. 1972].

———. *Eternal Life After Death*. Brooklyn: Ansaru Allah Community, 1977.

———. *The Fallacy of Easter*. Brooklyn: Ansaru Allah Community, 1980.

———. *The Fallacy of Easter*. 2nd ed. Brooklyn: Ansaru Allah Community, 1982.

———. *A Family Guide to Easy Arabic Phrases*. Brooklyn: Ansaru Allah Community, 1977.

———. *Fast of Ramadaan*. Brooklyn: Ansaru Allah Community, 1980.

———. *The Forgotten Tribe Kedar*. Brooklyn: Ansaru Allah Community, n.d. [1974].

———. *Hadith: Allah's Scripture Comes First*. Brooklyn: Ansaru Allah Community, 1979.

———. *Halloween: The Devil's (CH) Sabbat*. Brooklyn: Ansaru Allah Community, 1980.

———. *The Holy Gospel: The Revelation of Jesus the Messiah to the World, Book 2*. Brooklyn: Ansaru Allah Community, 1979.

———. *The Holy Gospel: The Revelation of Jesus the Messiah to the World, Book 3*. Brooklyn: Ansaru Allah Community, 1979.

———. *The Holy Qur'an: The Last Testament*. Vols. 1–3. Brooklyn: Ansaru Allah Community, 1977–81.

———. *Holy War*. Brooklyn: Ansaru Allah Community, 1979.

———. *How to Read the Qur'an in Arabic*. Brooklyn: Ansaru Allah Community, 1981.

———. *I Don't Claim to Be . . .* Brooklyn: Ansaru Allah Community, 1981.

———. *Al Imaam Isa vs. the Computer*. Brooklyn: Ansaru Allah Community, 1982.

———. *Islamic Music*. Brooklyn: Ansaru Allah Community, 1977.

———. *Islam the True Faith: The Religion of Humanity by Shaikh al Hajj Dauwd Ahmad Faisal (HWON) (1891–1980)*. Brooklyn: Ansaru Allah Community, 1980.

———. *Khutbat's of Al Hajj Al Imam Isa Abd'Allah Muhammad Al Mahdi, Book One*. Brooklyn: Ansaru Allah Community, n.d. [ca. 1977–79].

———. *Khutbat's of Al Hajj Al Imam Isa Abd'Allah Muhammad Al Mahdi, Book Two*. Brooklyn: Ansaru Allah Community, n.d. [ca. 1977–79].

———. *The Lost Children of Mu and Atlantis*. Brooklyn: Ansaru Allah Community, 1983.

———. *Muhammad Ahmad: The Only True Mahdi!* Brooklyn: Ansaru Allah Community, n.d. [1977].

———. *Muslim Funeral Rites.* Brooklyn: Ansaru Allah Community, 1983.

———. *Muslim Prayer Book, Part One.* Brooklyn: Ansaru Allah Community, 1983.

———. *The Muslim Woman.* Brooklyn: Ansaru Allah Community, 1977.

———. *The 99+1 Attributes of Allah.* Brooklyn: Ansaru Allah Community, 1983.

———. *Opening of the Seventh Seal: Secret Societies Unmasked.* Brooklyn: Ansaru Allah Community, n.d. [ca. 1974–77].

———. *Our Savior's Day: Dr. Malachi Z. York Family Reunion.* Eatonton: Holy Tabernacle Ministries, 1995.

———. *Our Symbol.* Brooklyn: Ansaru Allah Community, 1977.

———. *The Pale Man.* Brooklyn: Ansaru Allah Community, 1977.

———. *The Pictures of the Arabic Alphabet.* Brooklyn: Ansaru Allah Community, 1981.

———. *Polytheism: Worship of the Canaanites.* Brooklyn: Ansaru Allah Community, 1977.

———. *Prehistoric Man and Animals—Did They Exist?* Brooklyn: Ansaru Allah Community, 1980.

———. *The Raatib (Unshakable) of Imam Al Mahdi (AS).* Brooklyn: Ansaru Allah Community, 1980.

———. *Santa or Satan? The Fallacy of Christmas.* Brooklyn: Ansaru Allah Community, 1982.

———. *Science of the Pyramids.* Brooklyn: Ansaru Allah Community, 1983.

———. *Series of Hadiyth, Book One: Purification.* Brooklyn: Ansaru Allah Community, 1982.

———. *Series of Hadiyth, Book Two: Worship.* Brooklyn: Ansaru Allah Community, 1982.

———. *Teach Yourself Arabic.* Brooklyn: Ansaru Allah Community, 1980.

———. *Teach Yourself Qur'aan with Tape.* Brooklyn: Ansaru Allah Community, 1982.

———. *Thus Said: Al Imaam Muhammad Ahmad Al Mahdi (AS).* Brooklyn: Ansaru Allah Community, 1982.

———. *Tribal Encyclopedia.* Brooklyn: Ansaru Allah Community, 1977.

———. *The Tribe Israel Is No More!* Brooklyn: Ansaru Allah Community, n.d. [1975].

———. *The True Origin of the Martial Arts.* Brooklyn: Ansaru Allah Community, 1977.

———. *The True Story of Cain and Abel.* Brooklyn: Ansaru Allah Community, 1980.

———. *The True Story of Noah (PBUH).* Brooklyn: Ansaru Allah Community, 1978.

———. *The Turban Jewel: Catalog of Fine Jewelry.* Brooklyn: Ansaru Allah Community, 1979.

———. *Was Christ Really Crucified?* Brooklyn: Ansaru Allah Community, 1980.

———. *What Is a Masjid?* Brooklyn: Ansaru Allah Community, 1983.

———. *What Is a Muslim?* Brooklyn: Ansaru Allah Community, 1977.

———. *What's a Prophet?* Brooklyn: Ansaru Allah Community, 1981.

———. *Who Was Noble Drew Ali?* Brooklyn: Ansaru Allah Community, 1980.

———. *Who Was the Prophet Muhammad?* Brooklyn: Ansaru Allah Community, 1977.

———. *Why Allah Should Not Be Called "God."* Brooklyn: Ansaru Allah Community, 1979.

———. *Will Send Elijah Before the Coming of the Great and Dreadful Day of the Lord.* Brooklyn: Ansaru Allah Community, 1977.

———. *Yoruba.* Brooklyn: Ansaru Allah Community, 1978.

Malachizodok-El, Nayya. *People of the Sun.* Eatonton: Holy Tabernacle Ministries, n.d.

Malachizodok York-El, Nayya. *It's Alignment Time! At Wahanee!!* Eatonton: A.M.O.M., n.d.

Muhammad, Isa. *Science of Creation.* Brooklyn: Ansaru Allah Community, 1979.

———. *Talisman.* Brooklyn: Ansaru Allah Community, 1979.

NIHMA (Nubian Islamic Hebrew Mission in America). *Back to the Beginning: The Book of Names.* N.p., n.d. [1972].

———. *Did the Hog Come for Mankind?* N.p., n.d. [ca. 1975–77].

———. *The Fast of Ramadhan: Is It Good for You?* N.p., n.d.

———. *Founding Father of Islam in America Today, Here Since 1928 A.D.* Brooklyn: Masgid of the Nubian Islamic Hebrew Mission in America, n.d. [1972–73].

———. *From Allah to Man.* N.p., n.d.

———. *Hadith: Who's to Say Which Is the Right One?* N.p., n.d.

———. *Imam Isa.* Brooklyn: Masgid of the Nubian Islamic Hebrew Mission in America, n.d.

———. *Is Music and Dance Lawful for Muslims?* N.p., n.d. [ca. 1972].

———. *Is the Holy Qur'an a Product of Man?* N.p.: Ansar Printing, n.d.

———. *Learn the Importance of Muslim Prayer.* N.p., n.d.

———. *A Look at the Muslim Man.* N.p., n.d. [1972].

———. *A Look at the Muslim Woman.* N.p., n.d.

———. *Men Who Dress in Women's Clothes: Second City of Sadum (Sodom).* Brooklyn: Masgid of the Nubian Islamic Hebrew Mission in America, n.d.

———. *The Nubian Islamic Hebrew Mission in America.* N.p., n.d.

———. *The Nubian Islamic Hebrew Mission in America.* 3rd ed. N.p., n.d. [1972].

———. *The Nubian Islamic Hebrew Mission in America.* 4th ed. N.p., n.d.

———. *The Nubian Islamic Hebrew Mission in America.* 5th ed. N.p., n.d. [1972].

———. *Qur'anic Arabic.* N.p., n.d.

———. *The Spell of the Blacks Was Broken in the Year 1970 A.D. by the Seventh Seal Being Opened: Leviathan's 6,000 Years Are Up in the Year 2000.* N.p., n.d.

———. *Thou Shalt Not KILL!!* Brooklyn: Masgid of the Nubian Islamic Hebrew Mission in America, n.d. [1972].

———. *Was Christ Really Crucified?* Brooklyn: Masgid of the Nubian Islamic Hebrew Mission in America, n.d.

———. *Was Created with One Thought: The "Key" Is Within.* Brooklyn: Nubian Islamic Hebrew Mission in America, n.d. [ca. 1972].

———. *What Law Says the Veil?* Brooklyn: Masgid of the Nubian Islamic Hebrew Mission in America, n.d.

———. *Who's Leviathan—The Dollar Bill.* Brooklyn: Masgid of the Nubian Islamic Hebrew Mission in America, n.d.

Original Tents of Kedar. *Calendar of 1990.* Brooklyn: Original Tents of Kedar, 1989.

———. *The 12 Spiritual Disciples (1991 Calendar).* Monticello, N.Y.: Original Tents of Kedar, 1991.

Al Qutb. *Celestial Being or Terrestrial Being... Which One Are You?* N.p., n.d.

———. *The Second Step of the Sufi.* N.p., n.d.

———. *Secret Document: The Second Step of the Sufi.* N.p., n.d.

———. *Sons of the Green Light, the First Degree, Study Five.* N.p., n.d.

———. *Sons of the Green Light, the First Degree, Study Nine.* N.p., n.d.

———. *Sons of the Green Light, the First Degree, Study One.* N.p., n.d.

———. *Sons of the Green Light, the First Degree, Study Three.* N.p., n.d.

———. *You and the Sons of the Green Light.* N.p., n.d.

Raakhptah, Amunnubi. *Egiptian Magic: Charms and Amulets for Protection.* Athens, Ga.: Ancient Egiptian Order, n.d.

———. *Nuwaupic: The Ancient Egiptian Mystery Language.* Athens, Ga.: Ancient Egiptian Order, n.d.

———. *Pa Ashutat "The Prayer."* Athens, Ga.: Ancient Egiptian Order, n.d.

Rooakhptah, Amunnubi. *The Degree of Muhammad-ism.* Athens, Ga.: Tama-Re, Egypt of the West Embassy, n.d.

Ruakhptah, Amunnubi. *The Sacred Records of Neter: Aaferti Atum-Re.* N.p., n.d. [1998].

Tents of Abraham. *Nubian Village Bulletin, Edition 2: Women of the Scriptures.* Monticello, N.Y.: Tents of Abraham, 1992.

———. *Nubian Village Bulletin, Edition 4: The Truth of the Scriptures.* Monticello, N.Y.: Original Tents of Abraham, 1992.

———. *True Light Tape, the Lamb Speaks from Mount Zion: Nubian Woman.* Monticello, N.Y.: Tents of Abraham, n.d. [1992].

———. *True Light Tape, the Lamb Speaks from Mount Zion: Our Own Flag.* Monticello, N.Y.: Tents of Abraham, n.d.

———. *True Light Tape, the Lamb Speaks from Mount Zion: People of the Sun.* Monticello, N.Y.: Tents of Abraham, n.d.

———. *True Light Tape, the Lamb Speaks from Mount Zion: The Fallen Angelic Beings.* Monticello, N.Y.: Tents of Abraham, n.d.

———. *The Truth, Edition 2: Women of the Scriptures.* Atlanta: Tents of Abraham, 1992.

———. *The Truth, Edition 3.* Atlanta: Tents of Abraham, 1992.

———. *The Truth, Edition 5: The True Faces of the Men of the Holy Scriptures.* Atlanta: Tents of Abraham, 1992.

———. *The Truth, Edition 7: The True Faces of the People of the Scriptures.* Atlanta: Tents of Abraham, 1992.

———. *The Truth, Edition 8: Are There Orientals in the Bible?* Atlanta: Tents of Abraham, 1992.

———. *The Truth, Edition 9: The Making of the Disciples.* Atlanta: Tents of Abraham, 1992.

Tents of Nubia. *The Truth, Edition 12: 666—Mark of the Beast—Visa.* Atlanta: Tents of Nubia, 1993.

———. *The Truth, Edition 13: Are You Still Eating Pork?* Atlanta: Tents of Nubia, 1993.

———. *The Truth, Edition 14: The 7 Heads and the 10 Horns.* Atlanta: Tents of Nubia, 1993.

———. *The Truth, Edition 15: Prophecy Fulfilled.* Atlanta: Tents of Nubia, 1993.

———. *The Truth, Edition 16: Muhammad Was a Hebrew.* Atlanta: Tents of Nubia, 1993.

———. *The Truth, Edition 19: The Collage of Truth.* Atlanta: Tents of Nubia, 1993.

———. *The Truth, Special Edition: Who Do People Say I Am?* Atlanta: Tents of Nubia, 1992.

UNNM (United Nuwaubian Nation of Moors). *Nuwaubian Moors Newsletter*, August 3, 17, 24, 31, 1997; September 7, 14, 21, 28, 1997; October 5, 12, 19 (ed. 1, vols. 11 and 12), 1997; November 16, 1997; December 28, 1997; June 22, 1978; September 30, 1988.

York, Dwight. *360 Questions to Ask the Orthodox Sunni Muslims.* Monticello, N.Y.: Original Tents of Kedar, n.d.

York, Grandma. *Grandma's Words of Wisdom.* N.p., n.d.

———. *"They Say."* Eatonton: Holy Tabernacle Ministries, n.d.

York, Malachi Z. *Be Prepared for the Anti-Christ.* Eatonton: Holy Tabernacle Ministries, n.d.

———. *Could Jesus Transform Himself?* Eatonton: Holy Tabernacle Ministries, 1994.

———. *Does Dr. Malachi Z. York Try to Hide the Fact That He Was Imaam Issa?* Eatonton: Holy Tabernacle Ministries, n.d.

———. *Does God Help His Own?* Eatonton: Holy Tabernacle Ministries, 1994.

———. *Dr. Malachi Z. York Answers Questions on the Holy Tablets Series.* Book 15. Eatonton: Holy Tabernacle Ministries, n.d.

———. *Dr. Malachi Z. York Debates with the Nation of Islam.* Books 21 and 22. Eatonton: Holy Tabernacle Ministries, n.d.

———. *El's Holy Injiyl.* Eatonton: Holy Tabernacle Ministries, n.d. [1990s].

———. *El's Holy Qur'aan.* Eatonton: Holy Tabernacle Ministries, n.d. [1990s].

———. *El's Holy Tehillim (Zabuwr).* Eatonton: Holy Tabernacle Ministries, n.d. [1990s].

———. *El's Holy Torah.* Eatonton: Holy Tabernacle Ministries, n.d. [1990s].

———. *Exodus: Introduction.* Eatonton: Holy Tabernacle Ministries, n.d.

———. *The Fallacy of Easter.* Eatonton: Holy Tabernacle Ministries, n.d.

———. *The Glory of Jesus the Messiah.* Eatonton: Holy Tabernacle Ministries, 1994.

———. *God Gave the Sign to Jonah.* Eatonton: Holy Tabernacle Ministries, 1994.

———. *God Misinterpreted.* Eatonton: Holy Tabernacle Ministries, 1994.

———. *The Holy Tablets.* Eatonton: Holy Tabernacle Ministries, n.d. [1996].

———. *El Injiyl, Part 1, Chapter 1–11.* Eatonton: Holy Tabernacle Ministries, n.d.

———. *Is Haile Selassie the Christ?* Eatonton: Holy Tabernacle Ministries, 1994.

———. *Is Jesus the God of the Koran?* Eatonton: Holy Tabernacle Ministries, 1994.

———. *Jesus Found in Egipt*. Athens, Ga.: Ancient Egiptian Order, n.d. [1996].

———. *El Katub Shil el Mawut (The Book of the Dead): Coming Forth by Day*. Eatonton: Holy Tabernacle Ministries, n.d. [1990s].

———. *Malachi: I Will Send You Elijah, Part 1*. Eatonton: Holy Tabernacle Ministries, n.d.

———. *Malachi: I Will Send You Elijah, Part 2*. Eatonton: Holy Tabernacle Ministries, n.d.

———. *Man from Planet Rizq*. Eatonton: Holy Tabernacle Ministries, n.d.

———. *The Melanin-ite Children*. Eatonton: Holy Tabernacle Ministries, n.d. [1995].

———. *Muslim's Creeds: True or False*. Eatonton: Holy Tabernacle Ministries, 1995.

———. *Nuwaubian Taful*. Eatonton: Holy Tabernacle Ministries, n.d.

———. *Post Graduate: The Renewal of the Lessons*. Eatonton: Holy Tabernacle Ministries, n.d. [1996].

———. *The Problem Book*. N.p., n.d.

———. *The Raatib: The Unshakable Facts*. Eatonton: Holy Tabernacle Ministries, n.d.

———. *The Real Messiah*. Eatonton: Holy Tabernacle Ministries, n.d.

———. *The Resurrection*. Eatonton: Holy Tabernacle Ministries, 1994.

———. *Shaikh Daoud vs. W. D. Fard*. Eatonton: Holy Tabernacle Ministries, n.d.

———. *Shamballah and Aghaarta: Cities Within the Earth*. Eatonton: Holy Tabernacle Ministries, n.d.

———. *Sodom Misinterpreted*. Eatonton: Holy Tabernacle Ministries, 1994.

———. *360 Questions to Ask a Hebrew Israelite. Parts 1, 2, and 3*. Eatonton: Holy Tabernacle Ministries, 1994.

———. *The True Light Tapes: Who Named the Angels?* Eatonton: Holy Tabernacle Ministries, n.d.

———. *What Is God Doing for You?* Eatonton: Holy Tabernacle Ministries, 1994.

———. *What Is God's Language?* Eatonton: Holy Tabernacle Ministries, 1994.

———. *What Laws Did Y'ashua Follow?* Eatonton: Holy Tabernacle Ministries, n.d.

York-El, Malachi Z. *The Constitution of U.N.N.M.: "The United Nuwaubian Nation of Moors."* Milledgeville, Ga.: Yamassee Tribe of Native Americans, Seminole, Creek, Shushuni, Washita Mound Builders, 1992.

———. *The Holy Shroud: "Fact or Fiction."* Eatonton: Holy Tabernacle Ministries, n.d.

———. *The Holy Tablets*. Rev. ed. N.p., n.d.

———. *Is It Black Man's Christianity or White Man's Christianity?* Athens, Ga.: Egipt, n.d.

———. *Nuwaubu and Amunnubi Rooakhptah: Fact or Fiction?* Eatonton: Holy Tabernacle Ministries, n.d. [1996].

———. *Questions to Dr. Malachi Z. York-El About the Beginning*. Athens, Ga.: Ancient Egiptian Order, n.d.

———. *The Raatib for Shriners*. Macon, Ga.: International Supreme Council of Shriners, n.d.

———. *The Real Messiah*. Eatonton: Holy Tabernacle Ministries, n.d.

———. *The Real Trinity*. Eatonton: Holy Tabernacle Ministries, n.d.

———. *The Three Jesus'*. Eatonton: Holy Tabernacle Ministries, n.d.

———. *Who Rolled the Stone?* Eatonton: Holy Tabernacle Ministries, n.d.

———. *Women Who Changed the Course of History!* Eatonton: Holy Tabernacle Ministries, n.d.

York-El, Malachizodok. *El Maguraj: The Pilgrimage*. Eatonton: Holy Tabernacle Ministries, 1997.

OTHER SOURCES

Abdul Khabeer, Su'ad. "Black Arabic." In *Black Routes to Islam*, edited by Manning Marable and Hishaam D. Aidi, 167–89. New York: Palgrave Macmillan, 2009.

———. *Muslim Cool: Race, Religion, and Hip Hop in the United States*. New York: New York University Press, 2016.

Abdullah, Zain. *Black Mecca: The African Muslims of Harlem*. Oxford: Oxford University Press, 2010.

Abusharaf, Rogaia Mustafa. "Structural Adaptations in an Immigrant Muslim Congregation in New York." In *Gatherings in Diaspora: Religious Communities and the New Immigration*, edited by R. Stephen Warner and Judith G. Wittner, 235–62. Philadelphia: Temple University Press, 1998.

———. *Wanderings: Sudanese Migrants and Exiles in North America*. Ithaca: Cornell University Press, 2002.

Adefunmi, Oseijeman. *Tribal Origins of African-Americans*. New Oyo [Harlem]: Yoruba Temple, 1962.

Ahmed, Gubdi Mahdi. "Muslim Organizations in the United States." In *The Muslims of America*, edited by Yvonne Yazbeck Haddad, 11–24. Oxford: Oxford University Press, 1991.

Albanese, Catherine. *A Republic of Mind and Spirit: A Cultural History of American Metaphysical Religion*. New Haven: Yale University Press, 2007.

Ali, Abdullah Yusuf, trans. *The Meaning of the Holy Qur'an*. Brentwood, Md.: American Trust, 1977.

Ali, Maulana Muhammad, trans. *The Holy Qur'an, with English Translation and Commentary*. Dublin, Ohio: Ahmadiyya Anjuman Isha'at Islam Lahore, 2002.

Ali, Noble Drew. *The Holy Koran Circle Seven*. N.p.: Ancient and Mystic Order of Melchizedek, n.d.

Amen, Ra Un Nefer. "Oyotunji: Oyo Rises Again; Saga of the Rebirth of Yoruba Culture on American Soil." *Oracle of Tehuti* 2, no. 7 (1981): 10–24.

Amin, Mustafa el-. *Afrocentricity, Malcolm X, and al-Islam*. Newark, N.J.: El-Amin Productions, 1993.

———. *Freemasonry, Ancient Egypt, and the Islamic Destiny*. Jersey City: New Mind Productions, 1994.

Asante, Molefi. *Afrocentricity*. 1980. Trenton, N.J.: Africa World, 1988.

Aydin, Cemil. *The Idea of the Muslim World: A Global Intellectual History*. Cambridge, Mass.: Harvard University Press, 2017.

Baer, Hans A., and Merrill Singer. "Toward a Typology of Black Sectarianism as a Response to Racial Stratification." *Anthropological Quarterly* 54, no. 1 (1981): 1–14.

Ben-Jochannan, Yosef A. A. *African Origins of the Major "Western Religions."* 1970. Baltimore: Black Classic Press, 1991.

Ben Yahweh, Yahweh. *Yahweh Judges America*. Seguin: PEESS Foundation, 1985.

Berg, Herbert. *Elijah Muhammad and Islam*. New York: New York University Press, 2009.

Berman, Jacob Rama. *American Arabesque: Arabs and Islam in the Nineteenth-Century Imaginary*. New York: New York University Press, 2012.

Bey, R. A. Umar Shabazz. *We Are the Washitaw: The Indigenous Black Inhabitants of North America*. N.p.: Hotep, 1996.

Beynon, Erdmann Doane. "The Voodoo Cult Among Negro Migrants in Detroit." *American Journal of Sociology* 43, no. 6 (1938): 894–907.

Blum, Edward J., and Paul Harvey. "From Light to White: The Place and Race of Jesus in Antebellum America." *Historically Speaking* 13, no. 4 (2012): 13–15.

Blyden, Edward W. *Christianity, Islam, and the Negro Race*. 1887. Edinburgh: Edinburgh University Press, 1967.

Bowen, Patrick D. "Abdul Hamid Suleiman and the Origins of the Moorish Science Temple." *Journal of Race, Ethnicity, and Religion* 2, no. 13 (2011): 1–54.

———. *The African American Islamic Renaissance, 1920–1975*. Vol. 2 of *A History of Conversion to Islam in the United States*. Leiden: Brill, 2017.

———. "The Search for 'Islam': African-American Islamic Groups in NYC, 1904–1954." *Muslim World* 102, no. 2 (2012): 264–83.

Bruder, Edith, and Tudor Parfitt. "Introduction." In *African Zion: Studies in Black Judaism*, edited by Edith Bruder and Tudor Parfitt, 1–10. Newcastle upon Tyne: Cambridge Scholars, 2012.

Bushman, Richard Lyman. *Joseph Smith: Rough Stone Rolling*. New York: Vintage, 2007.

Calavito, Jason. *The Cult of Alien Gods: H. P. Lovecraft and Extraterrestrial Pop Culture*. Amherst, N.Y.: Prometheus Books, 2005.

Carter, Youssef J. "Islamic Party of North America." In *Encyclopedia of Muslim American History*, edited by Edward E. Curtis IV, 292–93. New York: Facts on File, 2010.

Chandler, Wayne B. "Ebony and Bronze: Race and Ethnicity in Early Arabia and the Islamic World." In *African Presence in Early Asia*, edited by Runoko Rashidi and Ivan van Sertima, 270–311. New Brunswick: Transaction, 1985.

Chireau, Yvonne. "Black Culture and Black Zion: African American Religious Encounters with Judaism, 1790–1930, an Overview." In *Black Zion: African American Religious Encounters with Judaism*, edited by Yvonne Chireau and Nathaniel Deutsch, 15–32. New York: Oxford University Press, 2000.

Clarke, Kamari Maxine. *Mapping Yoruba Networks: Power and Agency in the Making of Transnational Communities*. Durham: Duke University Press, 2004.

Clegg, Claude Andrew, III. *An Original Man: The Life and Times of Elijah Muhammad*. New York: St. Martin's Press, 1997.

Colla, Elliott. *Conflicted Antiquities: Egyptology, Egyptomania, Egyptian Modernity*. Durham: Duke University Press, 2007.

Collins, Robert O. *A History of Modern Sudan*. Cambridge: Cambridge University Press, 2008.

Curtis, Edward E., IV. *Black Muslim Religion in the Nation of Islam, 1960–1975*. Chapel Hill: University of North Carolina Press, 2006.

Curtis, R. M. Mukhtar. "Urban Muslims: The Formation of the Dar ul-Islam Movement." In *Muslim Communities in North America*, edited by Yvonne Yazbeck Haddad and Jane Idleman Smith, 51–74. Albany: SUNY Press, 1994.

Dannin, Robert. *Black Pilgrimage to Islam*. Oxford: Oxford University Press, 2002.

Daulatzai, Sohail. *Black Star, Crescent Moon: The Muslim International and Black Freedom Beyond America*. Minneapolis: University of Minnesota Press, 2012.

DeCaro, Louis A., Jr. *On the Side of My People: A Religious Life of Malcolm X*. New York: New York University Press, 1996.

Deutsch, Nathaniel. "'The Asiatic Black Man': An African American Orientalism?" *Journal of Asian American Studies* 4, no. 3 (2001): 193–208.

———. "The Proximate Other: The Nation of Islam and Judaism." In *Black Zion: African American Religious Encounters with Judaism*, edited by Yvonne Chireau and Nathaniel Deutsch, 91–117. New York: Oxford University Press, 2000.

Dew, Spencer. "'Moors Know the Law': Sovereign Legal Discourse in Moorish Science Religious Communities and the Hermeneutics of Supersession." *Journal of Law of Religion* 31, no. 1 (2016): 70–91.

———. "Washitaw de Dugdahmoundyah: Counterfactual Religious Readings of the Law." *Nova Religio: The Journal of Alternative and Emergent Religions* 19, no. 2 (2015): 65–82.

Diamant, Jeffrey. "Engagement and Resistance: African Americans, Saudi Arabia, and Islamic Transnationalisms, 1975 to 2000." PhD diss., City University of New York, 2016.

Dickson, William Rory. *Living Sufism in North America: Between Tradition and Transformation*. Albany: SUNY Press, 2015.

Donnelly, Ignatius L. *Atlantis: The Antediluvian World*. New York: Harper and Bros., 1882.

Dorman, Jacob S. *Chosen People: The Rise of American Black Israelite Religions*. Oxford: Oxford University Press, 2012.

———. "'A True Moslem Is a True Spiritualist': Black Orientalism and Black Gods of the Metropolis." In *The New Black Gods: Arthur Huff Fauset and the Study of African American Religions*, edited by Edward E. Curtis IV and Danielle

Brune Sigler, 116–42. Bloomington: Indiana University Press, 2009.
Dyrendal, Asbjørn. "Hidden Knowledge, Hidden Powers: Esotericism and Conspiracy Culture." In *Contemporary Esotericism*, edited by Egil Asprem and Kennet Granholm, 200–225. London: Routledge, 2014.
Elmasry, Shadee. "The Salafis in America: The Rise, Decline, and Prospects for a Sunni Muslim Movement Among African-Americans." *Journal of Muslim Minority Affairs* 30, no. 2 (2010): 217–36.
Ernst, Carl. "Situating Sufism and Yoga." *Journal of the Royal Asiatic Society of Great Britain and Ireland* 15, no. 1 (2005): 15–43.
Faisal, Daoud. *Islam, the True Faith, the Religion of Humanity: The Works of Hajj Shaykh Daoud Ahmed Faisal*. Edited by Muhammed el-Ahari. Chicago: Magribine Press, 2006.
Farrakhan, Louis. "Million Man March Address." In *The Columbia Sourcebook of Muslims in the United States*, edited by Edward E. Curtis IV, 130–39. New York: Columbia University Press, 2008.
Fluehr-Lobban, Carolyn. "Islamization in Sudan: A Critical Assessment." *Middle East Journal* 44, no. 4 (1990): 610–23.
Ford, Arnold Josiah. *Universal Ethiopian Hymnal*. New York: Beth B'nai, 1922.
Friedlander, Shems. *Ninety-Nine Names of Allah*. London: Wildwood House, 1978.
Gabriel, Theodore. "The United Nuwaubian Nation of Moors." In *UFO Religions*, edited by Christopher Partridge, 149–63. New York: Routledge, 2003.
Gardell, Mattias. *In the Name of Elijah Muhammad: Louis Farrakhan and the Nation of Islam*. Durham: Duke University Press, 1996.
Garnett, Ruby S. *Soul Sacrifice: One Story of Many*. Bloomington: AuthorHouse, 2012.
GhaneaBassiri, Kambiz. *A History of Islam in America: From the New World to the New World Order*. Cambridge: Cambridge University Press, 2010.

Gomez, Michael A. *Black Crescent: The Experience and Legacy of African Muslims in the Americas*. Cambridge: Cambridge University Press, 2005.
Gregorius, Fredrik. "Inventing Africa: Esotericism and the Creation of an Afrocentric Tradition in America." In *Contemporary Esotericism*, edited by Egil Asprem and Kennet Granholm, 49–71. London: Routledge, 2014.
Grewal, Zareena. *Islam Is a Foreign Country: American Muslims and the Global Crisis of Authority*. New York: New York University Press, 2014.
Griffin, Sean Patrick. *Black Brothers, Inc.: The Violent Rise and Fall of Philadelphia's Black Mafia Family*. Wrea Green, UK: Milo Books, 2005.
Haddad, Yvonne Yazbeck, and Jane Idleman Smith. *Mission to America: Five Islamic Sectarian Communities in North America*. Gainesville: University Press of Florida, 1993.
Halman, Hugh Talat. "Sufism in the West: Islam in an Interspiritual Age." In *Voices of Islam*, edited by Vincent J. Cornell, 169–98. Westport: Praeger, 2007.
———. *Where the Two Seas Meet: The Qur'anic Story of al-Khidr and Moses in Sufi Commentaries as a Model of Spiritual Guidance*. Louisville, Ky.: Fons Vitae, 2013.
Hammer, Olav. *Claiming Knowledge: Strategies of Epistemology from Theosophy to the New Age*. Leiden: Brill, 2004.
Haslip-Viera, Gabriel, Bernard Ortiz de Montellano, and Warren Barbour. "Robbing Native American Cultures: Van Sertima's Afrocentricity and the Olmecs." *Current Anthropology* 38, no. 3 (1997): 419–41.
Hermansen, Marcia. "Hybrid Identity Formations in Muslim America: The Case of American Sufi Movements." *Muslim World* 90 (Spring 2000): 158–97.
Hevesi, Dennis. "Muslims Leave Bushwick: The Neighbors Ask Why." *New York Times*, April 24, 1994.
Holt, P. M., and M. W. Daly. *A History of the Sudan: From the Coming of Islam to*

the Present Day. 6th ed. London: Routledge, 2011.

Hornung, Erik. *The Secret Lore of Egypt: Its Impact on the West*. Translated by David Lorton. Ithaca: Cornell University Press, 2001.

Houston, Drusilla Dunjee. *Wonderful Ethiopians of the Ancient Cushite Empire*. 1926. Baltimore: Black Classic Press, 1985.

Howe, Stephen. *Afrocentrism: Mythical Pasts and Imagined Homes*. London: Verso, 1999.

Howell, Sally. *Old Islam in Detroit: Rediscovering the Muslim American Past*. Oxford: Oxford University Press, 2014.

Hucks, Tracey E. "From Cuban Santeria to African Yoruba: Evolutions in African American Orisa History, 1959–1970." In *Òrìṣà Devotion as World Religion: The Globalization of Yorùbá Religious Culture*, edited by Jacob K. Olupona and Terry Rey, 337–54. Madison: University of Wisconsin Press, 2008.

Ibrahim, Hassan Ahmed. *Sayyid ʿAbd al-Rahman al-Mahdi: A Study of Neo-Mahdism in the Sudan, 1899–1956*. Leiden: Brill, 2004.

Islam, Amir al-. "Sunni Islam in the African American Experience: The Dialectic and Dialogic of Race, Ethnicity, and Islamicity; Mapping and Decoding the Mosque of Islamic Brotherhood, 1964–2001." PhD diss., New York University, 2010.

Jackson, Sherman. *Islam and the Blackamerican: Looking Toward the Third Resurrection*. Oxford: Oxford University Press, 2005.

Jameelah, Maryam. *Three Great Islamic Movements in the Arab World of the Recent Past*. Lahore: Mohammad Yusuf Khan, 1976.

James, George G. M. *Stolen Legacy: The Egyptian Origins of Western Philosophy*. 1954. Brooklyn: African Islamic Mission Publications, 1989.

Javid, Muhammad Asif. "Constructing Life Narratives: The Multiple Versions of Maryam Jameelah's Life." Master's thesis, Leiden University, 2018.

Johnson, Paul Nathaniel. *Holy Fahamme Gospel or Divine Understanding*. Houston: Fahamme Temples of Islam and Culture, 2003.

Johnson, Sylvester. *The Myth of Ham in Nineteenth-Century American Christianity: Race, Heathens, and the People of God*. New York: Palgrave Macmillan, 2004.

Joseph, Simon J. "Jesus in India? Transgressing Social and Religious Boundaries." *Journal of the American Academy of Religion* 80, no. 1 (2012): 161–99.

Karrar, Ali Salih. *The Sufi Brotherhoods in the Sudan*. Evanston: Northwestern University Press, 1992.

Khalifa, Rashad. *Quran: The Final Testament*. Fremont, Calif.: Universal Unity, 2000.

Khan, Adil Hussain. *From Sufism to Ahmadiyya: A Muslim Minority Movement in South Asia*. Bloomington: Indiana University Press, 2015.

Khan, Hazrat Inayat. *The Sufi Message of Hazrat Inayat Khan*. Vol. 10. Geneva: International Headquarters of the Sufi Movement, 1973.

Knight, Michael Muhammad. *Magic in Islam*. New York: Tarcher/Penguin, 2016.

———. *Why I Am a Five Percenter*. New York: Tarcher/Penguin, 2011.

Königshofer, Martina. *The New Ship of Zion: Dynamic Diaspora Dimensions of the African Hebrew Israelites of Jerusalem*. London: LIT Verlag, 2008.

Landing, James E. *Black Judaism: Story of an American Movement*. Durham: Carolina Academic Press, 2002.

Layish, Aharon. *Shariʿa and the Islamic State in Nineteenth-Century Sudan: The Mahdi's Legal Methodology and Doctrine*. Leiden: Brill, 2016.

Lewis, Tyson, and Richard Kahn. "The Reptoid Hypothesis: Utopian and Dystopian Representational Motifs in David Icke's Alien Conspiracy Theory." *Utopian Studies* 16, no. 1 (2005): 45–74.

Lieb, Michael. *Children of Ezekiel: Aliens, UFOs, the Crisis of Race, and the Advent of End Time*. Durham: Duke University Press, 1998.

MacKey, Albert Gullatin, and William James Hughan. *An Encyclopedia of Freemasonry and Its Kindred Sciences: Comprising the Whole Range of Arts, Sciences, and Literature as Connected with the Institution*. New York: Masonic History, 1913.

Maffly-Kipp, Laurie. *Setting Down the Sacred Past: African-American Race Histories*. Cambridge, Mass.: Belknap Press of Harvard University Press, 2010.

Mahmoud, Muhammad. "Sufism and Islamism in the Sudan." In *African Islam and Islam in Africa: Encounters Between Sufis and Islamists*, edited by Eva E. Rosander and David Westerlund, 162–92. London: C. Hurst, 1997.

Malcolm X. "Interview with *Al-Muslimoon*." In *The Columbia Sourcebook of Muslims in the United States*, edited by Edward E. Curtis IV, 96–104. New York: Columbia University Press, 2008.

Malcolm X and Alex Haley. *The Autobiography of Malcolm X*. New York: Grove Press, 1965.

McCloud, Aminah Beverly. *African American Islam*. New York: Routledge, 1995.

Melton, J. Gordon. "Daoud Ahmed." In *Encyclopedia of Islam*, edited by Juan Eduardo Campo, 181–82. New York: Facts on File, 2009.

Miyakawa, Felicia M. *Five Percenter Rap: God Hop's Music, Message, and Black Muslim Mission*. Bloomington: Indiana University Press, 2005.

Montserrat, Dominic. *Akhenaten: History, Fantasy, and Ancient Egypt*. London: Routledge, 2003.

Moses, Wilson Jeremiah. *Afrotopia: The Roots of African American Popular History*. Cambridge: Cambridge University Press, 1998.

Muhammad, Elijah. *Message to the Black Man in America*. Phoenix: Secretarius MEMPS, 1997.

———. *The Secrets of Freemasonry*. Phoenix: Secretarius MEMPS, 2005.

———. *Supreme Wisdom*. Phoenix: Secretarius MEMPS, n.d.

———. *The Theology of Time: The Secret of Time*. Edited by Nasir Makr Hakim. Phoenix: Secretarius MEMPS, 2002.

———. *The True History of Master Fard Muhammad*. Edited by Nasir Makr Hakim. Phoenix: Secretarius MEMPS, 1996.

———. "A Warning to the Black Man of America." *Final Call to Islam*, August 18, 1934.

———. "Warning to the MGT and GCC." *Muhammad Speaks*, April 19, 1974, 11.

Muhammad, Wallace Deen. *As the Light Shineth from the East*. Chicago: WDM, 1980.

———. "Bilalian." *Bilalian News*, November 14, 1975, 24.

———. "New Flag for the Nation of Islam." *Bilalian News*, March 12, 1976. http://nurallah.org/imams-corner/history-of-muslim-american-flag/.

Muir, Sir William. *The Life of Mahomet: With Introductory Chapters on the Original Sources for the Biography of Mahomet, and on the Pre-Islamite History of Arabia*. London: Smith, Elder, 1861.

Murphy, Joseph M. "Santa Barbara Africana: Beyond Syncretism in Cuba." In *Beyond Conversion and Syncretism: Indigenous Encounters with Missionary Christianity, 1800–2000*, edited by David Lindenfield and Miles Richardson, 137–66. New York: Berghahn Books, 2012.

Musa, Aisha Y. *Hadith as Scripture: Discussions on the Authority of Prophetic Traditions in Islam*. New York: Palgrave Macmillan, 2008.

Nance, Susan. "Mystery of the Moorish Science Temple: Southern Blacks and American Alternative Spirituality in 1920s Chicago." *Religion and American Culture: A Journal of Interpretation* 12, no. 2 (2002): 123–66.

Nash, M. Naeem. "Addeynu Allahe Universal Arabic Association." In *Encyclopedia of Muslim American History*, edited by Edward E. Curtis IV, 10–11. New York: Facts on File, 2010.

———. "Muhammad Ezaldeen." In *Encyclopedia of Muslim American History*, edited by Edward E. Curtis IV, 175–76. New York: Facts on File, 2010.

Nupu, Wu, Asa Nupu, and Naba Nupu. *The Nine Ball, Count 1.* New York: Those Who Care, 1971.

Nuruddin, Yusuf. "Ancient Black Astronauts and Extraterrestrial Jihads: Islamic Science Fiction as Urban Mythology." *Socialism and Democracy* 20, no. 3 (2006): 127–65.

Obaba, Imam. *Some Things Concerning Blacks (Only).* Miami: Helpers, IYH Mission, 1975.

O'Connor, Kathleen Malone. "The Nubian Islaamic Hebrews, Ansaaru Allah Community: Jewish Teachings of an African American Muslim Community." In *Black Zion: African American Religious Encounters with Judaism,* edited by Yvonne Chireau and Nathaniel Deutsch, 118–50. New York: Oxford University Press, 2000.

Palmer, Susan J. *The Nuwaubian Nation: Black Spirituality and State Control.* Burlington, Vt.: Ashgate, 2010.

Palmer, Susan J., and Steve Luxton. "The Ansaaru Allah Community: Postmodernist Narration and the Black Jeremiad." In *New Trends and Developments in the World of Islam,* edited by Peter B. Clarke, 353–70. London: Luzac Oriental, 1998.

Philips, Abu Ameenah Bilal. *The Ansar Cult in America.* Riyadh: Tawheed Publications, 1988.

Rahkaptah, Amunubi. *Bible Interpretations and Explanations.* Booklet 2. New York: Those Who Care, 1968.

Rogers, J. A. "Bilal Ibn Rahab—Warrior Priest." *Messenger* 9 (July 1927): 213–14.

———. *Negro-Caucasian Mixing in All Ages and All Lands.* 1940. Vol. 1 of *Sex and Race.* New York: Helga M. Rogers, 2014.

———. *World's Great Men of Color.* Vol. 1. New York: Simon and Schuster, 1996.

Rohan, Robert. *Holding York Responsible.* Johnson City, N.Y., 2014.

Salomon, Noah. "Undoing the Mahdiyya: British Colonialism as Religious Reform in the Anglo-Egyptian Sudan, 1898–1914." Religion and Culture Web Forum, Martin Marty Center for the Advanced Study of Religion, University of Chicago Divinity School, May 2004. https://sudaneseonline.com/board/15/msg/Undoing-the-Mahdiyya%3ABritish-Colonialism-as-Religious-Reform-in-the-Anglo-Egyptian-Sudan,1898-191...-1421934726.htm.

Schuon, Frithjof. "Paradoxical Aspects of Sufism." *Studies in Comparative Religion* 12, nos. 3–4 (1978): 131–75.

———. *Understanding Islam.* 1963. Bloomington: World Wisdom, 2011.

Sedgwick, Mark. *Against the Modern World.* Oxford: Oxford University Press, 2004.

———. *Western Sufism: From the Abbasids to the New Age.* Oxford: Oxford University Press, 2017.

Sesay, Chernoh M., Jr. "The Dialectic of Representation: Black Freemasonry, the Black Public, and Black Historiography." *Journal of African American Studies* 17 (2013): 380–98.

Sirriyeh, Elizabeth. *Sufis and Anti-Sufis: The Defence, Rethinking, and Rejection of Sufism in the Modern World.* London: RoutledgeCurzon, 1999.

Smith, Jane I. *Islam in America.* New York: Columbia University Press, 1999.

Spieth, Darius A. *Napoleon's Sorcerers: The Sophisians.* Newark: University of Delaware Press, 2007.

Trafton, Scott. *Egypt Land: Race and Nineteenth-Century American Egyptomania.* Durham: Duke University Press, 2004.

Van Sertima, Ivan. *They Came Before Columbus: The African Presence in Ancient America.* 1976. New York: Random House, 2003.

Vaughan, Delores A. *The Preeminence of Christ and the Motherland Religions.* Conshohocken, Pa.: Infinity, 2005.

wadud, amina. "American Muslim Identity: Race and Ethnicity in Progressive Islam." In *Progressive Islam,* edited by Omid Safi, 270–305. Oxford: Oneworld, 2003.

Wallace, Maurice O. *Constructing the Black Masculine: Identity and Ideality in African*

American Men's Literature and Culture, 1775–1995. Durham: Duke University Press, 2002.

Warburg, Gabriel. "Islam and State in Numayri's Sudan, Africa." *Journal of the International African Institute* 55, no. 4 (1985): 400–413.

———. *Islam, Sectarianism, and Politics in the Sudan Since the Mahdiyya.* Madison: University of Wisconsin Press, 2002.

Webb, Gisela. "Negotiating Boundaries: American Sufis." In *The Cambridge Companion to American Islam*, edited by Juliane Hammer and Omid Safi, 190–207. Cambridge: Cambridge University Press, 2013.

Webb, James Morris. *The Black Man the Father of Civilization, Proven by Biblical History.* Seattle: Acme Press, 1910.

Williams, Chancellor. *The Destruction of Black Civilization: Great Issues of a Race from 4500 B.C. to 2000 A.D.* Chicago: Third World Press, 1971.

Xavier, Merin Shobhana. *Sacred Spaces and Transnational Networks in American Sufism: Bawa Muhaiyaddeen and Contemporary Shrine Cultures.* London: Bloomsbury, 2018.

Index

Note: page numbers in italics refer to figures. Those followed by n refer to notes, with note number.

AAC/NIH (Ansaru Allah Community/Nubian Islamic Hebrews)
    Brooklyn flagship location of, 2
    changes in names and symbols, minimal doctrinal impact of, 21, 22, 122
    as community separate from Al Mahdi, 27
    desertions of 1970–74, 18
    and Faisal, competition for legacy of, 78–79
    FBI investigations of, 190–91
    flags used by, 21, 64–66, 90, 114, 130
    forfeiting of covenant with God, Al Mahdi on, 129, 132
    founding of, 12, 15–16, 60
    and gender equality, move toward, 191
    and hip-hop artists, sympathetic, favorable attention to, 230, 236
    history of, 12–23
    history of, in York's *Holy Tablets*, 214–15
    lack of mosque in early years, 18–19
    large revenue, changes prompted by, 20
    mission statement of, 18
    musicians associated with, 2, 231–32, 234–35
    names used by, 4, 21, 22, 23, 26, 64, 113, 114, 126, 130
    number of followers, 148
    Nuwaubians as term for, 4
    as only true version of Islam, 212, 213
    and other Muslim groups in Brooklyn: attacks and threats from, 188–89; early opposition from, 18; limited early engagement with, 83
    as preservers of 'Asim recitation in West, 48
    publications offered by, 1–2, *2*
    relocation to rural Georgia, 4, 23, 113–14, 187
    renaming as United Nuwaubian Nation of Moors (UNNM), 23, 187, 205
    reputation for holy madness, 114
    return to Africa as goal of, 18
    Sufi genealogies of, 148–54
    visibility in 1980s, 2
    See also Ansars (followers of AAC/NIH); Ansaru Allah Community; dress of Al Mahdi and followers; Nubian Islamic Hebrews (NIH); UNNM (United Nuwaubian Nation of Moors)

AAC/NIH beliefs and practices, 20–21
    and African religion, efforts to recover, 38
    American metaphysical traditions and, 165
    assumed incoherence of, 7
    broad consistency over time, 7, 16, 22, 132–34, 168, 206–7, 211, 220, 242, 243
    categorization of, as issue, 4, 6
    eclectic nature of: as characteristic of Black Islam, 240–42; as mix of Islamic, Christian, African, and other traditions, 1–2, 4; scholars' emphasis on, 238–40; as typical of all religions, 240
    loud dhikr and drumming, 13, 15, 18, 34
    as Nubian-centered Islam, 66
    opposition to Salafism, 225
    on origin of races and history of humankind, 39–44
    overlap with black Hebraism, 116–19
    phases of: Philips on, 6; York on, 23, 132, 207, 242
    rational, evidence-based debate characteristic of, 242
    and rejection of Muslim anti-Blackness, 66
    on return of Christ, 20
    See also Egyptosophy and AAC/NIH; Hebrew elements of AAC/NIH beliefs; Islam in AAC/NIH thought; metaphysical Africa; Sufism; Sufism and AAC/NIH

Abba Island in America (AAC), 228
Abdul Khabeer, Su'ad, 11, 44–45, 224–25
Abdul Uzza, 213
Abode, the, 151

About the Raatib: The Book of the Mahdi (1987), 66
Abraham
    all true Hebrews as descendants of, 70, 116, 119, 132, 180
    as Arabic speaker, 46
    as Black Muslim, 119, 123, 126, 180
    civilizing of white people as mission of, 177
    and genetic engineering of pigs, 173, 177, 178
    life and mission of, Al Mahdi on, 41–42
    and monotheism of ancient Egyptians, 178
    as origin of Judaism, Christianity, and Islam, 132
    and *Suhuf*, 180
    training by Egyptian elder/gods, 177
Abu Bakr
    and Bilal, freeing of, 139–40, 142, 144
    and false Islam, York on, 212
    Al Mahdi on, 49, 50, 53, 55, 56, 144
    as second pick as Muhammad's successor, 138, 144
Abusharaf, Rogaia Mustafa, 13, 59
Achamad, Paul J. *See* Johnson, Paul Nathaniel
Adam
    as Allah's *khalifa*, 40
    as Black man, 16, 29, 39, 116, 174, 251n6
    body of, as Black Stone in Ka'ba, 174
    and fall from grace, 105
    site of creation, 29, 39–40
    as source of baraka, 147
Adamski, George, 155
Addeynu Allahe Universal Arabic Association, 30
Adefunmi, Oseijeman, 15, 32–33
al-Afghani, Jamal ad-Din, 201
Africa, Elijah Muhammad's views on, 30–31
African Americans
    esoteric traditions of, as unknown to white New-Agers, 8
    as lost tribe of Kedar, 44
    See also entries under Black
African Hebrew Israelite community, 9, 116–17
African Islamic Mission (AIM), 17
African Lodge of Boston, 202
African Origins of the Major "Western Religions" (Ben-Jochannan), 36, 137–38
African Presence in Early Asia (Rashidi and van Sertima), 51
Africans, Muslim *vs.* pagan, Al Mahdi on, 72–73
African spirituality
    Afrocentrist effort to recover, 32–33, 38
    American version of, Yoruba revival movement and, 14
    elements of, 38–39
    non-Muslim, Al Mahdi's early encounters with, 14–15
African Times and Orient Review (Ali), 10
Afrocentricity (Asante), 38
Afrocentrism
    Bilal ibn Rabah as hero of, 137–38
    Black Islam's opposition to, 37
    and Christian and Islamic names, rejection of, 37, 38
    and Christianity, rejection of, as white supremacist, 36, 38
    Egyptosophy, 9, 38, 170
    Farrakhan and, 38
    foundational text of, 38
    on God as within human beings, 162
    Al Mahdi and, 34, 47, 49, 59
    non-Islamic, 36, 173
    on Nubian ancestry of Aztecs, Incas, and Mayas, 200
    W. D. Muhammad and, 38
    Yoruba tradition and, 9, 38
    See also Islam, Black (Afrocentrist) rejection of
ahl al-bayt (Muhammad's household)
    AAC/NIH allegiance to, 49
    Al Mahdi as self-declared successor of, 51
    Al Mahdi on, 50, 102
    and power struggle between true (Black) and false (white) lineages, 48–56
    in Revelations, 20, 50–51
    as true Shi'as, 119
    See also Shi'ism
Ahmad, Jesus' Khalifat (Successor) (Al Mahdi, 1980), 76, 152
Ahmad, Muhammad (Sudanese Mahdi)
    and AAC/NIH link to Nubian Islam, 29
    as avatar inhabiting body of Al Mahdi, 157
    claim to be awaited Mahdi, 58
    and defeat of Anglo-Egyptian colonial regime, 14, 29, 58–59, 101
    direct line to Muhammad, 50
    family of, 57
    life of, 57–58
    and Al Mahdi, AAC/NIH emphasis on ties to, 20
    Al Mahdi on lineage of, 212–13, 217
    as Al Mahdi role model, 14, 66

Ahmad, Muhammad (*continued*)
   Al Mahdi's claim to legacy of, as grandson, 17–18, 20, 21, 62, 63, 67, 101–2, 192–93, 199, 215, 217, 219, 246–47n83
   Al Mahdi's interest in Sufism of, 153
   in Al Mahdi's vision at junction of two Niles, 216
   and Sammaniyya order, 57–58
   shrine of, destroyed by British, 59
   son of, 59
   and Sudan as center of Allah's interest, 29
   and Sunni revivalism in Sudan, 58
   and true copy of Qur'an, possession of, 213
   in York's translation of Revelation, 29
   See also Ratib of Muhammad Ahmad
Ahmad Din. *See* Johnson, Paul Nathaniel
Ahmadiyya
   Bilal story and, 137
   on burial place of Jesus in Kashmir, 182
   Fahamme movement breakoff from, 171–72
   IMA and, 12
   and metaphysical Africa, 10
   recruitment of Black Masons, 203
   and Sufism in West, 150
AIM. *See* African Islamic Mission
A'isha, Al Mahdi on, 49, 50–51, 52, 53, 56, 212
Akhenaten, 178, 204, 208, 209
Albanese, Catherine, 7
Ali, Abdul Wali Farrad Muhammad
   assassination by government, Al Mahdi on, 92
   Al Mahdi on, 99–100
   Noble Drew Ali and, 99
   and Supreme Wisdom Lessons, 92
Ali, Duse Mohamed, 10, 100–101, 211
Ali, Maulana Muhammad, 251n6
Ali, Muhammad (Ahmadiyya scholar), 86
Ali, Noble Drew
   AAC/NIH Sufism and, 151–52
   absorption into AAC/NIH thought, 144
   assassination by government, Al Mahdi on, 92
   blending of Islam and Egyptian mysticism, 171
   claims to Native Americans heritage, 201
   on Egypt as origin of African Americans, 170–71
   and Egyptosophy, 170–71
   foretelling of Al Mahdi by, 96–97
   Holy Koran of (*Circle Seven Koran*), 10, 99, 155, 170, 181, 204; York's publication of edition of, 218

influence on Al Mahdi, 13
   on Jesus as example of enlightenment through learning, 181–82
   Al Mahdi on, 84, 93, 97–99
   Al Mahdi's claim to legacy of, 76, 77, 86, 96–100, 111, 187
   mingling of Freemasonry, Islam, and pharonic Egypt in, 203–4
   mingling of Islam and Egyptosophy in, 182, 185
   nationality and citizenship as themes of, 201
   perennialism of, 182
   teachings of, 10, 30
   and "Two Fards" conspiracy theory, 91
   York's *Holy Tablets* on, 211
'Ali
   AAC/NIH images of, 55
   as keeper of true Qur'an, 212
   as lineage of true Islam, 49–53, 212–13
   and *Suhuf*, 180
   See also Shi'ism; Fatima
Al Imaam Isa Visits Egypt 1981 (AAC,1981), 20, 69–70, 178–80, *179*
Al Imam Isa Visits the City of Brotherly Love (AAC/NIH poster, c. 1980), 3
Allah
   as Black god-scientist, in Nation of Islam theology, 155–56
   vs. God, in Al Mahdi's theology, 17, 40
   as within human beings, in Afrocentric theology, 162
   as name of God, Al Mahdi on, 46
   as self-perfected man, in Nation of Islam theology, 162
Allah (Clarence 13X), 103–11
   AAC/NIH portrait of, 107–8, *108*
   and Allah as name, 103
   assassination of, 103, 106
   founding of Five Percenter movement, 103
   Al Mahdi on, 77, 100, 105–6, 107–8, 110–11
   Al Mahdi's claim to legacy of, 106–11, 187
   Al Mahdi's separation from Five Percenter beliefs, 109
   teachings of, 103
   York's *Holy Tablets* on, 211
   See also Five Percenter movement
American metaphysical religion, white prejudices in, 7–8
American Muslims: Muslims in America (AAC, 1980), 89
Al-Amin, Muhammad, 121

el-Amin, Mustafa, 34
AMOM. *See* Ancient and Mystic Order of Melchizedek
Amorite race
  and African slavery, 73
  in Ansar musical theory, 225–27, 228, 233–34, 236
  Al Mahdi on, 39, 197
  oppression of Nubians, 56
Ancient and Mystic Order of Melchizedek (AMOM), 202, 214
Ancient Egypt and the Pharaohs (Al Mahdi, 1980), 156, 174–76, 178
Ancient Egyptian Arabic Order, Nobles of the Mystic Shrine, 171, 203
Ancient Egyptian Order, 202
Ancient Mystical Order Rosae Crucis, 171, 204
angels, as extraterrestrials, Al Mahdi on, 196
ankh, Al Mahdi on, 174
Ansaar Cult, The: Rebuttal to the Slanderers (Al Mahdi), 145, 163–65
Ansaar Village Bulletin, 50, 72
Ansar Cult in America, The (Philips)
  on AAC/NIH dress, 83
  AAC/NIH informants for, 20
  as attack on Al Mahdi, 6, 96, 163
  on Bilal and Muslim antiracism, 145
  damage to Al Mahdi's reputation, 126, 188, 192
  on four phases of AAC/NIH history, 6
  on Al Mahdi and Sufism, 153
  on Al Mahdi's birth, 246–47n83
  on Al Mahdi's conversion to Islam, 13, 77–78
  Al Mahdi's response to, 145–46, 163–65, 188
  publication of, 6, 145
  as source on Al Mahdi's early life, 15
Ansar hip-hop
  artists and albums of, 231–32, 234–35
  and Muslim International, 231
Ansar musical theory, 226–30, 236
  on Amorites' (whites') creation of poisonous music to destroy Nubians, 227, 228, 236
  on Amorites' efforts to erase Black musicality, 226, 236
  on Amorites' lack of souls and musical ability, 226, 227
  on Amorites' theft and corruption of Black musical traditions, 225–27, 233–34
  on dancing, as part of true Islam, 229
  on folk-songs as cultural heritage, 229
  on health benefits of music, 229
  influence on hip-hop, 233
  on music as part of Nubian spiritual gift, 226, 230, 236
  on music as part of true Islam, 228–29
  on music in worship and teaching, 229–30
  on origin of the blues, 226–27
  on Sunni's rejection of music as anti-Black, 228
  See also music, Al Mahdi's engagement with
Ansar Pure Sufi group
  founding of, 15, 59–60, 151
  name change to Nubian Islamic Hebrew Mission in America (NIHMA), 15
  and second wave of American Sufism, 151
  and Sufi genealogies of AAC/NIH, 148
Ansars (followers of AAC/NIH)
  Arabic as required knowledge for, 47
  attraction to Al Mahdi's claims and arguments, 220
  solicitation of donations, 2, 3
  See also dress of Al Mahdi and followers
Ansars (Mahdiyya). *See* Mahdiyya
Ansaru Allah Community
  links affirmed by, 19
  name as intended evocation of Faisal, 78
  as name used by AAC/NIH, 4, 19, 126
  period of name use, 4, 19, 21, 122
  See also AAC/NIH (Ansaru Allah Community/Nubian Islamic Hebrews)
Anunnaqi, 196, 197
Apology to the Nation of Islam, the True Followers of the Honorable Elijah Muhammad, An (Al Mahdi, 1990), 189
Aquarian Gospel of Jesus the Christ, The (Dowling), 181
Arabia, as colony of Ethiopia, Houston on, 30
Arabian Peninsula as once part of Africa, Al Mahdi on, 40, 100, 102, 116, 156, 176
Arabic
  Black origin of true form of, 45–48
  Al Mahdi on, 44–48
  as marker of legitimacy among Muslims, 44; African American resistance to, 44–45
  Nubic language and, 48
  as required learning for AAC/NIH members, 47
  teaching of, in AAC/NIH, 178
Arabic: The First Language (Al Mahdi, 1977), 47, 121

Index • 279

Arabs
  idolatry of Muhammad, Al Mahdi on, 126, 209
  as keepers of Islam, African American resistance to, 44–45, 53–54
  Al Mahdi's concerns about violent extremism of, 192
  as not original residents of Arabia, 30, 39
  origin of, Al Mahdi on, 44
  as white race corrupting Islam: Al Mahdi on, 44, 45, 52, 56, 74, 102, 119; W. D. Muhammad on, 35
  as white slave-trading invaders in Africa, 11, 31, 33, 37
Arab slave trade, 11, 31, 33, 37
  Black Islam's objection to characterization as Islamic practice, 37
  and Black rejection of Arab Islam, 33, 37
Are the Ansars (in the West) a Self-Made Sect?, 60, 63
Ark of the Covenant, Al Mahdi on, 176–77
Aryanism, and shift of white interest from Egypt to India and Tibet, 170
Aryans, Al Mahdi on origin of, 42
Asante, Molefi, 38, 162, 173, 200
As Sayyid Al Imaam Isa Al Haadi Al Mahdi Explains the Secret Meaning of Qur'aan to the A'immah of Ansaaru Allah, 47
Atlantis
  Blavatsky on, 170
  Al Mahdi on, 2, 147, 156, 200
  New Age works on, 200
Atlantis: The Antediluvian World (Donnelly), 200
Ausar Auset Society, 173
Aydin, Cemil, 10
Aztecs. *See* pre-Columbian civilizations

Baatinite movement, AAC/NIH and, 6
Back to the Beginning: The Book of Names (Al Mahdi, 1972), 16, 45–46, 121
Bambaataa, Afrika, 232, 233–34, 234
baraka, Al Mahdi on, 147
Barathary gland, human loss of, York on, 197
al-Bashir, 'Margaret Hasan Ahmad, 192
Ben Ammi, 9, 11, 111, *111*, 116–17
Bengalee, Sufi, 171–72
Ben-Jochannan, Yosef, 36, 137, 178–80
Bennett comet, 163
Beth B'nai Abraham, 117
Bible Interpretation and Explanations (Rahkaptah), 205, 207

Biggest Secret, The (Icke), 196
Bilaal, the Sceptre Bearer (Al Mahdi, 1985), 142, 143–44
Bilal (AAC, 1973), 140–41, 143, 144
Bilal ibn Rabah
  AAC/NIH misspelling of father's name, 138–39, 141
  Arab and Persian Muslims' removal from Islamic history, 138
  as bridge to Noble Drew Ali's followers, 146
  as bridge to Ras Tefar I followers, 146
  and colorblindness of Islam, 135–40, 143, 145–46
  as companion of Muhammad, 135
  and connection between Ethiopia and Islam, 135–36
  and construction of Nubian Islamic Hebraism, 146
  and Ethiopians as true Hebrews, 136, 141
  Farrakhan on, 140
  as first convert to Islam, 139
  as first to perform call to prayer, 136, 137
  as hero in Afrocentrist discourses, 137–38
  as Judahite, 136
  Al Mahdi on; as Black claimant to prophetic heritage, 141; claimed descent from, 199; as descendant of Judah, 144, 213; as figure of proto-Shi'ism, 144; in *Holy Tablets*, 213–14; and influence of Ben-Jochannan, 138; as learned man, 141, 142, 144; as link between Israelite and Ishmaelite lines, 136, 140–41; as link between Moses and Muhammad, 144; and Muhammad's conquest of Mecca, 143; as proof of Muhammad as Black man, 142; as relative of Muhammad, 142–43
  Malcolm X on, 139
  and Mihjan, 55, 141, 142, 143, 144, 158, 213
  Moses' prophesy of, 141
  as Muhammad's named successor, 138, 142, 144
  and Muslim view of paradise, 138
  Philips on, 145
  as prototypical Islamic Hebrew, 136
  rise to prominence among first Muslims, 137, 142
  as shaper of Islamic faith, 138
  and Shriners, origin of, 217
  slavery of, parallels to African American slavery, 139–40

sons of, as ancestors of all Black Moors, 144
story of life, 136, 141–42
as symbol of Black moral leadership, 140
W. D. Muhammad on, 94, 139–40
Blackamerica leaders
AAC/NIH poster of, 111–12, *112*
descriptions of, in York's *Holy Tablets*, 211
U.S. government plot to assassinate, Al Mahdi on, 92
Blackamerica leadership, Al Mahdi's claiming of, 75–77, 86, 111–12
Black leaders whose legacy Al Mahdi claimed, 76, 111–12, *112*, 126
claim to Allah (Clarence 13X) legacy, 106–11
claim to Daoud Ahmed Faisal legacy, 76, 77–84, 86, 111
claim to Elijah Muhammad legacy, 75–76, 77, 84–94, 111
claim to Malcolm X legacy, 77, 94–96, 111
claim to Marcus Garvey legacy, 77, 86, 100–103
claim to metaphysical Africa legacy, 101–2
claim to Noble Drew Ali legacy, 76, 77, 86, 96–100
claim to Ras Tefar I legacy, 125–26
claim to Shaikh Daa'wud legacy, 77
as resistance against white supremacy and Sunni hegemony, 111–12
and sources from both sides of heterodox-orthodox binary, 76
as struggle between Nubian awakening and opposition by whites and Arabs, 76
Black Atlantic, 117–19
Black Eagle, as name used by York, 199, 207
Black Hebraism
and Black Islam, long history of connections between, 117–21
as global phenomenon, 117–19
overlap of AAC/NIH beliefs with, 116–19
targeting of, in UNNM publications, 193
Black Hebrew Israelite movements, 9, 46, *46*
Al Mahdi on, 42, 46
Black Hebrews of the Seed of Abraham, Isaac, and Jacob of the Tribe of Judah, Benjamin, and Levi, After 430 Years in America, The (Jenkins), 116–17
Black Islam
and Black Hebraism, long history of connections between, 117
conflict between African American and immigrant Muslims, 33–35
defense of Islam from Afrocentric critics, 37
eclectic nature of theology in, 240–42
Nuwaubu as culmination of, York on, 217–18
York's claim to leadership of, 187
York's *Holy Tablets* on, 211
Black Israelite movements
AAC/NIH narrative on Bilal and, 146
history of, 117
influence of Freemasonry on, 205
Al Mahdi's rejection of, 122
Black liberation struggles, and Black metaphysical traditions, 8
Black Mafia Family, Nation of Islam ties to, 190
Black metaphysical traditions, 8
See also metaphysical Africa
Black Muslim Religion in the Nation of Islam, 1960-1975 (Curtis), 172
Black Orientalism, 11
Black race, Adam as origin of, 16, 29, 39
Black Salafism
and Afrocentrist recovery of African religion, 38
Al Mahdi on, 44–45
Saudi influence and, 36
Black Sunni communities
dress code, AAC/NIH criticisms of, 69
Al Mahdi's critique of, 95
and Salafiyya movement, 11
Blavatsky, Helena, 155, 169–70
Blyden, Edward, 10, 135, 136–37
Book of Lamb, The (Al Mahdi), Al Mahdi's order to burn all copies of, 189
Book of Lamb, The: The Message of the Messenger Is Right and Exact (Al Mahdi, 1979), 87, 88, 89, 90, 91, 93, 94, 104
Book of Lamb, The: To Whom It May Concern, Fear No Longer for I Have Arrived (1985), 93
Book of Lamb, The: To Whom It May Concern, Fear No Longer for I Have Arrived (1989), 93, 94–95, 105, 107, 109
Book of Mormon, 169
Book of the Five Percenters, The (Al Mahdi, 1991), 95–96, 106–10, 195
Book of the Glory of the Black Race, The (al-Jahiz), 52
Book of J: To Whom It May Concern: Fear No Longer for I Have Arrived (AAC. ca. 1978-79), 87, 90–91
Bowen, Patrick, 171–72

Brahamic orders, 162
Brand Nubian, 110, 231, 232
Breaking the Fast (1973), 78–79
Brotherhood of Imhotep, 202
Buddha, Al Mahdi on, 42, 43

Call of the Mahdi in America, The, 66
Campos, Pedro, 111, *111*
Canaan, as origin of white race, 41
Canaanites
 Al Mahdi on, 41, 42
 and origin of polytheism, 42
"Can You Be Sufi?" (Al Mahdi, 1972), 148
Caribbean migration, and Yoruba tradition in New York City, 14
Carver, George Washington, 9
Catholicism, Faisal on, 119
Catskills AAC/NIH settlement. *See* Jazzir Abba/Mount Zion AAC/NIH settlement (Catskill Mountains)
Celestial Being or Terrestrial Being ... Which One Are You! (Al Qutb), 161–62
Chandler, Wayne B., 51, 52
Christianity
 Abraham as origin of, 132
 Black (Afrocentrists) rejection of, as white supremacist ideology, 36, 38
 elements in AAC/NIH beliefs, 127–31; mixing with Egyptosophy, 129
 as false narrative produced by lizard aliens, 196
 as false Paulism, 127, 131
 necessity of including in teachings, Al Mahdi on, 127
 and Qur'an as completion of Christian scripture, Al Mahdi on, 125
 separation from Judaism and Islam as error, Ford on, 117
Christianity, Islam, and the Negro Race (Blyden), 136–37
Christ Is the Answer (Al Mahdi, 1977), 84, 193
Christmas, Al Mahdi rejection of, 116
"Christ Series" of AAC/NIH publications, cover images of, 127–29
Clarence 13X. *See* Allah (Clarence 13X)
Collins, Robert O., 57
communism, Nation of Islam and, 92
Confucius, Al Mahdi on, 43
Cuban migration to U.S., and United States encounters with Afro-Cuban traditions, 32–33

Curtis, Edward E. IV, 10, 31, 69, 172
Cushite race, Al Mahdi on, 39
Cush/Kush, as origin of Dongolawi Nubians, 39

Daa'wud, Shaikh, Al Mahdi's claim to legacy of, 77
al-Dahr, Muhammad Sa'im, 186
Dar ul-Islam movement, 12, 15, 34, 82, 83, 152–53
Daughters of Zoser, 202
Daulatzai, Sohail, 230–31
Destruction of Black Civilization, The (Williams), 36–37
Deutsch, Nathaniel, 120
dhikr, Al Mahdi on
 and baraka, 147
 eastern religions and, 158, 165
 Al Mahdi's early street performances of, 13, 15
 and music, 229
 proper form of, 34
Diamant, Jeff, 35
Disco Music: The Universal Language of Good or Evil? (Al Mahdi, 1979), 69–70, 226, 228
divine names, chanting of, Al Mahdi on, 150
Does Dr. Malachi Z. York Try to Hide The Fact That He Was Imaam Issa? (York), 207
Dogon Tribe (Mali), 9, 196, 211
Dongolawi Nubians
 Bilal ibn Rabah and, 213
 characteristics of, Al Mahdi on, 39
 as descendants of Kush, Al Mahdi on, 39
 Al Mahdi as descendant of, 213
 origin of, 217
 targeting by slave traders, 73
Donnelly, Ignatius, 200
Dorman, Jacob, 117–19, 205
Dowling, Levi H., 10, 99, 181
dress of Al Mahdi and followers, 2, 3, 34, 61, 69–72, 129–30, 168
 nose rings, significance of, 70–71
 as reclamation of Nubian body, 69
 women's modesty and, 69–70, 222
 York's *Holy Tablets* on changes in, 214

Easter, Al Mahdi rejection of, 116
Eden
 destruction of, 176
 site of, Al Mahdi on, 40, 116, 174
Edomite race, Al Mahdi on, 39
Egiptian [sic] Church of Karast, Malachi Z.York as founder of, 193

Egypt
and colonialism, 169
as colony of Ethiopia, Houston on, 30
images of Al Mahdi in, 174, 178–80, *179*
Al Mahdi visit to, 69–70
modern, as home to corrupted pale Arabs, 181
women's dress in, Al Mahdi criticisms of, 69–70
Egyptian *Book of the Dead*, 170
York's translation of, 208, *209*
Egyptians, whites' assumption of whiteness of, 170
Egyptosophy
and Afrocentrist recovery of African religion, 9, 38, 170
Ausar Auset Society and, 173
and Fahamme movement (Ethiopian Temples of Islam and Culture), 171–72
Freemasonry and, 202–4
and hieroglyphs, mystical associations with, 169
Nation of Islam and, 172–73, 185
Noble Drew Ali's interest in, 170–71, 185
non-Muslim Afrocentrists and, 173
and Nuwaubu, 206
W. D. Muhammad and, 167, 172–73
white interest in, 169–70
Egyptosophy and AAC/NIH
on afterlife, Egyptian misunderstanding of, 174
on Blackness of ancient Egyptians, 174
and Black perennialism, 182
consistency of AAC/NIH narratives on, 185
on death of Jesus, 183–85
early publications on, 173–74
on Egypt as technologically and spiritually advanced civilization, 174–77, 180
increased focus on after 1980s, 168, 174
and Islam, reconciling of, 168, 180
on Islamic faith of ancient Egyptians, 174, 178–80
on Jesus's education in Egypt, 156, 174, 181–85
and Al Mahdi's dress as pharaoh, 168
mixing with Christian imagery, 129
on monotheism of Egyptians, 178
polytheism of, as fabrication of Greeks and Babylonians, 178
on pyramids, origin, uses, and power of, 129, 174, 176–77, 237–38

similarity to other Muslim views of Egypt, 185–86
varying articulations of Islam-Egypt relationship, 173
on white devils' distortion of Egyptian wisdom, 178–80
on white people as subhuman evil animals, 177
on Zoser/Abdul Quddus, as god worshiped in many cultures, 176
Egyptosophy and UNNM symbolism, 193, 194, 195
El Din, Hamza, 62, 228
El-Haady, Rabboni Y'shua Bar, as name used by Al Mahdi, 113, 114, 130, 188, 191, 214
El's Holy Injiyl [book of Revelations] (York, tr.), 208
El's Holy Qur'aan (York, tr.), 208–10, 212
El's Holy Tehillim (Zabuwr) [the Psalms] (York, tr.), 208
El's Holy Torah (York, tr.), 208
Eternal Life After Death (Al Mahdi, 1977), 173–74, *175*
Ether (Creative Power), as root of "Ethiopian," 206
Ethiopia, as term, 206
Ethiopian Jews (Falashsas. Beta Israel), 117–19
Ethiopians, as true Hebrews, 136, 141
Ethiopian Temples of Islam and Culture. *See* Fahamme movement
extraterrestrials
Adam and Eve as, Al Mahdi on, 129
as avatars inhabiting Al Mahdi, 160
in Black Islamic narrative, 241
as builders of ancient marvels, melanin theory and, 9
chakra-powered ships of, 160
Elijah Muhammad on, 129, 198, 241
in hip-hop music, 233–34, *234*, *235*
images of, in AAC/NIH publications, 127, *128*
increased focus on, in 1980s, 129
influence on Earth, York on, 196–97
Al Mahdi on, 159–60
Al Mahdi's claim to be, 114, 195–96
in Al Mahdi's interpretation of Revelations, 22
Al Mahdi's power to contact, 21
and Muslim International, 231, 232
Sitchin on, 196
as Sufis, 160

Index • 283

extraterrestrials (*continued*)
    in UNNM beliefs, 196–98, 240–41, *241*
    in York's *El's Holy Qur'aan*, 209
    in York's *Holy Tablets*, 211
    York's narratives on, as staple of Black Islam, 198
    See also Salaam civilization
Ezaldeen, Muhammad, 30
Ezekiel's vision, and spacecraft, Al Mahdi on, 156

Fahamme movement (Ethiopian Temples of Islam and Culture), 171–72
Faisal, Daoud Ahmed
    Al-Islam, the Religion of Humanity, 119
    and Black Israelites, 119
    certification as teacher by Saudi Arabia and Jordan, 77
    and credentials of AAC/NIH and Al Mahdi, 17–18, 75, 77, 80
    critics of, 34
    eclectic theology of, 240–41
    and false Fard Muhammad, 218
    on Islam as original religion of Black people, 77
    and Islamic Mission of America, founding of, 12, 77
    and Islamic Propagation Center of America, 77
    on Jesus as Black man, 117
    Al Mahdi as defender of, 79
    Al Mahdi as student of, 13, 62, 77–78
    Al Mahdi on, 23, 99, 100
    Al Mahdi on failures of, 82–83
    Al Mahdi on religious education of, 83
    Al Mahdi's claim to legacy of, 76, 77–84, 86, 111, 187
    Al Mahdi's tying of Malcolm X to, 94
    and Medinat as-Salaam communal living experiment, 82–83
    and State Street Mosque, 12, 13, 77, 92
    York's *Holy Tablets* on, 211
Family Guide to Easy Arabic Phrases, A, 47
Fard, W. D., 84
    See also Muhammad, Fard
Farrakhan, Louis
    AAC/NIH concern about, 84
    and Afrocentrist recovery of African religion, 38
    on Bilal, 140
    eclectic theology of, 240

    and Egyptosophy, 172
    and hip-hop, 232, 233
    on Jesus as Black man, 117
    Al Mahdi on, 89, 100, 111, *111*, 112, 192
    mothership vision of, 198
    Saudi co-opting of, Al Mahdi on, 107
    and schism in Nation of Islam, 75, 84, 87, 89, 90, 93–94
    York's criticism of, 218
Father Divine, 84, 99
Fatima, Al Mahdi on, 56
    as Black woman, 49, 52–53, 54, 56
    flight to Sudan, 102
    as keeper of true Qur'an, 212
    as messiah figure, 219
    in Revelation, 50, 208
    as successor to Muhammad, 53
    and *Suhuf*, 180
Fatimid dynasty, refuge in Sudan, Al Madhi on, 47–48
FBI investigations of Al Mahdi and AAC/NIH, 190–91
Final Call newspaper, 198
Final Link, The (AAC, 1978), 60, 63, 64, 65
Final Messenger, The: Christ the Final Word (Al Mahdi, 1991), 127–28, 183–85
fiqh. *See* Muslim jurisprudence
Five Percenter movement
    and AAC/NIH, interactions of, 103–5
    hip-hop artists embracing, 103, 104, 106, 110, 231, 232
    importance in New York cultures, 103
    influence on Al Mahdi, 104–5, 163
    and knowledge of self as goal, 165
    Al Mahdi's critique of, 105–6, 108–11
    Al Mahdi's early life and, 59
    significance of name, 103
    York's publication of texts for, 218
    See also Allah (Clarence 13X)
Flugelrods, 197
flying saucers. *See* extraterrestrials
Ford, Arnold Josiah, 113, 117
Ford, Wallace Dodd, 91–92, 99–100
    See also Fard, W.D.; Muhammad, Fard
Forgotten Tribe Kedar, The (1974), 40, 44
Freemasonry
    Black: and Black view of Islam, 203; history of, 202–3; influence on Black Israelite movements, 205; influence on Al Mahdi, 204–5; influence on Nation of

Islam, 204; influence on Noble Drew
  Ali, 203–4
and Egyptosophy, 202–4
history of, 169
and Islam, 10
Al Mahdi and, 12
Masonic orders within UNNM, 202
and Moorish Science Temple, 203–4
York's adoption of, 202
York's recasting of ties to Islam and metaphysical Africa in terms of, 215–19
"Furqaan" power claimed by York, 207

Gabriel (angel), and death of Jesus, 183–85
Garnett, Ruby S. (wife of Al Mahdi)
  on Al Mahdi's turn from Islamic identity, 192
  responsibilities within AAC/NIH, 27
  on Sullivan County legal harassment, 189–90
Garvey, Marcus
  deportation of, 92
  and Duse Mohamed Ali, 10
  Al Mahdi on, 99, 100–101
  Al Mahdi's claim to legacy of, 77, 86, 100–103
  and pan-Africanist flag, 21, 66
Georgia facility of UNNM. *See* Tama Re UNNM facility, Eatonton, Georgia
Ghadir Khumm, Al Mahdi on, 50
GhaneaBassiri, Kambiz, 136–37
Ghulam Ahmad, Mirza, 150
Gospel of John, Chapter One (Al Mahdi), 184
Grand Lodge of Luxor, 203
Grandmaster Melle Mel, 66
Great Migration, and hoodoo tradition, 8
Great Pyramid, The (Taylor), 169
green light
  AAC/NIH sale of glow sticks with, 159
  healing power of, 161
  and Indian *prana*, 159
  Khidr and, 154, 160, 161, 162, 215
  in Al Mahdi's vision at junction of two Niles, 216
  See also Sons of the Green Light (SGL)
Griff, Professor, 232–33

Al Haadi Al Mahdi, Al Hajj Imam Isa. *See* Al Mahdi, Al Hajj Imam Isa Al Haadi
Hadith: Allah's Scripture Comes First (Al Mahdi, 1979), 48–49

hadiths
  anti-music, Al Mahdi's rejection of, 229
  Al Mahdi on, 43, 70, 109, 121, 123
  York's criticism of, in *Holy Tablets*, 212
Hadrat Faatimah (AS) (Al Mahdi), 52–53, 54–56
Haile Selassie, 101, 111, *111*, 112, 122, 125–26, 193
Hajar, 70–71, 173, 177, 180, 183
Halman, Hugh Talat, 154, 158
Ham, 30, 40–41
Hamid, Yusuf Muzaffaruddin, 35
Hammer, Olav, 155, 169
hanifs, Bilal and, 141
Hare Krishna movement, 42, 151
Hart-Celler Act of 1965, 34
Hasan, Al Mahdi on, 50, 55
  See also Shi'ism
Hasuwn, Sheikh Ahmad, 62
Hebrew elements of AAC/NIH beliefs, *118*, 121–34
  and Abraham as origin of Judaism, Christianity, and Islam, 132
  anticipation of Second Coming and, 130–31
  Biblical Tents of Kedar name and, 126
  community view of through Qur'anic lens, 133–34
  covenant, 123
  dress code changes and, 129–30, 131, 132
  early valorization of Hebrew language, 121
  and "Jewish period" of 1992-93, 114, 132, 133–34
  Al Mahdi's criticisms of Muslims for rejection of revealed Hebrew and Christian scriptures, 123–25
  and modern Jews as false sect, 131
  and Mohammad as Nubic Islamic Hebrew, 125
  and "19 Classes," 130
  and Nubians of Western Hemisphere as heirs to Israelite covenant, 122, 123
  and references to Allah as Eloh or Yahuwa, 131
  restoration of Torah sacraments, 130
  and sale of Jewish religious merchandise, 131
  six point star, use of, 121
  as theme throughout group's history, 114, 132, 133–34
  See also Israelites; Judaism
Hebrew identity of AAC/NIH, prioritization of Muslim identity over, 116
Hebrew Israelites, on extraterrestrials, 198
Hebrews, as Black, Malcolm X on, 119

Hermetic Brotherhood of Luxor, 169–70
Hindus, origin of, Al Mahdi on, 42
hip-hop
    Ansar musical theory and, 233
    artists sympathetic to AAC/NIH, 230
    embrace of Islam, 230–31
    and Five Percenter movement, 103, 104, 106, 110, 231, 232
    of golden age, as nonsectarian, 232
    Al Mahdi's embrace of, 230, 236
    and Al Mahdi's extraterrestrials, 233–34, 234, 235
    Al Mahdi's influence on, 232–35
    and Muslim Cool, 224–25
    and Nu-wop, 235
    and Zulu Nation movement, 233
    See also Ansar hip-hop
History of the Black Indians (Al Mahdi), 199
Holy Gospel, The: The Revelation of Jesus the Messiah to the World (Al Mahdi, 1984), 50, 121
Holy Tabernacle Ministries, as name used by UNNM, 23, 193
Holy Tabernacle of the Most High, as name used by AAC/NIH, 113, 114
Holy Tablets, The (York, 1996)
    AAC/NIH beliefs reflected in, 211
    on AAC/NIH history, 214–15, 220
    on Bilal, 213–14
    descriptions of Blackamerica leaders in, 211
    format of, 210–11
    as future scripture predicted Elijah Muhammad, 219
    on Islam, corruption of, 130, 212, 214
    on Islamic practice of AAC/NIH, ineffectiveness of, 214
    on Muhammad as false prophet, 211–12
    as original revelation, 210
    revised edition of, 211
    strong Islamic influence in, 211–12
    on Sufism, 214
    on true Qur'an in Sudan, 212
    on York's journey as full circle, 220
hoodoo tradition, and Great Migration, 8
Hopi Tribe, extraterrestrials in traditions of, 198
Houston, Drusilla Dunjee, 28, 29–30
How Many Muslims Really Follow the Holy Qur'an? (Al Mahdi), 122
Hu (Egyptian God), in UNNM beliefs, 193
Hucks, Tracey E., 14, 32
Humazah (Al Mahdi, 1979), 230

Husayn, Al Mahdi on, 50, 51, 52, 55
    See also Shi'ism

Iblis, 74
Ibn al-'Arabi, 154
Icke, David, 196
I Don't Claim to Be . . . (Al Mahdi, 1981), 20, 193
Idris/Enoch, Muslim scholars on, 186
al-Idrisi, 186
Id with the Ansars (Al Mahdi, 1977), 19–20, 80, 81, 149, 152
Ikhwaani Muslimuwn (Muslim Brothers), York on corruption of Islam by, 212
Illuminati, as lizard aliens ruling the Earth, 196
IMA. *See* Islamic Mission of America
Imhotep, 177–78
    Al Mahdi on, 41–42, 173
immigrants from Muslim countries, increase in, after Hart-Celler Act, 34
Incarnated in Human Form (AAC/NIH advertisement, 1987), 5
Incas. *See* pre-Columbian civilizations
Indian religions
    Al Mahdi on, 42–43
    Al Mahdi's adoption of parts of, 158–59
    white esotericists' interest in, Aryanism and, 170, 181
al-insan al-kamil, Dhikr and, 147
Intellectual Hoodlum. *See* Tragedy Khadafi
IPNA. *See* Islamic Party of North America
Iran, heretical innovation (*bida*) in, 44
Isa Muhammad, as name used by Al Mahdi, 163
Is Haile Selassie the Christ? (York, 1994), 193
Ishmaelites
    and forfeiture of covenant, 129, 132
    as heirs to Israelite covenant, 122, 123, 126
    prophetic heritage, 178
Isis Unveiled (Blavatsky), 170
Islam
    Abraham as origin of, 132
    and Afrocentrist recovery of African religion, 38–39
    Black (Afrocentrist) rejection of, 11, 33; after conflicts with Saudi influence, 36; as anti-Black, 28, 36, 38, 53; due to incompatibility with Black creativity and sophistication, 33; due to Muslim association with slavery, 33, 36, 37; as foreign to Africa, 11, 15, 33; as ideology of Arab racial supremacy, 36, 37, 38, 53

contemporary, as distorted "Muhammad-ism," AAC/NIH on, 131–32
corrupted forms of, as product of white devils, 73–74
criticisms of Blacks adopting, due to acceptability to whites, 33
egalitarianism of, 10
as false narrative produced by lizard aliens, 196
golden age of Black embrace of, 230–31
history of, in York's *Holy Tablets*, 211
Al Mahdi on: Black origins of, 12; on connections between Africa and, 16–17; early views, 34; opposition to sect labels in, 43
Al Mahdi's conversion to, 12–13
Al Mahdi's turn from, 23, 187–88, 191–92; and concerns about targeting of Muslims, 192; reasons for, 22–23
and metaphysical Africa: as issue for AAC/NIH, 12; range of origins and expressions of, 10–12
Nubia as origin of, Al Mahdi on, 48
and oppression of women, York on, 219
separation from Judaism, as work of the devil, 102
separation from Judaism and Christianity as error, Ford on, 117
takeover by red and pale Arabs, 29
true, as Religion of Abraham, Al Mahdi on, 131–32
true black version *vs.* corrupted form of Arabs, 102
See also Black Islam; Muslims; Shi'i; Sunni Islam
Al- Islam (journal), 36, 37
Islamic Center of Washington, D.C., 35–36
Islamic civilization
as product of Black civilization, Nation of Islam on, 30–31, 35
as product of Black civilization, Houston on, 30
Islamic Mission of America (IMA)
affiliations of, 12
conflict between African American and immigrant Muslims in, 77
founding of, 12, 77
NIHMA claim to be authorized branch of, 17–18
Islamic Music (Al Mahdi, 1977), 228

Islamic Party of North America (IPNA), 35–36, 37
Islamic Propagation Center of America, founding of, 77
Islamic Society of North America, 36
Islam in AAC/NIH thought
Al Mahdi on, 12
and Qur'an and Arabic as Nubian, 29
rejection of orthodox Islam as anti-Black, 12
relocation of Islam's heartland to Sudan, 12, 28–29, 39
Yorks' recasting through Freemasonry, 215–19
Islam the True Faith: The Religion of Humanity (Al Mahdi, 1980), 82
Ismael, lost tribe of, AAC/NIH as, 60
Is Music and Dance Lawful for Muslims? (NIHMA, ca. 1972), 228
Israelites
as Black Muslims, 119
Ethiopian Falashas as only modern descendants of, 42, 121–22, 123, 141
Nubians of Western Hemisphere as heirs to covenant, 122, 123, 126; forfeiting of covenant, 129, 132
See also Jews, modern

Jaaliyyan Nubians, characteristics of, 39
Jamaat al-Fuqra, 153, 189
Jameelah, Maryam, 13, 58
Jay-Z, 2, 221
Jaz, The, 2, 231
Jazzir Abba/Mount Zion AAC/NIH settlement (Catskill Mountains)
communal living experiment at, 82–83
forfeiting of covenant with God, Al Mahdi on, 129, 132
Al Mahdi's redesign of AAC/NIH ritual and aesthetics at, 191
and Al Mahdi's retreat from Islamic identity, 191–92
and "19 Classes" reorientation, 130
relocation to, 4, 22, 113–14, 126; motives for, 189, 191, 192; York on, 214
Sullivan County legal harassment of, 189–90
Jenkins, Clarke, 116–17, 251n7
Jesus Christ
AAC/NIH views on, 127, 129
angel Gabriel as father of, 183–85
as Black man, 117, 119

Index • 287

Jesus Christ (*continued*)
    burial place in Kashmir, Ahmadiyya on, 182
    connections to Black metaphysical traditions, 8
    death of, Al Mahdi on, 183–85
    education of: and Black perennialism, 182; enlightenment through learning, 181–83; in India, late-nineteenth-century narratives on, 181; and Khidr/Melchizedek as teacher, 156, 174, 183; at pyramids, 156, 174, 182, 183
    in Egypt, consistency of AAC/NIH narrative on, 185
    as follower of Mosaic law, 127
    Gospel (*Injil*) of, Al Mahdi on: in *Holy Gospel*, 50, 121; as limited to Revelation, 123, 131, 134, 208; translation of (*El's Holy Injiyl*), 208
    identification of Al Mahdi with, 130–31
    and metaphysical religions' narrative of revelations from superior beings, 155
    and Mihjan, 158
    as priest in Melchizedek's order, 183
    return to Earth, AAC/NIH publications on, 193
Jesus Found in Egipt (Al Mahdi, 1996), 185
Jews, modern
    as Canaanites, 52
    as false sect, 131, 136
    and Mosaic Law, failure to follow, 127
    and Qur'an as completion of Jewish scripture, 125
    ties to Islam, Elijah Muhammad on, 120
    as white: Elijah Muhammad on, 120; Faisal on, 119; Al Mahdi on, 42, 44, 121–22
al-Jilani, 'Abd al-Qadir, 154
Johnson, Paul Nathaniel (Ahmad Din, Paul J. Achamad), 171–72
John the Baptist
    AAC/NIH on, 129
    Al Mahdi on Elijah Muhammad as, 20, 84
Judaism
    Abraham as origin of, 132
    as false narrative produced by lizard aliens, 196
    names for God, as corruptions of "Allah," 46–47
    separation from Islam, as work of the devil, 102
    separation from Islam and Christianity as error, Ford on, 117

    See also Hebrew elements of AAC/NIH beliefs; Israelites
junction of two Niles
    inhabitants of, as Muslim, 79
    Al Mahdi's mystical vision at, 19, 130, 153, 159, 174, 185, 215, 216
    Moses and Khidr at, 154
    shuwba and, 158
    as site of creation of Adam, 29, 174

Ka'ba
    Black Stone in, as body of Adam, 174
    York on Egyptian origins of, 195
Kahane, Meir, 189
Karenga, Maulana, 162, 173, 200
El Katub Shil el Mawut (*The Book of the Dead*): *Coming Forth by Day* (York, tr.), 208, 209
Kedar
    Muhammad as descendant of, 48
    as origin of Nubians, 48, 126
    as origin of Nubians in America, 42, 121
Khalifa, Rashad, 106, 188–89
Khalwatiyya order, 153, 217
Khan, Hazrat Inayat, 147, 150, 151
Khidr, 154–58
    Al Madhi on, 12, 17, 19, 22, 23, 90
    as avatar inhabiting body of Al Mahdi, 156, 157, 158, 195
    as consistent theme in Al Mahdi's writings, 158
    as cosmological energy in Al Mahdi, 154, 160, 162
    Al Mahdi's consistency with other accounts, 154–55
    and Melchizedek, 154–55, 166
    and metaphysical religions' narrative of revelations from superior beings, 155
    and Mihjan, 157
    as Moses' teacher, 152, 154
    pyramids built around world by order of, 199–200
    as spiritual teacher to Al Mahdi, 215
    and Sufism, 154
    as superior being revealing truth to humans, 156
    as teacher of Jesus, 156, 174, 183
    as transrational sage, 154
Khutbat series, 85

Khutbat's of Al Hajj Al Imam Isa Abd'Allah Muhammad Al Mahdi, Book Two (Al Mahdi), 85–86
King, Martin Luther, Jr., 106, 111, *111*
KMD, 2, 232
Kush/Cush, as origin of Dongolawi Nubians, 39

Lamb, the
    and Elijah Muhammad's vision of the *lam*, 158
    as name used by Al Mahdi, 130, 158
Lamurudu, 73
letter esotericism of Al Mahdi, 162–63
Lewis, "Sufi Sam," 151, 154
Lieb, Michael, 198
Life of Mahomet (Muir), 136
lizard aliens, creation of humans by, 196
Lone Wolf, Wauneta, 198
Lost Children of Babylon/Egypt, 235
Lubavitcher Hasidim, 130

al-Madhi, Sayyid Sadiq
    claim to Ansar leadership, 192
    flight from Sudan, 14
    Al Mahdi's ties to, 61–66, 67
    return to power in Sudan, 64–66
    visit to Al Mahdi in Brooklyn, 63, 64, 67
El Maguraj ceremony
    events and symbolism in, 238
    similarity to other ceremonies within larger interstellar Blackness, 237–38
    York's reinstitution of, 237–38, 239
Mahbub, Hafis, 12, 79
Al Mahdi, Al Hajj Imam Isa Al Haadi
    and AAC/NIH, establishment of, 59
    AAC/NIH efforts to free from prison, 23
    addition of "Al Haadi" to name, 4
    adoption of name, 214
    and African spirituality, non-Muslim, early encounters with, 14–15
    appearance of, 1
    on Arabic, true form of, 44–48
    arrest (1987), 190
    arrest (2002), 4
    assassination attempt against, 189
    avatars inhabiting body of, 22, 156–57, 160, 176
    beliefs of: as Afrocentric Sufism, 34, 59; as Blackness-affirming Salafism, 43; influence of Nation of Islam on, 40, 41, 48; turn to eclectic mix after 1993, 23
    on Black god-scientists ruling universe, 156
    on Black Man as God (Gomar Oz Dubar), 17, 40, 104
    and Black Muslim agency, consistent advocacy of, 74
    and Black nationalist version of Islam, development of, 13
    on Black unity through Arabic language, 16
    brother of, 17
    characterization as unstable trickster, inaccuracy of, 240
    childhood of, and avatars inhabiting his body, 157
    commentaries on Qur'an suras, 47
    on connections between Islam and Africa, 16–17
    consistency of beliefs over time, 16, 132–34
    on continuity of AAC/NIH underlying message, 132–33
    conversion to Islam, 12–13
    conviction as sexual predator, 4
    conviction for racketeering and child sex abuse, 23
    early beliefs of, 17, 18
    extraterrestrial origin, claims of, 114
    FBI investigations of, 190–91
    and founding of AAC/NIH, 15–16, 59–60
    Freemasonry's influence on, 204–5
    identification with angel Michael/Khidr/Melchizedek, 90
    images of, 1, 2, 3, 5, 65, 67, 68, 112, 114, 115, 126–27, 128, 145, 179, 194, 201, 223
    and Indian religions, adoption of parts of, 158–59
    influence of, 148
    on Islam: Black origins of, 12; early views, 34; opposition to sect labels in, 43
    on Islamic, Christian, and Jewish scriptures, study of, 19–20
    and Jesus, identification with, 20
    Jewish phase of, 22
    the Lamb as designation for, 20, 22
    Masonic lodges led by, 12
    mingling of Judaism, Islam, and Christianity concepts, consistency across career, 132–34
    and Muhammad Ahmad (Sudanese Mahdi): AAC/NIH emphasis on ties to, 20; claim to be grandson of, 17–18, 20, 21, 29, 62, 63, 67, 101–2, 192–93, 199, 215, 217, 219, 246–47n83; as role model, 14, 66

murder accusations against, 190
as Muslim, Jew, and Christian, 129
mystical visions of, 19
name, first Islamic (Isa 'Abd'Allah ibn Abu Bakr Muhammad), 13, 16, 83
name at birth (Dwight York), 12
name change to Malachi Z. York, 22, 157
name change to Rabboni Y'shua Bar El Haady, 22
names used by, 26, 130, 168, 185, 191, 214
Nation of Islam attacks on, 189
NIHMA pamphlets by, 16
on Nubians as original humans, 40
on origin of races and history of humankind, 39–44, 93
on orthodoxy as white heresy, 43
on phases of his mission, 23, 132, 207, 242
poetry by, 149
as possessor of 76 trillion years of Khidriyya knowledge, 158
powers attributed to, 19; AAC/NIH turn to focus on, in 1970s, 20; power to contact ancient and extraterrestrial figures, 21
prison sentence, current, 4
prison sentence for assault (1965-67), 13
public profile of, 148
purported lineage and childhood in Sudan, 62–63, 77
on *Ratib* of Muhammad Ahmad, 64
recognition as Mahdi by Sudanese Ansar, 60
Saudi efforts to discredit, 6
on separation of Africa (Earth) and Asia (Moon), 40, 100, 102, 116, 156, 176
spiritual authority of, as genealogical inheritance, 119
and State Street Mosque: breakoff of Ansar Pure Sufi group from, 15, 83; Islamic education at, 12–14
on Sudan as center of divine creative activity, 17
and Sudanese community, identification with, 13–14
and Sunni hegemony, struggle against, 66
as temple of incarnated divinity, 159
ties to living Mahdiyya family, 61–66, 67
travel to Middle East and Africa, 19
trip to Egypt, 69–70
turn from Christianity and Judaism, 23
turn from Islamic identity, 22–23, 187–88, 191–92
and "Two Fards" conspiracy theory, 91–92, 218
on underlying unity of all religions, 152
on white people: as debased subhumans, 41; as devils, 41, 89; origin of, 40–41
and white supremacy, struggle against, 66, 69
wives of, responsibilities with AAC/NIH, 26–27
writings by, as largely plagerized or ghost-written, 26–27
and Yoruba Temple, connections to, 15
See also Blackamerica leadership, Al Mahdi's claiming of; dress of Al Mahdi and followers; Yanaan/Yaanuwn; York, Dr.; York, Malachi Z.; *other specific topics*
al-Mahdi, Hadi, 14
al-Mahdi, Sayyid 'Abd al-Rahman, 59, 60
Mahdiyya [followers of Muhammad Ahmad]
AAC/NIH adoption of flag of, 21, 64, 66, 102–3, 111–12, 112, 114, 221, 230, 231, 233, 242
Ansaru Allah Community name and, 19
and defeat of Anglo-Egyptian colonial regime, 14, 29, 51, 58–59, 101
Garvey's use of flag of, 101
Al Mahdi and AAC/NIH claimed ties to, 7, 21, 23, 49, 61, 69, 74, 83, 93, 174, 199;
Al Mahdi's later recasting of, within Egyptosophy/Freemasonry, 215, 242;
Mahdiyya's challenging of, 192–93
in Al Mahdi's interpretation of Revelation, 93
Al Mahdi's ties to living family of, 61–66, 67
and political turmoil in Sudan, 14
popularity with Black music artists, 221, 230, 231, 233
Sufis and, 58
See also Ahmad, Muhammad (Sudanese Mahdi)
Mahmuwd, as spiritual teacher of Al Mahdi, 216
Majid, Satti, 13
Malachi-Zodok, as name used by Al Mahdi, 130
Malachizodok-El, as name used by York, 193
Malcolm X
assassination of, Al Mahdi on, 95, 96, 106
The Autobiography of Malcolm X, 119
on Bilal, 139
on Hebrews as Black, 119

and hip-hop, 232, 233
Al Mahdi on, 76, 94–95, 96, 100
Al Mahdi's claim to legacy of, 77, 94–96, 111
Al Mahdi's insertion of himself into Malcolm X's life story, 94, 95, 96
and "moral geography of the Dark world," 29
post-Nation travels, new names acquired in, 32
two heartlands of, 32
Yoruba Temple and, 15
Mali, Afrocentrist rejection of Islam's influence on, 38
Malik ibn Anas, 43
Man of Miracles in This Day and Time, The (Al Mahdi), 156, 157, 159, 176
Man of Our Time, The (AAC, 1978), 49, 86
"Many Questions, One Answer" (Al Mahdi), 149
al-Maqrizi, 186
Marrant, John, 202
Maryam, Faatimah, 62
Maryamiyya, 151–52
al-Masih, Isa, as avatar inhabiting body of Al Mahdi, 156, 157
Masjid at-Taqwa (Brooklyn), 35
Masons. *See* Freemasonry
Mayas. *See* pre-Columbian civilizations
Medinat as-Salaam communal living experiment, 82–83
Melanin-ite Children, The (York, 1995), 196–97
melanin theorists, 9, 196–97
Melchisedek, as name used by Al Mahdi, 130
Melchizedek
  as avatar inhabiting body of Al Mahdi, 195
  and Egyptian pyramids, 169
  and Khidr, 154–55, 166, 183
  Al Mahdi on, 17, 19, 23, 90
Melle Mel, 231, 232
Merchants of Oyo, 17
metaphysical Africa
  AAC/NIH engagement with: through Al Mahdi's tie to Sudan, 192–93; turn to Egyptian connection in 1980s, 174; via Nubian connection in 1970s, 174; Yorks' recasting through Freemasonry, 215–19
  on Blacks' unique spiritual gifts and destiny, 9
  eclectic imaginary of, 241–42
  Egyptocentrism in, 9

and Islam: as issue for AAC/NIH, 12; range of origins and expressions of, 10–12
Al Mahdi's claim to legacy of, 101–2
and melanin theories, 9, 196–97
and Nation of Islam, 10–11
origin of term, 7
range of views on African spiritual tradition, 9
Sufism as expression of, 153
York's blending of Native American beliefs with, 199, 200
MIB. *See* Mosque of Islamic Brotherhood
Mihjan
  Bilal and, 55, 141, 142, 143, 144, 158, 213
  Jesus's possession of, 158
  Al Mahdi's claim to possess, 144–45, 145, 157, 158
  significance of, 157–58
Million Man March, 172
miracles performed by Al Mahdi, 157
Moabites, and Egyptian civilization, 171
monotheism, as Black, AAC/NIH on, 29, 42
Montserrat, Dominic, 199
Moorish Science Temple
  AAC/NIH Sufism and, 151–52
  AAC/NIH thought and, 144
  and Black Orientalism, 171
  and Egyptosophy, 171
  and exchange with East, 150
  Ford plan to destroy, Al Mahdi on, 92
  Freemasonry and, 203–4
  and metaphysical Africa, 10
  and narrative of revelations from superior beings, 155
  sovereignty claims of, 200–201
  York's publication of texts for, 218
  See also Ali, Noble Drew
Moorish Zionist Temple, 117, 204–5
moral geographies of blackness, African American debate over, 28–29
Moroccan Empire, Moabites and, 171
Moses
  and Egyptian wisdom, association with, 169, 203, 237
  Khidr as teacher of, 154, 162
  Masons and, 169
Mosque of Islamic Brotherhood (MIB), conflict with NIHMA, 18, 79–80
Mount Zion AAC/NIH settlement. *See* Jazzir Abba/Mount Zion AAC/NIH settlement (Catskill Mountains)

Index • 291

Mu (capital of Salaam), 2, 40, 102, 147, 156, 176
Muhaiyaddeen, Bawa, 151
Muhammad (prophet)
    as Black man, 29, 48, 49, 52, 55, 142
    as confirmer of timeless religion of prophets, 131
    death of, as poisoning by Jewish woman, 52, 212
    as descendant of Kedar, 48
    Elijah Muhammad on, 31–32
    as false prophet, York's *Holy Tablets* on, 211–12, 213
    as follower of Mosaic Law, 125, 127
    as Hebrew, Al Mahdi on, 132, *133*
    knowledge of atomic science, Al Mahdi on, 177
    and Mihjan, 158, 213
    Muslim's idolatry of, Al Mahdi on, 126, 209
    as Nubic Islamic Hebrew, 125
    See also ahl al-bayt (Muhammad's household)
Muhammad, Elijah
    on Black god-scientists ruling universe, 155–56
    on Black people on Mars, 187
    break with traditional Islam, 32
    as conscientious objector in World War II, 252n22
    correction of Al Mahdi in dream, 189
    criticism by traditional Muslims, 53–54
    distinction between Muslim and African identities, 31
    and Egyptosophy, 172–73, 185
    elements of Christianity in teachings of, 120
    on extraterrestrials, 129, 198, 241
    and false Fard Muhammad, 218
    on Fard Muhammad as Second Coming of Jesus, 120
    influence of Black Freemasonry on, 204
    on Islam and Freemasonry, 204
    on Jesus as Black man, 117
    on Jesus's education in Egypt, 182
    on Jews, 120
    Al Mahdi on, 20, 23, 100
    Al Mahdi's claim to be successor of, 75–77, 84–94, 111, 187, 219; cautious approach to, 86; and claimed Elijah prophesy of Al Mahdi's coming, 93; and claimed power to explain Elijah's misunderstood teachings, 87–89; and communication with Elijah in dreams, 219; and Elijah as Elijah the prophet, 89; and Elijah as John the Baptist figure, 20, 84; and Elijah's prophesy of successor, 89–90; and Elijah's teaching as interim step to Nubian Islam, 89; and Farrakhan-Muhammad schism, 93–94; and Supreme Wisdom Lessons, effort to fix, 92–93; and symbolism of *lam* vision of Elijah, 90; and "Two Fards" conspiracy theory, 91–92
    Al Mahdi's criticism of, 76, 85–86
    mothership vision of, 129, 198
    on Muhammad as Black, 31–32
    on new book replacing Qur'an in hereafter, 86, 87, 120, 219
    on New Islam led by Black Muslims, 32
    on non-Muslim African cultures, 11, 31
    on Qur'an, 120
    on separation of Earth and Moon, 40
    on shared Black and Islamic identity, 10–11, 13
    and Supreme Wisdom Lessons, 10, 92
    Theology of Time, The, 86, 87
    and "Two Fards" conspiracy theory, 91
    views on Africa, 30–31
    vision of the *lam*, 158
    on white people as devils, 89
    York's *Holy Tablets* on, 211
    York's Nuwaubian-era writings on, 218–19
    York's publication of sermons by, 219
Muhammad, Fard
    on Africa, 30
    elements of Christianity in teachings of, 120
    Elijah Muhammad's Biblical interpretation of, 120
    and Elijah Muhammad's education, 86
    Freemasonry's influence on, 204
    and Supreme Wisdom Lessons, 10
    and "Two Fards" conspiracy theory, 91–92, 218
    on white people as devils, 88–89
    York's *Holy Tablets* on, 211
    See also Fard, M. D.
Muhammad, Hashim, 190
Muhammad, Siddiq, 20
Muhammad, Silis, 100
Muhammad, Warith Dean. *See* Muhammad, W. D
Muhammad, W. D.
    AAC/NIH criticisms of, 143
    and Afrocentrist recovery of African religion, 38

on Bilal, 139–40
claim to legacy of father, 88
corruption by Wahhabi Sect, 96
and deracialization of Nation of Islam teachings, 140
and Egyptosophy, 167, 172–73
groups in opposition to, 35–36
Al Mahdi on, 100
Al Mahdi's criticism of, 90, 91
on original Muslims as Black, 35
and reinterpretation of father's teachings, 88–89
rejection of Arab influence on Islam, 34–35
relations with Saudi Arabia, 35
and schism in Nation of Islam, 75–76, 84, 86–87, 89, 90, 93–94
York's criticism of, 209, 218
York's effort to lure away followers of, 219
Muhammad Ahmad: The Only True Mahdi! (1977), 20, 49
Muhammad Speaks (newspaper), 31, 69–70, 79, 89, 172
Muhammad Was a Hebrew (Al Mahdi, 1993), 132, 133
Al Mukhlisina, 212
Muridiyya Order, 153
Musaylimat, 212
music, Islamic prohibitions on
Al Mahdi's rejection of, 225, 226, 228–29
racialized notion of Islamic tradition created by, 225
music, Al Mahdi's engagement with, 194
and anti-Black ideas about Islam and music, 225
Billboard ad, 222–23, 224, 230
and blessing of musical artists, 232
condemnation of Western music, 222, 227–28, 236
followers' lack of concern about, 224
and hip-hop, influence on, 232–35
and music in worship and teaching, 229–30
as outreach to troubled world, 230, 236
as performer, 222–24, 223, 235–36
as product of Nubian spiritual gifts, 230
as studio owner with record label, 222, 228, 233
See also Ansar musical theory; hip-hop; York, Dr.
music, traditional Nubian, Al Mahdi's support for, 222, 228
Muslim Cool (Abdul Khabeer), 225

Muslim Cool, and intersection of hip-hop and Islam, 224–25
Muslim International, Ansar hip-hop and, 231, 232
Muslim jurisprudence (*fiqh*)
Sons of the Green Light and, 162
York's criticism of, in *Holy Tablets*, 212
Muslims
and Mosaic Law, failure to follow, 127
origin of term, Al Mahdi on, 102, 156
rejection of Black African forms of Islam, 11–12
rejection of pan-Africanism, 28
See also Islam
Muslim World League (MWL), 32, 35, 126
mystery schools of ancient elders, 156, 165
Jesus as student at, 10, 129
and Jesus's education, 183
locations of, 176–77

names
AAC/NIH change from Muslim to scriptural names, 129–30
Christian and Islamic, Afrocentrists' rejection of, 37, 38
true Nubian, importance of recovering, Al Mahdi on, 45
Nance, Susan, 181, 203–4
Nation of Gods and Earths. *See* Five Percenter movement
Nation of Islam
on Allah as self-perfected man, 162
on Black African origin of Aztec wonders, 198
on Black god-scientists ruling universe, 155–56
on Black Man as father of civilization, 30–31, 35
and communism, 92
doctrine, Al Mahdi's criticism of, 90
dress code, AAC/NIH criticisms of, 69
and Egyptosophy, 172–73, 185
and exchange with East, 150
and extraterrestrials, 198
groups in opposition to, 35–36
influence of Black Freemasonry on, 204
and knowledge of self as goal, 165
Al Mahdi's apology to, 189, 218
Al Mahdi's minimal early engagement with, 84–85
Al Mahdi's refusal to confront, 83

Index • 293

Nation of Islam (*continued*)
  materials on Bilal, 139
  and metaphysical Africa, 10–11
  rejection of Arab influence on Islam, 34–35
  Saudi influence on, 35–36
  schism after Elijah Muhammad's death, 75, 84, 86–87, 89, 90
  symbols of, Al Mahdi's criticism of, 84–85, 89, 92–93
  teachings of, Al Mahdi's knowledge and use of, 83
  ties to Black Mafia Family, 190
  on time allotted to white people, 206
  and "Two Fards" conspiracy theory, 91–92, 218
  violent attacks on AAC/NIH and Al Mahdi, 189
  on white people, origin of, 41
  York's attacks on, 218
  York's criticism of, 218
  York's publication of texts for, 218, 219
Nation of Yahweh, on extraterrestrials, 198
Native American heritage
  Noble Drew Ali's claim to, 201
  UNNM claim to, 200, 202
  York's claim to, 199–202, 201
Native Americans
  Nubian ancestry of, as UNNM belief, 199–200
  theories of ancient Freemasonry among, 203
  Washitaw Muurs as, 201–2
Native Americans beliefs
  popularity in 1990s among New Agers, 199
  UNNM's blending with metaphysical Africa, 199, 200
New Age movement
  AAC/NIH resistance to, as white domain, 158
  elements of, throughout Al Mahdi's career, 165
  exclusion of Islam and African religions from, 8
  Al Mahdi phase of, as inaccurate, 165
  popularity of Native Americans beliefs in 1990s, 199
  and Sufism, 158
  white prejudices in, 7–8
New Religious Movement (NRM) studies, 7
Nibiru, 193, 196, 197, 198, 211

NIHMA. *See* Nubian Islamic Hebrew Mission in America
Nimatullahi Order, 151
Nine Ball, The (Nupu et al.), 205, 207
"19 Classes" reorientation, 130
Ninety-Nine Names of Allah (Friedlander), 150
99+1 Attributes of Allah (Al Mahdi, 1983), 148–50
Nommos, in York's *Holy Tablets*, 211
El Nosair, Sayyid, 189
Now!!! Receive the Answers (AAC/NIH poster, ca. 1980), 1, 2
Nubia
  Fatimid dynasty's refuge in, Al Madhi on, 47–48
  and flags used by AAC/NIH, 64–66
  as origin of Islam, Al Mahdi on, 48, 56
Nubian Islamic Hebrew Mission in America (NIHMA)
  beliefs of, 16–18
  characteristic dress of, 15, 16, 18
  consistency of views with later AAC/NIH, 16, 19
  as intended evocation of Faisal's IMA, 78
  opposition from New York Muslim groups, 18
  practices of, 16
  as successor group to Ansar Pure Sufi group, 15
  on Sufism, right of American Muslims to identify with, 17
Nubian Islamic Hebrews (NIH)
  on Black unity through Arabic language, 16
  on connections between Islam and Africa, 16–17
  limited doctrinal significance of name change, 116
  as one name of AAC/NIH, 4, 64, 126
  period of name use, 4, 21, 122
  See also AAC/NIH (Ansaru Allah Community/Nubian Islamic Hebrews)
Nubians
  and AAC/NIH dress code, 70
  Arabic as original language of, Al Mahdi on, 47
  claim to both Islamic and pre-Islamic Egypt, 180–81
  as first humans, 40
  Muslim, as learned and super-intelligent, 73
  northern, as keepers of Muslim culture, 48

oppression by Amorites, and white animosity for Black Islam, 56
as original inhabitants of Egypt and Arabia, 30, 39
southern, as degenerated, 48
superior spirituality of, Al Mahdi on, 161–62
three categories of, Al Mahdi on, 39
Nubians of Western Hemisphere
as Ishmaelite heirs to Israelite covenant, 122, 123, 126; and forfeiting of covenant, 129, 132
Kedar as origin of, 42
Nubic, Al Madhi on, 48
Nubic: The Language of the Nubian Americans, 48
al-Numayri, Ja'far Muhammad, 14, 60
Nuwaubians, as term for AAC/NIH, 4
See also UNNM (United Nuwaubian Nation of Moors)
Nuwaubu (Nuwaupu)
as always part of York's message, York on, 207
as culmination of Black Islam, York on, 217–18
meaning and origin of term, 205–6
Nuwaupianism anti-cult site, 258n109
Nuwaupic language, 206
Nu-wop, 235

Olmecs, Nubian ancestors of, York on, 200
Opening of the Seventh Seal (Al Mahdi), 204
orders, hierarchy of, Al Mahdi on, 162
Original Tents of Kedar
as name used by AAC/NIH, 21, 126
period of name use, 126
Origin and Objects of Ancient Freemasonry (Delany), 203
"The Originators" (The Jaz music video)
AAC/NIH images in, 221, 222
and corporate pop culture, 222
and status of Muslim women, 221–22
Our Flag: The True Banner of Al Islaam (Al Mahdi, 1989), 66, 107
Our Symbol (Al Mahdi, 1977), 84
Oyo, Obaba (David Piper York, Jr.), 17, 203, 246n59

Paleman, The (Al Mahdi, 1990s), 199–200
Palmer, Susan, 8, 116–17, 220, 240–41
Passion (music group), 222, 230
Paz, Vinnie, 234–35

Philips, Abu Ameenah Bilal
Al Mahdi on, 96, 107
study in Saudi Arabia, 36
See also The Ansar Cult in America (Philips)
pineal gland, melanin theorists on, 9
polytheism
as product of white perversity, Al Mahdi on, 42
of Yorubas, Al Mahdi on, 72–73
Polytheism: Worship of the Canaanites (1977), 39, 42
pope, Catholic, Faisal on, 119
Post Graduate: The Renewal of the Lessons (York, 1996), 219
pre-Columbian civilizations
Al Mahdi on Nubian ancestry of, 200
Nation of Islam on Black African origin of, 198
Nubian ancestry of, as common Afrocentric narrative, 200
Prehistoric Man and Animals — Did They Exist? (Al Mahdi, 1980), 123
Problem Book, The, York's publication of edition of, 218
Prophet Muhammad and Ali Were Nubian, The (Black), 52, 72
Psalms 68:31, 202
publications of AAC/NIH, author(s) of, as difficult to identify, 26
public image of AAC/NIH, as eclectic, incoherent sect, 4
pyramids
Al Mahdi on origin, uses, and power of, 129, 174, 176–77, 237–38
Muslim views of, 186
mystical associations with, 169
in South America: and Nubian origin of Aztecs, Incas and Mayans, 200; Washitaw Muurs as source of, 201
at UNNM Tama Re compound, 195

Quetzlcoatl
importance to Nation of Islam, 198
Zoser/Abdul Quddus as, 199
Qur'an
on Egypt as paradigm of human wickedness, 168
Egyptian origins of, York on, 195
on Jews' altering of Torah, AAC/NIH views on, 131
Al Mahdi as supreme interpreter of, 125

Qur'an (*continued*)
　Al Mahdi on, as continuation of Biblical revelation, 125
　true version of, in Sudan, 209, 212
　York on Muslim corruptions of, 209, 212
　York's accommodation of extraterrestrial narratives within, 197–98
　York's chronological arrangement of, 197–98
al Qutb, as avatar inhabiting body of Al Mahdi, 156, 160, 161, 219

Raatib for Shriners, The (York), 215–17
races, origin of, Al Mahdi on, 39–44, 93, 116
Rahkaptah, Amunubi, 205–6
Rahmah, as avatar inhabiting body of Al Mahdi, 157
Rakim (hip-hop artist), 104, 110
Ramadan fast, AAC/NIH "Jewish period" and, 134
Ras Tefar I
　Bilal ibn Rabah and, 136
　Al Mahdi on, 101, 122
　Al Mahdi outreach to, 125–26
　Al Mahdi's claim to legacy of, 125–26
　and Psalms 68:31, 202
Ratib of Muhammad Ahmad, 58
　AAC/NIH distribution and use of, 63–64
　Sudanese governments effort to ban, 63–64
　York's Nuwaubian edition of, 215
Resurrection, The (York, 1994), 127
Revelation
　ahl al-bayt in, 20, 50–51
　Jesus as Black man in, 117, 119
　Al Mahdi's interpretation of, 22, 50–51, 102, 129, 134
　on Qur'an, 125
　Qur'an's affirmation of, 123, 131, 134
Rizq (planet), as IMAM's home planet, 4, 195, 197
Rogers, J. A., 10, 28, 51, 135, 137, 138, 139
Rohan, Robert, 191, 202
Rooakptah, Amunnubi, as name used by Al Mahdi, 168, 205, 207, 214
Rutherford, Judge, 120, 252n22

Sabbath
　community view of through Qur'anic lens, 134
　Al Mahdi on, 123–24, 124
Sacred Records of Neter: Aaferti Atum-Re (York, 1998), 219

Sacred Society of Anubis, 202
Sadat, Anwar, 106
Sadiq, Muhammad, 203
Sai Baba, 157
Salaam civilization
　destruction of, 176
　Al Mahdi on, 102, 156
　See also Mu (capital of Salaam)
Salafism, AAC/NIH opposition to, 225
Salafiyya movement, 11
Salah bin Rega, 52
Sammaniyya Order, Muhammad Ahmad and, 153
Santeria, in New York City, 14
Saudi Arabia
　influence on Nation of Islam, 35–36
　religious training program for Americans, 11–12
Saudi Arabian Muslims, Al Mahdi on, 74
"The Savior" (York, 1993), 194
scholarship on AAC/NIH, 6–7
Schuon, Frithjof, 151–52, 154–55
Science of Healing (Al Mahdi, 1985), 156, 158, 159
Science of the Pyramids (Al Mahdi, 1983), 176, 178, 181, 185
Secret Document: The Second Steop of the Sufi (Al Qutb), 161, 165
Secret Teachings of All Ages, The (Hall), 143
Serapis Bey, 155, 170
seventh seal, opening of (1970), 20, 60, 90, 125, 134, 234
Sex and Race (Rogers), 51
sexism in Muslim communities, Al Mahdi's critiques of, 191
SGL. *See* Sons of the Green Light
Shabazz Bey, R. A. Umar, 201
Shabazz tribe
　Al Mahti on, 44
　and ancient Egypt, 172
　establishment of civilization by, Elijah Muhammad on, 31
　separation of Earth and Moon by, Elijah Muhammad on, 40
Shaikh Daoud vs. W. D. Fard (York), 218
Shaqiya Nubians, characteristics of, Al Mahdi on, 39
shariya, York's criticism of, in *Holy Tablets*, 212
Shi'ism
　Black Arabs as nucleus for, 52
　claims about Muhammad's successor, Al Mahdi on, 49

Should Muslims Observe the Sabbath? (1985), 123, 124, 141, 144
Shriners, York on origin of, 217
shuwba, Al Mahdi's claim to possess, 158
Signs of 73 (Al Mahdi), 104
Silsilati: My Lineage, 66
Sisters of Isis, 202
Sitchin, Zecharia, 196
slaves in United States, Muslim vs. pagan, 72, 73
Smith, Joseph, 169
Sons of Canaan (Al Mahdi), 44, 129
Sons of the Green Light (SGL), 158–65
    AAC/NIH advertisements for, 126, 159–60, *164*
    downplaying of Nubian metaphysical Africa in, 161–62
    emblem of, 160, *164*
    enlightenment promised to members of, 159
    founding of, 21
    initiation to, 160–61
    lineage back to Muhammad, 161
    Al Mahdi pamphlet on, 161
    Al Mahdi's letter esotericism and, 163
    Al Mahdi's use of music in lessons for, 229
    replacement by Ancient and Mystic Order of Melchizedek, 202, 204
    as Sufi lodge, 148, 153–54, 161–62
    Sunni antagonism against, 163
    as "universal" order spanning all traditions, 160, 161
Sphinx, loss of nose, 186
star, six-pointed
    Five Percenters' use of, 105
    Garvey's use of, 101
    use by AAC/NIH, 16, 19, 46, *46*, 89, 92–93, 114, *118*, 121, 122–23, 128, 129, 130, 143, 152, 173–74, *175*, 242–43
    use by UNNM, 193, *194*
State Street Mosque (Brooklyn)
    breakoff of Dar ul-Islam movement, 34
    breakoff of Al Mahdi faction, 15
    breakoff of Ya-Sin Mosque, 12, 34, 152–53
    conflict between African American and immigrant Muslims, 33–34, 77, 79
    Dongolowi influence in, 13–14
    founding of, 77, 92
    images of, in AAC/NIH publications, 127, *128*
    Al Mahdi's criticism of schism in, 82–83
    Al Mahdi's defense of Faisal against immigrant teachers, 79

    Al Mahdi's Islamic education and, 12–14, 59, 63, 77–78
    members' move to AAC/NIH, 83
    and origin of AAC/NIH, 12
    range of beliefs represented in, 13–14
    Sudanese-American community in, 13–14, 59
    teachings on Israelites as Muslim and Black, 119–20
Stolen Legacy: The Egyptian Origins of Western Philosophy (James), 203
Sudan
    in AAC/NIH materials, as mythical land of pure Islam, 61
    AAC/NIH relocation of Islam's heartland to, 12, 28–29, 39
    Anglo-Egyptian colonial regime: and banning of Ahmad's *Ratib*, 63–64; Al Mahdi on, 51; Muhammad Ahmad's defeat of, 14, 29, 101; reconquest by, 58–59
    as center of divine creative activity, Al Mahdi on, 17
    connections to ancient Egypt, Adefunmi on, 15
    Fatima's flight to, Al Mahdi on, 102
    Al Mahdi's cutting of ties to, 192–93, 214
    Al Mahdi travel to, 60, 62
    Muhammad's flight to, 29
    Muslim military coup in, 192
    in nineteenth century: Islamic orthodoxy imposed in, 57, 59; Sufism in, 57; Turko-Egyptian regime, 57
    northern, as origin of Black Americans, 48
    as site of Adam and Eve's creation, 29, 39–40, 43
    as site of Mahdi's rise, 29
    twentieth-century, political conflict in, 60
    See also Ahmad, Muhammad; Mahdiyya
Sudanese-American community, at State Street Mosque, 13–14, 59
Sudanese Madhi. *See* Ahmad, Muhammad
Sufi Order International, 151
Sufi Order of the West, 150
Sufi orders, Al Mahdi on, 162
Sufism, American
    first wave of, 150–51
    second wave of, 151–52
Sufism and AAC/NIH
    and AAC/NIH founding as Ansar Pure Sufi, 151–52

Sufism and AAC/NIH (*continued*)
    and AAC/NIH universalism, 152
    availability to Westerners, Al Mahdi on, 148–49
    definition of, Al Mahdi on, 149
    eastern religious practice and, 158, 165
    as engagement with existing local dialect, 165–66
    and esoteric perennialism, 151–52
    as expression of metaphysical Africa, 153
    growing diaspora communities and, 153
    and growth of Sufism in African American community, 152–53
    importance to Al Mahdi, 148
    Khidr and, 154
    Al Mahdi poem on, 149
    Al Mahdi's early embrace of, 165
    Al Mahdi's engagement with Sufism and, 148–50
    Al Mahdi's list of Sufi masters, 162
    Al Mahdi's Sufism, and return to knowledge of self, 165
    Al Mahdi's trip to Egypt and, 153
    and New Age movement, 158
    in nineteenth century Sudan, 57
    non-Muslim forms of, 151
    Philips on, 153
    and self-healing, 165
    as separate from Islam, in New Age view, 8
    Sons of the Green Light and, 161–62
    Sudanese community at State Street Mosque and, 153
    Sufi practices in AAC/NIH, 147–48
    as "universal" teaching, 160, 161, 165
    and York's consistent treatment of Sufism, 214
    See also Sons of the Green Light (SGL)
Suhuf, Al Mahdi on, 180
Sulaiman, Amir, 225
Suleiman, Abdul Hamid, 203
Sunni Islam
    AAC/NIH rejection of, 53
    antagonism against AAC/NIH, 163
    conversion to, as reclaiming of Hamitic-Arab racial heritage, 30
    false Hadiths spread by, Al Mahdi on, 48–49, 51
    Al Mahdi attacks on, 188
    Al Mahdi on origin of, 51
    Al Mahdi's leadership of Blackamerica as counter to hegemony of, 111
    and origin of AAC/NIH, 12
    racism against true Black Islam, AAC/NIH on, 56
    Saudi co-opting of, Al Mahdi on, 107
    violent attacks on AAC/NIH and Al Mahdi, 188–89
    as white form of Islam, Al Mahdi on, 48
superior beings revealing wisdom to humans, metaphysical religions' narrative of, 155–56
Supreme Wisdom Lessons
    on Africa as not true home of Blacks, 30–31
    and Elijah Muhammad as renewer of Islam, 219
    Five Percenters and, 103, 110
    influence of Black Freemasonry on, 204
    Al Mahdi on, 92–93, 110, 134
    and "Two Fards" theory, 92
Swahili, Al Mahdi on, 47
Sweet Daddy Grace, 84, 99

Tablighi Jama'at, 34, 79
al-Tabrizi, Shams ad-Din, 159
Talilsman (Al Mahdi, 1979), 163
Tama Re UNNM facility, Eatonton, Georgia
    El Aswud Mir (Black Pyramid) at, 237
    dress code at, 194–95
    government confiscation and bulldozing of, 23
    government raid on, 4, 23
    and El Maguraj ceremony, 237–38, 239
    Mahdi shrine at, 242–43
    move to, 4, 23, 113–14, 187; and departure from Brooklyn hip-hop culture, 234; motives for, 188–93, 202; and turn from Islamic identity, 187–88; York on, 214
    symbolism of architecture and art in, 195, 242–43; scholars' emphasis on eclectic nature of, 238–40, 242
Teach Yourself Qur'aan with Tape, 47
Temple, Robert K. G., 9
Tents of Abraham, as name used by AAC/NIH, 22, 114, 130, 187
Tents of Nubia, as name used by AAC/NIH, 22, 130
Theosophical Society, 169–70
They Came Before Columbus (van Sertima), 38, 200
Third World internationalism, and metaphysical Africa, 10
360 Questions to Ask A Hebrew Israelite (York), 193

360 Questions to Ask the Israeli Church (York), 193
360 Questions to Ask the Orthodox Sunni Muslims (Al Mahdi), 188
Three Wise Men, 158
Tibet, white esotericists' interest in, 170
Tijaniyya Order, 153
Torah, Qur'an on Jews' altering of, AAC/NIH views on, 131
Trafton, Scott, 203
Tragedy Khadafi (Intelligent Hoodlum), 230, 231, 235
Travels of a Sufi, The (Al Mahdi, 1987), 159
Tribal encyclopedia (Al Mahdi, 1977), 39, 42
Tribal Origins of African-Americans (Adefunmi), 15
Tribe Israel Is No More, The! (Al Mahdi, 1975), 121, 122
True Light (Al Mahdi cassette tape series), 44, 226
True Story of Noah, The (Al Mahdi, 1986), 234
Tuitit Bey, 155, 170

'Umar
  and false Islam, York on, 212
  Al Mahdi on, 52
Umayyad caliphate, Al Mahdi on, 52
Understanding Islam (Schuon), 154
UNIA. *See* Universal Negro Improvement Association
United Muslims in Exile, as name used by AAC/NIH, 21
United Nuwaubian Nation of Moors. *See* UNNM (United Nuwaubian Nation of Moors)
United States government, plan to assassinate Black leaders, Al Mahdi on, 92
Universal Ethiopian Hymnal (Ford), 117
Universal Negro Improvement Association (UNIA), 66, 101
UNNM (United Nuwaubian Nation of Moors)
  dress code of, 194–95
  Masonic orders within, 202
  names used by, 193, 214
  as Native Americans, in York's view, 200, 202
  and Nuwaupic language, 206
  publications of works by Black Muslims leaders, 218, 219
  and recovery of interstellar Blackness in science of Nuwaubu, 238
  renaming of AAC/NIH as, 23, 187, 205
  as stage begun in early and mid-1990s, 234
  as Sufi order, according to York, 214
  symbolism of, 193, *194*, 200
  See also Tama Re UNNM facility, Eatonton, Georgia
UNNM beliefs
  Afrofuturist perennialism, 235, 237–38
  blending of Native American spirituality with metaphysical Africa, 199, 200
  as consistent with earlier AAC/NIH beliefs, 132–34, 206–7, 211, 220, 242, 243
  on Egyptian roots of biblical and Islamic traditions, 193, 195
  Egyptian symbolism, 193, *194*, 195
  emphasis on Christ's return, 193
  extraterrestrials in, 196–98, 240–41, *241*
  on human origins, 196–97
  on immanent arrival of spacecraft to retrieve the 144,000 worthy persons, 197
  Islamic symbolism of, 193
  Native American symbolism of, 195, 200, *201*
  on Nubian ancestry of Native Americans, 199–200
  on Nubian superiority, 197
  and Nuwaubu, beliefs associated with, 205–6
  rituals, 195
  on Sumerian roots of biblical and Islamic traditions, 193, 195–96, 197
  targeting of Black Hebraism, 193
  on underground civilizations, 196, 197
  Washitaw Muurs narrative in, 202
Unto Thee I Grant (Ancient Mystical Order Rosae Crucis), 171, 204
Upper Room at AAC/NIH headquarters, 46, *46*
'Uthman, and false Islam, York on, 212

van Sertima, Ivan, 38, 51, 200

Wadhiyfah: The Science of Sound Healing (Al Mahdi), 229
Wahhabi Sect, Al Mahdi on, 96, 106, 188
Wahhaj, Siraj, 35, 96, 107, 126, 188, 192, 209
Was Christ Really Crucified? (Al Mahdi, 1980), 185
Was Created with One Thought: The "Key" Is Within (Al Mahdi), 149

Washitaw de Dughdahmoundyah movement, 201–2
Washitaw-Turner Goston El-Bey, Empress Verdiacee "Tiari," 201
Welsing, Frances Cress, 9, 196
Whatever Happened to the Nubian Islaamic Hebrews? (Al Mahdi, 1985), 122
Whatever Happened to the Nubian Islaamic Hebrews? (Al Mahdi, 1989), 126
What Laws Did Jesus Follow? (Al Mahdi, 1988), 127
Where Is the Tabernacle of the Most High? (Al Mahdi, 1986), 51, 82, 125–26
white people
    civilizing of, as mission of Abraham, 177
    as devils: Fard Muhammad on, 88–89; Al Mahdi on, 41, 89
    distortion of Egyptian wisdom by, 178–80
    effort to destroy Nation of Islam, Al Mahdi on, 92
    immodesty of, AAC/NIH on, 69–70
    interest in Egyptosophy, 169–70
    origin of, Al Mahdi on, 40–41
    as subhuman depraved animals, 177, 197
    time allotted to, in Nation of Islam tradition, 206
    See also Amorite race
white supremacy, Al Mahdi's leadership as counter to, 111
Who Was Jesus Sent To? (Al Mahdi, 1991), 127
Who Was Marcus Garvey? (Al Mahdi, 1988), 82, 98, 100–103, 127
Who Was Noble Drew Ali? (Al Mahdi, 1980), 82, 96–100, 144
Who Was Noble Drew Ali? (Al Mahdi, 1988), 97, 98, 104, 180
Who Was Shaikh Daww'ud?, 82
Why Do Muslim Women Wear the Face Covering (Veil)? (Al Mahdi, 1989), 70
"Why the Nosering?" (Al Mahdi, 1986), 70, 71
Williams, Chancellor, 36–37
Williams, Mary C. (mother of York), 199
Will Send "Elijah" Before the Coming of the Great and Dreadful Day of the Lord (Al Mahdi, 1973), 84
Wisemen, The (Al Mahdi, 1991), 127
Wonderful Ethiopians of the Ancient Cushite Empire (Houston), 29–30
"Wooly-Headed People by Nature," predisposition to spiritual insight, 205–6
World Assembly of Muslim Youth, 32

World's Columbian Exposition (Chicago, 1893), 171
World War II, Sudanese migration to U.S. in, 59

Yahweh Ben Yahweh, 111, *111*, 116, 198
Yamassee Indians, UNNM as, in York's view, 200
Yanaan/Yaanuwn
    as avatar inhabiting body of Al Mahdi, 156, 163, 195, 196
    first mention in AAC/NIH publications, 127
    as intergalactic sheikh inhabiting Al Mahdi's body, 22, 127
    in Al Mahdi's interpretation of Revelations, 22
    as name used by Al Mahdi, 130, 163
Ya-Sin Mosque
    founding of, 12, 34, 152–53
    Al Mahdi's criticism of, 82, 83–84
    shooting at (1974), 18
Yazid, Al Mahdi on, 53
York, Ben (Ibn Ali), as claimed ancestor of York, 199
York, David P. (father of York), 199
York, Dr.
    as Al Mahdi, as publicly known, 224
    on music as beyond racial boundaries, 230
    publicity photo, 223
    singing career of, 222–24, *223*
    See also music, Al Mahdi's engagement with
York, Dwight, as birth name of Al Mahdi, 12
York, Malachi Z.
    on adjustment of message to suit audience, 207
    avatars inhabiting body of, 195
    bar mitzvah at age 13 claimed by, 193
    claim to be angelic being, 196
    dress styles, range of, 187, 200, 201
    "Furqaan" power to distinguish between allegorical and decisive scripture, 207
    and Islam, claim to restore and purify, 219
    legacies of Black Islam leaders claimed by, 187
    Al Mahdi's renaming as, 187, 192, 193–94, 234
    names used by, 193, 199, 205, 207
    as name used by Al Mahdi, 185
    Native American heritage, claim to, 199, 200–201, *201*, 202
    on phases in AAC/NIH beliefs, 207

roles and titles claimed by, 187
and scripture: claimed power to correct and purify, 207–8, 220; mastery of, as signature claim, 207; new translations/corrections published by, 208–10
turn from Arab ties, 195, 219
turn from Islamic identity, 187–88, 191–92, 193, 219
York-El, Malachi Zodok, as name used by York, 193
Yoruba (1978), 72
Yorubas
Afrocentrism and, 9, 38
connections to ancient Egypt, Adefunmi on, 15
as degenerate former Muslims, Al Mahdi on, 72–73
New York City revival movement, 14
revivalism, Al Mahdi's criticisms of, 72–74
Yoruba Temple (Harlem), 15, 33
You and the Sons of the Green Light (Al Mahdi), 161

Zev Love X, 224
Zodoq, Aluhum Muhammad, 216
Zoroastrianism, Al Mahdi on, 43
Zoser/Abdul Quddus
as avatar inhabiting body of Al Mahdi, 156–57
and genetic engineering of pigs, 177
Al Mahdi on, 41–42, 174–76, 177, 180
as Quetzlcoatl, 199
Zulu Nation movement, 233

www.ingramcontent.com/pod-product-compliance
Lightning Source LLC
Chambersburg PA
CBHW032335300426
44109CB00041B/877